Other Books and Series by Jeff Bowen

Applications for Enrollment of Chickasaw Newborn Act of 1905
Volumes I thru VII

Cherokee Intermarried White 1906 Volume I, II, III, IV, V & VI

Visit our website at **www.nativestudy.com** to learn more about these and other books and series by Jeff Bowen

CHEROKEE INTERMARRIED WHITE 1906 VOLUME VII

TRANSCRIBED BY
JEFF BOWEN

NATIVE STUDY
Gallipolis, Ohio
USA

Copyright © 2014
by Jeff Bowen

ALL RIGHTS RESERVED
No part of this publication may be reproduced
or used in any form or manner whatsoever
without previous written permission from the
copyright holder or publisher.

Originally published:
Baltimore, Maryland
2014

Reprinted by:

Native Study LLC
Gallipolis, OH
www.nativestudy.com
2020

Library of Congress Control Number: 2020917307

ISBN: 978-1-64968-076-1

Made in the United States of America.

This series is dedicated to
Jerry Bowen
the Brave and the Strong.

DEPARTMENT OF THE INTERIOR

Commissioner to the Five Civilized Tribes

Muskogee, Indian Territory, March 9, 1907.

NOTICE IS HEREBY GIVEN that the undersigned, the Commissioner to the Five Civilized Tribes, has been designated by the Secretary of the Interior, as the official to make and approve appraisals of the value of improvements upon land in the Cherokee Nation which were made prior to November 5, 1906, by white persons who intermarried with Cherokee citizens prior to December 16, 1895, and who have the right under the Act of Congress approved March 2, 1907 (Public 180), to sell improvements.

NOTICE IS FURTHER GIVEN that former claimants to citizenship by intermarriage who have made permanent and valuable improvements on lands of the Cherokee Nation and who claim the right to sell the same under and by virtue of said Act of Congress of March 2, 1907 (Public 180), must appear before the Commissioner to the Five Civilized Tribes prior to April 1, 1907, and designate the land upon which are located the improvements which they claim the right to sell by virtue of said Act; and if any such intermarried citizen shall fail to appear before the Commissioner to the Five Civilized Tribes prior to April 1, 1907, it will be considered that he makes no claim to the benefits conferred by said Act. Such appearance and designation of improvements must be made before the Commissioner at his office in Muskogee, Indian Territory, at any time between Monday, March 11th, 1907, and Saturday, March 30th, 1907, inclusive, or at any of the following named places between the dates named at which places the Commissioner will have a representative to receive said designations and hear testimony relative thereto:

Bartlesville, Ind. Ter., Monday March 18th, 1907, to Saturday March 23rd, 1907, inclusive.
Tulsa, Ind. Ter., Monday March 25th, 1907, to Saturday March 30th, 1907, inclusive.
Claremore, Ind. Ter., Monday March 18th, 1907, to Saturday March 23rd, 1907, inclusive.
Nowata, Ind. Ter., Monday March 25th, 1907, to Saturday March 30th, 1907, inclusive.
Vinita, Ind. Ter., Monday March 18th, 1907, to Saturday March 23rd, 1907, inclusive.
Pryor Creek, Ind. Ter., Monday March 25th, 1907, to Saturday March 30th, 1907, inclusive.
Tahlequah, Ind. Ter., Monday March 18, 1907, to Saturday March 23rd, 1907, inclusive.
Sallisaw, Ind. Ter., Monday March 25th, 1907, to Saturday March 30th, 1907, inclusive.

Designations must be made in person by the intermarried white claimant, or in case proper proof is made that he is physically unable to appear, by some adult member of his immediate family, or in case proper proof is made of the fact that the intermarried white claimant is physically unable to appear and has no adult member of his immediate family, by a person holding a properly executed power of attorney; provided, that in every case the designation must be made by a party familiar with the character, ownership, location and value of the improvements to be designated. At the time of said designation the testimony of any competent person will be taken by the Commissioner as to the location, character and value of said improvements.

No former intermarried white claimant will be permitted to designate improvements upon more land than he would have been entitled to take in allotment for himself had he been admitted to citizenship. If any intermarried white claimant has made a tentative selection of a full allotment he will not be allowed to designate improvements upon other land.

NOTICE IS FURTHER GIVEN that if any citizen of the Cherokee Nation entitled to select an allotment shall claim that the improvements on land tentatively selected by a former intermarried white claimant, or held by him, do not belong to said intermarried white claimant, or makes any adverse claim to said improvements, or to the right of the intermarried white claimant to sell said improvements under the Act approved March 2, 1907 (Public 180), said citizen must appear before the Commissioner to the Five Civilized Tribes either at Muskogee, Indian Territory, prior to April 1, 1907, or at one of the places above designated and within the dates above designated and make formal complaint before the Commissioner to the Five Civilized Tribes of his contention. At Muskogee, Indian Territory, between March 11th and March 30th, 1907, inclusive, and at the other places herein named during the hearings at said places as herein fixed, plats will be open for inspection showing the location of tentative allotments made by former claimants to citizenship by intermarriage and all other land on which such claimants claim improvements, so far as indicated by the records of this office.

All persons interested should take careful note of the limitation of time herein provided for, within which designations and complaints may be made, and that they must be made by appearance before the Commissioner.

TAMS BIXBY,
Commissioner.

This particular notice concerns the appraisals of improvements on properties held by Cherokee intermarried whites. You would have found notices like this throughout the Nation to bring in people to finalize the allotment question, of who belonged and who did not.

E.C.M.

Cherokee 58.

DEPARTMENT OF THE INTERIOR,
COMMISSIONER TO THE FIVE CIVILIZED TRIBES.

In the matter of the application for the enrollment of ALBERTIN HAMPTON as a citizen by intermarriage of the Cherokee Nation.

DECISION

THE RECORDS OF THIS OFFICE SHOW: That at Fairland, Indian Territory, July 9, 1900, Albertin Hampton appeared before the Commission to the Five Civilized Tribes, and made application for the enrollment of himself as a citizen by intermarriage, and for the enrollment of his wife, Jane E. Hampton, et al. as citizens by blood of the Cherokee Nation. The application for the enrollment of the said Jane E. Hampton et al. as citizens by blood of the Cherokee Nation has been heretofore disposed of, and their rights to enrollment will not be considered in this decision. Further proceedings in the matter of said application were had at Muskogee, Indian Territory, September 3, 1902, October 14, 1902, and January 2, 1907.

THE EVIDENCE IN THIS CASE SHOWS: That the applicant herein, Albertin Hampton, a white man, was married, in accordance with Cherokee law, January 20, 1874, to his wife, Jane E. Hampton, nee Thomas, who was at the time of said marriage a recognized citizen by blood of the Cherokee Nation, and whose name appears on the approved partial roll of citizens by blood of the Cherokee Nation, opposite No. 195; that since said marriage the said Albertin Hampton and Jane E. Hampton have resided together as husband and wife, and have continuously lived in the Cherokee Nation. Said Albertin Hampton is identified on the Cherokee authenticated tribal roll of 1880, and the Cherokee census roll of 1896, as "Bert Hampton", an intermarried citizen of the Cherokee Nation.

IT IS, THEREFORE, ORDERED AND ADJUDGED: That in accordance with the decision of the Supreme Court of the United States, dated November 5, 1906, in the case of Daniel Red Bird et al. vs. the United States,

E.C.M.   - 2 -   Cherokee 58.

under the provisions of Section twenty-one, of the Act of Congress approved June 28, 1898 (30 Stat., 495), Albertin Hampton is entitled to enrollment as a citizen by intermarriage of the Cherokee Nation, and his application for enrollment as such is accordingly granted.

                                                    Commissioner.

Dated at Muskogee, Indian Territory, this JAN 18 1907

The above is an accepted decision of the Commissioner to the Five Civilized Tribes. The Attorney for the Cherokee Nation had fifteen days after the date of Commissioner's decision in which to protest.

Cherokee 58.

Attorney for the Cherokee Nation,
MUSKOGEE, I.T.   January 18, 1907.

The Commissioner to the Five Civilized Tribes,

Muskogee, Indian Territory.

Sir:

Receipt is acknowledged of the testimony and of your decision enrolling Albertin Hampton, as a citizen by intermarriage of the Cherokee Nation. Time for protesting said decision is waived and I consent that said person may be placed upon the schedule immediately.

Yours very truly,

W. W. Hastings

Attorney for Cherokee Nation.

The above is a notice of the Attorney waiving the time for protesting the Commissioner's decision (on the two previous pages) concerning Albertin Hampton's application and consenting to place the applicant upon schedule immediately.

INTRODUCTION

The *Cherokee Intermarried White*, National Archive film M-1301, Rolls 305-307, are found under the heading of Applications for Enrollment of the Commission to the Five Civilized Tribes. The genealogical value of this series concerning the relationships between many Cherokee tribesman and their marriages among another race is very important and virtually a treasure trove of information long sought after. While on the other hand what these cases are really about are the efforts of many to attain Cherokee land allotments. Referenced from the Supreme Court Decision, Cherokee Intermarriage Cases – 203 U.S. 76 (1906).

This collection of Intermarried claims involves two hundred and eighty-eight separate cases with a variety of scenarios from the divorced to the widowed to the deserving to the deceptive. During these times there were many that wanted what was rightfully only the Cherokees. You will see each case will be headed by the title from the first folder as an example: *Intermarried White I, Trans from Cher. 34*, the transfer number is the Dawes Commission number from the claimants spouse.

These cases are fascinating because of the generational bloodlines that can be verified by documentation rather than just word of mouth. From Kent Carter's book, *The Dawes Commission*, "The tribe also, continued to oppose the enrollment of whites who had married into the Cherokee tribe. That controversy dragged through the U.S. Court of Claims and then the Supreme Court, which finally ruled in favor of the tribe on November 05, 1906. The court upheld the Cherokee citizenship laws that denied rights to any white who had married into the tribe after November 1, 1877. It also upheld an 1839 law which stated that anyone who moved out of the nation lost their citizenship unless they were readmitted. The applications of 3,341 persons were rejected as a result of this ruling, and the allotment clerks were forced to undo a great deal of their work. With the issue finally settled by the courts, the commission was able to send the first schedule of Cherokees by intermarriage, containing fifty-five names, to the secretary of interior on June 10, 1907. Eventually only 286 people were enrolled as intermarried whites----far fewer than the number put on the rolls of the Choctaw and Chickasaw tribes, which had much more liberal laws on rights based on marriage." [1]

---

[1] The Dawes Commission and the Allotment of the Five Civilized Tribes, 1893-1914 by Kent Carter, pg. 121

In Cohen's Handbook of Federal Indian Law he states, "In the *Cherokee Intermarriage Cases,* the Supreme Court considered the claims of certain white persons, intermarried with Cherokee Indians, who wanted to participate in the common property of the Cherokee Nation. Such persons were permitted by tribal law to be tribal citizens with limited rights in tribal property. The tribe had also provided for the revocation of citizenship rights of a white person who intermarried with a Cherokee if the Cherokee spouse were abandoned or if a widower or widow married a non-Cherokee. The Court found that the Cherokee Nation had authority to qualify the rights of citizenship which it offered to its "naturalized citizens. Such tribal action defeated the claims of the plaintiffs:

The laws and usages of the Cherokees, their earliest history, the fundamental principles of their national policy, their constitution and statutes, all show that citizenship rested on blood or marriage; that the man who would assert citizenship must establish marriage; that when marriage ceased (with a special reservation in favor of widows or widowers) citizenship ceased; that when an intermarried white married a person having no rights of Cherokee citizenship by blood it was conclusive evidence that the tie which bound him to the Cherokee people was severed and the very basis of his citizenship obliterated."[2]

An important footnote that Cohen published within his pages for the above paragraph also needs to be studied. He noted, "Under Cherokee law white persons intermarrying with Cherokees before 1875 were tribal citizens for most purposes, including allotment of tribal land, but had no interest in tribal funds except those funds derived from tribal lands. A Cherokee law that became effective in 1875 provided that whites marrying Cherokees had no rights to tribal property but could obtain full citizenship by the payment of $500 to the tribe. In 1877 the tribe provided that no intermarried citizen could obtain any rights to tribal land or funds."[3]

During many years of study this author has found cases that should have been been accepted, especially with the particular documentation presented. All in all the outcome of the decision made should have rendered a different result. Also there have been many that numb the mind as to how they their cases were even considered. The years have given many the hopes that their ancestors were one of those that had a decent claim and an honest consideration. Like any time in history there are political struggles

---

[2] Felix S. Cohen's Handbook of FEDERAL INDIAN LAW 1982 ED. pgs 20-21.
[3] Felix S. Cohen's Handbook of FEDERAL INDIAN LAW 1982 ED. pg 21 footnote16.

and the human factor that points out man is not perfect. These pages were transcribed with the wish that another person somewhere along the line will find their relation from the past and give them the answers long hoped for.

Jeff Bowen
Gallipolis, Ohio
NativeStudy.com

Cherokee Intermarried White 1906
Volume VII

Cher IW 194

◇◇◇◇◇

E.C.M.

DEPARTMENT OF THE INTERIOR,

COMMISSIONER TO THE FIVE CIVILIZED TRIBES.

In the matter of the application for the enrollment of

WILLIAM CROWDER

As a citizen by intermarriage of the Cherokee Nation.

CHEROKEE NO. 231.

◇◇◇◇◇

DEPARTMENT OF THE INTERIOR,
COMMISSION TO THE FIVE CIVILIZED TRIBES,
WESTVILLE?[sic] I.T. JULY 16, 1900.

In the matter of the application of William Crowder et als., fir[sic] enrollment as Cherokee citizens, said Crowder being sworn by Commissioner Needles, testified:

Q   What is your name?   A   William Crowder.
Q   How old are you?   A   I don't know exactly, but I guess about 52.
Q   What is your postoffice?   A   Baptist.
Q   Make your residence there?   A   Yes.
Q   How long have you lived in the Cherokee Nation?   A   About 30 yeas continuously and have not lived out of it.
Q   For whom do you apply for citizenship?   A   For myself and wife and children.
Q   You are not a Cherokee?   A   No sir.
Q   You make application as a Cherokee citizen by intermarriage?   A   Yes.
Q   What's the name of your father?   A   Nelson Crowder.
Q   He is not living?   A   No sir.
Q   Is he on any of the rolls of the Cherokee Nation?   A   No sir.
Q   Does your name appear upon any of the authenticated rols[sic] of the Cherokee Nation?   A   Yes, on the roll of 80.
    On '80 roll, page 416, number 37.
        On '96 roll, page 819, number 37.
Q   Did you ever apply to the Cherokee tribal authorities for admission?   A   No sir.
Q   Are you married?   A   Yes.
Q   Under what law?   A   Cherokee law.

1

Cherokee Intermarried White 1906
Volume VII

Q What was your wife's name? A Polly Foreman.
Q When? A About 30 years ago.
Q Is your wife's name on the roll of '80? A Yes.
    Polly Crowder on '80 roll, page 416, number 311, as Mary Crowder.
    Polly Crowder on '96 roll, page 732, number 395.
Q How long has your wife lived in the Cherokee Nation? A Born and raised here and never lived out of it.
Q Have you any children under 21 years of age living with you? A Yes.
Q What is the name of the oldest one unmarried and living with you?
  A William Penn, 15 years old.
    On '96 roll, page 732, number 397, Goingsnake District.
    On Pay-roll of '94, page 650[sic], number 430. Page 630.
Q Does he live with you at home now? A Yes.

    William Crowder applies to be enrolled and makes application for himself, his wife, Polly, and his child, William Penn.

William Crowder is found upon the roll of '80 and also upon the roll of '9_ according to number and page as indicated in this testimony.

William P. Crowder, his son, is found upon the Census rolls of '96 and also upon the pay-roll of '94. Satisfactory proof having been made as to the residence of these parties, they are ordered enrolled; William Crowder as a citizen by intermarriage, and Polly Crowder and William P. Crowder, as citizens by blood of the Cherokee Nation, and their names entered upon the rolls now being made by this Commission.

    Brown McDonald, being sworn by Commissioner Needles, says as Stenographer to the Commission to the Five Civilized Tribes, he reported in full the testimony of the above named witness, and that the foregoing is a full, true and correct transcript of his notes.

                      Brown McDonald

Sworn to and subscribed before me this 17th day of July, 1900, at Westville, I.T.

                                  TB Needles
                                  Commissioner.

Cherokee Intermarried White 1906
Volume VII

R.
Cher. 231.

Department of the Interior.
Commission to the Five Civilized Tribes.
Tahlequah, I. T., September 29, 1902.

SUPPLEMENTAL TESTIMONY AND PROCEEDINGS in the matter of the application for the enrollment of William Crowder as a citizen by intermarriage of the Cherokee Nation.

WILLIAM CROWDER, being first duly sworn, and being examined, testified as follows:

BY COMMISSION: What is your name?   A William Crowder.
Q How old are you?   A About fifty-six.
Q What is your post office address?   A Baptist.
Q Are you a white man?   A Yes sir.
Q Have you heretofore made application to this Commission for enrollment as a citizen by intermarriage of the Cherokee Nation?   A I reckon I did. I was before the Dawes Commission at Westville. I enrolled up there.
Q What is the name of your wife?   A Polly Foreman.
Q Is she living?   A Yes sir.
Q Are you and she living together?   A Yes sir.
Q Have you lived together continuously since the date of your marriage?   A Yes sir.
Q Do you claim your fight to enrollment by reason of your marriage to her?   A Yes sir.
Q Are you and she living together now?   A Yes sir.
Q Were you ever married before you married her?   A No sir.
Q Was she ever married before she married you?   A Yes sir, she was married, they had one child.
Q What was the name of her former husband?   A Zeke Proctor.
Q Was he living when you married her?   A Yes sir.
Q Were they divorced?   A Those times, when we was married, in 1869, that was under the Cherokee law, in 1869, I don't know anything about that. We was married in August, 1869.
Q Had she lived with Zeke Proctor prior to that time as his wife?
Q[sic] They had been living together about two years, I guess.
Q Do you know anything about their marriage?   A No sir, I don't.
Q Do you know whether or not a divorce was obtained between them?   A No sir.
Q Are you on the 1880 roll?   A I m on every roll there is, I guess. I was married in 1869.

This testimony will be filed with and made a part of the record in the matter of the application for the enrollment of William Crowder as a citizen by intermarriage of the Cherokee Nation, Cherokee straight card field No. 231.

Cherokee Intermarried White 1906
Volume VII

Wm. Hutchinson, being first duly worn, states that as stenographer to the Commission to the Five Civilized Tribes he correctly recorded the testimony and proceedings in this case, and the foregoing is a true and correct transcript of his stenographic notes thereof.

Wm Hutchinson

Subscribed and sworn to before me this 29th day of September, 1902.

John O Rosson
Notary Public.

◇◇◇◇◇

Cherokee 231.

DEPARTMENT OF THE INTERIOR,
COMMISSIONER TO THE FIVE CIVILIZED TRIBES.
Muskogee, Ind. Ter., January 2, 1907.

In the matter of the application for the enrollment of William Crowder as a citizen by intermarriage of the Cherokee Nation.

William Crowder being first duly sworn by Frances R. Lane, a Notary Public for the Western District of Indian Territory, testified as follows:

By the Commissioner.
Q What is your name?   A William Crowder.
Q How old are you?   A I don't know how old.
Q About how old?   A I guess somewhere between 58 and 60.
Q What is your postoffice address?   A Westville, I. T.
Q Do you claim to be a citizen by intermarriage of the Cherokee Nation?   A Yes sir.
Q Through whom do you claim your right?   A My wife.
Q What is her name?   A Polly Foreman
Q When were you married to Polly Foreman?   A In 1869.
Q What date?   A I don't remember.
Q Did you get a license?   A Yes, July 5, 1869.
Q Were you ever married before you married Polly Foreman?   A No sir.
Q Was she ever married before her marriage to you?   A Yes, I think so.
Q What was the name of her husband?   A Zeke Proctor.
Q Was she married at the time she was married to you?   A Yes.
Q Was she married to Zeke Proctor at the time she married you?
A Not that I know of.
Q Was he living at the time you married her?   A Yes sir.
Q Where were you married to Polly Foreman?   A In Going Snake District, Cherokee Nation.

Cherokee Intermarried White 1906
Volume VII

Q I see from your marriage license which you hand me that the license was issued by the Cherokee nation[sic] for you to marry Polly Foreman. If she was married to Zeke Proctor why was the marriage license issued to Polly Foreman? A I don't know.
Q I she was the lawful wife of Zeke Proctor, how could she marry you without being divorced? A Well, now, I don't know anything about that. It was said that they had lived together. I don't know whether they had or not only what they[sic] people said.
Q Have you lived with Polly Foreman ever since you were married to her in 1869?
A Yes sir.
Q Living with her at the present time? A Yes sir.
Q Have you lived with her in the Cherokee Nation continuously since that time?
A Yes sir.
Q Was Polly Foreman a citizen of the Cherokee Nation at the time you married her?
A Yes sir.

> The applicant is identified on the 1880 Cherokee roll opposite No. 310. His wife, through whom he claims his citizenship is identified on said roll opposite No. 311. She is also identified on the final roll of citizens by blood of the Cherokee Nation opposite No. 709.
>
> The applicant also offers in evidence license issued by Aaron H. beck on July 5, 1869, Clerk of the District Court of Going Snake District, granting him the right to marry Polly Foreman, together with the certificate of George Whitmire, Judge of the District Court, showing that they were married according to law on July 25, 1869.

Q How long did Polly Foreman live with Zeke Proctor? A I don't know; I suppose 5 of 6 months; maybe a little longer. Not long.
Q Was it as much as a year? A No, I think not.
Q Did they keep house? A No, they didn't keep house. He lived one place and she lived another. Some say he had another wife. The license was issued in her maiden name. They never held themselves out as man and wife.
Q Was there any form of marriage ceremony gone through with.[sic]
A No, I think not.
Q Had they any children? A No sir.

Witness excused.

Frances R. Lane upon oath states that as stenographer to the Commissioner to the Five Civilized Tribes she reported the testimony in the above entitled cause and that the above and foregoing is an accurate transcript of her stenographic notes thereof.

Frances R Lane

Subscribed and sworn to before me this 4th day of January, 1907.

Edward Merrick
Notary Public.

Cherokee Intermarried White 1906
Volume VII

◇◇◇◇◇

(The Marriage License and Certificate below typed as given.)

Cherokee Nation)
)
Goingsnake Dist)

bee it known that authority is granted to any of the Judges and all ministers of all evangelical denominations having the care of soles to solemnise the rights of matrimony according to the cerimonies usely observed in such cases between Mr.W.P.Crowder to miss Polly Foreman an unmaried Cherokee citizen W.P.Crowder having complied with the law in such cases July 5th 1869 given under hand in office

Aaron H Beck

Clk Dist Court

this to certify that I doe this day performed and pronounced the right and cerimony as required by those licens and according to law July 25, 1i69

George Whitmire Judge Dist Court

Recorded on New book page 181 This 23 March 1880

W C Ghomly

Clk G S Dist

The undersigned being duly sworn states that as stenographer to the Commission to the Five Civilized Tribes, she made the above copy, and that the same is a true and correct copy of the instrument now on file in this office.

Mary Tabor Mallory

Subscribed and sworn to before me this 9 day of Jan 1907

Chas E Webster
Notary Public.

◇◇◇◇◇

Cherokee Intermarried White 1906
Volume VII

L. G. D.   Cherokee 231.

DEPARTMENT OF THE INTERIOR,
COMMISSION TO THE FIVE CIVILIZED TRIBES.
Muskogee, Indian Territory, January 18, 1907.

In the matter of the application for the enrollment of William Crowder as a citizen by intermarriage of the Cherokee Nation.

APPEARANCES: Polly Crowder for applicant.

Cherokee Nation represented by W. W. Hastings, Attorney.

Supplemental Testimony.

Polly Crowder being first duly sworn by B. P. Rasmus, Notary Public, testified as follows:

ON BEHALF OF COMMISSIONER.

Q   What is your name?   A   Polly Crowder.
Q   What is your age?   A   About 63.
Q   What is your post office address?
A   Westville.
Q   Are you acquainted with William Crowder?
A   Yes sir.
Q   Who is William Crowder?
A   William Crowder is my lawful husband.
Q   When was you married to William Crowder?
A   In '69; I think it was about the 5th of July.
Q   Was you ever married before you married William Crowder?
A   No sir.
Q   When William Crowder appeared before this office on January 2, 1907, he was asked whether you had ever married prior to your marriage to him and he replied that you was and that your former husband's name was Zeke Proctor. Is that correct?
A   Well, I wasn't married. You know how they just kind of made a contract; and I got dissatisfied; I saw I had got the worst end of it.
Q   Then you never was married to Zeke Proctor?
A   No, I never was. We lived together like the Indians did, about three months and I never left my mother's home at all.
Q   Then William Crowder was mistaken in his testimony of January 2, 1907, when he stated that you was formerly married to Zeke Proctor?
A   Yes, he was mistaken' I never was married to him lawfully at all. We lived together about three months in the Indian style there at my mother's home.

Cherokee Intermarried White 1906
Volume VII

A   Is Zeke Proctor living at this time?
A   Yes sir.
Q   Is he married?
A   Well, he is a widower now.
Q   He has been married?
A   Twice; his first wife died and he married again; then his wife died about a year ago.
Q   Did he marry his first wife before you and he lived together or afterwards?
A   Afterwards.

BY MR. HASTINGS.

Q   Did you and Zeke Proctor have any marriage contract?
A   No, there was no written contract or nothing; you know how people married them days.
Q   Did you have any verbal contract before witnesses?
A   No sir.
Q   Did you and he live together as husband and wife and hold each other out to the community as husband and wife during that time?
A   No, I reckon not; he would come there and stay at mother's a little,- maybe a couple of days, and he would be gone.
Q   Did you mother and the folks there at your home during that time regard him as your husband?
A   Well, mother never did; of course, my step-father, he never had nothing to say about it at all but my mother never did.
Q   Was there any children born of that union?
A   One.
Q   Was she born while you were living together?
A   No sir; not while I was living with him; we didn't live together long.
Q   About how long did you live together?
A   Not more than three months.
Q   And not continuously; only occasionally?
A   Yes sir; just occasionally.
Q   You never were married by a preacher?
A   No; never was married by nobody.
Q   You never did keep house in separate apartments?
A   No; never left my mother's home.

BY COMMISSIONER.

Q   Did Proctor ever make a home for you at all?
A   No sir.
Q   Did you ever live at his house?
A   No sir.
Q   You didn't live anywhere except with your own folks during the time of this connection of yours with Mr. Proctor?
A   Right in my mother's house; never left my mother's house.

Cherokee Intermarried White 1906
Volume VII

Q   Did your mother feel as if your were married to Proctor under the Indian custom or did she not?
A   I don't know what,-- she wasn't satisfied at all.
Q   She didn't look with favor on the arrangement?
A   No sir; she didn't.
Q   How did you look upon it as to whether or not you were married; did you expect any further ceremony or any ceremony at all to be--
A   I don't know that I thought much of anything; it was just sort of like a rat getting in a trap. I was into this trouble before I knew it.
Q   How old were you at the time?
A   I was about 20.
Q   You were old enough to know what you were doing?
A   Yes, of course; but you know how it is.
Q   Did Proctor pay any board while he was there at your mother's house?
A   No sir.
Q   How long did he ever stay there at any one time?
A   O[sic], a day and night.
Q   He stayed usually when he came, during the day or just during the night?
A   Sometime[sic] he would stay a day and sometime he would get in after noon and leave the next morning.

The undersigned being first duly sworn states that as stenographer to the Commission to the Five Civilized Tribes, she recorded the testimony taken in this case and that the foregoing is a full, true and correct transcript of her stenographic notes thereof.

Myrtle Hill

Subscribed and sworn to before me this the 18th day of January, 1907.

John E. Tidwell
Notary Public.

◇◇◇◇◇

Cherokee Intermarried White 1906
Volume VII

E C M

Cherokee 231.

DEPARTMENT OF THE INTERIOR,

COMMISSIONER TO THE FIVE CIVILIZED TRIBES.

In the matter of the application for the enrollment of WILLIAM CROWDER as a citizen by intermarriage of the Cherokee Nation.

_D_E_C_I_S_I_O_N_

THE RECORDS OF THIS OFFICE SHOW: That at Westville, Indian Territory, July 16th, 1900 application was received by the Commission to the Five Civilized Tribes for the enrollment of William Crowder as a citizen by intermarriage of the Cherokee Nation. Further proceedings in the matter of said application were had at Muskogee, Indian Territory, September 29th, 1902 and January 2nd, 1907, and January 18th, 1907.

THE EVIDENCE IN THIS CASE SHOWS: That the applicant herein, William Crowder, a white man, was married in accordance with Cherokee law July 25th, 1869 to his wife, Polly Crowder, who was at the time of said marriage a recognized citizen by blood of the Cherokee Nation, who is identified on the Cherokee authenticated tribal roll of 1880, Going Snake District No. 311 as a native Cherokee, and whose name appears on the approved partial roll of citizens by blood of the Cherokee Nation, opposite No. 709. If it further shown that, previous to her marriage with William Crowder, the said Polly Crowder had cohabited with one Zeke Proctor for a period of about three months; and that at no time during said co-habitation did the said Polly Crowder or Zeke Proctor hold themselves out as husband and wife, nor were they regarded as such in the community. It is further shown that since said marriage of said William Crowder and Polly Crowder they have resided together as husband and wife and continuously lived in the Cherokee Nation. Said applicant is identified on the Cherokee authenticated tribal roll of 1880 and the Cherokee census roll of 1896 as an intermarried citizen of the Cherokee Nation.

IT IS, THEREFORE, ORDERED AND ADJUDGED: That in accordance with the decision of the Supreme Court of the United States dated November 5th, 1906, in the cases of Daniel Red Bird, et al. vs. the United States, Nos. 125, 126, 127, and 128, the said applicant, William Crowder is entitled, under the provisions of Section Twenty-one of the Act of Congress approved June 28th, 1898 (30 Stats. 495), to enrollment as a citizen by intermarriage of the Cherokee Nation, and his application for enrollment as such is accordingly granted.

Tams Bixby
Commissioner.

Dated at Muskogee, Indian Territory,
this FEB 16 1907

◇◇◇◇◇

Cherokee Intermarried White 1906
Volume VII

Cherokee No 231

Muskogee, Indian Territory, February 16, 1907.

W. W. Hastings,
    Attorney for the Cherokee Nation,
        Muskogee, Indian Territory.

Dear Sir:

    There is enclosed herewith copy of the decision of the Commissioner to the Five Civilized Tribes, dated February 16, 1907, granting the application for the enrollment of William Crowder as a citizen by intermarriage of the Cherokee Nation.

    Respectfully,

    Commissioner.

Enc I-7

RPI

◇◇◇◇◇

Cherokee 231

Muskogee, Indian Territory, February 16, 1907

The Commissioner to the Five Civilized Tribes,
    Muskogee, Indian Territory.

Sir:

    Receipt is acknowledged of the testimony and of your decision, enrolling William Crowder as a citizen by intermarriage of the Cherokee Nation. Time for protesting said decision is waived and I consent that said person may be placed upon the schedule immediately.

    Respectfully,
    W. W. Hastings
    Attorney for the Cherokee Nation.

◇◇◇◇◇

Cherokee Intermarried White 1906
Volume VII

Cherokee No 231

Muskogee, Indian Territory, February 16, 1907.

William Crowder,
    Baptist, Indian Territory.

Dear Sir:

There is enclosed herewith copy of the decision of the Commissioner to the Five Civilized Tribes, dated February 16, 1907, granting the application for your enrollment as a citizen by intermarriage of the Cherokee Nation.

You will be advised when your name has been placed upon a schedule of citizens of the Cherokee Nation and approved by the Secretary of the Interior.

Respectfully,

Enc I-8

Commissioner.

RPI

◇◇◇◇◇

Cherokee
I.W. 194

Muskogee, Indian Territory, April 16, 1907.

William Crowder,
    Westville, Indian Territory.

Dear Sir:

Your marriage license and certificate filed in connection with your application for enrollment as a citizen by intermarriage of the Cherokee Nation is returned to you herewith, copies of the same being retained in the files of this office.

Respectfully,

Encl. W-23.
S.W.

Commissioner.

Cher IW 195

Cherokee Intermarried White 1906
Volume VII

◇◇◇◇◇

(Copy of original document from case.)

◇◇◇◇◇

DEPARTMENT OF THE INTERIOR
COMMISSIONER TO THE FIVE CIVILIZED TRIBES
CHEROKEE LAND OFFICE

Muskogee, Indian Territory, _____ **March 29**__, 190_7_

Testimony of _____ **William N. Littlejohn**_____
in the matter of the Application for Allotment and Homestead on the reverse side hereof.

Q. What is your name?   A. _____**William N. Littlejohn**_____

Q. What is your postoffice address?   A. _____**Sallisaw I.T.**_____

Q. W_**as**___ the person _____ for whom you make this application living on the first day of September, 1902?   A. _____**Yes**_____

Q. H_**as**_ the person _____ for whom you make this application ever been enrolled or recognized as ____

Cherokee Intermarried White 1906
Volume VII

citizen __ of the Choctaw, Chickasaw, Creek or Seminole Nation? A. **Yes**

Q. H **as** the person _____ for whom you make this application received or applied for _____ allotment of land in the Choctaw, Chickasaw, Creek or Seminole Nation? A. **Yes**

Q. Are there any improvements on the land you have selected for _____ **Yourself** _____ ? A. **Yes**

Q. What do the improvements consist of? A. **Homestead, 2 houses and barns with some out buildings. About all fenced and about 35 acres cultivated. Balance is fenced timber land. Allotment That in *(illegible...)* public domain except for a fence which was across the west side enclosing about 21 acres. This fence was put there by a non citizen named Bond of Owasso, I.T. who once had the place leased before Sarah London applied for the land. Since then she has lost her citizenship. In 12-24 about 3 acres fenced this fence was made by Doc Martin of Sallisaw. But he has certified his allotment and does not claim it any more.**

Q. Who is the owner of these improvements? A. **I am except as stated above.**

Q. Have you obtained permission of _____ **of the person above named** _____ to select the land on which _____ **their** _____ improvements are located? A. **No**

Q. Does any one else claim this land or any part of it? A. **No**

Q. Are there any churches, school houses or burial grounds on this land? A. **No**

Q. Is that portion of the land which you have designated as a homestead suitable for a home?
A. **Yes**

Cherokee Intermarried White 1906
Volume VII

Q. Have you obtained permission of ....
to select the land on which ....improvements are located?   A. ....

Q. Does any one else claim this land or any part of it?   A. ....

Q. Are there any churches, school houses or burial grounds on this land?   A. ....

Q. Is that portion of the land which you have designated as a homestead suitable for a home?
A. ....

Q. Are there any improvements on the land you have selected for ....
....................?   A. ....

Q. What do the improvements consist of?   A. ....

Q. Who is the owner of these improvement?   A. ....

Q. Have you obtained permission of ....
to select the land on which ....improvements are located?   A. ....

Q. Does any one else claim this land or any part of it?   A. ....

Q. Are there any churches, school houses or burial grounds on this land?   A. ....

Q. Is that portion of the land which you have designated as a homestead suitable for a home?
A. ....

Witnesses to mark:

....................**William N Littlejohn**....................

Cherokee Intermarried White 1906
Volume VII

INDIAN TERRITORY,
WESTERN DISTRICT

Subscribed and sworn to before me at Muskogee, Indian Territory, this ___29___ day of ___March___, 190_7_.

B.P. Rasmus
Notary Public.

◇◇◇◇◇

Application No. 5

212

ORIGINAL

DEPARTMENT OF THE INTERIOR
Commissioner to the Five Civilized Tribes
CHEROKEE ENROLLMENT OFFICE.

Muskogee, I. T. Mch 28 A.D. 1907

To the Chief Clerk of the Cherokee Land Office:

This is to certify that the names of the following persons

Roll Number	Card Number	Name	Relationship to Person First Named	Age	Degree of Blood
2A/195	1017	William N. Littlejohn		56	—

4:30 P.M.
3-28-07

All appear upon the records of the Commissioner to the Five Civilized Tribes as citizens of the Cherokee Nation.

_____
Commissioner.

_____
Roll Clerk.

(Copy of original document from case.)
◇◇◇◇◇

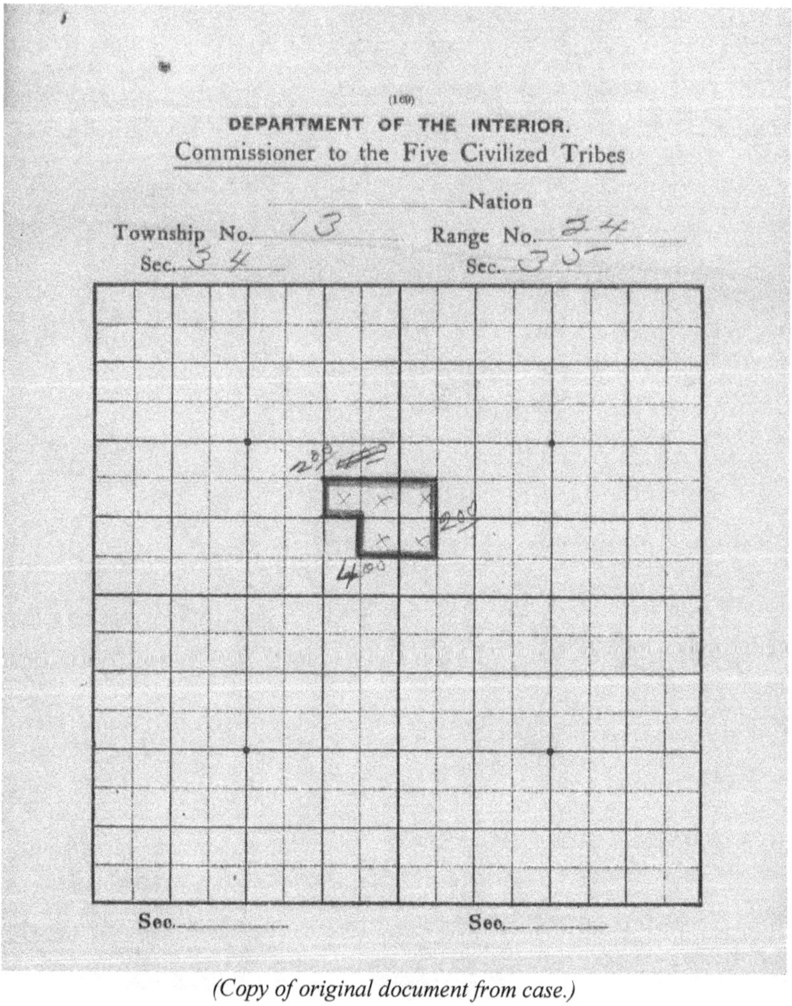

Cherokee Intermarried White 1906
Volume VII

(160)
DEPARTMENT OF THE INTERIOR.
Commissioner to the Five Civilized Tribes

................................Nation
Township No. 13   Range No. 54
Sec. 34   Sec. 35

(Copy of original document from case.)

Cherokee Intermarried White 1906
Volume VII

(Copy of original document from case.)

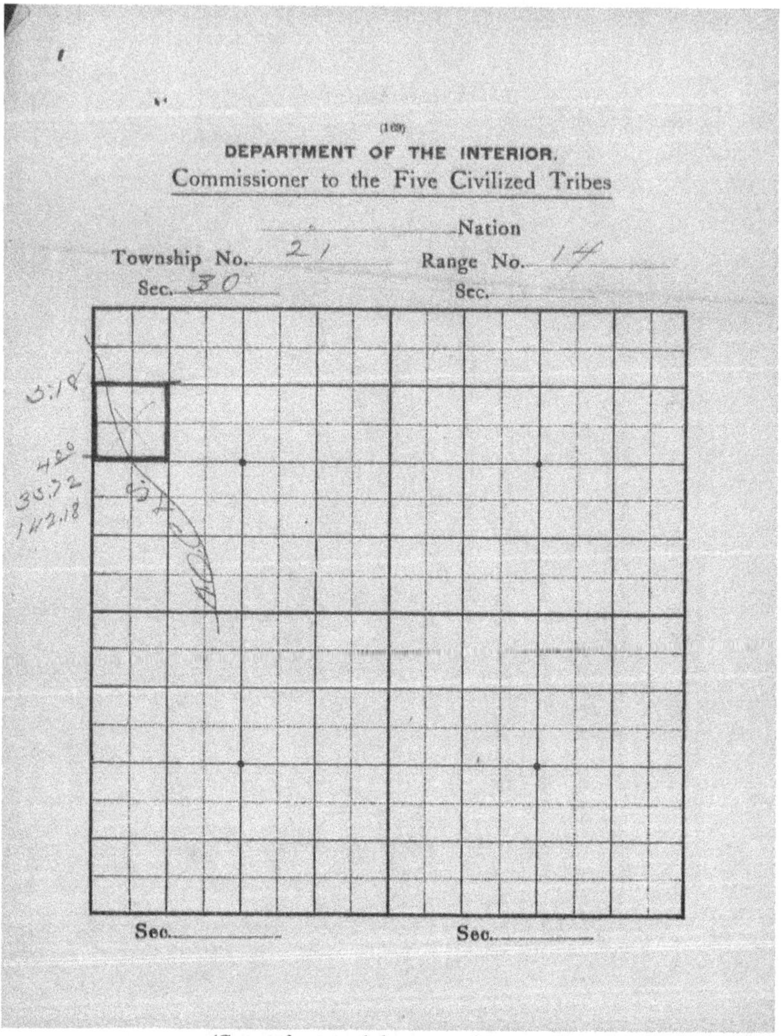

Cherokee Intermarried White 1906
Volume VII

(Copy of original document from case.)

Cherokee Intermarried White 1906
Volume VII

Allotment No.
2768.

December 30, 1904.
Tahlequah, Indian Territory,

Jesse McKnight,
    Alluwee[sic], Indian Territory.

Dear Sir:

    On July 22, 1904, Edward Derrick, of Hayden, Indian Territory, appeared before the Cherokee Land Office at Tahlequah, Indian Territory, and selected in[sic] allotment for Charley B. Derrick, the E/2 of the NW4 of the NE4 and the NE4 of the SW4 of the NE4 of Section 34, Township 26 North, Range 17 East of the Indian Meridian, containing 30 acres.

It appears that you also claim the above described tract of land, or a part thereof.

    Section 49 of the Act of Congress, approved July 1, 1902, (Public No. 241), provides as follows:

    "Sec. 69. After the expiration of nine months after the date of the original selection of an allotment by or for any citizen of the Cherokee tribe as provided in this Act, no contest shall be instituted against such selection, and as early thereafter as practicable patent shall issue therefore."

    You are, therefore, hereby notified that you may appear at the Cherokee Land Office at any time within nine months after the date of said selection and make application for the above described tract of land, or any part thereof claimed by you, and file contest therefor if you so desire.   Respectfully,

CWM

Register

Commissioner in Charge
Cherokee Land Office.

**Cherokee Intermarried White 1906
Volume VII**

I.W. No. 195

William N. Littlejohn

Record and Decision

Not in Cher. No. 1017

4/15/07

Cher IW 196

I.W. No. 196

Phoebe A. Adair

Record and Decision

Not in No 582 - 4/15/07

Cherokee Intermarried White 1906
Volume VII

Cher IW 197

◇◇◇◇◇

> I.W. No. 197
>
> William L. Wilder
>
> Record and Decision
>
> Not in No. 2538 - 4/15/07

Cher IW 198

◇◇◇◇◇

DEPARTMENT OF THE INTERIOR,
COMMISSION TO THE FIVE CIVILIZED TRIBES.
MULDROW, I. T., AUGUST 15th, 1900.

IN THE MATTER OF THE APPLICATION OF Joseph H. Alexander, wife and children, for enrollment as citizens of the Cherokee Nation, and he being sworn by Commissioner, T. B. Needles, testified as follows:

Q What is your name?   A Joseph H. Alexander.
Q What is your age?   A Fifty nine.
Q What is your Postoffice?   A Ft. Smith, Arkansas.
Q Are you a recognized citizen of the Cherokee Nation?   A Yes sir.
Q By blood or by intermarriage?   A By adoption.
Q You mean by intermarriage?   A Yes sir.
Q What District do you live in?   A Sequoyah.
Q How long have you lived there?   A Thirty two years.
Q Continuously in Sequoyah District?   A Yes sir.
Q For whom do you apply?   A My wife and children, and one child of my first wife, and myself.
Q What is your father's name?   A Silas Alexander.

Cherokee Intermarried White 1906
Volume VII

Q Is he living? A No sir.
Q Was he a non citizen? A Yes sir.
Q Are you married? A Yes sir.
Q What is your wifes[sic] name? A Sophronia E. Alexander.
Q When were you married? A The first of April, 1883.
Q What was her name before you married her? A Duncan.
Q Is she living? A Yes sir.
Q What is her father's name? A John Duncan.
Q Is he living? A No sir.
Q Was he a Cherokee citizen by blood? A Yes sir.
Q When did he die? A In 1881, I believe.
Q What is the name of her mother? A Betsey Duncan.
Q Is she living? A Yes sir.
Q What evidence have you of your marriage? A I have a marriage certificate.
Q Have you any children? A Yes sir.
Q What is the name of the oldest one at home? A Maud Alexander.
Q How old? A Sixteen.
Q Next one? A Fay Alexander.
Q How old? A Twelve.
Q Next one? A Kate Alexander.
Q How old? A Four.
Q What is the name of the next one? A That is all.
Q. These children are living, and living with you? A Yes sir.
Q You say you have some children by a former marriage? A Yes sir; one a little over twenty.
Q What is the ones[sic] names at home? A Lillian Alexander.
Q What is the name of Lillian's mother? A Cherokee C. Alexander.
Q Was she a Cherokee by blood? A Yes sir.
Q Is she living? A No sir.

(Applicant identified on the roll of 1880, Page 680, #6, Joseph H. Alexander, Sequoyah District)
(Applicant's present wife identified on the roll of 1880, Page 692, #399, Safrony Alexander, Sequoyah District)
(Lillian Alexander identified on the roll of 1880, Page 680, #13, Lillian Alexander, Sequoyah District)
(Applicant identified on the roll of 1896, Page 1111, #5, Joseph Alexander, Sequoyah District)
(Applicant's wife identified on the roll of 1896, Page 1050, #31, Sophenia Alexander, Sequoyah District)

Identification of applicant's children:
(1896 Roll, Page 1050, #33, Lillian Alexander, Sequoyah District)
(1896 Roll, Page 1050, #34, Maud Alexander, Sequoyah District)
(1896 Roll, Page 1050, #35, Fay Alexander, Sequoyah District)
(1896 Roll, Page 1050, #36, Kate Alexander, Sequoyah District)

Cherokee Intermarried White 1906
Volume VII

The name of Joseph H. Alexander appears upon the authenticated roll of 1880, as well as the census roll of 1896; the name of his wife, Sophronia Alexander appears on the authenticated roll of 1880 as Safrony Duncan, and on the census roll of 1896 as Sophronia Alexander: The names of his children, Lillian, Maude, Fay and Kate appear on the census roll of 1896, they all being in the testimony, and they having made satisfactory proof as to residence, said Joseph H. Alexander will be duly listed for enrollment by this Commission as a citizen by intermarriage; and his wife and children will be duly listed for enrollment by this Commission as Cherokees by blood.

R. R. Cravens, being sworn, states that as stenographer to the Commission to the Five Civilized Tribes, he reported the foregoing case, and that the above and foregoing is a true, full and correct transcript of his stenographic notes in said case.

R. R. cravens

Sworn to and subscribed before
me this 21st day of August, 1900.

T B Needles
COMMISSIONER.

◇◇◇◇◇

R.

DEPARTMENT OF THE INTERIOR.
Commission to the Five Civilized Tribes.
Muskogee, Indian Territory, October 27th, 1902.

In the matter of the application of Joseph H. Alexander for the enrollment of himself as a citizen by intermarriage of the Cherokee Nation and for the enrollment of his wife, Sophronia Alexander, and his children, Lillian, Maud, Fay and Kate Alexander, as citizens by blood of the Cherokee Nation.

Supplemental to #1450.

JOSEPH H. ALEXANDER, being duly sworn, testified as follows:
Examination by the Commission.

Q. What is your name?   A. Joseph H. Alexander.
Q. What is your age?   A. Near 62, as well as I can remember.
Q. What is your post office?   A. Fort Smith.
Q. Are you an applicant for enrollment as an intermarried citizen?   A. Yes, sir.
Q. What is your wife's name?   A. My present wife is named Sophronia.
Q. When were you married to her?   A. '83.
Q. Had you been married before you married this wife?   A. Yes, sir.

Cherokee Intermarried White 1906
Volume VII

Q. What was your first wife's name?   A. Cherry C. Thompson.
Q. Was she a Cherokee by blood?   A. Yes, sir.
Q. Were you married to your first wife under a Cherokee license?
A. Yes, sir; the second time I was. I remarried. Married in Texas and remarried in January, 1868.
Q. Do you appear on the eighty roll with her?   A. Yes, sir.
Q. When did she die?   A. She died the 11th day of April, 1881.
Q. After her death you married your wife Sophronia?   A. Yes, sir.
Q. Is she also a Cherokee?   A. Yes, sir.
Q. Did you and your first wife live together until her death?   A. Yes, sir.
Q. Have you and your present wife always lived together as husband and wife?
A. Yes, sir.
Q. Never have been separated?   A. No, sir.
Q. Has your home been in the Cherokee Nation?   A. It has been our home all the time, although my wife has occasionally moved to Fort Smith to send our children to school.
Q. How many times did you go to Fort Smith?   A. About 5 times.
Q. When did you go there first?   A. I took my first family there in 1873. Then I married again and went there in 1884, then in 1887.
Q. Then did you go in 1887 again?   A. Yes, sir, and stayed two years. Then I went about in 1892 and I have been there ever since.
Q. Your family has been in Fort Smith since 1892?   A. Yes, sir. My home is in the bottom and we can't live there. It is close to town.
Q. How far from town?   A. About 2 miles. I work my farm myself and have been for 34 years.
Q. As a matter of fact, since 1892 your wife and children have spent their time in Fort Smith?   A. Yes, sir.
Q. Do you have a house--keep house in Fort Smith?   A. Yes, sir.
Q. Never kept house with your family over in the Nation since 1892?
A. Not the last time. I have kept house in the bottom; me and my son.
Q. You have stayed, yourself, at the farm for the last 3 or 4 years?   A. Yes, sir; I run the farm for 34 years. The family has only been there part of the time.
Q. Where have you spent most of the time?   A. On the farm and at Muldrow. I have got a gin there.
Q. Which son is it that is there with you?   A. Joe.
Q. But your wife and the younger children stay at Fort Smith?   A. Yes, sir.
Q. And you go over Saturday and stay until Monday morning, as a rule?   A. Yes, sir.
Q. These children, Lillian, Maud, Fay and Kate, are you children by your present wife?
A. No, sir; Lillian is the youngest by my first wife.
Q. The other three are children by your present wife?   A. Yes, sir
Q. All four of these children are living?   A. Yes, sir; Lillian has been teaching in the seminary.
Q. Which seminary?   A. Female seminary at Tahlequah.
Q. Do you know how long she has been teaching there?   A. 2 or 3 years. After he quit school. She went east to school.

Cherokee Intermarried White 1906
Volume VII

Q. Where did she go to school?   A. Columbia 5 years ago and Vanderbilts[sic] the neat[sic] year, then came back and went to teaching in the seminary.
Q. Since she quit school she has been teaching over in the seminary?   A. Yes, sir.
Q. The other three children have been with their mother in Fort Smith?
A. Yes, sir. One of them is off to school in Virginia.
Q. What is true as to your wife and yourself is true as to your children?   A. Yes, sir.
Q. As to residence?   A. Yes, sir.

++++++++++++++++++++++++++++++++++

Jesse O. Carr, being first duly sworn, states that as stenohrapher[sic] to the Commission to the Five Civilized Tribes he reported the above entitled case and that the foregoing is a true and complete transcript of his stenographic notes thereof.

Jesse O. Carr

Subscribed and sworn to before me this 28th day of October, 1902.

PG Reuter
Notary Public.

◇◇◇◇◇

Cherokee 1450.

DEPARTMENT OF THE INTERIOR,
COMMISSION TO THE FIVE CIVILIZED TRIBES.
Muskogee, I. T., October 29, 1902.

In the matter of the application of Joseph H. Alexander for the enrollment of himself as a citizen by intermarriage, and for the enrollment of his wife, Sophronia Alexander, and his four minor children, Lillian, Maud, Fay and Kate Alexander, as citizens by blood, of the Cherokee Nation.

SUPPLEMENTAL PROCEEDINGS.

JOSEPH H. ALEXANDER, being sworn, testified as follows:

By the Commission,

Q What is your name, please?   A Joseph H. Alexander.
Q How old are you, Mr. Alexander?   A Sixty-two.
Q You appeared before the Commission on last Monday and gave some testimony in regard to your application?   A Yes, sir.
Q You were married to your first wife when, Mr. Alexander?
A Originally in Texas and we married in '68; afterward we came to the Nation in the fall of '68, and married under Cherokee law.

Cherokee Intermarried White 1906
Volume VII

Q How long did she live after you were married?   A She died in '81.
Q She appears on the '80 roll?   A Yes, sir, her and her children.
Q Then when did you marry your second wife?   A In 1883.
Q In 1883?   A Yes, sir.
Q She was also a Cherokee?   A Yes, sir, she was raised here.
Q You did not take out a license to marry the second time?   A No, sir, I had a marriage certificate down at the hotel. I exhibited that before.
Q Have you and your second wife lived together since your marriage to the present time?   A Yes, sir.
Q Where have you lived, Mr. Alexander, since 1880?   A I have lived in Sequoyah District near Fort Smith.
Q Where has your wife, Sophronia, lived all that time?   A Part of the time there and part of the time in Fort Smith sending the children to school.
Q When did you first take your family to Fort Smith?   A My family stayed there a little while in the summer of '84 and back there in the year '87, and then in '92 we moved back.
Q Has your wife and children been living in Fort Smith, Arkansas keeping house there, since 1892?   A Yes, sir, but I have not been keeping house there. I have been on my farm, had my own house there, that is, cook and run the place there the whole time.
Q How far is your farm from fort Smith?   A About two and a half miles above the bridge on this side and another mile to the town across the river.
Q Who's living on your farm at this time?   A I and my son, Joe.
Q How old is Joe?   A He is about thirty.
Q He a married man?   A No.
Q He baches[sic] there?   A He keeps cooks hired. We run the farm with hired hands.
Q You say your wife and children have lived in Fort Smith since '92?   A Yes, sir.
Q The got a house, keep house, there?   A Yes, sir.
Q And you claim you have been yourself in the Territory since '92?   A Yes, sir, all my business is there.
Q You and your wife are not separated at all, are you?   A No.
Q Still living together?   A We are not separated at all, I visit them still.
Q How often do you go?   A In busy time I go Saturday night and stay until Monday morning.
Q From Staurday[sic] night until Monday morning?   A Yes, sir, I stay all the week in Muldrow. I have a cotton gin.
Q How far is Muldrow from your farm?   A About eight miles.
Q Do you stay on the farm while you run the gin at Muldrow?   A No, sir.
Q Do you keep house there?   A Yes, sir.
Q How much of the year do you stay at Muldrow?   A I stay all the fall of the year from September to the last of February. I buy cotton and attend to the business. My son runs the farm or part of it, he has charge of the farm.
Q He has charge of the hands and you and he share in the profits of the farm?   A I assist him in running the farm and we share in the profits. I furnish the stock and everything is mine.
Q Well, have you got - do you keep a cook of your own over here on the farm?
A Yes, sir, I keep a family there hired.

Cherokee Intermarried White 1906
Volume VII

Q Keep a hired family? A Yes, sir.
Q And you only spend Saturday night and Sunday over in Fort Smith?
A As a rule.
Q Well, isn't it a matter of fact, Mr. Alexander, that your home is in Fort Smith since '92? A No, I don't pretend to have any family there, they can't live there. We buried one child and my wife said she would go to Fort Smith and raise the children.
Q Did you have a house in Fort Smith? A Yes, sir, but I do not vote there. I have repeatedly sworn that I am not a citizen of Arkansas. I am a citizen of the Cherokee Nation. I have always been recognized as a Cherokee and voted always at every election for thirty-four years since I have been here and have never been challenged or disputed.
Q You keep up the expenses of the house there in Fort Smith of your wife and children, don't you? A Yes, sir, of course.
Q Do you have your washing done over there? A No, not much of the time. My washing is done at the farm.
Q At the farm? A yes, sir.
Q Where do you spend the summers, Mr. Alexander? A I spend them mostly on the farm.
Q Where do you spend July and August? A On the farm. Just as busy a time as any other time - potato raising - we raise a crop of potatoes in the summer. My family sometimes go off in the summer.
Q Your children all living there with your wife? A All but one was born on the farm.
Q And the youngest was born at Fort Smith? A Yes, sir.
Q But the oldest children have lived with your wife in Fort Smith ever since '92, except the time when the others were off at school? A Yes, sir, there at school, that's the object in taking them there. We never considered we were violating the Cherokee law, that is, as long as we were loyal to the Cherokee. All my effects are here.
Q Your family, your wife and children, with you, have never kept house ever in the Cherokee Nation since 1892, have they? A They have not. They did come over and spend the summer in '96, I believe, and then went back but they have not kept house since '92 there, jot except that summer.
Q In '96? A Yes, sir.
Q How long were they over there in '96? A About five month.
Q Did you move all your furniture from Fort Smith to the farm? A All that we had room for.
Q How much of a house, Mr. Alexander, have you got there on the farm where your son, Joe, stays? A Well, we have got a number of houses but the one we live in is a two story house, six rooms, yellow, big enough for a family that does the work and the hands.
Q Who owns the house there? A I do.
Q Your son has no interest? A I think not of that kind, only his clothes. I had it all there before he was old enough to work.
Q Your son has lived there all the time since he has been grown?
A Yes, sir, he never was out only he went to school in Fort Smith four or five months and in Virginia a while, but he has been here ever since.
Q How much of the time, Mr. Alexander, out of the year do you spend in Fort Smith?
A Well, I don't know in a year, let's see, when I am not very busy one or two days in the week. I have nothing to do in Fort Smith and I don't like to stay there. I have work in the

Cherokee Intermarried White 1906
Volume VII

woods on my own farm. I always have plenty to do. I have stock there and have nothing in the world to do in Fort Smith. I don't like to loaf.

    Retta Chick, being first duly sworn, states that, as stenographer to the Commission to the Five Civilized Tribes, she recorded the testimony and proceedings in the matter of the foregoing application, and that the above is a true and complete transcript of her stenographic notes thereof.

                                           Retta Chick

Subscribed and sworn to before me this 29th day of November, 1902.

                                           BC Jones

                                                                   Notary Public.

◇◇◇◇◇

Cher
Supp'l to # 1450

                              Department of the Interior,
                   Commission to the Five Civilized Tribes,
                       Muskogee, I. T., October 31, 1902.

    In the matter of the application of JOSEPH H. ALEXANDER, for the enrollment of himself as a citizen by intermarriage, and his wife, SAPHRONIA ALEXANDER, and his children, LILLIAN, MAUD, FAY and KATE ALEXANDER, as citizens by blood, of the Cherokee Nation:

    JOE ALEXANDER, being duly sworn and examined by the Commission, testified as follows:

Q What is your name ? A Joe Alexander.
Q What is your post office address ? A Fort Smith.
Q How old are you ? A Thirty years old.
Q What is the name of your father ? A Joseph H. Alexander.
Q What is the name of your mother ? A Cherokee Alexander.
Q Is your mother living ? A No sir.
Q Has your father married since her death ? A Yes sir.
Q What is his present wife's name ? A Saphronia.
Q You want to give testimony in the matter of your father's application for enrollment ? A Yes sir.
Q Now, do you live in Fort Smith, Mr. Alexander ? A No sir.
Q How far do you live from Fort Smith ? A About three miles.
Q Do you live on a farm ? A Yes sir.
Q Who does the farm belong to ? A It belongs to my father.
Q Are you a married man Mr. Alexander ? A No sir.
Q Do you keep house there on the farm ? A Yes sir, we hire a cook and I keep house.

29

Cherokee Intermarried White 1906
Volume VII

Q You hire a cook ? A Yes sir.
Q Where does your father's wife and his younger children live ?
A They are in Fort Smith.
Q How long have they been living there in Fort Smith ?
A They have been over there since about 1892.
Q Have they got a house, and keep house over there, do they ?
A Yes sir, they have got a house. The children are going to school over there.
Q Your father and his wife Saphronia live together over there don't they ? A They have never parted; he lives on the farm with me, and goes over there occasionally.
Q He don't pretend to live with his family ?
A He goes over there; they are over there with the children going to school.
Q Is the school going on all the time over there ?
A Yes sir, nine months in the year.
Q Have your father Joseph H. Alexander and his wife Saphronia kept house in the Cherokee Nation since 1892 ? A Yes sir.
Q Where ? A Up on the prairie. We keep house in the bottom all the time.
Q Has your father and his wife Saphronia kept house in the Cherokee Nation since they went to Fort Smith in 1892 ? A Yes sir.
Q Where ? A Up on the prairie about seven or eight miles from Fort Smith. They lived up there.
Q How long at any one time ? A About seven months was the longest time.
Q When was that ? A In 1896
Q What time of the year was it ? A In the summer.
Q Have they, since 1896, kept house in the Cherokee Nation for as much as a month at any one time ? A Well, the folks have been over.
Q That is his wife, your step-mother, and their children ? A No sir.
Q Since 1896 ? A No sir.
Q They come over sometimes on the farm for two or three days, and then go back to town, don't they ? A Yes sir.
Q And since 1896 they have never stayed as much as a month on the Cherokee side of the river, at any one time, to keep house ? A I don't believe they have.
Q Your father and his wife still live together as man and wife ? A Yes sir.
Q They haven't been separated ? A No sir.
Q Do you mean to say that your father lives on the farm with you and his wife and children stay at Fort Smith ? A We keep house there, and his business is there.
Q How far is your farm from Fort Smith ? A Three miles.
Q Don't your father, in the summer, stay over at Fort Smith at night, and drive out to the farm in the morning ? A No sir.
Q He stays on the farm all the week and goes over to town on Saturday and stays in town until Monday ? A That's generally the way.
Q During the cotton seas,[sic] say from September until spring, where does he stay ?
A Mostly at Muldrow.
Q He doesn't stay on the farm any during the winter does he ?
A No much. He comes down sometimes and stays a day or two.
Q Mr. Alexander, isn't it a fact that your farm is run pretty nearly exclusively by you ?
A No sir, we are partners.

Cherokee Intermarried White 1906
Volume VII

Q You are partners in the farming business ?
A He pays his part of the expenses, yes sir.
Q So far as the working of the crops, and everything of that kind, isn't that done directly under your supervision ? A No sir, he does about as much of it as I do.
Q You are there all the time aren't you ? A Not all the time; sometimes I go away, and he's there.
Q How long do you stay away ? A All night sometimes.
Q You never stay away as much as a week do you ? A Sometimes I do.
Q Does that occur very often ? A Not very often.
Q You are there on the farm a good deal more than your father ?
A He goes over to town more than I do.
Q He goes to town a great deal more than you do ? He doesn't pay you for staying there? Doesn't he go to town a great deal oftener than you do ? A No sir.
Q How often do you go over to Fort Smith ?
A Two or three times a week.
Q You don't spend the night there do you ? A Once in a while.
Q How often ? A Once a week, on Saturday night sometimes.
Q Your father in the winter time and fall stays up at Muldrow in the morning ?
A Sometimes he stays at Muldrow.
Q Qhile[sic] he is up there running the gin you stay on the farm ? A Yes sir.
Q You try to make it convenient for one of you to be on the farm all the time ?
A Yes sir.
Q You don't have anything to do with the ginning business at Muldrow ? A Yes sir, I am interested some; I go up there some myself.
Q Do you go up there and see about the business of ginning ?
A Yes sir sometimes I do.
Q Do you take charge of the ginning business ?
A Not as much as I do on the farm.
Q Do you take any charge of the gin up there ?
A When I am up there I do.
Q About how often do you go up there ?
A About once a week.
Q To Muldrow ? A Yes sir.
Q How long do you usually stay as a general proposition ?
A About half a day.
Q Just to look around to see how things are going on ?
A Yes sir.
Q You don't figure on what the ginning business is dong; whether it is running at a profit or a loss ? A Yes sir, I can stay in the bottom and do that.
Q Your step-mother, and these children, these younger children of your father's, your half-brothers and sisters, they keep house of your father's, your half-brothers and sisters, they keep house over there in Fort Smith, Arkansas don't they ? A Yes sir.
Q And they have kept house over there since they went there in 1892, haven't they ?
A Yes sir, except what time they are over in the Indian Territory.
Q When they are over in the Indian Territory they still keep their house in Fort Smith ?
A Yes sir.

Cherokee Intermarried White 1906
Volume VII

Q They have got their furniture over there and all ?
A They moved their furniture over there when they come over into the Territory.
Q That was in 1896 ? A Yes sir.
Q And they came over and stayed two or three months on the prairie there ?
A I think it was several months.
Q They stayed over there one summer, didn't they ? A Yes sir.
Q They didn't stay there during the winter and fall ? A No sir.
Q They went back to Fort Smith did they, so the children could go to school ?
A Yes sir.
Q Since then they haven't moved their furniture over into the Cherokee Nation to live, have they ? A No sir, but I carried some of the furniture over to the farm.
Q How long have Mrs. Alexander or the children stayed over there on the farm since 1896 ? A They haven't stayed over a night or two at a time.
Q Have they ever stayed over there, you since, since 1896, as much as a week at any one time ? Over on the farm ? A I don't remember that they have stayed that long.
Q Your father and your step-mother have never been separated since they were married, have they ? A No sir.
Q They were living together as man and wife on the first day of September, 1902 ?
A Yes sir.

GABRIEL L. PAYNE, called as a witness, being duly sworn and examined by the Commission, testified as follows:

Q What is your name ? A Gabriel L. Payne.
Q How old are you ? A Forty six years old.
Q Where do you live ? A In Sequoyah District, Cherokee Nation.
Q What is your post office address ? A Fort Smith.
Q How far from Fort Smith do you live ?
A I suppose it is in the neighborhood of seven or eight miles. It is right across the river.
Q Are you a citizen of the Cherokee Nation ? A Yes sir.
Q Are you an intermarried citizen or a citizen by blood ?
A By adoption.
Q You want to give some testimony in the matter of the application of Joseph H. Alexander ? A Mr. Alexander asked me to come up and testify in regard to his living in the Cherokee Nation.
Q How long have you known Mr. Alexander ? A Since 1869.
Q Do you know his present wife ? A Yes sir.
Q Where has Mr. Alexander lived for the past ten years ?
A Well, he has always claimed Sequoyah District, right above me, his home is right adjoining my farm.
Q Where has his wife and younger children lived since 1892 ?
A Well, they have been principally in Fort Smith.
Q Haven't they been in Fort Smith all the time with the exception of two or three months in 1896 ? A Maybe they have.
Q You can't say ? A No sir.

Cherokee Intermarried White 1906
Volume VII

Q How long do you know, of your own knowledge, of Mr. Alexander and his wife keeping house in the Cherokee Nation ?
A He was married in the Cherokee Nation.
Q I mean since 1892 ? A Now just wait until I tell you. He was married to his wife in the Cherokee Nation, and my recollection is that it was about 1891 or 1892 that he moved his family to Fort Smith. And then he moved back once after that time, but how long he stayed back I can't say.
Q That was about 1896 that he brought the family back up on the prairie ? A Probably so, that's where they lived. He has got a home up on the prairie where they lived before he took them to town.
Q With the exception of that one time, that you speak of, when he moved his family back over there, has Mr. Alexander, with his wife and younger children, jept[sic] house in the Cherokee Nation or Indian Territory since 1892 ? A I can't say positively whether they have or not.
Q Don't you know his family and the children have lived in Fort Smith all the time ?
A No sir, I do not know that. I know they came back over on this side of the river, but whether that was in 1896----
Q With the exception of that one time you speak of, haven't his wife and children lived in Fort Smith, Arkansas ?
A I can't say positively, but I think so.
Q Mr. Alexander has a farm on this side of the river right close to you, and only a short distance from Fort Smith ?
A Yes sir.
Q And he stays on the farm a good deal himself ? A Yes sir.
Q And he goes over once a week to see his family ?
A I can't say that he goes to see his family, but I suppose it would be natural that he should; out business is mostly donw[sic] at Fort Smith.
Q They were no separated ? A No sir.
Q They were living together as husband and wife on the first day of September, 1902 ?
A Yes sir.
Q They have never separated ? A No sir, I am pretty well acquainted with them; he is a brother-in-law of mine.

E. C. Bagwell, on oath states that, as stenographer to the Commission to the Five Civilized Tribes, he correctly recorded the testimony and proceedings had in the above entitled cause, and that the foregoing is an accurate transcript of his stenographic notes thereof.

E.C. Bagwell

Subscribed and sworn to before me this December 1, 1902.

PG Reuter
Notary Public.

◇◇◇◇◇

Cherokee Intermarried White 1906
Volume VII

Cher
Supp'l to # 1450

Department of the Interior,
Commission to the Five Civilized Tribes,
Muskogee, I. T., December 22, 1902.

In the matter of the application of JOSEPH H. ALEXANDER, for the enrollment of himself as a citizen by intermarriage, and his wife, SAPHRONIA ALEXANDER, and his children, LILLIAN, MAUD, FAY and KATE ALEXANDER, as citizens by blood of the Cherokee Nation.

Appearances:
    Applicant present in person, and by his attorneys, W. T. Hutchings and W. P. Thompson;

JOSEPH H. ALEXANDER, being duly sworn and examined by the Commission, testified as follows:

Examined by Mr. Hutchings:

Q State your name ?   Joseph H. Alexander.
Q You are the applicant that applied in August, 1900, for yourself and family ?
A Yes sir.
Q You have testified twice before in this case ?   A Yes sir.

By Mr. Hutchings: I want to offer in evidence Section Two, Article One, of the Constitution of the Cherokee Nation.

Witness further examined by Mr. Hutchings, as follows:

Q How long have you resided in the Cherokee Nation ?
A Thirty four years.
Q Did you ever hold any office in the Cherokee Nation ?   A Yes sir.
Q What was that ?   A Clerk of the district for two years.
Q Where has your family resided for the last ten years outside of yourself ?
A In Fort Smith.
Q Why did you carry your family to Fort Smith at that time ?
A At that time she was an invalid, and the physician, Dr. Bailey, Indian Territory stated that he would have to see her every day, and that she would have to go to the hospital, and requested that she come to town. We were living nine miles from Fort Smith on the prairie farm.
Q Did he perform any operations upon your wife ?   A Yes sir.
Q Has it been necessary that she be constantly under his treatment ever since that time?
A Yes sir, he performed three operations upon her in three or four years; they were only partially successful, and he is still treating her.

Cherokee Intermarried White 1906
Volume VII

Q   Doctor W. W. Bailey ?   A Yes sir.
Q   Could you have procured such medical services where you then lived as were necessary for her to have ?   A   No sir I could not. There was no one that could possibly perform the operations he does.
Q   Doctor Bailey is an eminent physician in Fort Smith ?
A   Yes sir, known as one, and a surgeon.
Q   What property did you have in the Cherokee Nation in 1892 when you moved your wife and children to Fort Smith ?
A   I had one farm of five hundred and fifty acres in cultivation on the farm; and one of one hundred, and one of sixty, separate ones in the bottom, and a prairie farm of two hundred acres in cultivation, besides a prairie pasture and hay pasture, of one hundred acres.
Q   What sort of improvements were on these places, and about what value ?
A   The prairie farm had about a $1000.00 dwelling house, and three tenant houses worth perhaps $200.00 a piece, and three or four good wells; and the one hundred acre farm had a good four room dwelling and three or four smaller tenant houses; and the small sixty acre farm had one three room house and out-buildings.
Q   What chattel and property ?
A   On the five hundred and fifty acre farm I have one good big dwelling for tenant house worth five or six hundred dollars, and had a house we kept for keeping house in, was furnished and everything, seven rooms, two story house, and five other common tenant houses, worth one hundred and fifty dollars a piece, I reckon, besides stock sheds and hay sheds. The buildings alone, I value at about $3000.00 altogether, actual cost; and I have about $2000.00 worth of farming machinery. Do you want to know what it consists of ?
Q   No; that $2000.00 worth of machinery.
A   I have a steam gin on the farm worth about $3000.00; at Muldrow I have a steam gin worth about $3500.00, and a small dwelling house worth about $200.00.
Q   Did you have these last things in 1892 when you sent your wife to Fort Smith ?
A   I had everything but that little dwelling at Muldrow. And in addition to that I bought some more land in the bottom.
Q   Now, what chattel property, in the way of horses, cattle, and one thing and another, have you had down on these places during the last ten years ?   A In 1892 I had one hundred head of cattle and about sixteen mules and thirty head of stock mares, and a stallion and a jack, and hogs, about one hundred head.
Q   Well ?   A Since then I have disposed of the most of the cattle, got about twenty five or thirty head now, and the stock mares. I have now about thirty head of work mules. I work that six hundred acre farm with hired hands, with my own stock.
Q   Then you have all the time, since 1892, had these farms and gins, and everything in the way of stock, on the farms ?   A Yes sir.
Q   Who has looked after this business in the Cherokee Nation ?
A   With the help of my son, I have. He stays on the bottom farm, and I help him, and these other farms I attend to myself without assistance, and in the fall I run the Muldrow gin, and I by cotton and manage it.

Cherokee Intermarried White 1906
Volume VII

Q   How do you live over in the Nation, and have lived since 1892 ?
A   While I run the prairie farm I had a straw berry farm there, and put in the most of my time there; I hired a man and his wife to cook, and the last four years I rented that farm out, and I moved the balance of my furniture to the bottom farm, and made that my headquarters when I wasn't at Muldrow.
Q   In what district of the Cherokee Nation are all these places ?
A   In Sequoyah.
Q   Have you all the time, since 1892, has reserved a furnished room for yourself in the Cherokee Nation ?   A   Yes sir, I have two places, one in the bottom, and one on the prairie. For the last four years I have been in the bottom.
Q   How much of your time in the last ten years have you spent in the city of Fort Smith, Arkansas ?
A   I suppose about two days in the week. I go there on business about the same as I did when my family lived in the Nation.
Q   The rest of the time you spent in the Cherokee Nation ?
A   Yes sir.
Q   Have you, at any time since 1892, had any business interests in the city of Fort Smith ?   A   No sir, I haven't done a dollar's worth of business interest in my life in Fort Smith.
Q   Has your business interests in the Nation occupied your time constantly during all that time ?   A   Yes sir, I have had more than I could do well.
Q   Did you by a home for your wife in Fort Smith ?   A   Yes sir.
Q   Have your children been going to school in Fort Smith since they were large enough to go to school ?   A   Yes sir, that's one of the motives for going there; we had no schools.
Q   Have you kept your children in school up to the present time in Fort Smith during the school year ?   A   Yes sir.
Q   Were there any schools where you could have sent them where you then resided in the Cherokee Nation ?
A   No sir, not since '92.
Q   Did you ever vote in the city of Fort Smith, or State of Arkansas ?
A   No sir.
Q   Were you at one or more times summoned to serve on juries in the city of Fort Smith, Arkansas in the Circuit Court there ?
A   Yes sir.
Q   Who was presiding judge at that time ?
A   Edgar E. Bryant.
Q   Were you sworn to answer questions in court ?   A   Yes sir.
Q   What statement did you make, and with what result ?
A   That I was a citizen of the Cherokee Nation, and not a citizen of Arkansas. The judge said of course I was not a competent juror and to stand aside.
Q   Did you ever pay poll tax in the city of Fort Smith ?
A   I paid poll tax once.
Q   What was the circumstance ?   A   I was assessed without my knowledge, and when they went to collect it I objected to it, and the Sheriff insisted, and said I could protest it, and he would write the protest across the receipt.

Cherokee Intermarried White 1906
Volume VII

Q It was just a dollar wasn't it ?   A Yes sir.
Q Did he give you a receipt with your protest marked on it ?
A He did.
Q That's the only time you ever paid it ?   A Yes sir, the only time I ever did. I was negligent in giving in my personal tax and they took it themselves.
Q When you moved your family what property did you take to Fort Smith ?   A Part of my furniture, after leaving enough in my house over there.
Q What was the value of the furniture you left on the Cherokee side ?
A Worth about $150.00 on the two places.
Q Have you always kept that furniture over there ?   A Yes sir.
Q And used it ?   A Yes sir.
Q How are you living now, and have been living for the last two or three years ?
A In the bottom, we hired a cook, and furnish board and rooms for the hands, and my son and I have rooms to ourselves.
Q You have got that room furnished ?   A Yes sir.
Q How much of your time do you spend there ?
A I spend; in the spring I stay there nearly all the time and in potatoe[sic] planting time; and in the fall I put in the biggest part of my time at Muldrow.
Q How often do you go to Fort Smith to see your family ?   And have for the last ten years ?   A Once or twice a week. If I am busy I go Saturday evening and stay until Monday morning; not any oftener than I would go if they were living on this side, for my business has to be transacted there.
Q Have you kept a sort of a store there, a commisary[sic] on your farm ?
A Yes sir, I have kept one for ten years I reckon.
Q Do you run it yourself ?   A Yes sir.
Q Have you acquired any other property besides that you mentioned, over there ?
A I bought an adjoining piece of land to straighten out the lines last year.
Q How much did you give for that ?
A There forty four acres, I gave $1100.00 for it cash.
Q Have you kept up your farms and improvements and everything in good shape ?
A Yes sir.
Q Well, have you at any time ever had any intention of acquiring citizenship in the state of Arkansas ?   A No sir.
Q Have you ever abandoned or intended to abandon your citizenship in the Cherokee Nation ?   A No sir.
Q Have you always expressed yourself to your friends and everybody else, that you kept your citizenshop[sic] in the Cherokee Nation ?   A Yes sir.
Q Did you for for[sic] the treaty ?   Did you vote the last time in the treaty election?
A I voted in the election.
Q What is the total value of all the property you now own in the Cherokee Nation ?
A I estimate it at $44,000.00
Q What is the value of the land too ?
A Yes sir, that the value of the clearing of the land.
Q That's the value of the improvements on the places, and the improvements you have put on them, including the breaking of it, and everything to date ?   A Yes sir.
Q It stands you $43,800.00 ?   A Yes sir.

Cherokee Intermarried White 1906
Volume VII

Mr. Hutchings: I desire to introduce in evidence the following itemized statement:

Bottom farm,	$ 22,500.00	
Prairie farm,	4,000.00	
Houses,	5,000.00	
Machinery,	2,000.00	
Horses and mules,	3,000.00	
Muldrow gin,	3,500.00	
Bottom gin,	3,000.00	
Household goods,	300.00	
Cattle and hogs,	500.00	
		$ 43,800.00
Residence at Muldrow,		200.00
		$ 44,000.00

Witness further examined by Mr. Hutchings as follows:

Mr. Hutchings: Doctor Bailey, whose certificate we have offered in evidence, had to go to New York on account of the illness of his wife, and for that reason he couldn't possibly come here.

The Commission: The applicant offers in evidence certificate of W. W. Bailey, M.D., under date of November 25, 1902.

By the Commission:

Q Mr. Alexander, your family have been in Fort Smith ever since 1892, have they ?
A Yes sir.
Q With the exception of one year ?   A With the exception of two or three months they come out on the lower prairie place and stayed there.
Q Your family have kept house in Fort Smith during all that time ?
A Yes sir.
Q You have paid taxes on your property in Fort Smith ?
A Yes sir.
Q You own a house in Fort Smith ?   A Yes sir.
Q You pay taxes on that and on personal property you own there ?
A Yes sir.
Q You have spent the greater portion of your time, however, in the Cherokee Nation during that time ?   A Yes sir.
Q How often, Mr. Alexander, do you go to Fort Smith, that is since your family has been living there ?   A Well, about as often as my business requires me, about twice a week or once a week.
Q How far is your place from Fort Smith ?   A The bottom place where I am staying now is about three miles. And I am six months at Muldrow. I stay there sometimes all the week and Sunday too.

Cherokee Intermarried White 1906
Volume VII

Q   These four children[sic], Lillian, Maud, Fay and Kate, have been with your wife in Fort Smith all the time, until the older one went to Tahlequah ?   A Lillian went to Columbia, Tennessee in '98.
Q   Her home has been with your wife ?   A Yes sir, until she left there to go to school.
Q   Until she left there and went out on her own hook ?
A   Yes sir. When she started off to school you might say, for she paid her own way.
Q   Did you ever vote in Fort Smith ?   A No sir.
Q   Never voted in the State of Arkansas at all ?   A No sir. I never voted any place in my life except in the Cherokee Nation.
Q   You paid poll tax one time in the city of Fort Smith, and State of Arkansas ?
A   Yes sir.
Q   Do you know what year that was ?   A I do not; I think it was about three years ago, during that late Sheriff's last term.

By Mr. Hutchings:

Q   What became of the receipt the Sheriff gave you ?
A   I lost it
Q   State whether you have had it during the pendency of this case ?
A   Yes sir, I had it when I was here the second time.
Q   It showed your protest on the face of it ?   A Yes sir, and the reason for it, and the Sheriff states on it that he was compelled to collect it.
Q   Have you served on the United States juries in the Indian Territory ?   A Yes sir.
Q   Where ?   A At Wagoner. Three years ago I served, and was summoned again last year and was excused on account of age.

WILLIAM H. NORRID, being duly sworn by the Commission, and examined, testified as follows:

Examined by Mr. Hutchings:

Q   State your name ?   A William H. Norrid.
Q   Where is your post office ?   A Muldrow.
Q   You are a citizen of the Cherokee Nation ?   A Yes sir.
Q   How long have you known Mr. Alexander, the applicant here ?
A   I have known Mr. Alexander--well, nearly ever since I can remember. Twenty years I guess.
Q   Do you know about the time his family removed to the city of Fort Smith ?
A   Yes sir, I know about what time.
Q   State if you know about how he has lived since that time ?
A   Since that time Mr. Alexander, since he moved his family to Fort Smith, Arkansas has stayed at Muldrow. Now he comes to Muldrow about the first or the middle of September, as soon as the ginning season opens up he comes to Muldrow, and stays there

Cherokee Intermarried White 1906
Volume VII

the biggest part of the time; he is there and buys cotton, and he is there all the time continuously until about the last of January or first of February, the ginning season is over, and then in the spring of the year Mr. Alexander is on his farm, and is planting potatoes along about the first of April, and stays there on his farm and looks after his farm, and he has a little commissary there, and I think they furnish quite a good many people around the country. He has got a little store on the place. He has a residence there, and a place where he boards his hands, and a two story building, and he has his room there and his furniture and bed, and he stays there the biggest part of his time. The fact of the business is he is over there, I guess, nearly every day.

Q If you should go to look for Mr. Alexander at any time, where would you go as his usual place of abode ?   A I would go to the farm if he wasn't at Muldrow.

Q What proportion of his time do you consider he is in the Indian Territory at one of these places ?   A At the very least, three-fourths of his time. At the very least, and maybe more. Sometimes probably he don't go to Fort Smith more than once a week.

Q Do you know whether he has had all this time, cattle, horses, and things of that sort over there ?   A Yes sir, I suppose Mr. Alexander has between three and five thousand dollars worth of mules and horses there on his farm, and milk cows and hogs, and implements; he has got one of the very best farms in the country; I expect he has got more plow things, and things of that sort, more than all the rest of the farmers put together in that country; he buys the best tools, and up-to-date tools that people farm with. He is a very extensive potatoe[sic] raiser, and everything that comes out that he thinks would be of advantage, he buys it.

Q Did you ever know of his voting in the Cherokee Nation ?

A Yes sir, I have been at the polls with him at different times.

Q And have seen him vote ?   A Yes sir.

By the Commission:

Q How much of the time has Mr. Alexander's family spent in the Cherokee Nation since they went to Fort Smith ?   A His family; now I can't say much about his family, his minor children or his family, of course his first set of children, they have been here in the Territory the biggest part of the time, Joe--

Q What you mean by his first set of children, is his children by his former wife ?

A Yes sir.

Q So the residence of his wife; where his wife has been, and his children by his second wife, you don't know anything about where they have been ?   A No sir.

HENRY HARDIN, being duly sworn by the Commission, and examined, testified as follows:

Examined by Mr. Hutchings:

Q What is your name ?   A Henry Hardin.

Q What is your post office address ?   A Fort Smith.

Cherokee Intermarried White 1906
Volume VII

Q How long have you know Mr. Alexander, the applicant here ?
A I have known Mr. Alexander a good long while, about fifteen years I reckon. I have been at work for him seven, or eight, or nine years.
Q When did you commence to work for him ?
A In 1894 I believe it was.
Q How long did you continue to work for him ?
A I worked for him up until 1897.
Q What were you doing for him ? A I was at work for him on the farm; farming for him; seeing after the farm for him when he wasn't there.
Q Were you working for him on the farm in 1898 ?
A I wasn't working for him in the year '97 though, that's the only year I have missed since 1894.
Q Where was Mr. Alexander during the year 1898 ?
A He was on the farm. He was on the prairie farm, and he was there a good deal of the time; in straw berry time he was there pretty near all the time; he stayed there a good deal until ginning season, and then he went to Muldrow.
Q Where was he most of the time, so far as the Cherokee Nation is concerned, was he in the Cherokee Nation ? A Yes sir, I think so.
Q Where did he room ? A He roomed there at this place on the prairie, he kept a room there for himself.
Q Have his own furniture in it ? A Yes sir.
Q His house ? A Yes sir.
Q Do you know whether he kept any rooms for hands he hired, and does yet ?
A He kept some bedding there, I guess, on that place. He keeps beds in the bottom.
Q Did he have any place furnished for himself and hands on the farm ?
A Yes sir.
Q What sort of a house did he have down there ?
A Why he has a dwelling there with six or seven rooms to it.
Q All furnished with his furniture ? A Yes sir.
Q How much stock and things of that kind has he always had won there since you remember ? A I don't remember, I guess about thirty head of mules and horses, and a good many hogs and cattle.
Q Has he always had hogs, and cattle and stock since you have known him ?
A Yes sir.
Q Over in the Cherokee ? A Yes sir.
Q During the time that you worked for him, which was '94-5-6 and 8, as I understand--
A Yes sir.
Q How much of the time did he spend in the Cherokee Nation ? And on his farms looking after his business ?
A I suppose he spent three fourths of the time.
Q You have been living since 1898 on what place ?
A On the bottom farm.
Q Has he spent about the same amount of time since then in the Cherokee Nation as before ? A Yes sir, he's there most every day, I see him around there.

Cherokee Intermarried White 1906
Volume VII

By the Commission:

Q   When did you commence to work for Mr. Alexander ?   A   In '94.
Q   Where has his family been since '94 ?   A   In Fort Smith.
Q   Practically all the time ?   A   Yes sir I think so.
Q   Kept house there ?   A   Yes sir.
Q   Mr. Alexander goes over to see them once or twice a week ?   A   Yes sir.
Q   Stays over the balance of the time to look after his farms and property in the Cherokee Nation ?   A   Yes sir.
Q   Where was his family in the year 1898 ?   A   They were in Fort Smith, Arkansas I suppose.
Q   They were there all during that year ?   A   They have never lived in the Cherokee Nation since I have been working for him, that I know of.

ANDREW RUSSELL, being duly sworn by the Commission, and examined, testified as follows:

Examined by Mr. Hutchings:

Q   What is your name ?   A   Andrew Russell.
Q   What is your post office ?   A   Gans.
Q   You are a citizen by blood of the Cherokee Nation ?   A   Yes sir.
Q   Ever hold any office in the Cherokee Nation ?   A   Yes sir.
Q   What ?   A   Deputy Sheriff twelve years, and Judge of the district court three years.
Q   Have you known Mr. Alexander during that time ?   A   Yes sir.
Q   Was he clerk of the court there while you were holding office ?
A   Yes sir, while I was deputy sheriff.
Q   Has he always been recognized as a citizen of the Cherokee Nation ?
A   I never knew of anything to the contrary.
Q   Do you know of his voting ?   A   Yes sir.
Q   Do you know these places he has had down there ?
A   Why yes, I am acquainted with them, I haven't been upon the bottom place for several years.
Q   If you had occasion to look for him in those days where would you go to find him ?
A   At Muldrow or in the bottom.
Q   Did you see enough of him to say what proportion of his time he spent in the Cherokee Nation looking after his interests there ?
A   All the time so far as I know, occasionally I would go over to Fort Smith on Saturday, and see him, sometimes meet him on the road, and we would go into Fort Smith together; and sometimes I would meet him coming away from Fort Smith.
Q   Has he ever had any business of any kind in Fort Smith so far as you know ?
A   No sir, he has not.

Cherokee Intermarried White 1906
Volume VII

By the Commission:

Q   Where do you live Mr. Russell ?   A Gans, Indian Territory.
Q   How far is that from where Mr. Alexander's farm is ?   A About fifteen miles.
Q   Do you know where Mr. Alexander's wife and family have been for the last ten years ?   A No sir, I haven't paid any attention to them, but I have heard that they was living away, but I don't know.
Q   You haven't seen them over in the Nation ?   A No sir, I haven't lately.

J. B. GOODMAN, being duly sworn by the Commission, and examined, testified as follows:

Examined by Mr. Hutchings:

A   What is your name ?   A J. B. Goodman.
Q   What is your post office address ?   A Muldrow.
Q   How long have you know Mr. Alexander, the applicant ?   A Since 1886.
Q   Did you ever work for him any ?   A I worked in '94, I think, a month, for him. In October or September.
Q   How close have you lived to him in the last seven or eight or ten years ?   A about eight or nine miles I reckon it is; somewhere along there, I don't know; I live in close to Muldrow, Indian Territory and his farm is seven or eight miles below.
Q   Did you ever see him at Muldrow any ?
A   All the time during the winter season
Q   Do you know the years he had the straw berry farms ?   A Yes sir.
Q   How much attention did he give to that ?
A   He must have give[sic] pretty near all.
Q   Do you know of his having property in the Cherokee Nation all the time for the last ten years ?   A Yes sir, ever since I have known him.
Q   Do you know about how much of his time he has spent at Muldrow, Indian Territory or how much he spent on the other farm ?   A No sir, I can't get exactly at that, but all through the week while work was going on I could always see Mr. Alexander passing bachwards[sic] and forwards at Muldrow and going to the farm.
Q   During the week you saw him attending to his business in the Nation pretty much all the time ?   A Yes sir.
Q   What sort of work did you do for Mr. Alexander ?
A   I started in to weigh cotton for him at the gin, and I was called for as a witness in a murder case at Fort Smith.

By the Commission:

Q   Where is Mr. Alexander's wife and children been living for the last ten years ?
A   Actually I am not acquainted with Mr. Alexander's family.
Q   You don't know where they are ?   A No sir.

Cherokee Intermarried White 1906
Volume VII

<u>Mr. Hutchings</u>: We desire to offer a certificate of J. T. Parks, executive secretary of the Cherokee Nation, showing that, for the years '95, '97, '99 and 1901, being regular elections, that Mr. Alexander's name appears on the records as a legal voter; and also as a legal voter in 1902;

We have the certificate of the deputy collector who collected poll tax from Mr. Alexander, and he states that it was paid under protest by Mr. Alexander; and listed without consulting him;

Also the certificate of the Mayor of Fort Smith, Arkansas stating that Mr. Alexander took no part in politics in Fort Smith, Arkansas and did not vote at elections.

Certificate, also, of one of the judges of election, Michael O'Connell, stating that he did not vote at elections in the 4th ward where he resided for the last ten years;

Also certificate of Matthew Gray, an election judge, and W. H. Jacobs, as election judge, during those times, that he did not vote in the ward where he resides.

And the certificate of Edgar E. Bryant, Indian Territory Judge of the Sebastian Circuit Court, that Mr. Alexander was summoned and excused as a juror, because he was a citizen of the Indian Territory, and not of the State of Arkansas.

<u>The</u> <u>Commission</u>: Applicant asks that letter, under date of November 25, 1902, addressed to the Commission to the Five Civilized Tribes, by T. M. Buffington, Principal Chief of the Cherokee Nation, be filed with the record in this case, and that it may be considered for what it may be worth.

E. C. Bagwell, on oath states that, as stenographer to the Commission to the Five Civilized Tribes, he correctly recorded the testimony and proceedings had in the above entitled cause, and that the foregoing is an accurate transcript of his stenographic notes thereof.

E.C. Bagwell

Subscribed and sworn to before me this December 30, 1902.

S.R. Walkingstick
Notary Public.

Cherokee Intermarried White 1906
Volume VII

C. F. B. Cherokee 1450.

DEPARTMENT OF THE INTERIOR,
COMMISSIONER TO THE FIVE CIVILIZED TRIBES.
Muskogee, Indian Territory, January 14, 1907.

In the matter of the application for the enrollment of Joseph H. Alexander as a citizen by intermarriage of the Cherokee Nation.

APPEARANCES:

Thomas J. Watts, representing applicant.

Joe Alexander being first duly sworn by B. P. Rasmus, Notary Public, testified as follows:

ON BEHALF OF COMMISSIONER.

Q What is your name? A Joe Alexander.
Q What is your age? A 33 years old.
Q What is your post office address?
A Fort Smith.
Q Are you a citizen by blood of the Cherokee Nation?
A Yes sir.
Q What was the name of your father?
A Joseph H. Alexander.
Q Is he living or dead? A He is dead.
Q When did he die? A December 10, 1905.
Q He was a white man? A Yes sir.
Q He had no Cherokee blood that you ever heard of?
A No sir.
Q Your father, Joseph H. Alexander, is an applicant for enrollment before this office as a citizen by intermarriage of the Cherokee Nation?
A Yes sir.
Q What was the name of your mother?
A Cherokee Alexander.
Q Is she living? A No sir.
Q When did she die? A She died in 1880.
Q Was she a Cherokee by blood? A Yes sir.
Q Since her death, your father married a second time?
A Yes sir.
Q What was the name of his second wife?
A Saphronia Duncan.
Q She is a Cherokee by blood? A Yes sir.

Cherokee Intermarried White 1906
Volume VII

Q You know of your own prsonal[sic] knowledge, that from the time your father, Joseph H. Alexander, married Saphronia Alexander, they lived together as husband and wife until his death?
A Yes sir.
Q Since you can first remember, did your father continuously reside in the Cherokee Nation up to and including September 1, 1902?
A Yes sir.

BY MR. WATTS.

Q When did your father marry Saphronia Duncan?
A In April, '83.
Q Did he ever marry any other woman? A No sir.
Q Was he a resident of the Cherokee Nation at the time of his death?
A Yes sir.

J. H. Bowers being first duly sworn by B. P. Rasmus, Notary Public, testified as follows:

ON BEHALF OF COMMISSIONER.

Q What is your name? A J. H. Bowers.
Q What is your age? A 68.
Q What is your post office address?
A Muldrow, Indian Territory.
Q Did you ever know a person in the Cherokee Nation by the name of Joseph H. Alexander?
A Yes sir.
Q Is he living? A No sir.
Q When did he die? A About a year ago.
Q When did you first become acquainted with him?
A 1868
Q Was he a married man at the time of his death?
A Yes sir.
Q Did you know him before he was married?
A No sir; not before he married his first wife?[sic]
Q What was her name? A Cherokee Alexander.
Q Do you know of your own personal knowledge when Joseph H. Alexander was married to Cherokee Alexander?
A No; he came from Texas with his first wife.
Q He was married to this woman in Texas?
A Yes sir.
Q And then removed to the Cherokee Nation?
A Yes sir; about Christmas, 1868.
Q Did you become acquainted with him soon after that?
A Yes sir; in a month after they moved into the country.

Cherokee Intermarried White 1906
Volume VII

Q   On his coming to the Cherokee Nation, was his wife Cherokee, recognized as a citizen of the Nation?
A   Yes sir.
Q   It wasn't necessary for her to go before the Courts and be re-admitted?
A   I don't think at that time.
Q   Was she ever re-admitted?
A   I don't know anything about that.
Q   Did Joseph H. Alexander, after coming to the Cherokee Nation with his wife, Cherokee, secure a license and marry her in accordance with the law of the Cherokee Nation?
A   That was my understanding; I lived in the same neighborhood.
Q   You didn't see his license[sic]?   A   No sir.
Q   You didn't see his petition?   A   No sir.
Q   But it is your understanding that he did secure a license and that they were married in accordance with the laws of the Cherokee Nation?
A   Yes sir.
Q   Do you know of your own personal knowledge that since that time, Joseph H. Alexander enjoyed the rights and privileges of a citizen by intermarriage of the Cherokee Nation?
A   Yes sir.
Q   He was always recognized as such?
A   Yes sir.
Q   Did he ever hold any office?
A   Yes sir.
Q   What office in the Cherokee Nation did he hold?
A   Clerk of the District Court.
Q   And[sic] other that you know of?   A   No sir.
Q   What district was that?   A   Sequoyah District.
Q   And it was in Sequoyah District that he secured his marriage license?
A   Yes sir.
Q   Can you give me approximately the date that he secured that last license?
A   It was in '69.
Q   When did Cherokee Alexander die?
A   About '80.
Q   From the time you became acquainted with them, did they reside together as husband and wife until the death of Cherokee Alexander?
A   Yes sir.
Q   After her death, did Joseph H. Alexander marry again?
A   Yes sir; he married in two or three years.
Q   What was the name of his second wife?
A   Saphronia Duncan.
Q   She is a Cherokee by blood?   A   Yes sir.
Q   Joseph H. and Saphronia Alexander resided together as husband and wife continuously from the time of their marriage until the time of the death of Joseph H. Alexander?
A   Yes sir.

Cherokee Intermarried White 1906
Volume VII

Q And lived all these years in the Cherokee Nation?
A Yes sir.
Q Did Joseph H. Alexander to your knowledge ever marry any one besides these two women you have mentioned?
A No sir.

An examination of the original marriage records Sequoyah district, Book "A", which is in the possession of this office, shows on page 11, that on February 4, 1869, license as issued by George Benge, Clerk Sequoyah District, Cherokee Nation, in accordance with the Cherokee law, authorizing the marriage of J. H. Alexander, a white man, and Mrs. C. C. Alexander, a Cherokee, and that said parties were united in marriage in accordance with the terms of said license, March 9, 1869, by Franklin Falkner, Judge Sequoyah District Court, Cherokee Nation.

Joseph H. Alexander is identified on the Cherokee authenticated tribal roll of 1880, Sequoyah District, number 8.

BY MR. WATTS.

Q Mr. Bowers, at the time you speak of Mr. Alexander coming to the Cherokee Nation from Texas, were you a recognized citizen of the Cherokee Nation?
A Yes sir.
Q Do you know whether or not J. H. Alexander from the time of his marriage in '69 to the time of his death, exercised the rights of citizenship in the Cherokee Nation by voting?
A Yes sir; I registered his name several times.
Q Did you ever serve as an election officer of the Cherokee Nation prior to November, 1875?
A Yes sir; in August, '75.
Q When was it that Mr. Alexander was elected to office in the Cherokee Nation?
A In August, '75.
Q Did he enter upon the duties of that office?
A Yes sir.
Q Did he fill out his term of office?
A Yes sir.

C. A. Fargo being first duly sworn by B. P. Rasmus, Notary Public, testified as follows:

ON BEHALF OF COMMISSIONER.

Q What is your name?   A C. A. Fargo.
Q What is your age?   A 60.
Q What is your post office address?
A Muldrow.

Cherokee Intermarried White 1906
Volume VII

BY MR. WATTS.

Q   Did you know Joseph H. Alexander during his life time?
A   I did.
Q   When and where did you first get acquainted with him?
A   At his place of residence and around through the neighborhood in 1869.
Q   In what district?   A   Sequoyah District.
Q   How far did you live from Mr. Alexander?
A   About 5 miles.
Q   Do you have any recollection of his marriage to his first wife?
A   No; I don't know anything about his marriage. I know he was around getting up a petition to marry.
Q   Did you see that petition?   A   Yes.
Q   Where were you, Mr. Fargo, when you saw it?
A   I was at home. He came there with it getting signers.
Q   Can you state the name or names of any that signed that petition?
A   Well, I know I signed it, and my brother Calvin Fargo signed it.
Q   Can you state about what year it was that you signed that petition?
A   I think it was along in February of '68 or '69.
Q   You can't be certain as to the exact time?
A   No sir.
Q   Do you know whether or not Mr. Alexander went ahead and procured his license and married?
A   I understood he did.
Q   Do you know whether or not he exercised the rights and privileges as a citizen of the Cherokee tribe?
A   He did.
Q   In what particular or particulars did he do so?
A   Well, he was our clerk of Sequoyah district.
Q   When was he elected Clerk?
A   I think in '75.
Q   In what month of the year, under the law, did you hold those elections?
A   First Monday in August.
Q   Then state in what month in '75 Mr. Alexander was elected to office?
A   The first Monday in August, '75.
Q   Do you know whether or not he entered upon the duties of that office and filled the term of office to which he was elected?
A   Yes sir.
Q   Do you know whether or not Mr. Alexander lived continuously in the Cherokee Nation from the time of your acquaintance with him in 1868 or 1869, to the time of his death?
A   Yes sir; he resided there continuously.
Q   When did he die?
A   I think he died in 1904.
Q   You can't be positive as to the exact time?
A   No sir.

Cherokee Intermarried White 1906
Volume VII

Q   Is his first wife living?
A   No sir.
Q   Did he ever marry again?
A   Yes.
Q   To whom?
A   Saphronia Duncan
Q   Did he ever marry to any other woman?
A   Not that I know of.
Q   How close did you live to him?
A   Well, part of the time I only lived about three miles; I was living where I am now; part of the time I was down in the bottom; I was about five miles from him there.
Q   Will ask you if from the time of your acquaintance with Mr. Alexander up to the time of his death, he exercised the rights of an elector in the Cherokee Nation by voting?
A   Yes sir.

ON BEHALF OF COMMISSIONER.

Q   You didn't know Joseph H. Alexander prior to the time he removed from Texas to the Cherokee Nation?
A   No sir.
Q   You can't testify then as to whether Cherokee Alexander was his first wife or not?
A   No sir.
Q   But you never did hear anything to the contrary?
A   No sir.
Q   You never heard that Cherokee Alexander was ever married prior to her marriage to Joseph H. Alexander?
A   No.

John Faulkner being first duly sworn by B. P. Rasmus, Notary Public, testified as follows:

ON BEHALF OF COMMISSIONER.

Q   What is your name?
A   John Faulkner.
Q   What is your age?
A   59.
Q   What is your post office address?
A   Muldrow.
Q   Did you know one Joseph H. Alexander during his life time?
A   Yes sir.
Q   When did he die?
A   It has been over two years.
Q   Since September 1, 1902?
A   Yes sir.
Q   When did you first become acquainted with him?
A   About '69.
Q   Was he married at that time?
A   He got married; my father told me he married him but I can't recollect the date.
Q   What was his wife's name?
A   I can't state.
Q   What was your father's name?
A   Frank Faulkner.

Cherokee Intermarried White 1906
Volume VII

Q   Your father, Frank Faulkner, was Judge of Sequoyah District Court and married Joseph H. Alexander?
A   Yes; that's what he told me.
Q   You don't remember just the year?
A   It was in '69; I can't recollect the date.
Q   Did you know these parties subsequent to that time?
A   Yes sir.
Q   Has he lived since that time in the Cherokee Nation?
A   I think so; probably he might have taken his family over to school them[sic]; he was continually on his farm though.
Q   But the Cherokee Nation has been his home since that time?
A   Yes sir.
Q   When did his first wife die?
A   I can't recollect; about '80 or '81.
Q   After her death, did he marry?
A   Yes sir.
Q   What is the name of his second wife?
A   Saphronia Duncan.
Q   She is a Cherokee by blood?   A   Yes sir.
Q   These two women, Cherokee Alexander and Saphronia Alexander, are the only wives that Joseph H. Alexander to you knowledge ever had?
A   Yes sir.

An examination of the Cherokee authenticated tribal roll of 1880 shows that Cherokee Alexander is identified on said roll at Page 680, Number 9, Sequoyah District, marked "dead".

The undersigned being first duly sworn states that as stenographer to the Commission to the Five Civilized Tribes, she recorded the testimony taken in this case and that the foregoing is a full, true and correct transcript of her stenographic notes thereof.

Myrtle Hill

Subscribed and sworn to before me this the 19th day of January, 1907.

John E. Tidwell
Notary Public.

Cherokee Intermarried White 1906
Volume VII

E C M

Cherokee-1450.

DEPARTMENT OF THE INTERIOR,
COMMISSIONER TO THE FIVE CIVILIZED TRIBES.

In the matter of the application for the enrollment of JOSEPH H. ALEXANDER as a citizen by intermarriage of the Cherokee Nation.

D E C I S I O N.

THE RECORDS OF THIS OFFICE SHOW: That at Muldrow, Indian Territory, August 15, 1900 application was received by the Commission to the Five Civilized Tribes for the enrollment of Joseph H. Alexander as a citizen by intermarriage of the Cherokee Nation. Further proceedings in the matter of said application were had at Muskogee, Indian Territory, October 27, 1902, October 29, 1902, October 31, 1902, December 22, 1902 and January 14, 1907.

THE EVIDENCE IN THIS CASE SHOWS: That the applicant herein, Joseph H. Alexander, a white man, was married in accordance with Cherokee law March 9, 1869 to one Cherokee Alexander, since deceased, who was at the time of said marriage a recognized citizen by blood of the Cherokee Nation, who is identified on the Cherokee authenticated tribal roll of 1880, Sequoyah District, Page 680, No. 9, as a native Cherokee; that from the time of said marriage until the death of said Cherokee Alexander, which occurred in 1880, the said Joseph H. Alexander and Cherokee Alexander resided together as husband and wife and continuously lived in the Cherokee Nation. It is further shown that on April 1, 1883 the said Joseph H. Alexander was married to one Saphronia Alexander, nee Duncan, who was at the time of said marriage a recognized citizen by blood of the Cherokee Nation, who is identified on the Cherokee authenticated tribal roll of 1880, Sequoyah District, Page 692, No. 399 as a native Cherokee, and whose name is included on the approved partial roll of citizens by blood of the Cherokee Nation opposite No. 3941; that from the time is said marriage the said Joseph H. Alexander and Saphronia Alexander resided together as husband and wife, and that said Joseph H. Alexander continuously remained a resident of the Cherokee Nation, until his death on December 10, 1905. Said applicant is identified on the Cherokee authenticated tribal roll of 1880 and the Cherokee census roll of 1896 as an intermarried citizen of the Cherokee Nation.

IT IS, THEREFORE, ORDERED AND ADJUDGED: That in accordance with the decision of the Supreme Court of the United States, dated November 5, 1906, in the cases of Daniel Red Bird, et al. vs. the United States, Nos. 125, 126, 127, and 128, the said applicant, Joseph H Alexander, is entitled, under the provisions of Section Twenty-one of the Act of Congress approved June 28, 1898 (30 Stats. 495), to enrollment as a citizen by intermarriage of the Cherokee Nation, and his application for enrollment as such is accordingly granted.

Cherokee Intermarried White 1906
Volume VII

Tams Bixby
Commissioner.

Dated at Muskogee, Indian Territory,
this   FEB 19 1907

◇◇◇◇◇

Cherokee 1450.

Muskogee, Indian Territory, February 19, 1907.

W. W. Hastings,
    Attorney for the Cherokee Nation,
        Muskogee, Indian Territory.

Dear Sir:

      There is enclosed herewith a copy of the decision of the Commissioner to the Five Civilized Tribes, dated February 19, 1907, granting the application for the enrollment of Joseph H. Alexander as a citizen by intermarriage of the Cherokee Nation.

Respectfully,

Enc I-108.   Commissioner.

RPI

◇◇◇◇◇

Cherokee 1450.

Muskogee, Indian Territory, February 19, 1907.

The Commissioner to the Five Civilized Tribes,
        Muskogee, Indian Territory.

Sir:

      Receipt is acknowledged of the testimony and of your decision enrolling Joseph H. Alexander as a citizen by intermarriage of the Cherokee Nation. Time for protesting said decision is waived and I consent that said person may be placed upon the schedule immediately.

Respectfully,
W. W. Hastings
Attorney for the Cherokee Nation.

◇◇◇◇◇

Cherokee Intermarried White 1906
Volume VII

Cherokee 1450

Muskogee, Indian Territory, February 19, 1907.

Sophronia Alexander,
    Fort Smith, Arkansas.

Dear Madam:

    There is enclosed herewith a copy of the decision of the Commissioner to the Five Civilized Tribes, dated February 19, 1907, granting the application for the enrollment of your husband, Joseph H. Alexander, as a citizen by intermarriage of the Cherokee Nation. Your attorney, W. P. Thompson, Vinita, Indian Territory, has heretofore been furnished with a copy of the record of proceedings had in the case, and there has this day been forwarded to him a copy of the Commissioner's decision.

    You will be advised when the name of your husband has been placed upon a schedule of citizens of the Cherokee Nation and approved by the Secretary of the Interior.

                              Respectfully,

Enc I-110   Commissioner.

RPI

◇◇◇◇◇

Cherokee 1450

Muskogee, Indian Territory, February 19, 1907.

W. P. Thompson,
    Attorney for Joseph H. Alexander,
        Vinita, Indian Territory.

Dear Sir:

    There is enclosed herewith a copy of the decision of the Commissioner to the Five Civilized Tribes, dated February 19, 1907, granting the application for the enrollment of Joseph H. Alexander as a citizen by intermarriage of the Cherokee Nation. You have heretofore been furnished a copy of the record of proceedings had in the case.

                              Respectfully,

Enc I-109   Commissioner.

RPI

Cherokee Intermarried White 1906
Volume VII

Cher IW 199

◇◇◇◇◇

Department of the Interior,
Commission to the Five Civilized Tribes,
Pryor Creek, I.T., Sept. 11, 1900.

In the matter of the application of John H. Baugh for the enrollment of himself as a Cherokee citizen; being sworn and examined by Commissioner Breckinridge he testified as follows:

Q What is your full name? A John H. Baugh.
Q What is your age? A Seventy-five years the 3rd day of last March.
Q What is your post-office? A I am receiving my mail now at Muskogee; I formerly lived at Chouteau, and got a good deal of mail from Chouteau that is forwarded down.
Q But you call your post-office now Muskogee? A Yes sir, at the present time I am staying down there with my son.
Q What district do you call your district? A Cooweescoowee.
Q You wish to make application for the enrollment of yourself?
A Yes sir.
Q Any one else? A No one.
Q Do you apply as a Cherokee by blood? A No sir.
Q Intermarriage? A Yes sir.
Q Have you a marriage license? A No sir. I was married before there was any license law here.
Q Were you married before 1880? A Oh, yes, I was married in 1854.
Q You claim under that marriage? A Yes sir.
Q Is your wife still living? A Oh, no, dead.
Q Have you ever married since? A No, I was married at that time and I went then- they made this marriage law shortly after I was married and I went then to the District Clerk and qualified to all that was necessary in regard to intermarriage in this country.
Q You married in 1854 and that's the marriage you claim under? A Yes sir.
Q And that wife is dead is she? A Yes sir, she died in 1871.
Q Have you ever re-married? A No sir.
Q Never married since the wife you married in 1854 died? A Never have.
Q You are not married at this time? A No sir.
Q Have you continued to make your residence in the Cherokee Nation ever since 1880? A Yes sir, of course I sometimes go out on account of my health; take a little trip around.
1880 roll page 73 #361 J. H. Baugh Cooweescoowee District.
1896 roll page 294 #39 John H. Baugh Cooweescoowee District, adopted Cherokee.
Q Give me the name of your father? A My father's name was Mitchell Baugh?
Q White man? A Yes sir.
Q He is dead is he? A Yes sir.
Q What is your mother's given name? A Cynthia.
Q She is a white woman? A Yes sir.
Q Is she dead or alive? A They are dead.

Cherokee Intermarried White 1906
Volume VII

Com'r Breckinridge: The applicant is identified on the roll of 1880 and also on the roll of 1896 as a Cherokee by adoption; his Cherokee wife is dead, but he has never remarried; he has lived continuously in the Cherokee Nation since 1880 and he will be listed now for enrollment as a Cherokee by adoption.

M.D. Green, being first duly sworn, states that as stenographer to the Commission to the Five Civilized Tribes he correctly recorded the testimony and proceedings in this case and that the foregoing is a true and complete transcript of his stenographic notes thereof.

MD Green

Subscribed and sworn to before me this 11 day of Sept 1900.

C R Breckinridge

Commissioner.

◇◇◇◇◇

COOWEESCOOWEE.
Statement of Applicant Taken Under Oath.

CHEROKEE BY BLOOD AND ADOPTION.

(75) Date **SEP 11 1900** 1900.

Name ......**John H. Baugh, Muskogee, I.T.**......
District......**COOWEESCOOWEE**...... Year ......**1880**...... Page ......**73**...... No. ......**361**......
Citizen by blood ......**No**...... Mother's citizenship { **Mitchell Baugh - white - dead**
Intermarried citizen ......**Yes**...... Parents { **Cynthia " - " - "**
Married under what law......................................Date of marriage ......**1854**......
License......................................Certificate......................................
Wife's name......................................
District......................................Year......................Page......................No......................
Citizen by blood......................Mother's citizenship......................
Intermarried citizen......................
Married under what law......................................Date of marriage......................
License......................................Certificate......................................

    Names of Children:

......................................Dist.......................Year......................Page......................No......................Age......................
......................................Dist.......................Year......................Page......................No......................Age......................
......................................Dist.......................Year......................Page......................No......................Age......................
......................................Dist.......................Year......................Page......................No......................Age......................
......................................Dist.......................Year......................Page......................No......................Age......................

On 1880 Roll as J.H. Baugh

#2464

◇◇◇◇◇

Cherokee Intermarried White 1906
Volume VII

Cherokee 2464.

Department of the Interior,
Commission to the Five Civilized Tribes,
Muskogee, I. T., October 3, 1902.

In the matter of the application of John H. Baugh for the enrollment of himself as a citizen by intermarriage of the Cherokee Nation; he being sworn and examined by the Commission, testified as follows:

Q What is your name? A John H. Baugh.
Q What is your age at this time? A 77 years old last March.
Q What is your postoffice address? A This town, Muskogee.
Q Are you the same John H. Baugh who made application for enrollment to this Commission as an intermarried citizen on September 11, 1900?
A At Pryorcreek[sic], yes sir.
Q What is your Cherokee wife's name? A Her name was Bryant[sic], Charlotte Bryant.
Q Is she living or dead? A She died in 1871.
Q When were you and she married? A We were married in July, '54.
Q Did you and she live together from the time of your marriage until her death?
A We did.
Q She died prior then to the making of the 1880 roll? A Yes sir.
Q Have you ever remarried any one since her death? A Never have.
Q You remained single from the time of her death until the present time? A Yes sir.
Q Were you a widower on the first day of September, 1902? A I was and am yet.
Q You have lived in the Cherokee Nation all the time since 1880?
A I come to the Cherokee Nation in '53 and I lived there up until the war and then I drifted out to Red River and after the war I lived in Mexico and stayed two years, and then I came to the Cherokee Nation and lived until three years ago when I come to this nation (Creek). I was in the drug business at Chouteau until three years ago.
Q Were you in the Cherokee Nation in 1880? A Yes sir.
Q Did you remain there until three years ago? A Yes sir.
Q And the last three years you lived in the Creek Nation, Muskogee? A Yes sir.
Q But still in the Indian Territory? A Yes sir.

The undersigned, being duly sworn, states that as stenographer to the Commission to the Five Civilized Tribes he correctly recorded the testimony and proceedings in this case, and the foregoing is a true and correct transcript of his stenographic notes thereof.

E.G. Rothenberger

Subscribed and sworn to before me this 21st day of October, 1902.

BC Jones
Notary Public.

Cherokee Intermarried White 1906
Volume VII

◇◇◇◇◇

Cherokee Field Card
No. 2464.

DEPARTMENT OF THE INTERIOR

COMMISSIONER TO THE FIVE CIVILIZED TRIBES,

MUSKOGEE, INDIAN TERRITORY, JANUARY 3, 1907.

IN THE MATTER of the application for the enrollment of John H. Baugh, as a citizen by intermarriage of the Cherokee Nation.

JOHN H. BAUGH, being first duly sworn by Walter W. Chappell, Notary Public, testified as follows:

EXAMINATION

ON BEHALF OF THE COMMISSIONER:

Q What is your name? A John H. Baugh.
Q How old are you? A I will be 82 3rd day of March.
Q What is your postoffice address? A Muskogee.
Q You claim citizenship in the Cherokee Nation by intermarriage, do you?
A Yes sir.
Q Through whom do you claim such citizenship? A Charlotte E. Bryan.
Q Is she living? A No sir, she is not.
Q What was her citizenship? A She was a Cherokee by blood.
Q When were you married to her? A I was married the 19th day of July, 1854,
Q Where were you married? A Married at J. M. Bryan's, her father's place.
Q What District? A Saline at that time.
Q Were you married under a Cherokee license? A No sir, there was no license law at that time I was married. The license law was passed after that time, and then I went before the District Clerk and made affidavit to support the constitution of the Cherokee Nation, that was the oath that was required by intermarried citizens.
Q By whom were you married? A I was married by David Foreman, a minister of the Gospel and a half-breed Cherokee.
Q Was your marriage to her in accordance with the customs of the Cherokee Nation at that time? A It was.
Q Was any one present at this marriage? A. Yes, Mrs. Lindsey.
Q Any one else? A No one living that I know of, except a colored man upon Lynch's Prairie, and some very small children, that couldn't recollect about the matter.
Q When did your wife die? A She died in March 1871.

Cherokee Intermarried White 1906
Volume VII

Q Did you live with her continuously from the date of your marriage until the time of her death? A Yes sir.
Q In the Cherokee Nation? A Yes sir, part of the time. We wasn't here all the time. The civil war came up and of course we had to drift down, - in the Choctaw Nation part of the time.
Q Was your wife identified on any Cherokee rolls?
A She was on the old settler's rolls and drew money on the old settler payment.

ON BEHALF OF THE COMMISSIONER:

  The applicant, John H. Baugh, is listed for enrollment on Cherokee card field No. 2664. He is identified on the 1880 authenticated roll of citizens of the Cherokee Nation as J. H. Baugh, opposite No. 361, Coowees Coowee District.

(Witness dismissed).

MARIAH LINDSEY, being first duly sworn by Walter W. Chappell, Notary Public, testified as follows:

EXAMINATION
ON BEHALF OF THE COMMISSIONER:

Q What is your name? A Mariah Lindsey.
Q What is your age? A Sixty-four.
Q What is your postoffice address? A Choteau.
Q Are you a citizen of the Cherokee Nation by blood? A Yes sir.
Q Do you know John H. Baugh? A Yes sir.
Q Were you present at his marriage? A Yes sir.
Q Where and to whom was he married? A Married to my sister Charlotte Bryan.
Q Where were they married? A Saline Postoffice, - Saline District, now Coowees Coowee District.
Q What year was it? A 1854, - I am not sure. I wasn't grown then, I wasn't more than twelve years old then I guess.
Q Do you know whether they were married under a Cherokee license? A I don't think they had any license then.
Q By whom were they married? A David Foreman, Cherokee minister.
Q Is his wife living? A No sir.
Q When did she die? A I don't know exactly. She has been dead, about. I don't know exactly, - I can't tell you how long ago it has been.
Q Did Baugh and his wife live together continuously in the Cherokee Nation from the time of their marriage up until her death? A Yes sir.
Q As husband and wife? A Yes sir.
Q Held themselves out to the community as such? A Yes sir.
Q Was their marriage in accordance with the customs and laws of the Cherokee Nation at that time? A Yes sir.

Cherokee Intermarried White 1906
Volume VII

(Witness dismissed).

R. W. LINDSEY, being first duly sworn by Walter W. Chappell, Notary Public, testified as follows:

EXAMINATION

ON BEHALF OF THE COMMISSIONER:

Q   What is your name?   A   R W Lindsey.
Q   What is your age?   A   Seventy-four.
Q   What is your postoffice address?   A   Choteau.
Q   Do you know John H. Baugh?   A   Yes sir.
Q   How long have you known him?   A   Forty-seven years.
Q   When was he married?   A   I can't tell.
Q   Do you know to whom he was married?   A   Yes, Charlotte Bryan.
Q   Is she related to you in any way?   A   She is my wife's sister.
Q   When was she married to Mr. Baugh?   A   I can't tell you, more than hearsay, sir.
Q   Please state, Mr. Lindsey, what if anything you know respecting this marriage?
A   In the first place I will state since I have known Mr. Baugh, he has been recognized as a citizen of the Cherokee Nation; and as he states he was married before there was a marriage law, and whilst I have a pretty good memory with those matters, they had a certain date I think it was 1856, they passed this intermarriage law with those restrictions, and then after that they required men who had been married to go before the District Clerk, and take the oath to support the constitution and laws of the Cherokee Nation, in accordance with the oath that was taken in the intermarriage law. They required in addition a signed petition for a party to get married legally. And then to take the oath to support the constitution. In accordance with this ace to enable those who married prior had to go before the District Clerk and take this oath.
Q   Do you know any of the signers of that petition?   A   He had none. This was previous to this license law.

(Witness dismissed).

I, S. T. Wright, stenographer to the Commissioner to the Five Civilized Tribes, on oath, state that I recorded the testimony and proceedings had in the above entitled cause on January 3, 1907, and that the above and foregoing is a true and correct transcript of my stenographic notes thereof taken on said date.

S.T. wright

Subscribed and sworn to before me this January 4th, 1907.

B.P. Rasmus
NOTARY PUBLIC.

Cherokee Intermarried White 1906
Volume VII

Cherokee-2464.

DEPARTMENT OF THE INTERIOR,
COMMISSIONER TO THE FIVE CIVILIZED TRIBES.

In the matter of the application for the enrollment of John H. Baugh as a citizen by intermarriage of the Cherokee Nation.

D E C I S I O N.

THE RECORDS OF THIS OFFICE SHOW: That at Pryor Creek, Indian Territory, September 11, 1900, application was received by the Commission to the Five Civilized Tribes for the enrollment of John H. Baugh as a citizen by intermarriage of the Cherokee Nation. Further proceedings in the matter of said application were had at Muskogee, Indian Territory, matter of said application were had at Muskogee, Indian Territory, October 3, 1902 and January 3, 1907.

THE EVIDENCE IN THIS CASE SHOWS: That the applicant herein, John H. Baugh, a white man, was married on July 19, 1854, to one Charlotte E. Baugh, nee Bryan, since deceased, who was at the time of said marriage a recognized citizen by blood of the Cherokee Nation; that said applicant, John H. Baugh, claims his right to enrollment as a citizen of the Cherokee Nation by reason of his said marriage; that at the time of said marriage there was no law in force in the Cherokee Nation requiring white men marrying Cherokee women to obtain a license before marrying or to take an oath of allegiance to the Cherokee Nation; that after the passage of the license Act of October 15, 1855, which required, among other things, that a white man so marrying should first obtain a license and take a certain oath of allegiance prescribed by that act, it was the custom in the said Cherokee Nation to require, as to intermarried white man who had, previous to the passage of said act married their Indian spouses, that they take the oath of allegiance before becoming recognized citizens by intermarriage of the Cherokee Nation and that upon the taking of said oath, the said white man who had lawfully married prior to October 15, 1855, became and were recognized as intermarried white citizens of the Cherokee Nation; that soon after the passage of the Act of October 15, 1855, John H. Baugh went before a district clerk of the Cherokee Nation and took the oath prescribed by that act; that from the time of his marriage in 1854 until the death of said Charlotte E. Baugh, which occurred in March, 1871, the said John H. Baugh and Charlotte E. Baugh resided together as husband and wife and continuously lived in the Cherokee Nation; that since the death of said Charlotte E. Baugh the said John H. Baugh has remained unmarried and continuously lived in the Cherokee Nation since 1854. Said applicant is identified on the Cherokee authenticated tribal roll of 1880 and the Cherokee census roll of 1896 as an intermarried citizen of the Cherokee Nation.

IT IS, THEREFORE, ORDERED AND ADJUDGED: That in accordance with the decision of the Supreme Court of the United States dated November 5, 1906, in the cases of Daniel Red Bird, et al, vs. the United States, Nos. 125, 126, 127, and 128, the said applicant, John H. Baugh, is entitled, under the provisions of Section Twenty-one of the

Cherokee Intermarried White 1906
Volume VII

Act of Congress approved June 28, 1898 (30 Stats. 495), to enrollment as a citizen by intermarriage of the Cherokee Nation, and his application for enrollment as such is accordingly granted.

Tams Bixby
Commissioner.

Dated at Muskogee, Indian Territory,
this FEB 19 1907

◇◇◇◇◇

Cherokee
2464

Muskogee, Indian Territory, December 24, 1906.

John H. Baugh,
    Muskogee, Indian Territory.

Dear Sir:

November 6, 1906, the United States Supreme Court held that white persons who intermarried with Cherokee citizens according to Cherokee law prior to November 1, 1875, are entitled to enrollment and allotments of land as citizens of the Cherokee Nation.

You are advised that to properly determine your right to enrollment as a citizen by intermarriage of the Cherokee Nation, it will be necessary for you to appear before the Commissioner for the purpose of giving testimony as to the date of your marriage and whether or not your wife, by reason of your marriage to whom you claim the right to enrollment as a citizen of the Cherokee Nation, was a recognized citizen of the Cherokee Nation at the time of your marriage to her, and whether or not you were married to her in accordance with Cherokee laws.

You are, therefore, directed to appear before the Commissioner at Muskogee, Indian Territory, at 9 o'clock A. M., on Thursday, January 3, 1907, and give testimony as above indicated.

Respectfully,

JMH   Acting Commissioner.

◇◇◇◇◇

Cherokee Intermarried White 1906
Volume VII

Cherokee 2464.

Muskogee, Indian Territory, February 19, 1907.

W. W. Hastings,
    Attorney for the Cherokee Nation,
        Muskogee, Indian Territory.

Dear Sir:

    There is enclosed herewith copy of the decision of the Commissioner to the Five Civilized Tribes, dated February 19, 1907, granting the application for the enrollment of John H. Baugh as a citizen by intermarriage of the Cherokee Nation.

        Respectfully,

RPI   Commissioner.
Enc I-100

◇◇◇◇◇

Cherokee 2464.

Muskogee, Indian Territory, February 19, 1907.

The Commissioner to the Five Civilized Tribes,
    Muskogee, Indian Territory.

Sir:

    Receipt is acknowledged of the testimony and of your decision, enrolling John H. Baugh as a citizen by intermarriage of the Cherokee Nation. Time for protesting said decision is waived and I consent that said person may be placed upon the schedule immediately.

        Respectfully,
           W. W. Hastings
           Attorney for the Cherokee Nation.

◇◇◇◇◇

Cherokee Intermarried White 1906
Volume VII

Cherokee 2464.

Muskogee, Indian Territory, February 19, 1907

John H. Baugh,
     Muskogee, Indian Territory.

Dear Sir:

There is enclosed herewith copy of the decision of the Commissioner to the Five Civilized Tribes, dated February 19, 1907, granting the application for your enrollment as a citizen by intermarriage of the Cherokee Nation.

You will be advised when your name has been placed upon a schedule of citizens of the Cherokee Nation and approved by the Secretary of the Interior.

Respectfully,

Enc I-101   Commissioner.

RPI

Cher IW 200

◇◇◇◇◇

DEPARTMENT OF THE INTERIOR.
COMMISSION TO THE FIVE CIVILIZED TRIBES.
VINITA, I. T., SEPTEMBER 18th, 1900.

IN THE MATTER OF THE APPLICATION OF Caleb Conner, wife and grand son for enrollment as citizens of the Cherokee Nation, and he being sworn by Commissioner, T. B. Needles, testified as follows:

Q What is your name?   A Caleb Conner.
Q What is your age?   A Sixty one.
Q What is your Postoffice?   A Afton.
Q What is your District?   A Delaware.
Q Are you a recognized citizen of the Cherokee Nation?   A Yes sir.
Q By blood?   A No sir.
Q By intermarriage?   A Yes sir.
Q For whom do you apply for enrollment?   A Myself, wife and one grand son.
Q You say you are a white man?   A Yes sir.
Q Your father and mother are non citizens?   A Yes sir.
Q What is the name of your wife?   A My present wife is Lucy Jane Conner.

Cherokee Intermarried White 1906
Volume VII

Q Is she a citizen by blood?   A Yes sir.
Q What was her name before you married her?   A Countryman.
Q When did you marry her?   A In 1880.
Q Were you married before that to any one?   A Yes sir.
Q What was the name of your first wife?   A Mary Ann.
Q Mary Ann what?   A Cary.
Q Was she a citizen by blood?   A Yes sir.
Q Is she living?   A No sir.
Q What is the name of Lucy Jane Countryman's father?   A I can not tell you.
Q Is he living?   A No sir., I believe his name was John.
Q What is the name of her mother?   A I do not know.
Q Is she living?   A No sir.
Q What is the age of your wife?   A About fifty.
Q What degree of blood do you claim for her?   A I am not able to tell you.
Q You say she is a citizen by blood?   A She was always recognized to be, and always claimed to be.
Q What are the name of your children at home?   A I have one grand son.
Q What is his name?   A Caleb Willis Cowels[sic].
Q How old is he?   A He was nineteen his last birth day.
Q What is the name of his father?   A Cowells; Frank Cowells.
Q Was he an Indian by blood?   A No sir.
Q What was the name of his mother?   A Jane Conner.
Q Is she living?   A No sir.
Q Was she a citizen by blood?   A Yes sir.
Q She afterwards married Frank Cowelss[sic]?   A Yes sir.
Q Is your name on the roll of 1880?   A Yes sir; I guess it is.

   (1880 Roll, Page 78, #467, Caleb Conner, Cooweescoowee Dis't)
   (1880 Roll, Page 78, #468, Lucy Conner, Cooweescoowee Dis't)
   (1896 Roll, Page 567, #101, Caleb Conner, Delaware District)
   (1896 Roll, Page 447, #501, Lucy Jane Conner, Delaware District)
   (1896 Roll, Page 447, #502, Caleb Willis Cowells, Delaware)
   (1880 Roll, Page 236, #545, Jane Cowells, Delaware District)

Q Is the Caleb Willis Cowells, for whom you apply for enrollment the son of Jane Cowells, whose name appears upon the authenticated roll of 1880?   A Yes sir.
Q And Frank Cowells is his father?   A Yes sir.
Q And the name of Frank Cowells appears upon the roll of 1880?   A Yes sir.

   The name of Caleb Conner appears upon the authenticated roll of 1880, as well as the census roll of 1896, as an intermarried white. The name of his wife, Lucy Jane, appears upon the authenticated roll of 1880, and the census roll of 1896, as Lucy Conner: The name of his grand child, Caleb Willis Cowells appears upon the census roll of 1896, and he avers that the said Caleb Willis Cowells is a son of Jane Conner, whose name appears on the authenticated roll of 1880, and who is now deceased. Proof to that effect being satisfactory, the said Caleb Willis Cowells will be duly listed for enrollment by this Commission as a Cherokee citizen by blood. And the said Caleb Conner will be enrolled

Cherokee Intermarried White 1906
Volume VII

as a Cherokee citizen by intermarriage, and his wife, Lucy Jane Conner, as a Cherokee citizen by blood.

The undersigned, being sworn, states that as stenographer to the Commission to the Five Civilized Tribes, he correctly recorded the testimony and proceedings in this case, and that the foregoing is a true and complete transcript of his stenographic notes thereof.

R R Cravens

Subscribed and sworn to before me this 20th day of September, 1900.

TB Needles
COMMISSIONER.

◇◇◇◇◇

R.

DEPARTMENT OF THE INTERIOR.
Commission to the Five Civilized Tribes.
Muskogee, Indian Territory, September 29th, 1902.

In the matter of the application of Caleb Conner for the enrollment of himself as a citizen by intermarriage of the Cherokee Nation; for the enrollment of his wife Lucy J. Conner and for the enrollment of his grandson Caleb W. Cowells as citizens by blood of the Cherokee Nation.

Supplemental to #2979.

Appearances:
James S. Davenport for Applicant.
J. C. Starr for Cherokee Nation.

JAMES S. DAVENPORT, being duly sworn, testified as follows:
Examination by the Commission.
Q. State your name, age and post office? A. James S. Davenport; 38, post office, Vinita, I. T.
Q. Are you a citizen of the Cherokee Nation? A. I am a citizen by adoption, yes, sir.
Q. Are you acquainted with the applicant in this case? A. Yes, sir.
Q. How long have you known him? A. I have known Mr. Conner since 1891.
Q. Where does he live? A. Living in Delaware district, Cherokee Nation.

Cherokee Intermarried White 1906
Volume VII

Q. Has he been living there since 1891?   A. He may have been out but he has been there I [sic] have known him.
Q. Do you know his wife?   A. Yes, sir.
Q. Have they lived----   A. Lived together as man and wife, or so held themselves out.
Q. Do you know his nephew, or grandchild?   A. No, sir. There is some child around there but I don't know that child.
Q. He is living with his wife Lucy J. at this time?   A. Yes, sir.
Q. Lived with her ever since you have known him?   A. Ever since I have known him; ever since I been around his place.
Q. They were living together on the first of September, 1902?
A. Yes, sir.

Jesse O. Carr, being first duly sworn, states that as stenographer to the Commission to the Five Civilized Tribes he reported the above entitled case and that the foregoing is a true and complete transcript of his stenographic notes thereof.

Jesse O Carr

Subscribed and sworn to before me this 6th day of October, 1902.

BC Jones
Notary Public.

◇◇◇◇◇

R.

DEPARTMENT OF THE INTERIOR.
Commission to the Five Civilized Tribes.
Muskogee, Indian Territory, October 7th, 1902.

In the matter of the application of Caleb Conner for the enrollment of himself as a citizen by intermarriage of the Cherokee Nation and for the enrollment of his wife, Lucy J. Conner, and his grandson, Caleb W. Cowells, as citizens by blood of the Cherokee Nation.

Supplemental to #2979.

Applicant appears in person.
Cherokee Nation by J. C. Starr.

Cherokee Intermarried White 1906
Volume VII

CALEB CONNER, being duly sworn, testified as follows:
Examination by the Commission.

Q. State your full name, Mr. Conner? A. Caleb Conner.
Q. How old are you? A. I am 63 past.
Q. What is your post office? A. Afton.
Q. Are you the same Caleb Conner who made application to this Commission September 8th, 1900, to be enrolled as a citizen by intermarriage? A. Yes, sir.
Q. What is the name of your wife? A. My first wife? My first wife is dead. Mary A.
Q. Your first wife in[sic] the one through whom you claim citizenship?
A. Yes, sir.
Q. When were you married to her? A. '59.
Q. When did she die? A. 35 years ago.
Q. She died before the 1880[sic] roll was made? A. Yes, sir.
Q. Did you live with Mary A. continuously until she died? A. Yes, sir.
Q. When did you marry your present wife, Lucy J.? A. '71, I believe. I just forget the date.
Q. She is on the eighty roll? A. Yes, sir.
Q. You are on the eighty roll? A. Yes, sir.
Q. Have you been living with your wife Lucy J. ever since you were married?
A. Yes, sir.
Q. In the Cherokee Nation? A Yes, sir.
Q. She is alive? A. Yes, sir.
Q. Living together in the Cherokee Nation at this time? A. Yes, sir.
Q. Had this wife Lucy J. been married before? A. Yes, sir.
Q. Was he[sic] husband dead when you married her? A. Yes, I guess so.
Q. Do you know for certain? A. No, I don't know. I didn't know her before I married her. She always said he said.[sic]
Q. You have one grandson living with you? A. Yes, sir.
Q. Caleb W. Cowells? A. Yes, sir.
Q. Been living with you in the Cherokee Nation? A. Tes[sic], sir.
Q. How long has he been living with you? A. His mother died when he was only a month old.
Q. He is your daughter's son? A. Yes, sir.
Q. What is your daughter's name? A. Jane.
Q. A daughter of yours by your first wife? A Yes, sir.
Q. When did your daughter Jane die? A. She has been dead 22 years. She died when the boy was only a month old; he is 22 years old now.
Q. Had she lived in the Cherokee Nation all her live? A. Yes, sir.
Q. You have never been out of the Cherokee Nation to make your home elsewhere?
A. No, sir; never have.

Jesse O. Carr, being first duly sworn, states that as stenographer to the Commission to the Five Civilized Tribes he reported the above entitled case and that the foregoing is a true and complete transcript of his stenographic notes thereof.

Jesse O. Carr

Cherokee Intermarried White 1906
Volume VII

Subscribed and sworn to before me this 11th day of November, 1902.

BC Jones
Notary Public.

◇◇◇◇◇

C. F. B.   Cherokee 2979.

DEPARTMENT OF THE INTERIOR,
COMMISSION TO THE FIVE CIVILIZED TRIBES.
Muskogee, Indian Territory, January 8, 1907.

In the Matter of the Application for the Enrollment of Caleb Conner as a citizen by intermarriage of the Cherokee Nation.

APPEARANCES: Applicant appears in person.
W. W. Hastings, Attorney.

Caleb Conner being first duly sworn by John E. Tidwell, Notary Public, testified as follows:

ON BEHALF OF COMMISSIONER.

Q What is your name? A Caleb Conner.
Q What is your age? A 68.
Q What is your post office address?
A Afton.
Q You claim the right to enrollment as a citizen by intermarriage of the Cherokee Nation?
A Yes sir.
Q You have no Cherokee blood?
A No sir; not that I know of.
Q Your only claim to the right to enrollment as a citizen of the Cherokee Nation is by virtue of your marriage to a citizen by blood of the Nation?
A Yes sir.
Q What was the name of your citizen wife?
A Mary Ann Carey?
Q Is she living or dead? A Dead.
Q When did she die?
A In '69 or '70; I don't remember which.
Q When were you married to her?
A July '58.
Q Was she a recognized citizen of the Cherokee Nation at the time you married her?
A Yes sir.

Cherokee Intermarried White 1906
Volume VII

Q Living in the Cherokee country?
A Yes sir.
Q Where were you married?   A[sic]
A Carey's Ferry, Delaware District, Cherokee Nation.
Q Did you secure a license and marry your wife in accordance with Cherokee law?
A Yes sir.
Q Who married you?
A A man by the name of Phillips.
Q Was this your first wife?   A Yes sir.
Q Were you her first husband?   A Yes sir; so far as I know.
Q You never heard of her having been married before she married you?
A No sir.
Q Have you any reason to believe that she was?
A No sir.
Q From the time of your marriage to her did you and she continuously live together as husband and wife until the time of her death?
A Yes sir.
Q Since her death, have you re-married?
A Yes sir.
Q When did you marry?   A '71.
Q What was her name?
A Lucy McDowell. Her maiden name was Countryman.
Q Was she a recognized citizen of the Cherokee Nation?
A Yes sir.
Q citizen by blood?
A Yes sir. She was on the '51 roll.
Q How long did you and she live together?
A We are living together now.
Q She is living at this time?   A Yes sir.
Q She was married before her marriage to you?
A Yes sir.
Q Was her former husband dead at the time you married her?
A Yes sir; she said he was and I have no reason to doubt it.
Q From the time of your marriage to your first wife until the present time, have you continuously made your home in the Cherokee Nation?
A Yes sir; never lived anywhere else only in the territory.

The applicant, Caleb Conner, is identified on the Cherokee authenticated tribal roll of 1880, Cooweescoowee District, No. 467.

Thomas J. McGee being first duly sworn by John E. Tidwell, Notary Public, testified as follows:

ON BEHALF OF COMMISSIONER.

Q What is your name?   A Thomas J. McGee.

Cherokee Intermarried White 1906
Volume VII

Q	What is your age?	A	62.

Q   What is your post office address?
A   Afton, Indian Territory.
Q   You desire to give testimony in the matter of the application for the enrollment of Caleb Conner as a citizen by intermarriage of the Cherokee Nation?
A   Yes sir.
Q   How long have you known him?
A   Well, I have known him ever since '61.
Q   He is a citizen by intermarriage of the Cherokee Nation?
A   He has always been recognized as a citizen by intermarriage of the Cherokee Nation.
Q   Did you know his first wife?   A   Yes sir.
Q   What was her maiden name?   A   Lucy Ann Carey.
Q   Do you know when they were married?
A   No, I do not.
Q   They were married before coming to the Cherokee Nation?
A   They were living together when I first got acquainted with them in '61.
Q   From the time you first became acquainted with them in 1861, did they live together as husband and wife until the death of Mrs. Conner in 1869 or '70?
A   Yes sir; lived in Delaware District on this side of the river.
Q   Do you know Caleb Conner's second wife?
A   Yes sir.
Q   She is a Cherokee by blood?
A   Yes sir; her maiden name was Lucy Countryman.
Q   Do you know of your own personal knowledge that Mr. Conner has been recognized as a citizen by intermarriage of the Cherokee Nation and enjoyed all the rights and privileges of that class of citizens?
A   Yes sir.
Q   He has been enjoying those privileges for the last 30 or 40 years to your knowledge?
A   Yes sir; his citizenship has never been doubted since I have known him, in '61.

The undersigned being first duly sworn states that as stenographer to the Commission to the Five Civilized Tribes, she recorded the testimony taken in this case and that the foregoing is a full, true and correct transcript of her stenographic notes thereof.

Myrtle Hill

Subscribed and sworn to before me this the 12th day of January, 1907.

Chas E Webster
Notary Public.

Cherokee Intermarried White 1906
Volume VII

F. B. Cherokee 2979.

DEPARTMENT OF THE INTERIOR,
COMMISSIONER TO THE FIVE CIVILIZED TRIBES.
Muskogee, I. T., February 2, 1907.

In the matter of the application for the enrollment of Caleb Connor as a citizen by intermariage[sic] of the Cherokee Nation.
Cherokee Nation represented by H. M. Vance.

Thomas J. McGhee, being first duly sworn, testified as follows: Sworn by Frances R. Lane, a Notary Public for the Western District of Indian Territory.

By the Commissioner:
Q What is your name? A Thomas J. McGhee.
Q Your age? A Sixty-two.
Q Postoffice address? A Afton, I. T.
Q Do you know one Caleb Connor in the Cherokee nation?
A Yes sir.
Q How long have you known him? A I have known Caleb Connor, I can go back to 1860; I believe '60 or '61.
Q At the time you first knew him was he a married man?
A Yes sir.
Q What is the name of his wife? A Her maiden name was Carey. Nancy, I think they called her.
Q Was she a recognized citizen by blood of the Cherokee Nation? A Yes, she was recognized.
Q At the time you first knew them they were living together as husband and wife in the Cherokee nation? A Yes, near the banks of the Grand river[sic], what they called Carey's ferry.
Q What is your understanding as to the date of that marriage?
A Well, it is from a record book that came into my possession in 1867.
Q What office did you hold in 1867? A Clerk of Delaware District, Cherokee Nation, and this book showed the record of Caleb Connor's license being issued, - in the book.
Q What became of that book? A I turn the book over to the Clerk that succeeded me with all the other papers that belonged to the clerk's office.
Q And you remember at this time that that book showed the record of the marriage license having been issued to Caleb Connor and Mary Ann Carey? A Yes sir. Some called her Nancy. I was going to state that this book was used prior to the war as a probate book, and most of the record was written in the Cherokee language. Judge Thompson and Judge Owen, and the English language was written by Hooley Bell and another clerk by the name of Dolphus Daniel, and Springston was the one that issued this Connor license.
Q The record of the Connor license was in Cherokee or English[sic]
A It was in English.

Cherokee Intermarried White 1906
Volume VII

Q Do you know about when Mrs. Connor died?   A She died along about 1868; somewhere along there.
Q Caleb Connor and his wife lived together until her death, did they?   A Yes, they lived together up until her death.
Q Caleb Connor then married agan[sic] did he?   A Yes, his second wife was named Lucy Cotterman.
Q At the time he married this second woman, she was a recognized citizen of the Cherokee nation, was she?   A Yes sir.
Q She is living at this time?   A Yes sir.
Q She and Mr. Connor are living together?   A Yes sir.
Q From the time of their marriage up to the present time?
A Yes sir.
Q You have never heard of that old marriage record which you turned over to your successor since that time, have you? Since you turned it over to him?   A No, I have not; I have heard of none of them until I heard of it here. Mr. Shelton was the one I turned it over to. He said it was no use to him. It was in 1887 or '88 I turned those records over to Mr Shelton and then I was elected clerk again in 1891, and I got these same old papers back again, all put into a sack. And then I turned the papers over again to the next clerk that succeeded me. I forget who that was. It seems to me like it was John Duncan or Pete Hastings; I don't know which. I have reason to think by these other books appearing here that that book must have been here somewhere too.
Q You remember positively that that old book contained the record of the marriage of Caleb Connor and Mary Ann Carey?   A Yes sir, I do.

Frances R. Lane upon oath states that as stenographer to the Commissioner to the Five Civilized Tribes she reported the testimony in the above entitled cause and that the foregoing is an accurate transcript of her stenographic notes thereof.

Frances R Lane

Subscribed and sworn to before me this February 4, 1907.

Walter W. Chappell
Notary Public.

Cherokee Intermarried White 1906
Volume VII

E C M

Cherokee 2979.

DEPARTMENT OF THE INTERIOR,

COMMISSIONER TO THE FIVE CIVILIZED TRIBES.

In the matter of the application for the enrollment of CALEB CONNOR as a citizen by intermarriage of the Cherokee Nation.

D E C I S I O N

THE RECORDS OF THIS OFFICE SHOW: That at Vinita, Indian Territory September 18, 1900 application was received by the Commission to the Five Civilized Tribes for the enrollment of Caleb Conner as a citizen by intermarriage of the Cherokee Nation. Further proceedings in the matter of said application were had at Muskogee, Indian Territory, September 29, 1902, October 7, 1902, January 8, 1907 and February 2, 1907.

THE EVIDENCE IN THIS CASE SHOWS: That the applicant herein, Caleb Conner, a white man, was married in accordance with Cherokee law in July, 1858 to one Mary Ann Conner, nee Cary, since deceased, who was at the time of said marriage a recognized citizen by blood of the Cherokee Nation. It is also shown that from the time of said marriage until the death of said Mary Ann Conner, which occurred about the year 1868, the said Caleb Connor and Mary Ann Conner resided together as husband and wife and continuously lived in the Cherokee Nation. It is further shown that about the year 1880 the said Caleb Conner was married to one Lucy Conner, nee Countryman, who was at the time of said marriage a recognized citizen by blood of the Cherokee Nation, who is identified on the Cherokee authenticated tribal roll of 1880, Cooweescoowee District No. 468 as a native Cherokee, and whose name is included on the approved partial roll of citizens by blood of the Cherokee Nation opposite No. 23726. It is further shown that from the time of said marriage the said Caleb Conner and Lucy Conner resided together as husband and wife and continuously lived in the Cherokee Nation up to and including September 1, 1902. Said applicant is identified on the Cherokee authenticated tribal roll of 1880 and the Cherokee census roll of 1896 as an intermarried citizen of the Cherokee Nation.

IT IS, THEREFORE, ORDERED AND ADJUDGED: That in accordance with the decision of the Supreme Court of the United States dated November 5, 1906 in the cases of Daniel Red Bird, et al. vs. the United States, Nos. 125, 126, 127, and 128, the said applicant, Caleb Conner is entitled, under the provisions of Section Twenty-one of the Act of Congress approved June 28, 1898 (30 Stats. 495), to enrollment as a citizen by intermarriage of the Cherokee Nation, and his application for enrollment as such is accordingly granted.

Cherokee Intermarried White 1906
Volume VII

Tams Bixby
Commissioner.

Dated at Muskogee, Indian Territory,
this   FEB 18 1907

◇◇◇◇◇

Cherokee 2979

Muskogee, Indian Territory, February 18, 1907.

W. W. Hastings,
    Attorney for the Cherokee Nation,
        Muskogee, Indian Territory.

Dear Sir:

      There is enclosed herewith a copy of the decision of the Commissioner to the Five Civilized Tribes, dated February 18, 1907, granting the application for the enrollment of Caleb Conner as a citizen by intermarriage of the Cherokee Nation.

Respectfully,

Encl. H-30   Commissioner.
  JMH

◇◇◇◇◇

Cherokee 2979

Muskogee, Indian Territory, February 18, 1907.

The Commissioner to the Five Civilized Tribes,
        Muskogee, Indian Territory.

Sir:

      Receipt is acknowledged of the testimony and of your decision enrolling Caleb Conner as a citizen by intermarriage of the Cherokee Nation. Time for protesting said decision is waived, and I consent that said person may be placed upon the schedule immediately.

Respectfully,
W. W. Hastings
Attorney for Cherokee Nation.

◇◇◇◇◇

Cherokee Intermarried White 1906
Volume VII

Cherokee 2979

Muskogee, Indian Territory, February 18, 1907.

Caleb Conner,
Afton, Indian Territory.

Dear Sir:

There is enclosed herewith a copy of the decision of the Commissioner to the Five Civilized Tribes, dated February 18, 1907, granting the application for your enrollment as a citizen by intermarriage of the Cherokee Nation.

You will be advised when your name has been placed upon a schedule of citizens of the Cherokee Nation and approved by the Secretary of the Interior.

Respectfully,

Encl. H-21
JMH

Commissioner.

Cher IW 201

◇◇◇◇◇

DEPARTMENT OF THE INTERIOR.

COMMISSION TO THE FIVE CIVILIZED TRIBES.

Vinita, I.T. September 22nd, 1900.

IN THE MATTER OF THE APPLICATION OF FRANK SKINNER FOR ENROLLMENT AS A CHEROKEE CITIZEN.

The said Frank Skinner, being sworn and examined by Commissioner T. B. Needles, testified as follows:

Q What is your name? A Frank Skinner.
Q What is your age? A Fifty-six.
Q What is your post office address? A Big Cabin, I.T.
Q What district do you live in? A Cooweescoowee.
Q Are you a recognized citizen of the Cherokee Nation? A I guess so. If these are correct I guess I am (indicating papers)

Cherokee Intermarried White 1906
Volume VII

Q   Are you a citizen by blood or intermarriage?   A   Intermarriage, sir.
Q   For whom do you apply for enrollment?   A   Just myself, my wife is dead.
Q   Are your father and mother non citizens?   A   Yes, sir; they are both dead. My father was a citizen, my mother was not.

1880 Roll, page 170, No. 2525, Frank Skinner, Cooweescoowee District.
1896 Roll, page 325, No. 980, Frank Skinner, Cooweescoowee District.

Q   How long have you lived in the Cherokee Nation, Mr. Skinner?
A   I came here in 1871, and have lived here ever since.
Q   You have not mrried[sic] since your wife died?   A   No, sir.

THE COMMISSIONER: The name of Frank Skinner appears upon the authenticated roll of 1880 as well as the census roll of 1896 as an intermarried citizen. He having made satisfactory proof as to his residence, he will be duly listed for enrollment by this Commission as a Cherokee citizen by intermarriage.

----o----

The undersigned, being sownn[sic], states that as stenographer to the Commission to the Five Civilized Tribes he correctly recorded the testimony and other proceedings in the above application for enrollment and that the foregoing is a correct and complete transcript of his stenographic notes thereof.

Wm S Meeshean

Subscribed and sworn to before me this 4th day of October A D 1900.

CR Breckinridge
Commissioner.

◇◇◇◇◇

R.

DEPARTMENT OF THE INTERIOR.
Commission to the Five Civilized Tribes.
Muskogee, Indian Territory, October 8th, 1902.

In the matter of the application of Frank Skinner for the enrollment of himself as a citizen by intermarriage of the Cherokee Nation.

Supplemental of #3288.

Applicant appears in person.
Cherokee Nation by J. C. Starr.

Cherokee Intermarried White 1906
Volume VII

FRANK SKINNER, being duly sworn, testified as follows:
Examination by the Commission.

Q. State you[sic] name? A. Frank Skinner.
Q. How old are you? A. 57.
Q. What is your post office? A. Big Cabin.
Q. You are a white man, are you? A. Yes, sir.
Q. You are the same Frank Skinner who made application on September 22nd, 1900, to be enrolled as a citizen by intermarriage? A. Yes, sir.
Q. What is the name of the wife through whom you claim citizenship?
A. Mattie Skinner.
Q. Is she your first wife? A. No, sir.
Q. You were married before? A. Yes, sir.
Q. What is the name of your first wife? A. Katie.
Q. White woman or Cherokee? A. White woman.
Q. Was she dead? A. Yes, sir.
Q. Died before you married this wife? A. Yes, sir.
Q. Was your present wife ever married before? A. No, sir.
Q. How long have you lived in the Cherokee Nation? A. Ever since '71.
Q. Continuously? A. Yes, sir.
Q. Never made your home elsewhere? A. No, sir.
Q. When did you marry your present wife? A. I think it was in '64.
Q. Under a Cherokee marriage license? A. Yes, sir.
Q. Have you been living with her continuously in the Cherokee Nation ever since you married her? A. No, sir; she is dead.
Q. When did she die? A. About 15 years ago.
Q. Did you live with her continuously from the time you were married up until the time of her death? A. Yes, sir.
Q. In the Cherokee Nation? A. Yes, sir.
Q. Have you married since? A. No, sir.
Q. Have you been living in the Cherokee Nation ever since your wife died?
A. Yes, sir.
Q. You have got no children? A. Yes, sir; one.
Q. Living with you? A. Yes, sir.

Q. What is its name? A. Dora. Dora Drake. She is married now.

BY MR. STARR:
Q. When did you second wife die? A. I think it was--I can't tell the day of the month now.
Q. You have never been married to any other woman since that time?
A. No, sir.

Cherokee Intermarried White 1906
Volume VII

Jesse O. Carr, being first duly sworn, states that as stenographer to the Commission to the Five Civilized Tribes he reported the above entitled case and that the foregoing is a true and complete transcript of his stenographic notes thereof.

Jesse O. Carr

Subscribed and sworn to before me this 24th day of November, 1902.

B C Jones
Notary Public.

◇◇◇◇◇

Statement of Applicant Taken Under Oath.

CHEROKEE BY BLOOD AND ADOPTION.

(56)
Date **SEP 22 1900** 1900.
Name **Frank Skinner** Big Cabin I.T.
District **COOWEESCOOWEE.** Year **1880** Page **170** No. **2525**
Citizen by blood **yes** Mother's citizenship
Intermarried citizen **Yes**
Married under what law .... Date of marriage
License .... Certificate
Wife's name
District .... Year .... Page .... No.
Citizen by blood .... Mother's citizenship
Intermarried citizen
Married under what law .... Date of marriage
License .... Certificate

Names of Children:
.... Dist. .... Year .... Page .... No. .... Age
.... Dist. .... Year .... Page .... No. .... Age
.... Dist. .... Year .... Page .... No. .... Age
.... Dist. .... Year .... Page .... No. .... Age
.... Dist. .... Year .... Page .... No. .... Age

#3288

◇◇◇◇◇

Cherokee Intermarried White 1906
Volume VII

C.F.B. Cherokee 3288

DEPARTMENT OF THE INTERIOR,
COMMISSIONER TO THE FIVE CIVILIZED TRIBES,
MUSKOGEE, IND. TER., JANUARY 4, 1907

In the matter of the application of FRANK SKINNER for enrollment as a citizen by intermarriage of the Cherokee Nation.

Applicant appears in person:

APPEARANCES:
Cherokee Nation represented by H.M. Vance, on behalf of W. W. Hastings, Attorney.

FRANK SKINNER being first duly sworn by B. P. Rasmus, a Notary Public, testified as follows:

ON BEHALF OF COMMISSIONER:

Q. What is your name? A. Frank Skinner.
Q. What is your age? A. Sixty-four.
Q. What is your postoffice address? A. Big Cabin Indian Territory, or Oklahoma.
Q. You are an applicant for enrollment as a citizen by intermarriage of the Cherokee Nation? A. Yes sir.
Q. You have no Cherokee blood? A. No sir.
Q. Your only claim to enrollment as a citizen of the Cherokee Nation is by reason of your marriage to a citizen of that Nation? A. Yes sir.
Q. What is the name of the person through whom yu[sic] claim the right to enrollment?
A. Mattie Bell.
Q. Is she living or dead? A. She is dead.
Q. When did she die? A. She has been dead about eighteen--nineteen-- years.
Q. When were you married to her? A. I was married to her in the fall of '74 as well as I remember; I was robbed in Texas and lost my license with all my other papers.
Q. Where was she living at the time you married her? A. At Vinita.
Q. Was she a recognized citizen of the Cherokee Nation at that time? A. Yes sir, I suppose so; she talked Cherokee language. I traded with the Indians and she acted as interpreter for me.
Q. Did you secure a license and marry her in accordance with Cherokee laws?
A. Yes sir.
Q. Where did you secure the license? A. In Delaware District; I was married in Cooweescoowee District, just across the line.
A. But you got the license in Delaware District? A. Yes sir
Q. Were you ever married before you married her? A. Yes sir.
Q. Was your former wife living or dead at the time you married her? A. Dead, sir. I married her in Missouri.
Q. Was your second wife ever married before her marriage to you? A. No, sir.

Cherokee Intermarried White 1906
Volume VII

Q. From the time of your marriage to your second wife did you and she continuously reside together as husband and wife until her death? A. Yes sir.
Q. Have you married since her death? A. No sir.
Q. Where have you lived since 1874? A. On Rough Creek, three miles and a half west of Big Cabin, Indian Territory.
Q. You have made your home continuously in the Cherokee Nation since that time?
A. Yes sir.
Q. Have you any documentary evidence showing your marriage to your wife? A. No sir, as I said awhile ago I lost my license when I was robbed in Texas. I can bring witnesses to prove it is[sic] necessary.

The applicant, Frank Skinner, is identified on the Cherokee authenticated tribal roll of 1880, Cooweescoowee District, No. 2525.

Q. Are there any persons present here to-day who have actual personal knowledge of your marriage?
A. There are persons here that know that we were married but there are only two people living who were at our wedding.
Q. Are they living in the Territory? A. Yes sir; they live at Vinita. My wife's father, James M. Bell, and my wife's sister, Dee Jordon are living in Vinita now. They are the only two persons living who saw us married; were at our wedding.

The undersigned, being first duly sworn, states that as stenographer to the Commission to the Five Civilized Tribes she correctly recorded the testimony taken in this case, and that the above and foregoing is a full, true, and correct transcript of her stenographic notes thereof.

Lucy M. Bowman

Subscribed and sworn to before me this 5th day of January, 1907

John E. Tidwell
Notary Public.

◇◇◇◇◇

Cherokee Intermarried White 1906
Volume VII

E. C. M.   Cherokee 3288.

DEPARTMENT OF THE INTERIOR,

COMMISSIONER TO THE FIVE CIVILIZED TRIBES.
Muskogee, Indian Territory, February 15, 1907.

In the matter of the application for the enrollment of Frank Skinner as a citizen by intermarriage of the Cherokee Nation.

SUPPLEMENTAL.

Delia P. Jordan being first duly sworn by Walter W. Chappell, testified as follows:

Q   What is your name?   A   Delia P. Jordan.
Q   What is your age?   A   50 years.
Q   What is your post office address?
A   Vinita, Indian Territory.
Q   Mrs. Jordan, you appear here forethe[sic] purpose of giving testimony relative to the right of Frank Skinner to enrollment as a citizen by intermarriage of the Cherokee Nation?
A   Yes sir.
Q   What relation are you to Mr. Skinner?
A   Why, he married my sister; my brother-in-law.
Q   What was your sister's name?   A   Mattie Bell.
Q   When were they married?
A   Well, they were married about '73 or '74; '74.
Q   They were married under a Cherokee license?
A   Yes sir.
Q   Your sister was a Cherokee by blood?   A   Yes sir.
Q   Was she born and raised in the Cherokee Nation?
A   Yes sir.
Q   Mrs. Jordan, were you present at the marriage?
A   Yes sir; present at the marriage.
Q   Did you see the license under which they were married?
A   No, I don't remember ever seeing the license; I don't think I did; I might have seen the license; I know he had a license.
Q   Can you swear positively, that Frank Skinner, the applicant in this case, was married to your sister, Mattie Bell, under a license secured from the authorities of the Cherokee Nation?
A   Well, I think I can. I think I can swear positively, although I didn't see the license; I don't think I did.
Q   Do you have positive knowledge that the license was procured?
A   Yes, I think I do because he had to have the license or he couldn't have married according to law.

Cherokee Intermarried White 1906
Volume VII

Q In what district did he secure the license?
A Cooweescoowee --- Delaware; we lived in Cooweescoowee.
Q In what district were they married?
A Cooweescoowee.
Q Mr. Jordan, was Frank Skinner your sister's first husband?
A Yes sir.
Q Was she his first wife?
A No, she wasn't his first wife; he had been married before in Missouri.
Q Was his former wife living at the time he was married to your sister?
A No sir.
Q How long had she been dead before he married your sister?
A Well, I don't know.
Q Are you sure she was dead?
A Yes, I am sure she was dead; the family all lived here.

(Witness Excused)

The undersigned being first duly sworn states that as stenographer to the Commission to the Five Civilized Tribes, she recorded the testimony of Delia P. Jordan taken in this case and that the above and foregoing is a true and correct transcript of her stenographic notes thereof.

Myrtle Hill

Subscribed and sworn to before me this the 15th day of February, 1907.

Chas[sic]. W. Chappell
Notary Public.

Cherokee Intermarried White 1906
Volume VII

E.C.M.   Cherokee 3288.

DEPARTMENT OF THE INTERIOR,
COMMISSIONER TO THE FIVE CIVILIZED TRIBES.
MUSKOGEE, I. T., FEBRUARY *(illegible)*, 1907.

In the matter of the application for the enrollment of FRANK SKINNER as a citizen by intermarriage of the Cherokee Nation.

SUPPLEMENTAL.

JAMES M. BELL, being first duly sworn by Walter W. Chappell, Notary Public, testified as follows:

Q What is your name? A James M. Bell.
Q What is your age? A 74.
Q What is your post office address? A *(Illegible)*
Q Do you appear here today for the purpose of giving testimony relative to the right of Frank Skinner to enrollment as a citizen by intermarriage of the Cherokee Nation? A Yes sir.
Q What relationship are you to Frank Skinner? A He married my daughter.
Q Are you a Cherokee by blood? A Yes sir.
Q Do you remember when Mattie Bell and Frank Skinner were married?
    A I can't give the exact date; I can give it approximately.
Q Give the approximate date. A About the fall of 1874.
Q Were they married under a license issued by the authorities of the Cherokee Nation?
    A Yes sir, I have always supposed so; Mr. Skinner has exercised all the rights and privileges of a citizen since that time.
Q Did you see the license? A No sir.
Q Were you present at the marriage? A Yes sir.
Q You say Mr. Skinner has exercised all the rights and privileges of a citizen of the Cherokee Nation since the marriage?
    A That is what I have understood.
Q Did he enjoy those privileges before his marriage? A No sir.
Q Then it was by virtue of his marriage to your daughter that he acquired these rights?
    A Yes sir.
Q Since the marriage of your daughter and Frank Skinner have they continuously resided together as husband and wife, and continuously lived in the Cherokee Nation?
    A Up to her death.
Q She is dead, is she? A Yes sir.
Q When did she die? A In about '89.
Q Since her death, has the applicant, Frank Skinner, remained unmarried? A Yes sir.
Q Has he lived in the Cherokee Nation continuously since her death?
    A Yes sir.

Cherokee Intermarried White 1906
Volume VII

The undersigned, being duly sworn, states that as stenographer to the Commission to the Five Civilized Tribes, she correctly reported the above and foregoing testimony, and that the same is a full, true and complete transcript of her stenographic notes thereof.

Sarah Waters

Subscribed and sworn to before me this *(remainder illegible)*

Walter W. Chappell
Notary Public.

◇◇◇◇◇

(There two pages that are completely illegible.)

◇◇◇◇◇

Cherokee No. 3288

Muskogee, Indian Territory, January 22nd, 1907.

Frank Skinner,
      Big Cabin, Indian Territory.

Dear Sir:

      In the matter of your application for enrollment as a citizen by intermarriage of the Cherokee Nation you are informed that it will be necessary that you furnish this office either with the original or a certified copy of your marriage license or the evidence of witnesses who have actual knowledge of your marriage to Mattie Skinner. As this matter is important, you are requested to give it your immediate attention.

Respectfully,

(Illegible Initials)   Commissioner.

◇◇◇◇◇

Cherokee Intermarried White 1906
Volume VII

Form No. 260.
THE WESTERN UNION TELEGRAPH COMPANY.
INCORPORATED
23,000 OFFICES IN AMERICA. CABLE SERVICE TO ALL THE WORLD.
ROBERT C. CLOWRY, President and General Manager.

Receiver's No.	Time Filed	Check
		Cherokee 3288

SEND the following message subject to the terms on back hereof, which are hereby agreed to.

R.C.W.   Muskogee, Indian Territory, February 12, 1907

Frank Skinner,

    Vinita, Indian Territory.

        Affidavits insufficient. Bring witnesses

immediately.

              Bixby,

G.P.G.E.Paid   Commissioner.

☞ READ THE NOTICE AND AGREEMENT ON BACK. ☜

(Copy of original document from case.)

◇◇◇◇◇

ALL MESSAGES TAKEN BY THIS COMPANY ARE SUBJECT TO THE FOLLOWING TERMS:

    To guard against mistakes or delays, the sender of a message should order it REPEATED; that is, telegraphed back to the originating office for comparison. For this, one-half the regular rate is charged in addition. It is agreed between the sender of the following message and this Company, that said Company shall not be liable for mistakes or delays in the transmission or delivery, or for non-delivery of any UNREPEATED message, beyond the amount received for sending the same; nor for mistakes or delays in the transmission or delivery, or for non-delivery of any REPEATED message, beyond fifty times the sum received for sending the same, unless specially insured, nor in any case for delays arising from unavoidable interruption in the working of its lines, or for errors in cipher or obscure messages. And this Company is hereby made the agent of the sender, without liability, to forward any message over the lines of any other Company when necessary to reach its destination.
    Correctness in the transmission of a message to any point on the lines of this Company can be INSURED by contract in writing, stating agreed amount of risk, and payment of premium thereon, at the following rates, in addition to the usual charge for repeated messages, viz, one per cent. for any distance not exceeding 1,000 miles, and two per cent. for any greater distance. No employee of the Company is authorized to vary the foregoing.
    No responsibility regarding messages attaches to this Company until the same are presented and accepted at one of its transmitting offices; and if a message is sent to such office by one of the Company's messengers, he acts for that purpose as the agent of the sender.
    Messages will be delivered free within the established free delivery limits of the terminal office. For delivery at a greater distance, a special charge will be made to cover the cost of such delivery.
    The Company will not be liable for damages or statutory penalties in any case where the claim is not presented in writing within sixty days after the message is filed with the Company for transmission.

                              ROBERT C. CLOWRY, President and General Manager.

(Copy of original document from case.)

◇◇◇◇◇

Cherokee Intermarried White 1906
Volume VII

REFER IN REPLY TO THE FOLLOWING:

Cherokee 3288

DEPARTMENT OF THE INTERIOR,
COMMISSIONER TO THE FIVE CIVILIZED TRIBES.

Special

Muskogee, Indian Territory, February 12, 1907

Frank Skinner,
    Vinita, Indian Territory.

Dear Sir:

    The Commissioner sent you this day a telegram as follows:

    "Affidavits insufficient. Bring witnesses immediately."

    The Act of Congress approved April 26, 1906, provides that the Secretary of the Interior shall have no jurisdiction to approve the enrollment of any person as a citizen of the Cherokee Nation after March 1, 1907.

    This matter, therefore, demands your immediate attention.

    Respectfully,

    Tams Bixby   Commissioner.

MMP

◇◇◇◇◇

Cherokee 3288

Muskogee, Indian Territory, February 20, 1907.

W. W. Hastings,
    Attorney for the Cherokee Nation,
        Muskogee, Indian Territory.

Dear Sir:

    There is enclosed herewith a copy of the decision of the Commissioner to the Five Civilized Tribes, dated February 20, 1907, granting the application for the enrollment of Frank Skinner as a citizen by intermarriage of the Cherokee Nation.

Cherokee Intermarried White 1906
Volume VII

Respectfully,

Enc I-237   Commissioner.

RPI

◇◇◇◇◇

Cherokee 3288

Muskogee, Indian Territory, February 20, 1907.

The Commissioner to the Five Civilized Tribes,
    Muskogee, Indian Territory.

Sir:

    Receipt is acknowledged of the testimony and of your decision enrolling Frank Skinner as a citizen by intermarriage of the Cherokee Nation. Time for protesting said decision is waived and I consent that said person may be placed upon the schedule immediately.

Respectfully,
W. W. Hastings
Attorney for the Cherokee Nation.

◇◇◇◇◇

Cherokee 3288

Muskogee, Indian Territory, February 20, 1907.

Frank Skinner,
    Big Cabin, Indian Territory.

Dear Sir:

    There is enclosed herewith a copy of the decision of the Commissioner to the Five Civilized Tribes, dated February 20, 1907, granting the application for your enrollment as a citizen by intermarriage of the Cherokee Nation.

    You will be advised when your name has been placed upon a schedule of citizens of the Cherokee Nation and approved by the Secretary of the Interior.

Respectfully,

Enc I--238   Commissioner.

RPI

Cherokee Intermarried White 1906
Volume VII

Cher IW 202

◇◇◇◇◇

DEPARTMENT OF THE INTERIOR.
COMMISSION TO THE FIVE CIVILIZED TRIBES.
VINITA, I.T., SEPTEMBER 26th, 1900.

IN THE MATTER OF THE APPLICATION OF Hugh McAffrey, wife and children for enrollment as citizens of the Cherokee Nation, and he being sworn by Commissioner, T.B. Needles, testified as follows:

Q What is your name?   A Hugh McAffrey.
Q What is your age?   A Sixty four.
Q What is your Postoffice?   A Klaus.
Q What district do you live in?   A Delaware.
Q Are you a recognized citizen of the Cherokee Nation?   A Yes sir.
Q By blood or intermarriage?   A Intermarriage.
Q For whom do you apply for enrollment?   A Myself and wife and children.
Q What is the name of your wife?   A Fannie McAffrey.
Q What was her name before you married her?   A Fannie Cordrey.
Q When did you marry ?   A In 1873.
Q What are the names of your children?   A James Albert.
Q How old is James Albert?   A Twenty.
Q What is the name of the next one?   A Hugh.
Q Any middle name?   A No sir.
Q Same name as you?   A Yes sir.
Q Hugh Jr.?   A Yes sir.
Q How old?   A Seventeen.
Q What is the name of the next one?   A Napoleon.
Q Just Napoleon?   A Yes sir.
Q How old is Napoleon?   A Thirteen.
Q What is the name of the next one?   A Walter T.
Q How old is Walter T.?   A Ten.
Q What is the name of the next one?   A Rhoda Savannah.
Q How old is Rhoda?   A Five.
Q Name of the next one?   A That is all.
Q Five children?   A Yes sir.
Q Are these children all living and living with you at this time?   A Yes sir.
Q Have you lived in the Cherokee Nation continuously since 1880?
A Yes sir; since 1873.
   (1880 Roll, Page 287, #1721, Hugh McAffrey, Delaware D'st)
   (1880 Roll, Page 287, #1722, Fannie McAffrey, Delaware D'st)
   (1896 Roll, Page 582, #389, Hugh McAffrey, Delaware D'st)
   (1896 Roll, Page ~~1911~~ 499, #1911, Fannie McAffrey, Delaware District)
   (1896 Roll, Page 499, #1912, James A. McAffrey, Delaware D'st)
   (1896 Roll, Page 499, #1913, Hugh McAffrey, Delaware D'st)

Cherokee Intermarried White 1906
Volume VII

#1915 (1896 Roll, Page 499, (#1924), Napoleon McAffrey, Delaware D'st)
    (1896 Roll, Page 499, #1916, Walter T. McAffrey, Delaware D'st)
    (1896 Roll, Page 499, #1917, Rhoda S. McAffrey, Delaware D'st)
    (1880 Roll, Page 499, #1726, Albert M. McAffrey, Delaware D'st)

The name of Hugh McAffrey, and his wife, Fannie McAffrey, appears upon the authenticated rolls of 1880, and the census roll of 1896, and the name of his oldest son, James A. appears upon the authenticated roll of 1880, as Albert McAffrey, and upon the census roll of 1896, as James A. McAffrey: The names of his children, Hugh, Napoleon, Walter T. and Rhoda S. appear upon the census roll of 1896, they all being duly identified according to the page and number of the roll, as indicated in the testimony; and having made satisfactory proof of their residence, the said Hugh McAffrey will be duly listed for enrollment by this Commission as a Cherokee citizen by intermarriage, and his wife, Fannie and children, as enumerated in the testimony, as Cherokee citizens by blood.

The undersigned, being sworn, states that as stenographer to the Commission to the Five Civilized Tribes, he correctly recorded the testimony and proceedings in this case, and that the foregoing is a true and correct transcript of his stenographic notes thereof.

                                              R R Cravens

Subscribed and sworn to before me
this 28th day of September, 1900.

                                              TB Needles
                                              COMMISSIONER.

◇◇◇◇◇

DEPARTMENT OF THE INTERIOR.
Commission to the Five Civilized Tribes.
Muskogee, Indian Territory, October 15th, 1902.

In the matter of the application of Hugh McAffrey for the enrollment of himself as a citizen by intermarriage of the Cherokee Nation and for the enrollment of his wife, Fannie McAffrey, and his children, James A., Hugh, Jr., Napoleon, Walter T., Rhoda S. and Loran R. McAffrey, as citizens by blood of the Cherokee Nation.

Supplemental to #3542.

HUGH McAFFREY, being duly sworn, testified as follows:
Examination by the Commission.

Cherokee Intermarried White 1906
Volume VII

Q. What is your name?   A. Hugh McAffrey.
Q. How old are you?   A. 67.
Q. What is your post office?   A. Cleora.
Q. Are you a Cherokee by blood?   A. No, sir.
Q. You are claiming as a citizen by intermarriage, are you?
A. Yes, sir.
Q. What is your wife's name?   A. Fannie.
Q. Is she a Cherokee by blood?   A. Yes, sir.
Q Is her name on the roll of 1880?   A. Yes, sir.
Q. How long has Fannie been living in the Cherokee Nation?
A. Born and raised here.
Q. Lived in the Cherokee Nation all her life?   A. Yes, sir.
Q. When were you married to her?   A. '74.
Q. Are you on the roll of 1880?   A. Yes sir.
Q. Fannie is your first wife?   A. Yes, sir.
Q. Have you and your wife Fannie lived together ever since 1880?
A. Yes, sir.
Q. She is living?   A. Yes, sir.
Q. You have never been separated?   A. No, sir.
Q. You are living together now?   A. Yes, sir.
Q. Any children living at home with you?   A. Four.
Q. All under age?   A. Yes, sir.
Q. How many children did you enroll two years ago?   A. Enrolled five.
Q. Has there been any deaths in your family within the last two years and a half?
A. No, sir.
Q. All the children that you applied for are living now?
A. Yes, sir.

++

Jesse O. Carr, being first duly sworn, states that as stenographer to the Commission to the Five Civilized Tribes he reported the above entitled case and that the foregoing is a true and complete transcript of his stenographic notes thereof.

Jesse O. Carr

Subscribed and sworn to before me this 10th day of January, 1903.

Samuel Foreman
Notary Public.

◇◇◇◇◇

Cherokee Intermarried White 1906
Volume VII

R.

DEPARTMENT OF THE INTERIOR.
Commission to the Five Civilized Tribes.
Muskogee, Indian Territory, September 29th, 1902.

In the matter of the application of Hugh McAffrey for the enrollment of himself as a citizen by intermarriage of the Cherokee Nation and for the enrollment of his wife Fannie McAffrey and his children James A., Hugh, Jr., Napoleon, Walter T., Rhoda S. and Loran R. McAffrey as citizens by blood of the Cherokee Nation.

Supplemental to #3542.

Appearances:
James S. Davenport for Applicant.
J. C. Starr for Cherokee Nation.

JAMES S. DAVENPORT, being duly sworn, testified as follows:
Examination by the Commission.

Q. What is your name, age and post office?
A. James S. Davenport, 38, Vinita, I. T.
Q. Are you acquainted with Hugh McAffrey, the applicant in this case? A. Yes, sir.
Q. How long have you known him? A. Known him since 1894.
Q. Are you acquainted with his wife? A. Yes, sir.
Q. How long have you known her? A. I met her at the same time. The first time I met him was during the 1894 payment.
Q. Is she a citizen by blood? A. Yes, sir.
Q. He is a citizen by intermarriage? A. He claims by intermarriage; yes, sir.
Q. Has he lived since 1894 as her husband? A. Yes, sir.
Q. Were they living together as husband and wife on the first of September, 1902?
A. Yes, sir.
Q. Is his wife still living at this time? A. Yes, sir.

Jesse O. Carr, being first duly sworn, states that as stenographer to the Commission to the Five Civilized Tribes he reported the above entitled case and that the foregoing is a true and complete transcript of his stenographic notes thereof.

Jesse O. Carr

Cherokee Intermarried White 1906
Volume VII

Subscribed and sworn to before me this 6th day of October, 19o2[sic].

BC Jones
Notary Public.

◇◇◇◇◇

C. F. B.   Cherokee 3542.

DEPARTMENT OF THE INTERIOR,
COMMISSIONER TO THE FIVE CIVILIZED TRIBES.
Muskogee, Indian Territory, January 21, 1907.

In the matter of the application for the enrollment of Hugh McAffrey as a citizen by intermarriage of the Cherokee Nation.

Hugh McAffrey being first duly sworn by B. P. Rasmus, Notary Public, testified as follows:

Q What is your name?   A Hugh McAffrey.
Q What is your age?   A 70 years old.
Q What is your post office address?
A Afton.
Q You are an applicant for enrollment as a citizen by intermarriage of the Cherokee Nation?
A Yes sir.
Q You have no Cherokee blood?   A No sir.
Q You claim the right to enrollment as a citizen of the Cherokee Nation by virtue of your marriage to a citizen by blood?
A Yes sir.
Q What is the name of the citizen through whom you claim the right to enrollment?
A Fannie Cordrey
Q Is she living?   A Yes sir.
Q When did you marry her?   A In March, '73.
Q Was she a recognized citizen of the Cherokee Nation at that time?
A Yes sir; born and raised here.
Q And living in the Cherokee country?
A Yes sir.
Q Did you secure a license and marry her in accordance with the law of the Cherokee Nation?
A Yes sir.
Q In what district was the license issued?
A Tahlequah.
Q Who issued it?
Q Tom Wolfe, Deputy; Bill Turner was the Clerk.

93

Cherokee Intermarried White 1906
Volume VII

Q And you were married soon after that?
A Yes sir.
Q In accordance with the terms of that license?
A Yes sir.
Q Who married you?
A A. J. Cove, Baptist preacher; he lived in Benton County.
Q Were you ever married prior to that marriage?
A No sir.
Q Was your wife ever married before she married you?
A No sir.
Q Since your marriage, have you and your wife continuously lived in the Cherokee Nation?
A Yes sir.
Q And resided together as husband and wife continuously?
A Yes sir.

The applicant, Hugh McAffrey, is identified on the Cherokee authenticated tribal roll of 1880, Delaware District, No. 1721. His wife, Fannie McAffrey, is identified on said roll at No. 1722, and her name appears upon the approved partial roll of citizens by blood of the Cherokee Nation, opposite No. 8625.

Q Have you any evidence of a documentary character showing your marriage to your wife?
A I have not; there was nobody but her and me together and this A. J. Cove who married us has been gone for many years.
Q Since your marriage to your wife have you exercised all the rights and enjoyed all the privileges of a citizen by intermarriage of the Cherokee Nation?
A I have.
Q Voted at elections?   A Yes; all the time.
Q Have you ever held any office?
A No sir.
Q Have you serve on juries?   A Yes sir.

William H. Miller being first duly sworn by John E. Tidwell, Notary Public, testified as follows:

Q What is your name?   A William H. Miller.
Q What is your age?   A About 67 years old.
Q What is your post office address?
A Weimer.
Q Are you acquainted with a person in the Cherokee Nation by the name of Hugh McAffrey?
A Yes sir.
Q He is living at this time?   A Yes sir.
Q How long have you known him?
A Ever since about '73 as well as I recollect. He married my first cousin.

Cherokee Intermarried White 1906
Volume VII

Q   What was her name?
A   Fannie Cordrey.
Q   Cordrey was her maiden name?
A   Yes sir.
Q   Is it your understanding that Hugh McAffrey secured a license and married his wife, Fannie McAffrey, in accordance with the law of the Cherokee Nation?
A   Yes sir.
Q   Did you see them married?
A   No sir, I wasn't there; but I know of it.
Q   They were married about what year?
A   It has been so long ago, I don't hardly remember.
Q   Are you positive it was before November 1, 1875?
A   Yes, I think it was.
Q   Since their marriage Hugh McAffrey has been recognized as a citizen by intermarriage of the Cherokee Nation?
A   I guess so; yes sir.
Q   Do you know of your own personal knowledge that he has exercised the rights and enjoyed the privileges of a citizen by intermarriage of the Cherokee Nation?
A   Yes sir.
Q   Hugh and Fannie McAffrey are living together as husband and wife at this time?
A   Yes sir.
Q   And have continuously lived together as such since their marriage?
A   Yes sir.

The undersigned being first duly sworn states that as stenographer to the Commission to the Five Civilized Tribes, she recorded the testimony taken in this case and that the foregoing is a full, true and correct transcript of her stenographic notes thereof.

Myrtle Hill

Subscribed and sworn to before me this the 24th day of January, 1907.

John E. Tidwell
Notary Public.

◇◇◇◇◇

Cherokee Intermarried White 1906
Volume VII

E C M

Cherokee 3542.

DEPARTMENT OF THE INTERIOR,

COMMISSIONER TO THE FIVE CIVILIZED TRIBES.

In the matter of the application for the enrollment of HUGH McAFFREY as a citizen by intermarriage of the Cherokee Nation.

O R D E R

An examination of the Cherokee autnehticated[sic] tribal roll of 1880 shows that said applicant and his family appear on said roll, their names and ages being as follows:

1880 Roll, Page 287, No. 1721, Hugh McAffrey, Adopted white, Delaware District.
1880 Roll, Page 287, No. 1722, Fannie McAffrey, Native Cherokee, Delaware District.
1880 Roll, Page 287, No. 1723, Andrew McAffrey, Native Cherokee, six years, Delaware District.
1880 Roll, Page 287, No. 1724, John McAffrey, Native Cherokee, four years, Delaware District.
1880 Roll, Page 287, No. 1725, Mary McAffrey, Native Cherokee, two years, Delaware District.
1880 Roll, Page 287, No. 1726, Albert McAffrey, Native Cherokee, two months, Delaware District.

It is so ordered that this statement be filed with and made a part of the record in the matter of the application for the enrollment of Hugh McAffrey as a citizen by intermarriage of the Cherokee Nation.

Tams Bixby
Commissioner.

Dated at Muskogee, Indian Territory, this FEB 4 1907

◇◇◇◇◇

Cherokee Intermarried White 1906
Volume VII

Cherokee 3542.

DEPARTMENT OF THE INTERIOR.

COMMISSIONER TO THE FIVE CIVILIZED TRIBES.

Muskogee, I.T. February 13, 1907.

Supplemental proceedings in the matter of the application for the enrollment of Hugh McAffrey as a citizen by intermarriage of the Cherokee Nation.

Hugh McAffrey being first duly sworn by Frances R. Lane, a Notary Public, testified as follows:

By the Commissioner:

Q What is your name? A Hugh McAffrey.
Q How old are you? A 70 years old.
Q Your Post Office address? A Afton.
Q Mr. McAffrey you appear here today for the purpose of giving testimony relative to your right as a citizen by intermarriage of the Cherokee Nation? A Yes sir.
Q Where were you married? A In Going Snake District about half a mile of the state line and the Cherokee Nation.
Q Were you married under a license issued by the authorities of the Cherokee Nation?
A Yes sir.
Q Where was the license issued? A Tahlequah.
Q What district was it in? A Tahlequah District.
Q Then the license was issued in Tahlequah district and you went over into Going Snake district and were married? A Yes, we went on up next to the state line and were married there.
Q Mr. McAffrey do you think that you could be mistaken about having secured a license in Tahlequah District? A No sir, not a bit of a mistake.
Q You couldn't have had that recorded in Going Snake District? A No sir, I took my license right back and returned it in to the Clerk. I was to do this within thirty days.
Q Then you can swear positively that you secured a marriage license after having obtained the requisite number of signers to your petition, in the Tahlequah district, and were married under that license in Going Snake District? A Yes sir.

A careful examination of Book C of the Marriage Records of Tahlequah District for the years 1870 to 1892 inclusive; fails to show any record of a marriage license having been issued to the applicant herein.

Q What was the date of your marriage? A The 23rd day of March '73.
Q Since your marriage have you and your wife continuously resided together as husband and wife and lived in the Cherokee Nation? A Yes sir, never moved out of it.

Cherokee Intermarried White 1906
Volume VII

Q Has[sic] either of you ever been married before? A I never have, I don't think she ever has.

Witness Excused.

Fannie McAffrey being duly sworn by Frances R. Lane, a Notary Public, testified as follows:

By the Commissioner:

Q What is your name? A Fannie McAffrey.
Q Your age? A 53.
Q Your Post Office address? A Afton.
Q Are you the wife of the applicant in this case, Hugh McAffrey? A Yes sir.
Q Mrs. McAffrey, I'll ask you the date of your marriage? A The 23d day of March, 1873.
Q Were you and your husband married under a license issued in the Cherokee Nation? A Yes sir.
Q In what district? A Tahlequah district.
Q Were you married in Tahlequah district? A No sir, in Going Snake district.
Q Mrs. McAffrey, you can't be mistaken as to where that license was secured can you? A No sir.
Q Can you testify positively that your husband before securing the license secured the requisite number of signers to the petition? A (No answer)
Q Did you see the petition? A Yes sir, but there's where the trouble is; I didn't read it; I had it but I didn't read it. I saw two of the parties sign it. I saw the preacher sign the license.
Q Did you see the license after he secured it? A Yes sir, but I didn't look over it and I had the license in my possession.
Q Have you ever been married but one time? A No sir.
Q Since your marriage, have you resided together as husband and wife and continuously resided in the Cherokee Nation? A Yes sir.

Witness Excused.

I, Cora E. Glendenning, a stenographer to the Commissioner to the Five Civilized Tribes, on oath state that I reported the foregoing proceedings in the above entitled cause, and that the foregoing is a true and correct transcript of my stenographic notes therein.

Cora E Glendenning

Subscribed and sworn to before me this 13th day of February 1907.

Frances R. Lane
Notary Public.

Cherokee Intermarried White 1906
Volume VII

E.C.M.   Cherokee 3542

DEPARTMENT OF THE INTERIOR,

COMMISSIONER TO THE FIVE CIVILIZED TRIBES.

In the matter of the application for the enrollment of Hugh McAffrey as a citizen by intermarriage of the Cherokee Nation.

D E C I S I O N

THE RECORDS OF THIS OFFICE SHOW: That on September 26, 1900, application was received by the Commission to the Five Civilized Tribes for the enrollment of Hugh McAffrey as a citizen by intermarriage of the Cherokee Nation. Further proceedings in the matter of said application were had at Muskogee, Indian Territory, October 15 and September 29, 1902, and January 21 and February 13, 1907.

THE EVIDENCE IN THIS CASE SHOWS: That the applicant herein, Hugh McAffrey, a white man, was married in accordance with Cherokee law, in 1873, to his wife, Fannie McAffrey, nee Cordrey, who was at the time of said marriage, a recognized citizen by blood of the Cherokee Nation, who is identified on the Cherokee authenticated tribal roll of 1880, Delaware District, No. 1722, as a native Cherokee, and whose name is included on the approved partial roll of citizens by blood of the Cherokee Nation opposite No. 8625. It is further shown that from the time of said marriage, the said Hugh McAffrey and Fannie McAffrey resided together as husband and wife and continuously lived in the Cherokee Nation up to and including September 1, 1902. Said applicant is identified on the Cherokee authenticated tribal roll of 1880, and the Cherokee census roll of 1896 as an intermarried citizen of the Cherokee Nation.

IT IS, THEREFORE, ORDERED AND ADJUDGED: That in accordance with the decision of the Supreme Court of the United States, dated November 5, 1906, in the cases of Daniel Red Bird, et al., vs. the United States, Nos. 125, 126, 127, and 128, the said applicant, Hugh McAffrey, is entitled, under the provisions of Section twenty-one of the Act of Congress approved June 28, 1898 (30 Stats. 495), to enrollment as a citizen by intermarriage of the Cherokee Nation, and his application for enrollment as such is accordingly granted.

                  Tams Bixby
                     Commissioner.

Dated at Muskogee, Indian Territory,
this   FEB 21 1907

Cherokee Intermarried White 1906
Volume VII

Cherokee
3542.

COPY

Muskogee, Indian Territory, February 21, 1907.

W. W. Hastings,
    Attorney for the Cherokee Nation,
        Muskogee, Indian Territory.

Dear Sir:

    There is enclosed herewith copy of the decision of the Commissioner to the Five Civilized Tribes, granting the application for the enrollment of Hugh McAffrey as a citizen by intermarriage of the Cherokee Nation.

        Respectfully,

Enc. I-35.

RPI

        SIGNED   *Tams Bixby*
                Commissioner.

◇◇◇◇◇

Cherokee
3542

Muskogee, Indian Territory, February 21, 1907.

The Commissioner to the Five Civilized Tribes,
    Muskogee, Indian Territory.

Sir:

    Receipt is acknowledged of the testimony and of your decision enrolling Hugh McAffrey as a citizen by intermarriage of the Cherokee Nation. Time for protesting said decision is waived and I consent that said person may be placed upon the schedule immediately.

        Respectfully,
        W. W. Hastings
        Attorney for the Cherokee Nation.

◇◇◇◇◇

Cherokee Intermarried White 1906
Volume VII

Cherokee
3542.

Muskogee, Indian Territory, February 21, 1907.

Hugh McAffrey,
    Afton, Indian Territory.

Dear Sir:

    There is enclosed herewith a copy of the decision of the Commissioner to the Five Civilized Tribes, dated February 21, 1907, granting your application for enrollment as a citizen by intermarriage of the Cherokee Nation.

    You will be advised when your name has been placed upon a schedule of citizens of the Cherokee Nation and approved by the Secretary of the Interior.

Respectfully,

Enc. I-34.

RPI   Commissioner.

Cher IW 203

DEPARTMENT OF THE INTERIOR.
COMMISSION TO THE FIVE CIVILIZED TRIBES.
VINITA, I.T., SEPTEMBER 26th, 1900.

IN THE MATTER OF THE APPLICATION OF John T. Brackett, wife and child for enrollment as citizens of the Cherokee Nation, and he being sworn by Commissioner, C.R. Breckinridge, testified as follows:

Q What is your full name?   A John T. Brackett.
Q What is your age?   A Fifty eight.
Q What is your Postoffice?   A Vinita.
Q What district do you live in?   A Delaware.
Q Who is it you want to have put on the roll?   A Myself, wife and little girl.
Q One child?   A Yes sir.
Q Do you applu[sic] for yourself as a Cherokee by blood ?   A No sir; I am a white man.
Q If your wife a Cherokee by blood?   A Yes sir.
Q Have you your marriage license and certificate?   A No sir; I was married in 1874.
Q Same wife still living?   A Yes sir.

Cherokee Intermarried White 1906
Volume VII

Q How long have you lived in the Cherokee Nation?   A Since 1873.
Q Have you lived with your wife all the time?   A Yes sir; ever since I married.
Q What district were you in in 1880?   A Canadian.
Q In 1896, what district?   A Delaware.
Q Give me your wifes[sic] name please?   A Margaret.
Q How old is she?   A Sixty five.
Q Now give ne the name of your child please?   A Bessie.
Q How old is she?   A Eleven.
    (1880 Roll, Page 6, #162, J. T. Bracket[sic], Canadian District)
    (1880 Roll, Page 6x[sic] #163, Margaret Bracket, Canadian District)
    (1896 Roll, Page 565, #10, John Thomas Brachet[sic], Delaware D'st)
    (1896 Roll, Page 442, #383, Margaret Bracket, Delaware D'st)
    (1896 Roll, Page 442m[sic] Bessie Bracket, Delaware D'st)
Q The child, Bessie, is living now, is she?   A Yes sir/[sic]

    The applicant applies for the enrollment of himself, his wife and one child: His wife is identified on the rolls of 1880 and 1896, as a Native Cherokee, and she will be listed now for enrollment as a Cherokee by blood.
    The applicant is identified on both of said rolls; and has lived with his Cherokee wife ever since their marriage, and has continued to live in the Cherokee Nation, and he will be listed now for enrollment as a Cherokee by adoption.
    The child, Bessie, is living at this time, and is identified with her parents on the roll of 1896. She will be listed now for enrollment as a Cherokee by blood.

    The undersigned, being sworn, states that as stenographer to the Commission to the Five Civilized Tribes, he correctly recorded the testimony and proceedings in this case, and that the foregoing is a true and complete transcript of his stenographic notes thereof.

R R Cravens

Subscribed and sworn to before me
this 29th day of September, 1900.

C R Breckinridge

COMMISSIONER.

◇◇◇◇◇

Cherokee Intermarried White 1906
Volume VII

Cherokee 3573?[sic]

DEPARTMENT OF THE INTERIOR,
COMMISSION TO THE FIVE CIVILIZED TRIBES.
Muskogee, I. T., October 28, 1902.

In the matter of the application of John T. Brackett for the enrollment of himself as a citizen by intermarriage, and for the enrollment of his wife, Margaret Brackett, as a citizen by blood, of the Cherokee Nation.

SUPPLEMENTAL PROCEEDINGS.

JOHN T. BRACKETT, being sworn, testified as follows:

By the Commission.

Q What is your name?   A John T. Brakett[sic].
Q How old are you, Mr. Brackett?   A Fifty-nine years old.
Q What's your postoffice address?   A Vinita.
Q Are you an applicant for enrollment as an intermarried citizen?   A Yes, sir.
Q What's your wife's name?   A Margaret.
Q Is she living?   A Yes, sir.
Q When were you married to your wife, Margaret?   A '74.
Q You're on the '80 roll with her?   A Yes, sir, Canadian District
Q Have you and your wife, Margaret lived together as husband and wife since 1880 up to the present time?   A Yes, sir.
Q Never have been separated?   A No, sir.
Q You were living together as husband and wife on the first day of September, 1902? A Yes, sir.
Q Have you and your wife resided in the Cherokee Nation all the time since '80 to the present time?   A Yes, sir, since '74.
Q All the time since '74?   A Yes, sir/[sic]

Retta Chick, being first duly sworn, states that, as stenographer to the Commission to the Five Civilized Tribes, she recorded the testimony and proceedings in the matter of the foregoing application, and that the above is a true and complete transcript of her stenographic notes thereof.

Retta Chick

Subscribed and sworn to before me this 2nd day of December, 1902.

PG Reuter
Notary Public.

Cherokee Intermarried White 1906
Volume VII

C. F. B.	Cherokee 3573.

DEPARTMENT OF THE INTERIOR,
COMMISSION TO THE FIVE CIVILIZED TRIBES.
Muskogee, Indian Territory, January 9, 1907.

In the Matter of the Application for the Enrollment of John T. Brackett as a citizen by intermarriage of the Cherokee Nation.

John T. bracket being first duly sworn by Chas. E. Webster, Notary Public, testified as follows:

ON BEHALF OF COMMISSIONER.

Q What is your name? A John T. Brackett.
Q What is your age? A 63.
Q What is your post office address?
A Vinita, Indian Territory.
Q You claim the right to enrollment as a citizen by intermarriage of the Cherokee Nation?
A Yes sir.
Q You have no Cherokee blood?
A No sir.
Q Your only claim to the right to enrollment as a citizen of the Cherokee Nation is by virtue of your marriage to a citizen by blood of the Nation?
A Yes sir.
Q What is the name of the citizen through whom you claim that right[sic]?
A Margaret Merrill.
Q Is she living? A Yes sir.
Q When did you marry her? A January, 1874.
Q Was she a recognized citizen of the Cherokee Nation at the time you married her?
A Yes sir.
Q Living in the Cherokee country?
A Yes sir.
Q Did you procure a license and marry your wife in accordance with the laws of the Cherokee Nation?
A Yes sir.
Q In what district was that license issued?
A Canadian.
Q Who married you? A Judge Woodall.
Q Was Margaret Brackett your first wife?
A Yes sir.
Q Are you her first husband? A No sir.
Q She was married prior to the time she married you?
A Yes sir.

Cherokee Intermarried White 1906
Volume VII

Q Was her former husband dead at the time you married her?
A Yes sir.
Q Since your marriage to your wife Margaret Brackett, have you and she continuously lived together as husband and wife?
A Yes sir.
Q And lived all the time in the Cherokee Nation?
A Yes sir.

John T. Brackett is identified on the Cherokee authenticated tribal roll of 1880, Canadian District, No. 162. His wife, Margaret Brackett, is identified on said roll at No. 163 and her name appears on the final roll of citizens of the Cherokee Nation approved by the Secretary of the Interior, at No. 8684.

Q Since your marriage to your wife have you been recognized by the Cherokee authorities as an intermarried citizen of the Cherokee Nation?
A Yes sir.
Q As an intermarried citizen of the Cherokee Nation, have you ever drawn money from the Cherokee authorities?
A In 1874 and one other time later; I don't remember when.
Q You drew what was called "bread money" in 1874?
A Yes sir.

W. H. Barker being first duly sworn by John E. Tidwell, Notary Public, testified as follows:

ON BEHALF OF COMMISSIONER.

Q What is your name?
A W. H. Barker.
Q What is your age?
A 56 years old.
Q What is your post office address?
A Muskogee, Indian Territory.
Q You appear here for the purpose of giving testimony relative to the right to enrollment of John T. Brackett?
A Yes sir.
Q How long have you known him?
A Since the Spring of '74.
Q Is he a married man?
A I suppose he is; he was living with his present wife as man and wife when I knew him first.
Q What was his wife's name?
A Mrs. Margaret Carter.
Q They have been living together as man and wife ever since you have known him?
A I can't say. I was in Texas 10 or 12 years since I knew them.
Q You didn't know of them being married?
A I didn't see them married.

Cherokee Intermarried White 1906
Volume VII

Q But it is your understanding and you believe that they were married prior to the time you became acquainted with them in 1874?
A Yes sir.
Q They were living together as husband and wife at that time?
A Yes sir.
Q Where were they living? A In Fort Gibson.
Q Have you know them since that time?
A Yes sir.
Q Has John T. Brackett been recognized as a citizen of the Cherokee Nation and enjoyed all the rights and privileges of that class of citizens, since you have known him?
A Yes sir.
Q He has been allowed to vote, has he?
A Well, I have always known him as an intermarried citizen. I don't know whether he voted or not.

      J. C. Jordan being first duly sworn by John E. Tidwell, Notary Public, testified as follows:

ON BEHALF OF COMMISSIONER.

Q What is your name? A J. C. Jordan.
Q What is your age? A 41.
Q What is your post office address?
A Muskogee, Indian Territory.
Q Do you know a person in the Cherokee Nation by the name of John T. Brackett?
A Yes sir.
Q How long have you known him?
A As far back as '74.
Q You remember that you knew him in 1874?
A Yes sir.
Q What is his wife's name? A Margaret Brackett.
Q Did you know her before they were married?
A I don't remember.
Q Do you remember when they were married?
A I don't remember when they were married. I lived with them in '75.
Q What part of the year in '75? A In the winter.
Q In the early part of the year? A Yes sir.
Q Were they living together as husband and wife at that time?
A Yes sir.
Q And were so recognized by all those who knew them?
A Yes sir.
Q Have you known them since then?
A Yes sir.

Cherokee Intermarried White 1906
Volume VII

Q Do you know of your own personal knowledge that since 1874 John T. Brackett has been recognized as a citizen by intermarriage of the Cherokee Nation, and has enjoyed the rights and privileges of that class of citizens?
A Yes sir.
Q You can testify to that of your own personal knowledge?
A Yes sir.
Q Do you know that he has voted in the Cherokee elections?
A Yes sir.
Q You did not witness the marriage,- you were not present when they were married?
A No; I was small.

Belle Rush being first duly sworn by B. P. Rasmus, Notary Public, testified as follows:

ON BEHALF OF COMMISSIONER.

Q What is your name? A Belle Rush.
Q What is your age? A 57.
Q What is your post office address?
A Muskogee.
Q Are you acquainted with a person in the Cherokee Nation by the name of John T. Brackett?
A Yes sir.
Q How long have you known him? A Since '74.
Q He claims the right to enrollment as a citizen by intermarriage of the Cherokee Nation?
A Yes sir.
Q Do you know his wife? A Yes sir.
Q What is her name? A Margaret.
Q She is a citizen by blood? A Yes sir.
Q Did you know her prior to her marriage to Mr. Brackett?
A Yes sir.
Q You knew her as a Cherokee by blood?
A Ever since I can remember.
Q You were not a witness at the marriage?
A No sir; my husband was though.
Q When were they married? A In 1874.
Q Is your husband living? A No sir; he's dead.
Q Did you live near those parties when they were married?
A No, I was living on Grand River and they were down in Canadian District.
Q But your husband was a witness to their marriage?
A Yes sir; he was there.
Q He told you did he that he was present at their marriage and saw them married?
A Yes sir.
Q You have every reason to believe then that they were married at that time, in 1874?
A Yes sir.

Cherokee Intermarried White 1906
Volume VII

Q   Have you known them since that time?
A   Yes sir.
Q   And you know of your own personal knowledge that since then they have resided together as husband and wife?
A   Yes sir.
Q   And they have always lived in the Cherokee Nation?
A   Yes sir.
Q   You don't know anything about Mr. Brackett obtaining a marriage license; you didn't see the license.
A   No sir.
Q   You know of their marriage by the information received from your husband, who witnessed the marriage?
A   Yes sir.

The undersigned being first duly sworn states that as stenographer to the Commission to the Five Civilized Tribes, she recorded the testimony taken in this case and that the foregoing is a full, true and correct transcript of her stenographic notes thereof.

Myrtle Hill

Subscribed and sworn to before me this the 14th day of January, 1907.

John E. Tidwell
Notary Public.

◇◇◇◇◇

E.C.M.   Cherokee 3573.

DEPARTMENT OF THE INTERIOR,
COMMISSIONER TO THE FIVE CIVILIZED TRIBES.
MUSKOGEE, I. T., FEBRUARY 12, 1907.

In the matter of the application for the enrollment of JOHN T. BRACKETT as a citizen by intermarriage of the Cherokee Nation.

JOHN T. BRACKETT, being first duly sworn by Walter W. Chappell, Notary Public, testified as follows:

ON BEHALF OF THE COMMISSIONER:

Q   What is your name?   A   John T. Brackett.
Q   What is your age?   A   63.
Q   What is your post office address?   A   Vinita.

Cherokee Intermarried White 1906
Volume VII

Q   Are you an applicant for enrollment as a citizen by intermarriage of the Cherokee Nation?   A Yes sir.
Q   Do you appear here today to give testimony relative to your right to enrollment as a citizen by intermarriage of the Cherokee Nation?   A Yes sir.
Q   What is the name of your wife?   A Margaret.
Q   When were you married?   A In January, 1874.
Q   Where?   A In Canadian District.
Q   Did you go to the Cherokee authorities and receive a license to marry your wife?
    A First I went and got a petition, with 10 Cherokees by blood, and then I went to the Clerk of Canadian District and got the license and paid $10.00 for it.
Q   Have you a copy of that license?   A No sir.
Q   Did you ever have a copy of it?   A No sir.
Q   Did you have a certificate of marriage?   A Yes sir
Q   Have you it now?   A No sir, it was lost.

A careful examination of Book "B", of the marriage records of Canadian District for the years 1869 to 1890, fails to disclose that a marriage license was ever ~~granted~~ issued to the applicant, John T. Brackett.

Q   Have you been recognized as a citizen of the Cherokee Nation ever since you were married?   A Yes sir. I drew money in the spring of '76, and should be on that 1874 or 1875 roll; I have drawn money once since then, but I have forgotten where it was; I voted for William P. Ross; Chief of the Cherokee Nation, and for every officer in every District I have lived in since.
Q   Why does your wife not appear here?   A She is 89 years old, and she is ill.
Q   Do you wish to present this affidavit, made by A. M. Clinkscales, that he has examined your wife, and finds that she is unable to appear here for the purpose of giving testimony?   A Yes sir.

The same will be filed with, and made a part of the record in this case.

You also wish to present in evidence an affidavit made by your wife, Margaret Brackett, sworn to and subscribed before E. M. Probasco, Notary Public?   A Yes sir.

The same will be filed with, and made a part of the record in this case.

BY W. W. HASTINGS, ATTORNEY FOR CHEROKEE NATION:

Q   Was your wife ever married prior to her married to you?
    A Yes sir.
Q   What was the name of her first husband?   A Williamson.
Q   Was he dead at the time of your marriage to your wife?   A Yes sir.
Q   What clerk of Canadian District issued you your license?
    A I think it was Rocky Smith, I am not sure.
Q   But you swear positively that a license was issued?   A Yes sir.

Cherokee Intermarried White 1906
Volume VII

Q You swear positively that you got up the necessary petition?
    A The man that helped me was Henderson Holt.
Q He helped you to get up your petition? A Yes sir.
Q You were married under this license in 1874? A Yes sir.
Q That was your first marriage? A Yes sir.
Q Who married you? A Judge Woodall.
Q He was Judge of Canadian District at that time? A Yes sir.
Q You and your wife are living together now, are you? A Yes sir.

ON BEHALF OF THE COMMISSIONER:

Q Why didn't you bring some witnesses here today to testify in your case?
    A I couldn't prove only by John Jordan, William Barker and Mrs. Rush. I supposed 3 was all right.
Q Are any witnesses alive today who were present at your marriage?
    A No sir; there was Henry Parris and Jeff Starr.
Q Who are both dead? A Yes sir.
Q Then it will be impossible for you to procure the testimony of witnesses, or a copy of the license issued to you permitting your marriage to your wife, Margaret Brackett? A Yes sir. But I can produce 50 witnesses to prove that we have been living together since 1874.

(Witness excused).

The undersigned, being first duly sworn, states that, as stenographer to the Commissioner to the Five Civilized Tribes, she correctly reported the above and foregoing testimony, and that the same is a full, true and complete transcript of her stenographic notes thereof.

Sarah Waters

Subscribed and sworn to before me this 14th day of February, 1907.

Frances R Lane
Notary Public.

Cherokee Intermarried White 1906
Volume VII

COPY.

United States of America)
   Indian Territory   ) SS.
Northern District   )

I, A. M. Clinkscales being duly sworn on oath say that I am a practicing Physician residing at Vinita, I. T., and that I have been engaged in the practice of my profession at said place 15 years and that I am the family physician for John T. Brackett, and that I am waiting upon his wife Margaret Brackett and that her physical condition is such that she cannot leave her home. She is suffering with attack of Lagrippe and is also aged and feeble and has been in such feeble condition that she has not been able to leave her home for many months and it is now impossible for her to appear at Muskogee and it will doubtless never be so that she can appear there. She is very feeble and almost helpless owing to physical disabilities that at her age will never be cured.

(Signed) A. M. Clinkscales, M. D.

Subscribed to before me and sworn to before me by the above named A. M. Clinkscales, M. D. this 11th day of February 1907.

(Signed) E. M. Probasco.
Notary Public.

◇◇◇◇◇

COPY.

Affidavit.

United States of America)
Indian Territory   ) SS.
Northern District   )

I, Margaret Brackett being duly sworn on oath state that my post office address is Vinita, Indian Territory that I am 78 years of age and will be 79 in April 1907, that my name was Margaret Carter before my last marriage, that I am now the wife of John T. Brackett, that I was married to John T. Brackett in the month of January 1874. That we were married in what was then known as Canadian District by Judge Woodall, who was at that time Judge of that district. That the said marriage was performed under and in accordance with the Cherokee Law.

Cherokee Intermarried White 1906
Volume VII

That the persons who witnessed said Marriage are dead. That said marriage was performed in the Indian Territory.

I further state that I and the said John T. Brackett have lived together as husband and wife in the Indian Territory ever since said marriage.

I further state that our marriage certificate has been lost so that it cannot be produced. I further state that we received a marriage certificate at the time of our marriage.

All of these statements are made of my own knowledge and by me know to be true.

(Signed) Margaret Brackett.

Subscribed to in my presence and sworn to before me by Margaret Brackett at her residence three miles east of Vinita, Indian Territory this 12th day of February 1907.

(Signed) E. M. Probasco.

Notary Public

◇◇◇◇◇

E.C.M. Cherokee 3573

DEPARTMENT OF THE INTERIOR,

COMMISSIONER TO THE FIVE CIVILIZED TRIBES.

In the matter of the application for the enrollment of John T. Brackett as a citizen by intermarriage of the Cherokee Nation.

D E C I S I O N

THE RECORDS OF THIS OFFICE SHOW: That on September 26, 1900, application was received by the Commission to the Five Civilized Tribes for the enrollment of John T. Brackett as a citizen by intermarriage of the Cherokee Nation. Further proceedings in the matter of said application were had at Muskogee, Indian Territory, October 28, 1902, January 9 and February 12, 1907.

THE EVIDENCE IN THIS CASE SHOWS: That the applicant herein, John T. Brackett, a white man, was married in accordance with Cherokee law in January, 1874, to his wife, Margaret Brackett, nee Carter, who was, at the time of said marriage, a recognized citizen by blood of the Cherokee Nation, who is identified on the Cherokee authenticated tribal roll of 1880, Canadian district, No. 163 as a native Cherokee, and whose name is included on the approved partial roll of citizens by blood of the Cherokee Nation opposite No. 8684. It is further shown that from the time of said marriage the said

Cherokee Intermarried White 1906
Volume VII

John T. Brackett and Margaret Brackett resided together as husband and wife, and continuously lived in the Cherokee Nation up you and including September 1, 1902. Said applicant is identified on the Cherokee authenticated tribal roll of 1880, and the Cherokee census roll of 1896, as an intermarried citizen of the Cherokee Nation.

IT IS, THEREFORE, ORDERED AND ADJUDGED: That in accordance with the decision of the Supreme Court of the United States, dated November 5, 1906, in the cases of Daniel Red Bird, et al., vs. the United States, Nos. 125, 126, 127, and 128, the said applicant, John T. Brackett, is entitled, under the provisions of Section twenty-one of the Act of Congress approved June 28, 1898 (30 Stats. 495), to enrollment as a citizen by intermarriage of the Cherokee Nation, and his application for enrollment as such is accordingly granted.

Tams Bixby
Commissioner.

Dated at Muskogee, Indian Territory,
this   FEB 19 1907

◇◇◇◇◇

Cherokee 3573.

Muskogee, Indian Territory, February 19, 1907.

W. W. Hastings,
Attorney for the Cherokee Nation,
Muskogee, Indian Territory.

Dear Sir:

There is enclosed herewith a copy of the decision of the Commissioner to the Five Civilized Tribes, dated February 19, 1907, granting the application for the enrollment of John T. Brackett as a citizen by intermarriage of the Cherokee Nation.

Respectfully,

Enc I-102   Commissioner.

RPI

◇◇◇◇◇

Cherokee Intermarried White 1906
Volume VII

Cherokee 3573

Muskogee, Indian Territory, February 19, 1907.

The Commissioner to the Five Civilized Tribes,
 Muskogee, Indian Territory.

Sir:

Receipt is acknowledged of the testimony and of your decision enrolling John T. Brackett as a citizen by intermarriage of the Cherokee Nation. Time for protesting said decision is waived and I consent that said person may be placed upon the schedule immediately.

Respectfully,
W. W. Hastings
Attorney for the Cherokee Nation.

◇◇◇◇◇

Cherokee 3573

Muskogee, Indian Territory, February 19, 1907.

John T. Brackett,
 Muskogee, Indian Territory.

Dear Sir:

There is enclosed herewith a copy of the decision of the Commissioner to the Five Civilized Tribes, dated February 19, 1907, granting the application for your enrollment as a citizen by intermarriage of the Cherokee Nation.

You will be advised when your name has been placed upon a schedule of citizens of the Cherokee Nation and approved by the Secretary of the Interior.

Respectfully,

Commissioner.

Enc I-103

RPI

Cher IW 204

◇◇◇◇◇

Cherokee Intermarried White 1906
Volume VII

Department of the Interior.
Commission to the Five Civilized Tribes.
Nowata, I. T., October 17, 1900.

In the matter of the application of Alfred M. Gott for the enrollment of himself, wife as Cherokee citizens: he being sworn and examined by Commissioner T. B. Needles, testified as follows:

Q What's your name?   A Alfred M. Gott.
Q How old are you?   A 56.
Q What is your postoffice address?   A Nowata.
Q What district do you live in?   A Cooweescoowee.
Q Are you a recognized citizen of the Cherokee Nation?   A Yes.
Q By blood?   A No sir.
Q Intermarriage?   A Yes.
Q For whom do you apply for enrollment?   A Myself, wife and one girl, we have raised.
Q What's the name of your wife?   A Susan T. Gott.
Q When did you marry her?   A About 31 years ago.
Q She a white woman?   A Cherokee.
Q By blood?   A Yes sir.
Q What the name of your child?   A Lou Harris, a niece of ours. We raised her.
Q How old is she?   A 15 years.
Q Got no children of your own?   A No, sir.
Q What's the mother's name of Lou Harris?   A Emma Harris.
Q She a Cherokee?   A Yes sir.
Q What was her maiden name?   A Emma Walker.
Q Would that be her name twenty years ago, in 1880?   A I don't know.
Q Is she living?   A Yes sir.
Q Who the mother of this child?   A Yes sir.
Q Is the mother going to enroll herself?   A Yes sir. (She must enroll her own child.)
   1880 roll; page 111, #1283, A. M. Gott, Cooweescoowee.
   1880 roll; page 111, #1284, Sue T. Gott,   "
   1896 roll; page 306, #428, Alfred M. Gott,   "
   1896 roll; page 171, #2079, Sue T. Gott,   "
Q How long have you lived in the Cherokee Nation?   A Thirty years.
Q Living here now are you?   A Yes.
Q Living with your wife all this time?   A Yes.
Q Living with your wife now?   A Yes sir.
Commissioner-

The name of Alfred M. Gott appears upon the authenticated roll of 1880 as well as the Census roll of 1896. The name of his wife, Susan T. Gott, also appears upon the Census roll of 1896 and the authenticated roll of 1880 ad Sue T. Gott as a Cherokee citizen by blood. Being duly identified according to page and number of the rolls, the said Alfred M. Gott will be duly listed for enrollment as a Cherokee citizen by intermarriage, and his wife, Sue T. Gott, as a Cherokee citizen by blood.

Cherokee Intermarried White 1906
Volume VII

E. G. Rothenberger, being duly sworn, states that as stenographer to the Commission to the Five Civilized Tribes, he reported in full all proceedings in the above case, and that the foregoing is a true and complete translation of his stenographic notes in said case.

E.G. Rothenberger

Subscribed and sworn to before me this 17th day of October, 1900.

C R Breckinridge
Commissioner.

◇◇◇◇◇

DEPARTMENT OF THE INTERIOR.
Commission to the Five Civilized Tribes.
Muskogee, Indian Territory, October 13th, 1902.

In the matter of the application of Alfred M. Gott for the enrollment of himself as a citizen by intermarriage and his wife, Susan T. Gott, as a citizen by blood of the Cherokee Nation.

Supplemental to #4515.

ALFRED M. GOTT, being duly sworn, testified as follows:
Examination by the Commission.

Q. What is your name? A. Alfred M. Gott.
Q. How old are you? A. 58.
Q. What is your post office? A. Nowata.
Q. Are you a white man? A. Yes, sir.
Q. You are on the eighty roll as an intermarried white?
A. Yes, sir.
Q. What is your wife's name? A. Susan Harris.
Q. Has she any middle name--"T"? A. Yes, sir; Susan T.
Q. Was she your wife in 1880? A. Yes, sir.
Q. Have you and your wife Susan T. lived together in the Cherokee Nation ever since 1880? A. Yes, sir.
Q. You were living together on the first day of last September?
A. Yes, sir; lived together ever since we were married.
Q. You have no children? A. No, sir; none of our own, just a child that we raised.

IIIIIIIIIIIIIIIIIIIIIIIIIIIII

Cherokee Intermarried White 1906
Volume VII

Jesse O. Carr, being first duly sworn, states that as stenographer to the Commission to the Five Civilized Tribes he reported the above entitled case and that the foregoing is a true and complete transcript of his stenographic notes thereof.

Jesse O. Carr

Subscribed and sworn to before me this 20th day of December, 1902.

B.C. Jones
Notary Public.

◇◇◇◇◇

C. F. B.   Cherokee 4515.

DEPARTMENT OF THE INTERIOR,
COMMISSION TO THE FIVE CIVILIZED TRIBES.
Muskogee, Indian Territory, January 17, 1907.

In the matter of the application for the enrollment of Alfred M. Gott as a citizen by intermarriage of the Cherokee Nation.

APPEARANCES: Applicant appears in person.

                     Cherokee Nation, represented by
                     W. W. Hastings, Attorney.

Alfred M. Gott being first duly sworn by B. P. Rasmus, Notary Public, testified as follows:

ON BEHALF OF COMMISSIONER.

Q What is your name?   A   Alfred M. Gott.
Q What is your age?   A   63, I was born in '44.
Q What is your post office address?
A Nowata.
Q You are an applicant for enrollment as a citizen by intermarriage of the Cherokee Nation?
A Yes sir.
Q You have no Cherokee blood?   A   None.
Q Your only claim to the right to enrollment as a citizen of the Cherokee Nation, is by virtue of your marriage to a citizen by blood?
A Yes sir.
Q What is the name of the citizen through whom you claim that right?
A Susan T. Harris.
A Susan T. Harris.[sic]
Q Is she living at this time?   A   Yes sir.

Cherokee Intermarried White 1906
Volume VII

Q When did you marry her? A November 8, '69.
Q Was she a recognized citizen of the Cherokee Nation at the time you married her?
A Yes sir.
Q Living in the Cherokee country?
A Yes sir.
Q Since your marriage to her, have you and she continuously lived together as husband and wife?
A We have.
Q And lived in the Cherokee Nation all the time?
A Yes sir.
Q Did you secure a license and marry your wife in accordance with the law of the Cherokee Nation?
A I did.
Q In what district was that license issued?
A Illinois; at Fort Gibson. I think George Sanders was the clerk then.
Q You have no witnesses here today who have actual knowledge of your marriage license having been issued to your?
A I can't say that there is anybody here who saw the license. The preacher and the clerk are the only ones I know of who saw it.
Q Did you ever have a copy of the license?
A I don't recollect as to that, whether I ever did or not. It is only an accident that I have this certificate. I had a lot of papers burned, but this didn't happen to be among them.

The applicant presents a marriage certificate showing that on November 8, 1869, he was married to one Susan Harris by Evan Jones, a Minister of the Gospel.

BY MR. HASTINGS.

Q You say you had a license? A Yes sir.
Q And you were married under that license?
A Yes sir.
Q The license was procured prior to this marriage in accordance with the Cherokee law?
A Yes sir
Q Do you remember any of the people who signed your petition for a license?
A I recollect some of them; there was Byrd Harris and George Sanders.
Q You state positively that you did get a license and that this marriage was under that license?
A Yes sir.

ON BEHALF OF COMMISSIONER.

The applicant, Alfred M. Gott, is identified on the Cherokee authenticated tribal roll of 1880, Cooweescoowee District, No. 1283. His wife, Susan T. Gott is

Cherokee Intermarried White 1906
Volume VII

identified on said roll at No. 1284, and her name is included in the approved partial roll of citizens by blood of the Cherokee Nation, opposite No. 10, 825.

Q Since your marriage in 1869, you have enjoyed all the rights and exercised all the privileges of a citizen by intermarriage of the Cherokee Nation?
A Yes sir.
Q Have you ever held any office in the Cherokee Nation?
A No sir; I don't think I have.
Q But you voted at the elections?
A Yes, I voted; have been on juries, and everything of that sort; exercised all the rights and privileges of a citizen.
Q Were you ever married prior to your marriage to your wife, Susan T. Gott?
A No sir.
Q Was she ever married prior to her marriage to you?
A No sir.
Q You don't remember the clerk's name?
A No, I am not positive; I think it was George Sanders.

James M. Keys being first duly sworn by John E. Tidwell, Notary Public, testified as follows:

ON BEHALF OF COMMISSIONER.

Q What is your name?
A James M. Keys.
Q What is your age?
A 63.
Q What is your post office address?
A Pryor Creek, Indian Territory.
Q Do you know a person in the Cherokee Nation by the name of Alfred M. Gott?
A I do.
Q How long have you known him?
A Ever since 1868 or '69.
Q What is his wife's name?
A Susan T. Gott. Her maiden name was Harris.
Q Alfred M. Gott is a citizen by intermarriage of the Cherokee Nation?
A Yes sir.
Q Did you know Susan T. Gott before her marriage to her husband, Alfred M. Gott?
A Yes sir; I knew her prior to the war.
Q She was a recognized citizen by blood of the Cherokee Nation?
A She was.
Q Do you remember when these parties were married?
A I remember about the time; they were married in '69 I think.
Q Since that time, do you know of your own personal knowledge that Alfred M. Gott has exercised all the rights and enjoyed all the privileges of a citizen by intermarriage of the Cherokee Nation?
A Yes sir; he has.

Cherokee Intermarried White 1906
Volume VII

The undersigned being first duly sworn states that as stenographer to the Commission to the Five Civilized Tribes, she recorded the testimony taken in this case and that the foregoing is a full, true and correct transcript of her stenographic notes thereof.

Myrtle Hill

Subscribed and sworn to before me this the 19th day of January, 1907.

John E. Tidwell
Notary Public.

◇◇◇◇◇

C. F. B.   Cherokee 4515.

(COPY)

November 8th, 1869.

This is to Certify that the rites of Matrimony between Mr. A. M. Gott of Falls County, Texas, and Miss Susan Harris of Fort Gibson in the Cherokee Nation were by me this day duly solemnized.

Evan Jones
Minister of the Gospel.

Witness:
    Chas. Harris, M. D.
    Minerva Kerr.
    G. W. Elliott.

The undersigned being first duly sworn states that the above is a true and correct copy of the original marriage certificate of said A. M. Gott and Susan Harris.

Myrtle Hill

Subscribed and sworn to before me this the 21st day of January, 1907.

B. P. Rasmus
Notary Public.

◇◇◇◇◇

Cherokee Intermarried White 1906
Volume VII

E. C. M.   Cherokee 4515.

DEPARTMENT OF THE INTERIOR.
COMMISSIONER TO THE FIVE CIVILIZED TRIBES.
Muskogee, Indian Territory, February 9, 1907.

In the matter of the application for the enrollment of Alfred M. Gott as a citizen by intermarriage of the Cherokee Nation.

SUPPLEMENTAL.

Cherokee Nation represented by W. W. Hastings, Attorney.

Henry Eiffert being first duly sworn by S. C. Pitts, Notary Public, testified as follows:

ON BEHALF OF COMMISSIONER.

Q What is your name?   A Henry Eiffert.
Q What is your age?   A 57.
Q What is your post office address?   A Fort Gibson.
Q You appear here for the purpose of giving testimony relative to the right of Alfred M. Gott to enrollment as a citizen by intermarriage of the Cherokee Nation?
A Yes sir.

BY MR. HASTINGS.

Q How long have you known the applicant, Alfred M. Gott?
A My recollection is I got acquainted with him about 1868.
Q Was that before his marriage?
A Yes sir; I knew him before his marriage.
Q Where did he live at that time?
A I think he was living with Capt. Jackson; near Fort Gibson; he was in the cattle business.
Q Did you know his wife?   A Yes sir.
Q Did you know her previous to her marriage?
A Yes sir.
Q What was her maiden name?
A Harris; Sir, I think.
Q Did you know of the circumstances of their marriage?
A Yes sir.
Q Were you acting in any official capacity at that time?
A As deputy clerk under William P. Boudinot, District Clerk, Cherokee Nation.
Q What district?   A Illinois District.

Cherokee Intermarried White 1906
Volume VII

Q Do you remember the circumstance of issuing a marriage license to the applicant, Alfred M. Gott?
A No sir; I don't remember the issuance.
Q You were at that time, however, deputy clerk of Illinois District?
A Yes sir.
Q Do you remember the circumstance of their marriage?
A Yes sir.
Q You know that they were married?
A Well, I know it in a sense; parties that went to the wedding told me they were married and I was at the ball they had that night in honor of his marriage; I didn't see them married.
Q It was a well known fact throughout the neighborhood that they were married?
A Yes sir; that was the rumor.
Q Do you know where they were said to have been married?
A I think over at Capt. Jackson's residence near Fort Gibson.
Q Did they live together as husband and wife after that time?
A Yes sir; have continuously ever since; I have visited them at their house.
Q But you cannot remember the circumstance of the issuance of the license?
A No sir, I can't; that is so long ago that I have no personal recollection of issuing the license.
Q William P. Boudinot was the regularly appointed clerk and you was his deputy?
A Yes sir.
Q Do you know whether Mr. Gott and his wife have continuously lived together as husband and wife since that time?
A Well, I have visited them off and on ever since they were married, and a month or two ago I was at their house, and I heard nothing to the contrary.
Q Had either of them been previously married to your knowledge?
A Not that I know of; no sir. I don't think his wife was married previous. I don't know anything about Mr. Gott, he came from Texas.

Charles Harris being first duly sworn by S. C. Pitts, Notary Public, testified as follows:

ON BEHALF OF COMMISSIONER.

Q What is your name?
A Charles Harris.
Q What is your age?
A 65.
Q What is your post office address?
A Muskogee, Indian Territory.
Q Mr. Harris, are you acquainted with the applicant in this case, Alfred M. Gott, and his wife, Susan Gott?
A Yes sir.
Q How long have you known them?
A 40 years.
Q Were you present at their marriage, Mr. Harris?
A Yes sir.

Cherokee Intermarried White 1906
Volume VII

Q   Were they married under a license issued by the authorities of the Cherokee Nation?
A   To the best of my knowledge they were.
Q   Did you see the license?
A   I can't recollect now that I saw the license but I am confident in my mind that they were married under a license of the Cherokee Nation, because it was at a period in our history here that everything of that kind was attended to strictly.
Q   You think it wouldn't have been possible for him to have been married without a license?
A   No; the friends and relatives of his wife would not have suffered it.
Q   Do you remember who married them, - who the minister was?
A   No sir, I don't remember; 40 years is a long time.
Q   You were present at the marriage?   A   Yes sir.
Q   Saw them married?   A   Saw them married; yes sir.
Q   Since their marriage have they continuously resided together as husband and wife?
A   Yes sir.
Q   What was Susan Gott's name before she was married?
A   Harris.
Q   She was a Cherokee, was she?
A   Yes sir; Cherokee by blood.
Q   You are willing to swear, Mr. Harris, that to the best of your knowledge they were married under a Cherokee license?
A   Yes sir.

The undersigned being first duly sworn states that as stenographer to the Commission to the Five Civilized Tribes she recorfed[sic] the testimony taken in this case and that the foregoing is a true and correct transcript of her stenographic notes thereof.

Myrtle Hill

Subscribed and sworn to before me this the 13th day of February, 1907.

Walter W. Chappell
Notary Public.

Cherokee Intermarried White 1906
Volume VII

COPY.

November 8th 1869

This is to Certify that the rites of Matrimony beween[sic] Mr A. M. Gott of Falls County Texas and Miss Susan Harris of Fort Gibson in the Cherokee Nation were by me this day duly Solemnized.

(Signed) Evan Jones
Minister of the Gospel

Witnesses
Chas. Harris M. D.
Minerva Kerr
G W Elliott

This certifies that the undersigned, being duly sworn, states that as stenographer to the Commission to the Five Civilized Tribes she made the above and foregoing copy and that the same is a full, true and correct copy of the original instrument now on file in this office.

Georgia Coberly

Subscribed and sworn to before me this 23rd day of January, 1907.

Frances R Lane
Notary Public.

Cherokee Intermarried White 1906
Volume VII

E.C.M.

Cherokee 4515

DEPARTMENT OF THE INTERIOR,

COMMISSIONER TO THE FIVE CIVILIZED TRIBES.

In the matter of the application for the enrollment of Alfred M. Gott as a citizen by intermarriage of the Cherokee Nation.

D E C I S I O N

THE RECORDS OF THIS OFFICE SHOW: That at Nowata, Indian Territory, October 17, 1900, application was received by the Commission to the Five Civilized Tribes for the enrollment of Alfred M. Gott as a citizen by intermarriage of the Cherokee Nation. Further proceedings in the matter of said application were had at Muskogee, Indian Territory, October 13 and January 17 and February 9, 1907.

THE EVIDENCE IN THIS CASE SHOWS: That the applicant herein, Alfred M. Gott, a white man, was married in accordance with Cherokee law November 8, 1869, to his wife, Susan T. Gott, nee Harris, who was, at the time of said marriage, a recognized citizen by blood of the Cherokee Nation, who is identified on the Cherokee authenticated tribal roll of 1880, Cooweescoowee District, No. 1284 as a native Cherokee, and whose name is included on the approved partial roll of citizens by blood of the Cherokee Nation opposite No. 10825. It is further shown that from the time of said marriage the said Alfred M. Gott and Susan T. Gott resided together as husband and wife and continuously lived in the Cherokee Nation up to and including September 1, 1902. Said applicant is identified on the Cherokee authenticated tribal roll of 1880, and the Cherokee census roll of 1896 as an intermarried citizen of the Cherokee Nation.

IT IS, THEREFORE, ORDERED AND ADJUDGED: That in accordance with the decision of the Supreme Court of the United States, dated November 5, 1906, in the cases of Daniel Red Bird, et al., vs. the United States, Nos. 125, 126, 127, and 128, the said applicant, Alfred M. Gott, is entitled, under the provisions of Section twenty-one of the Act of Congress approved June 28, 1898 (30 Stats. 495), to enrollment as a citizen by intermarriage of the Cherokee Nation, and his application for enrollment as such is accordingly granted.

            Tams Bixby
            Commissioner.

Dated at Muskogee, Indian Territory,
this   FEB 19 1907

Cherokee Intermarried White 1906
Volume VII

Cherokee 4515

Muskogee, Indian Territory, February 19, 1907.

W. W. Hastings,
    Attorney for the Cherokee Nation,
        Muskogee, Indian Territory.

Dear Sir:

    There is enclosed herewith copy of the decision of the Commissioner to the Five Civilized Tribes, dated February 19, 1907, granting the application for the enrollment of Alfred M. Gott as a citizen by intermarriage of the Cherokee Nation.

        Respectfully,

Enc I-104.   Commissioner.

RPI

◇◇◇◇◇

Cherokee 4515.

Muskogee, Indian Territory, February 19, 1907.

The Commissioner to the Five Civilized Tribes,
    Muskogee, Indian Territory.

Sir:

    Receipt is acknowledged of the testimony and of your decision enrolling Alfred M. Gott as a citizen by intermarriage of the Cherokee Nation. Time for protesting said decision is waived, and I consent that said person may be placed upon the schedule immediately.

        Respectfully,
        W. W. Hastings
        Attorney for the Cherokee Nation.

◇◇◇◇◇

Cherokee Intermarried White 1906
Volume VII

Cherokee 4515.

Muskogee, Indian Territory, February 19, 1907.

The Commissioner to the Five Civilized Tribes,
Muskogee, Indian Territory.

Sir:

    Receipt is acknowledged of the testimony and of your decision enrolling Alfred M. Gott as a citizen by intermarriage of the Cherokee Nation. Time for protesting said decision is waived, and I consent that said person may be placed upon the schedule immediately.

                  Respectfully,
                  W. W. Hastings
            Attorney for the Cherokee Nation.

◇◇◇◇◇

Cherokee 4515.

Muskogee, Indian Territory, February 19, 1907.

Alfred M. Gott,
    Nowata, Indian Territory.

Dear Sir:

    There is enclosed herewith copy of the decision of the Commissioner to the Five Civilized Tribes, dated February 19, 1907, granting the application for your enrollment as a citizen by intermarriage of the Cherokee Nation.

    You will be advised when your name has been placed upon a schedule of citizens of the Cherokee Nation and approved by the Secretary of the Interior.

                  Respectfully,

Enc I-105   Commissioner.

RPI

◇◇◇◇◇

Cherokee Intermarried White 1906
Volume VII

Cherokee
I.W. 204

Muskogee, Indian Territory, April 16, 1907.

Alfred M. Gott,
 Nowata, Indian Territory.

Dear Sir:

Your marriage license and certificate filed in connection with your application for enrollment as a citizen by intermarriage of the Cherokee Nation is returned to you herewith, copies of the same being retained in the files of this office.

Respectfully,

Encl. W-22.   Commissioner.
S.W.

Cher IW 205

◇◇◇◇◇

Department of the Interior.
Commission to the Five Civilized Tribes,
Nowata, I. T., October 17, 1900.

In the matter of the application of Elizabeth Riley for enrollment as a Cherokee citizen; she being sworn and examined by Commissioner T. B. Needles, testified as follows:

Q What's your name?   A Elizabeth Riley.
Q How old are you?   A 55.
Q What's your postoffice address?   A Nowata, I.T.
Q What district do you live in?   A Cooweescoowee.
Q Are you a recognized citizen of the Cherokee Nation?   A Yes sr[sic].
Q By blood?   A No.
Q By intermarriage?   A Intermarriage.
Q For whom do you apply for enrollment?   A Just myself.
Q What is your husband's name?   A Rufus Riley.
Q Is he living?   [sic] No sir.
Q When did you marry him?   A In '65.
Q When did he die?   A He's been dead about 10 or 12 years.
Q Have you married since his death?   A No sir.

Cherokee Intermarried White 1906
Volume VII

Q You lived with him until he died?   A Yes sir.
  1880 roll; page 162, #2353, Betty Riley, Cooweescoowee.
  1896 roll; page 321, #847, Bettie Riley, Cooweescoowee
Q You lived in the Cherokee Nation do you?   A Yes sir.
Q You have since you were married?   A Yes
Commissioner-
  The name of Elizabeth Riley appears upon the authenticated roll of 1880 as Betty Riley as an intermarried white; also on the Census roll of 1896 as Bettie Riley. She being duly idetified[sic] and having made satisfactory proof as to her residence, the said Elizabeth Riley will be duly listed for enrollment by this Commission as a Cherokee citizen by intermarriage.

  E. G. Rothenberger, being duly sworn, states that as stenographer to the Commission to the Five Civilized Tribes, he reported in full all proceedings in the above case, and that the foregoing is a true and complete translation of his stenographic notes in said case.

              E.G. Rothenberger

  Subscribed and sworn to before me this 18th day of October, 1900.

            C R Breckinridge
                 Commissioner.

◇◇◇◇◇

Cherokee 4521.

       Department of the Interior,
     Commission to the Five Civilized Tribes,
      Muskogee, I. T., October 6, 1902.

  In the matter of the application of Elizabeth Riley, for the enrollment of herself as a citizen by intermarriage of the Cherokee Nation,
  Samuel R. Riley, being sworn and examined by the Commission, testified as follows:
Q What is your name?   A Samuel R. Riley.
Q What is your age?   A Thirty-three years.
Q Do you know Elizabeth Riley who is an applicant for enrollment as an intermarried citizen of the Cherokee Nation?   A Yes sir.
Q Are you related to her in any way?   A I am her son.
Q She is your mother?   A Yes sir.
Q Do you know her age, Mr. Riley?   A She is in the fifties some place, about fifty-five.
Q You don't know her exact age?   A No sir.
Q What is her postoffice address?   A Nowata.
Q What was her husband's name?   A Rufus Riley.
Q Is he living or dead?   A Dead.

Cherokee Intermarried White 1906
Volume VII

Q Your mother and your father were married prior to 1880, were they not? A Yes sir.
Q How long has Rufus Riley been dead? A Close to fifteen years.
Q Did your mother Elizabeth Riley and her husband Rufus Riley live together from 1880 up until the time of his death as husband and wife? A Yes sir.
Q They were never separated during that time? A No sir.
Q Has your mother ever been married to any other man since her marriage to Rufus Riley? A No sir.
Q Was she still a widow and single on the first day of September, 1902? A Yes sir.
Q How long has she lived in the Cherokee Nation, do you know? A Lived there all of her life.
Q Has she lived in the Cherokee Nation all the time from 1880 up to the present time?
A Yes sir.

The undersigned, being duly sworn, states that as stenographer to the Commission to the Five Civilized Tribes he correctly recorded the testimony and proceedings in this case, and the foregoing is a true and correct transcript of his stenographic notes thereof.

E.G. Rothenberger

Subscribed and sworn to before me this 23rd day of October, 1902.

BC Jones
Notary Public.

◇◇◇◇◇

COOWEESCOOWEE.

Statement of Applicant Taken Under Oath.

CHEROKEE BY BLOOD AND ADOPTION.

Date **OCT 17 1900** 1900.
Name **Nowata I.T.**
District _____ Year _____ Page _____ No. _____
Citizen by blood _____ Mother's citizenship _____
Intermarried citizen _____
Married under what law _____ Date of marriage _____
License **55** _____ Certificate _____
Wife's name **Elizabeth Riley**
District **COOWEESCOOWEE.** Year **1880** Page **162** No. **2353**
Citizen by blood **No** Mother's citizenship _____
Intermarried citizen **Yes**
Married under what law _____ Date of marriage _____
License _____ Certificate _____

Names of Children:
_____ Dist. _____ Year _____ Page _____ No. _____ Age _____
_____ Dist. _____ Year _____ Page _____ No. _____ Age _____

Cherokee Intermarried White 1906
Volume VII

	Dist.	Year	Page	No.	Age
	Dist.	Year	Page	No.	Age
	Dist.	Year	Page	No.	Age

1 on 1880 Roll as Betty Riley

C. F. B.   Cherokee 4521.

DEPARTMENT OF THE INTERIOR,
COMMISSIONER TO THE FIVE CIVILIZED TRIBES.
Muskogee, Indian Territory, January 29, 1907.

In the matter of the application for the enrollment of Elizabeth Riley as a citizen by intermarriage of the Cherokee Nation.

APPEARANCES.
                      Applicant appears in person.

                      Cherokee Nation represented by
                      W. W. Hastings, Attorney.

Elizabeth Riley being first duly sworn by Chas. E. Webster, Notary Public, testified as follows:

ON BEHALF OF COMMISSIONER.

Q What is your name?   A Elizabeth Riley.
Q What is your age?   A 63.
Q What is your post office address?
A Nowata.
Q You are an applicant for enrollment as a citizen by intermarriage of the Cherokee Nation?
A Yes sir.
Q You have no Cherokee blood?   A No.
Q You claim the right to enrollment as a citizen of the Cherokee Nation by virtue of your marriage to a citizen by blood?
A Yes sir.
Q What is the name of the citizen through whom you claim that right?
A Rufus Riley.
Q Is he living?   A No, he's dead.
Q When were you married to Rufus Riley?
A The 12th day of July, 1865.
Q Was he a recognized citizen of the Cherokee Nation at the time you married him?
A Yes sir.

Cherokee Intermarried White 1906
Volume VII

Q   Living in the Cherokee country?
A   We were in the Choctaw Nation; he went South during the war.
Q   You were married in the Choctaw Nation?
A   We were married there and came back here.
Q   You removed to the Cherokee Nation immediately after your marriage?
A   Yes sir
Q   Was he your first husband?
A   He was my first husband and only husband.
Q   Were you his first wife?   A   I was his first wife.
Q   When did he die?
A   It has been 15 or 20 years.
Q   Did you and he continuously live together as husband and wife until his death?
A   Yes sir; we never was apart any.
Q   Since his death have you married?
A   No, indeed; I have never been married but once.
Q   Has your residence been continuously in the Cherokee Nation?
A   Here and nowhere else.
Q   You have lived continuously in the Cherokee Nation since you removed here immediately after your marriage?
A   Yes sir; never have been nowhere else.

BY MR. HASTINGS.

Q   Was your husband a resident of the Cherokee Nation immediately prior to the war?
A   Yes sir.
Q   And had gone down in the Choctaw Nation during the war?
A   Yes sir.
Q   And you returned back here directly after your marriage?
A   Yes sir.
Q   In what year did you return?   A   In '67.

ON BEHALF OF COMMISSIONER.

Q   Were you ever known by the name of Bettie Riley?
A   Yes sir.
Q   Did you have any children in 1880?
A   I had four children; I have three living and one dead.
Q   What was the name of your oldest child?   A   George.
Q   The next one?   A   Samuel.
Q   The next one?   A   Rufus.
Q   The next one?   A   Atwood.

The applicant, Elizabeth Riley, is identified on the Cherokee authenticated tribal roll of 1880, Cooweescoowee District, No. 2353. Her husband, Rufus Riley, by virtue of her marriage to whom she claims the right to enrollment as a citizen by intermarriage of the Cherokee Nation, is identified on said roll of said district at No.

Cherokee Intermarried White 1906
Volume VII

2352. Immediately following the names of Rufus Riley and his wife on the 1880 roll, appear the names of the following children: George Riley, age 13; Samuel Riley, age 10; and Atwood Riley, age 3.

Q   Have you any evidence of documentary character showing your marriage to Rufus Riley?
A   I guess I have some.

The applicant present what purports to be a leaf taken from the family bible, showing that on the 12th day of July, 1865, Rufus R. Riley was married to Elizabeth Risner, in the presence of Rev. Hodskins.

Q   When was this record made in the Bible?
A   I can't tell you when, hardly; it has been a long time ago.
Q   Can you approximate the date? Give about the date if you can.
A   I can't do that.
Q   By whom was the marriage ceremony performed?
A   By Hodskins, Presbyterian.

The record from the family bible presented by the applicant, will be filed with and made a part of the record in this case.

The undersigned being first duly sworn that as stenographer to the Commissioner to the Five Civilized Tribes, she recorded the testimony taken in this case and that the foregoing is a true and correct transcript of her stenographic notes thereof.

                                       Myrtle Hill

Subscribed and sworn to before me this 1st day of February, 1907.

                                       John E. Tidwell
                                       Notary Public.

Cherokee Intermarried White 1906
Volume VII

Cherokee 4521.

DEPARTMENT OF THE INTERIOR,
COMMISSIONER TO THE FIVE CIVILIZED TRIBES,
Muskogee, Indian Territory,
February 11, 1907.

SUPPLEMENTAL:
In the matter of the application for the enrollment of ELIZABETH RILEY as a citizen by intermarriage of the Cherokee Nation.

J. M. Chaney, being first duly sworn by Walter W. Chappell, a Notary Public, testifies as follows:

ON BEHALF OF COMMISSIONER:
Q What is your name?
A J. M. Chaney.
Q What is your age?
A 58 years.
Q Your post-office address?
A Ruby, Indian Territory.
Q You appear here for the purpose of giving testimony relative to the right of Elizabeth Riley to enrollment as a citizen by intermarriage of the Cherokee Nation?
A Yes sir.
Q How long have you been acquainted with Elizabeth Riley?
A Since about September, 1873.
Q Were you acquainted with her husband, Rufus Riley?
A Yes sir.
Q Were they married when you first became acquainted with them?
A They were living together as man and wife.
Q Did they hold themselves out as husband and wife?
A Yes sir.
Q Were they regarded as citizens of the Cherokee Nation?
A Yes sir.
Q Are they both living now?
A No sir?
Q Both dead?
A No sir, Mr. Riley is dead.
Q Do you remember when he died?
A No sir, I do not, exactly.
Q About how long ago was it?
A I think about twenty-five years ago.

Cherokee Intermarried White 1906
Volume VII

Q Can you testify positively that Rufus Riley was a citizen by blood of the Cherokee Nation?
A Yes sir, he always was recognized as that
Q Did they continuously reside together as husband and wife and live in the Cherokee Nation until the death of Rufus Riley?
A Yes sir.
Q Since the death of Rufus Riley has Elizabeth Riley re-married?
A No sir.
Q You don't know whether either of them had ever been married before?
A No sir, I do not.

(Witness excused)

This certifies that the undersigned, being duly sworn, states that as stenographer to the Commission to the Five Civilized Tribes she reported the above entitled cause and that the above and foregoing is a full, true and correct transcript of her stenographic notes thereof.

Georgia Coberly
Stenographer.

Subscribed and sworn to before me this 12th day of February, 1907.

Walter W. Chappell
Notary Public.

Cherokee 4521.

DEPARTMENT OF THE INTERIOR,
COMMISSIONER TO THE FIVE CIVILIZED TRIBES,
Muskogee, Indian Territory,
February 11, 1907.

SUPPLEMENTAL:
In the matter of the application for the enrollment of ELIZABETH RILEY as a citizen by intermarriage of the Cherokee Nation.

A. H. Norwood, being first duly sworn by Walter W. Chapell[sic], a Notary Public, testifies as follows:

ON BEHALF OF THE COMMISSIONER:

Q What is your name?
A A. H. Norwood.

Cherokee Intermarried White 1906
Volume VII

Q Your age?
A 56 years.
Q Your post-office address?
A Dewey, I T.
Q Are you acquainted with the applicant in this case, Elizabeth Riley?
A Yes sir.
Q Were you acquainted with her husband, Rufus Riley?
A Yes sir.
Q How long have you known them?
A I got acquainted with them in February, 1873.
Q Were they living together as husband and wife at that time?
A Yes sir.
Q Was he regarded as a citizen by blood of the Cherokee Nation?
A Yes sir.
Q Is he living now?
A No sir.
Q When did he die?
A I don't remember the time, but it has been a number of years ago.
Q As many as twenty years?
A I can't fix the date exactly.
Q Have you been acquainted with Elizabeth Riley since the death of Rufus Riley?
A Yes sir.
Q Is she a widow?
A Thats[sic] my understanding.

(Witness excused)

This certifies that the undersigned, being duly sworn, states that as stenographer to the Commission to the Five Civilized Tribes she reported the above entitled cause and that the above and foregoing is a full, true and correct transcript of her stenographic notes thereof.

Georgia Coberly
Stenographer.

Subscribed and sworn to before me this 11th day of February, 1907.

Walter W. Chappell
Notary Public.

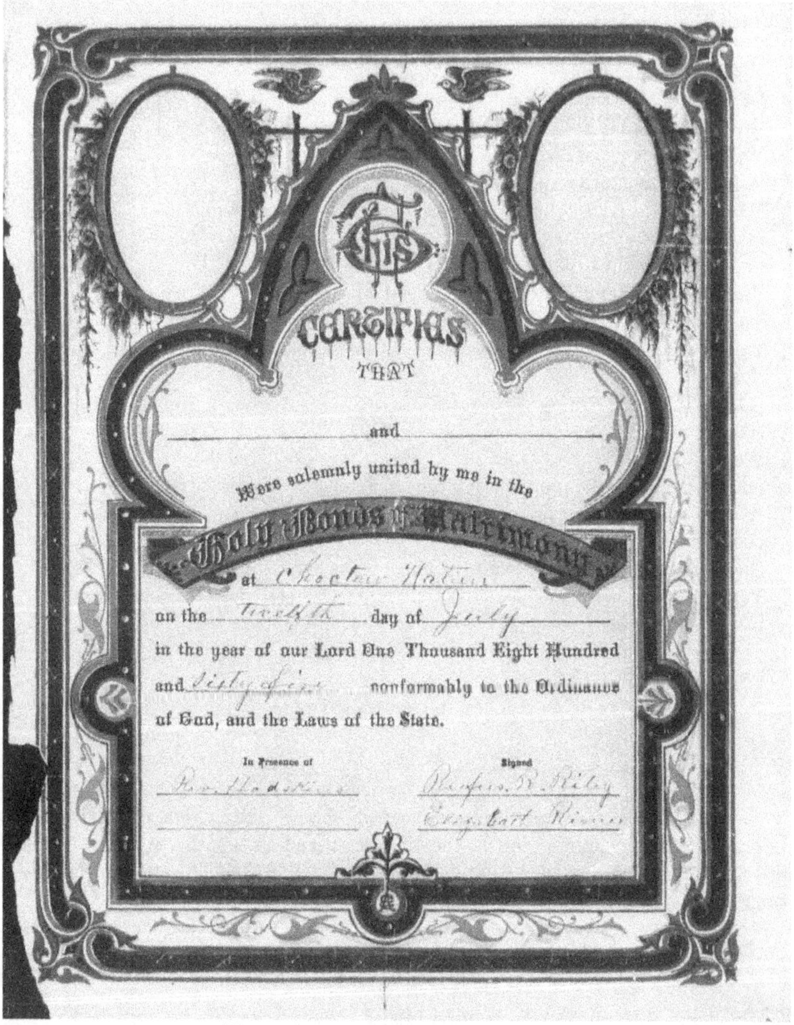

Cherokee Intermarried White 1906
Volume VII

(Copy of original document from case.)

Cherokee Intermarried White 1906
Volume VII

CERTIFIED COPY.

This

CERTIFIES

THAT _____ and _____ were solemnly united by me in the Holy Bonds of Matrimony at Choctaw Nation on the twelfth day of July in the year of our Lord One Thousand Eight Hundred and Sixty five conformably to the Ordinance of God, and the Laws of the State.

In Presence of
Rev. Hodskins.

(Signed)
Rufus R. Riley
Elizabeth Risner.

This certifies that the undersigned being duly sworn, states that as stenographer to the Commission to the Five Civilized Tribes she made the above and foregoing copy and that the same is a full, true and correct copy of the original instrument now on file in this office.

Georgia Coberly
Stenographer.

Subscribed and sworn to before me this 14th day of February, 1907.

Walter W. Chappell
Notary Public.

Cherokee Intermarried White 1906
Volume VII

E C M
Cherokee 4521.

DEPARTMENT OF THE INTERIOR,

COMMISSIONER TO THE FIVE CIVILIZED TRIBES.

In the matter of the application for the enrollment of ELIZABETH RILEY as a citizen by intermarriage of the Cherokee Nation.

D E C I S I O N

THE RECORDS OF THIS OFFICE SHOW: That at Nowata, Indian Territory October 17, 1900, application was received by the Commission to the Five Civilized Tribes for the enrollment of Elizabeth Riley as a citizen by intermarriage of the Cherokee Nation. Further proceedings in the matter of said application were had at Muskogee, Indian Territory, October 6, 1902, January 29, 1907 and February 11, 1907.

THE EVIDENCE IN THIS CASE SHOWS: That the applicant herein, Elizabeth Riley, a white woman, was married on July 12, 1865 to one Rufus Riley, since deceased, who was at the time of said marriage a recognized citizen by blood of the Cherokee nation, who is identified on the Cherokee authenticated tribal roll of 1880, Cooweescoowee District No. 2352, as a native Cherokee. It is further shown that from the time of said marriage until the death of said Rufus Riley, which occurred about the year 1887, the said Rufus Riley and Elizabeth Riley resided together as husband and wife and continuously lived in the Cherokee Nation; that since the death of said Rufus Riley the said Elizabeth Riley has remained unmarried and continuously lived in the Cherokee Nation up to and including September 1, 1902. Said applicant is identified on the Cherokee authenticated tribal roll of 1880 as "Betty Riley" and the Cherokee census roll of 1896 as an intermarried citizen of the Cherokee Nation.

IT IS, THEREFORE, ORDERED AND ADJUDGED: That in accordance with the decision of the Supreme Court of the United States, dated November 5, 1906 in the cases of Daniel Red Bird, et al. vs. the United States, Nos. 125, 126, 127, and 128, the said applicant, Elizabeth Riley is entitled, under the provisions of Section Twenty-one of the Act of Congress approved June 28, 1898 (30 Stats. 495), to enrollment as a citizen by intermarriage of the Cherokee Nation, and her application for enrollment as such is accordingly granted.

Tams Bixby
Commissioner.

Dated at Muskogee, Indian Territory,
this   FEB 18 1907

Cherokee Intermarried White 1906
Volume VII

REFER IN REPLY TO THE FOLLOWING:
Cherokee
4521.

DEPARTMENT OF THE INTERIOR,
COMMISSIONER TO THE FIVE CIVILIZED TRIBES.

Muskogee, Indian Territory, December 27, 1906.

Elizabeth Riley,
    Nowata, Indian Territory.

Dear Madam:

    November 6, 1906, the United States Supreme Court held that white persons who intermarried with Cherokee citizens according to Cherokee law prior to November 1, 1875, are entitled to enrollment and allotments of land as citizens of the Cherokee Nation.

    You are advised that to properly determine your right to enrollment as a citizen by intermarriage of the Cherokee Nation, it will be necessary for you to appear before the Commissioner for the purpose of giving testimony as to the date of your marriage and whether or not your husband, by reason of your marriage to whom you claim the right to enrollment as a citizen by intermarriage of the Cherokee Nation, was a recognized Cherokee citizen at the time of your marriage to him.

    You are therefore directed to appear before the Commissioner at Muskogee, Indian Territory, at 9 o'clock A. M., on Friday, January 4, 1907, and give testimony as above indicated.

                    Respectfully,

                      Wm O. Beall
H.J. .[sic]   Acting Commissioner.

Cherokee Intermarried White 1906
Volume VII

Form No. 260.

THE WESTERN UNION TELEGRAPH COMPANY.
INCORPORATED
23,000 OFFICES IN AMERICA.   CABLE SERVICE TO ALL THE WORLD.
ROBERT C. CLOWRY, President and General Manager.

Receiver's No.	Time Filed	Check
		Cherokee 4521

SEND the following message subject to the terms on back hereof, which are hereby agreed to.

E.C.M.

Muskogee, Indian Territory, 8, 1907

Elizabeth Riley,

Nowata, Indian Territory.

Intermarried case incomplete. Testimony of witnesses having knowledge of date of your marriage necessary. Produce same at once.

Bixby,

C.B.C.R.Paid   Commissioner

☞ READ THE NOTICE AND AGREEMENT ON BACK. ☜

(Copy of original document from case.)

◇◇◇◇◇◇

ALL MESSAGES TAKEN BY THIS COMPANY ARE SUBJECT TO THE FOLLOWING TERMS:

To guard against mistakes or delays, the sender of a message should order it REPEATED; that is, telegraphed back to the originating office for comparison. For this, one-half the regular rate is charged in addition. It is agreed between the sender of the following message and this Company, that said Company shall not be liable for mistakes or delays in the transmission or delivery, or for non-delivery of any UNREPEATED message, beyond the amount received for sending the same; nor for mistakes or delays in the transmission or delivery, or for non-delivery of any REPEATED message, beyond fifty times the sum received for sending the same, unless specially insured, nor in any case for delays arising from unavoidable interruption in the working of its lines, or for errors in cipher or obscure messages. And this Company is hereby made the agent of the sender, without liability, to forward any message over the lines of any other Company when necessary to reach its destination.

Correctness in the transmission of a message to any point on the lines of this Company can be INSURED by contract in writing, stating agreed amount of risk, and payment of premium thereon, at the following rates, in addition to the usual charge for repeated messages, viz, one per cent. for any distance not exceeding 1,000 miles, and two per cent. for any greater distance. No employee of the Company is authorized to vary the foregoing.

No responsibility regarding messages attaches to this Company until the same are presented and accepted at one of its transmitting offices; and if a message is sent to such office by one of the Company's messengers, he acts for that purpose as the agent of the sender.

Messages will be delivered free within the established free delivery limits of the terminal office. For delivery at a greater distance, a special charge will be made to cover the cost of such delivery.

The Company will not be liable for damages or statutory penalties in any case where the claim is not presented in writing within sixty days after the message is filed with the Company for transmission.

ROBERT C. CLOWRY, President and General Manager.

(Copy of original document from case.)

◇◇◇◇◇◇

Cherokee Intermarried White 1906
Volume VII

Cherokee 4521

Muskogee, Indian Territory, February 8, 1907.

Special

Elizabeth Riley,
    Nowata, Indian Territory.

Dear Madam:

    The Commissioner sent you this day a telegram as follows:

> "Intermarried case incomplete. Testimony of witnesses having knowledge of date of your marriage necessary. Produce same at once."

    The Act of Congress approved April 26, 1906, provides that the Secretary of the Interior shall have no jurisdiction to approve the enrollment of any person as a citizen of the Cherokee Nation after March 4, 1907.

    This matter, therefore, demands your immediate attention.

    Respectfully,

MMP   Commissioner.

◇◇◇◇◇

Cherokee 4521

Muskogee, Indian Territory, February 18, 1907.

W. W. Hastings,
    Attorney for the Cherokee Nation,
        Muskogee, Indian Territory.

Dear Sir:

    There is enclosed herewith a copy of the decision of the Commissioner to the Five Civilized Tribes, dated February 18, 1907, granting the application for the enrollment of Elizabeth Riley as a citizen by intermarriage of the Cherokee Nation.

    Respectfully,

Encl. H-35   Commissioner.
JMH

Cherokee Intermarried White 1906
Volume VII

◇◇◇◇◇

Cherokee 4521

Muskogee, Indian Territory, February 18, 1907.

The Commissioner to the Five Civilized Tribes,
    Muskogee, Indian Territory.

Sir:

    Receipt is acknowledged of the testimony and of your decision enrolling Elizabeth Riley as a citizen by intermarriage of the Cherokee Nation. Time for protesting said decision is waived, and I consent that said person may be placed upon the schedule immediately.

                  Respectfully,
                        W. W. Hastings
                        Attorney for Cherokee Nation.

◇◇◇◇◇

Cherokee 4521

Muskogee, Indian Territory, February 18, 1907.

Elizabeth Riley,
    Nowata, Indian Territory.

Dear Madam:

    There is enclosed herewith a copy of the decision of the Commissioner to the Five Civilized Tribes, dated February 18, 1907, granting the application for your enrollment as a citizen by intermarriage of the Cherokee Nation.

    You will be advised when your name has been placed upon a schedule of citizens of the Cherokee Nation and approved by the Secretary of the Interior.

                  Respectfully,

Encl. H-36   Commissioner.
JMH

Cherokee Intermarried White 1906
Volume VII

Cher IW 206

Department of the Interior,
Commission to the Five Civilized Tribes,
Muskogee, I. T. January, 18th 1901.

In the matter of the application of Charles Henry DeLano, for the enrollment of himself and wife as Cherokee citizens. He being sworn before Commissioner Breckinridge testified as follows-

Q What is your name? A. Charles Henry DeLano.
Q How old are you? A. 50.
Q What is your post office? A. Texanna.
Q What district do you live in? A. Canadian.
Q Who is it that you want to have enrolled, yourself and family? A. Yes sir.
Q Have you a wife? A. Yes sir.
Q How many children? A. Haven't any,
Q Are you a Cherokee by blood? A. Yes sir.
Q Full blood? A. Yes sir.
Q Is your wife a Cherokee by blood? A. She is a Cherokee but her blood has never been proven, so she is considered as a white woman.
Q You apply for her then as a white woman? A. Yes sir.
Q Have you lived in the Cherokee Nation all your life? A. Yes sir.
Q Give me the name of your father? A. Youngduck.
Q Is Youngduck dead? A. Yes sir.
Q Give me the name of your mother? A. As well as I remember, her name was Mariah.
Q Dead? A. Yes sir both of them died when I was young.
Q Give me the name of your wife? A. Mary E.
Q How old is your wife? A. Somewhere between 47 and 50 years old.
Q When did you and she marry? A. 1873.
Q Have you lived together ever since your marriage? A. Yes sir.

1880 roll, page 14 No 372, C. H. Delano, Canadian district.
1880   14   373   Mary Delano,   "   "
1896   19   527   Charles H. Delano, "   "
1896   86   68   Mary Delano,   "   "

***The applicant applies for the enrollment of himself and wife; he is identified on he[sic] 1880 and 1896 rolls as a native Cherokee; he has lived in the Cherokee Nation all his life and he will be listed now for enrollment as a Cherokee by blood. He applies for his wife as a white woman, she is identified with him on the 1880 and 1896 rolls as an adopted Cherokee; she has lived with her husband ever since their marriage in 1873; and she will be listed for enrollment as a Cherokee by adoption.

Cherokee Intermarried White 1906
Volume VII

Chas. von Weise, being sworn states that as stenographer to the Commission to the Five Civilized Tribes he reported in full all the proceedings in the above cause and that the foregoing is a full, true and correct transcript of his stenographic notes therein.

Chas von Weise

Subscribed and sworn to before me this the 18th of January, 1901.

TB Needles
Commissioner.

◇◇◇◇◇

Cher # 7091

Department of the Interior,
Commission to the Five Civilized Tribes,
Muskogee, I. T., October 2, 1902.

In the matter of the application of CHARLES DE LANO, for the enrollment of himself as a citizen by blood of the Cherokee Nation, and his wife Mary E. De Lano, as a citizen by intermarriage, of the Cherokee Nation:

MOLLIE DE LANO, called as a witness, being duly sworn and examined by the Commission, testified as follows:

Q What is your name ? A Mollie De Lano.
Q What is your age at this time ? A 48 years old. I don't know how my husband give it in, he made application for me before.
Q If he gave your age as 48 then, he made a mistake ? A Yes sir.
Q What is your post office address Mrs. De Lano ? A Texana[sic], Indian Territory.
Q Are you the same person for whom application was made on January 18, 1900, for enrollment as an intermarried citizen under the name of Mary E. De Lano ? A Yes sir; sometimes they sign it that way.
Q What is your right name ?
A My ma called me Mary, but they all call me Mollie Elizabeth.
Q Do you want to be enrolled as Mollie Elizabeth or as Mary E ?
A I want to be enrolled as Mollie. Nobody called me Mary but my mother.
Q What is your husband's name ? A Charles Henry.
Q Is he a citizen by blood of the Cherokee Nation ? A Yes sir.
Q When were you and he married ? A In 1873, November 30th.
Q Were you married prior to your marriage to him ? A No sir.
Q Was he married prior to his marriage to you ? A No sir.
Q You are his first wife ? A Yes sir.
Q And he is your first husband ? A Yes sir.
Q You have never been separated since your marriage ? A No sir.
Q Living together as husband and wife on September 1, 1902 ? A Yes sir.

Cherokee Intermarried White 1906
Volume VII

Q How long have you lived in the Cherokee Nation ?
A ever since I was about two years old.
Q Have you lived here all the time since 1880 in the Cherokee Nation ? A Yes sir.
Q Has your husband lived here all the time since 1880 in the Cherokee Nation ?
A Yes sir.

E. C. Bagwell, on oath states that, as stenographer to the Commission to the Five Civilized Tribes, he correctly recorded the testimony and proceedings had in the above entitled cause, and that the foregoing is an accurate transcript of his stenographic notes thereof.

E.C.Bagwell

Subscribed and sworn to before me this October 12, 1902.

BC Jones
Notary Public.

◇◇◇◇◇

Cherokee No. 7091.

DEPARTMENT OF THE INTERIOR.

COMMISSIONER TO THE FIVE CIVILIZED TRIBES.

MUSKOGEE, INDIAN TERRITORY, JANUARY 5, 1907.

IN THE MATTER of the application for the enrollment of Mollie E. Delano as a citizen by intermarriage of the Cherokee Nation.

MOLLIE E. DELANO, being first duly sworn by John E. Tidwell,
   testified as follows:

EXAMINATION

ON BEHALF OF THE COMMISSIONER:

Q What is your name?   A Mollie Elizabeth Delano.
Q You want your name to go down as Mollie E. Delano?   A Yes sir.
Q What is your age?   A Fifty-two.
Q What is your postoffice address?   A Texana[sic], Oklahoma, now.
Q Are you an applicant for enrollment as a citizen by intermarriage of the Cherokee Nation?   A Yes sir.

Cherokee Intermarried White 1906
Volume VII

Q   You have no Cherokee blood?   A   No sir; well, I can't say anything about that because we never proved our rights.

Q   Your only claim to the right to enrollment as a citizen of the Cherokee Nation is by virtue of your marriage to a citizen by blood of the Cherokee Nation?   A   Yes sir.

Q   What is the name of the citizen through whom you claim your right to citizenship?

A   C. H. Delano.

Q   Is he living or dead?   A   Yes sir, he is here.

Q   When did you marry him?   A   We married in November 29th, 1873.

Q   Was he a recognized citizen of the Cherokee Nation at the time you married him?

A   Yes sir.

Q   Living in the Cherokee country, was he?   A   Yes sir, he was born and raised in the Cherokee country, and never been outside except to go on little trips.

Q   He is your first husband?   A   Yes sir.

Q   You were his first wife?   A   Yes sir.

Q   Since you were married to Charles H. Delano in 1873 have you and he continuously resided together as husband and wife?   A   Yes sir.

Q   And always lived in the Cherokee Nation?   A   Yes sir, right there in Texana[sic], Indian Territory.

Q   Have you any documentary evidence, showing your marriage to your husband?   A   Well, I know, it is hard for me. We were married by the Cherokee law by a Circuit Judge or District Judge; our marriage was recorded in the clerk's office at Webbers Falls; we haven't but one witness living now and that is my sister. There was a witness, but a man told me awhile ago that he was dead; they are all dead except my sister.

Q   Where is she living?   A   In Texana[sic], Indian Territory, about thirty-five miles from here.

Q   Was she present?   A   Yes sir.

Q   This Judge didn't give you any certificate?   A   No sir.

Q   You think it is a matter of record there?   A   Yes, I know our marriage is recorded.

Q   What District is that in?   A   Canadian District, Cherokee Nation.

ON BEHALF OF THE COMMISSIONER:

    The applicant, Mollie E. Delano, is identified on the authenticated Cherokee tribal roll of 1880, Canadian District, opposite No. 373. The name of her husband Charles H. Delano is enrolled in an approved partial roll of citizens by blood of the Cherokee Nation opposite No. 16909.

(Witness dismissed).

Cherokee Intermarried White 1906
Volume VII

CHARLES H. DELANO, being first duly sworn by John E. Tidwell, Notary Public, testified as follows:

EXAMINATION

ON BEHALF OF THE COMMISSIONER:

Q What is your name? A Charles Henry Delano.
Q What is your name? A I never did know for certain; I have always put it down as so and so.
Q The records of this office show you to be about 56 years old, do you think that is about right? A Some where in the neighborhood.
Q What is your postoffice address? A Texana[sic], Indian Territory.
Q Are you a citizen by blood of the Cherokee Nation? A Yes; I have been taught that all my life.
Q What is your wife's name? A Mollie Elizabeth Delano.
Q When were you married to her? A In 1873.
Q Where were you married? A We was married at Judge Taylor's residence, on what was called Dirty Creek, about seven or eight miles north of Webbers Falls.
Q In Canadian District? A Yes sir.
Q Did the preacher give you a certificate? A No sir, we didn't get any; we was married by a Judge.
Q Since your marriage to your wife, have you and she lived together continuously as husband and wife? A Yes sir.
Q And always lived in the Cherokee Country? A Yes sir; never been out of it.

(Witness dismissed).

I, S. T. Wright, stenographer to the Commissioner to the Five Civilized Tribes, on oath, state that I reported the testimony and proceedings had in the above entitled cause on January 5, 1907, and that the above and foregoing is a true and correct transcript of my stenographic notes thereof taken on said date.

S.T. Wright

Subscribed and sworn to before me this January 5th, 1907.

Edward Merrick
NOTARY PUBLIC.

Cherokee Intermarried White 1906
Volume VII

E.C.M.   Cherokee 7091.

DEPARTMENT OF THE INTERIOR,
COMMISSIONER TO THE FIVE CIVILIZED TRIBES.
Muskogee, Indian Territory, February 6, 1907.

In the matter of the application for the enrollment of Mollie Delano as a citizen by intermarriage of the Cherokee Nation.

Fannie E. McClure being first duly sworn by Mrs. Lyman K. Lane, Notary Public, testified as follows:

Q What is your name?   A Fannie E. McClure.
Q What is your age?   A 55.
Q What is your post office address?   A Texanna.
Q What relation are you to the applicant, Mollie Elizabeth Delano?
A I am her sister.
Q You can here for the purpose of giving testimony in the matter of the application for the enrollment of your sister?
A Yes sir.
Q What is the name of your sister's husband?
A C. E[sic]. Delano.
Q Is he a Cherokee?   A Yes sir.
Q When were they married?   A In 1873.
Q Can you give the date of the month?
A 29th of November, I think.
Q Were you present at the marriage?
A Yes sir.
Q Was her husband a recognized citizen of the Cherokee Nation at the time she married him?
A Yes sir.
Q Living in the Cherokee country?   A Yes sir.
Q Is he her first husband?   A Yes sir.
Q Is she his first wife?   A Yes sir.
Q Since her marriage to Charles E[sic]. Delano, have they continuously resided in the Cherokee Nation as husband and wife?
A Yes sir.
Q They have never been out of the Nation?
A No sir.
Q Were you acquainted with Charles E. Delano before you sister married him?
A Yes sir.
Q How long had you known him prior to his marriage?
A Quite a while; ever since he was a school boy.

Cherokee Intermarried White 1906
Volume VII

Q   Has he always been recognized as a citizen of the Cherokee Nation?
A   Yes sir.
Q   Are you the only witness to the marriage who is now living?
A   The only one that I know of. Mr. Riley and Mr. Jim Alexander are dead; and the Taylor family, I don't know of any of the children who are living.

The undersigned being first duly sworn states that as stenographer to the Commission to the Five Civilized Tribes, she recorded the testimony taken in this case and that the foregoing is a full, true and correct transcript of her stenographic notes thereof.

                                                    Myrtle Hill

Subscribed and sworn to before me this the 12th day of February, 1907.

                                                    Walter W. Chappell

E.C.M.   Cherokee 7091

DEPARTMENT OF THE INTERIOR,

COMMISSIONER TO THE FIVE CIVILIZED TRIBES.

In the matter of the application for the enrollment of Mollie Delano as a citizen by intermarriage of the Cherokee Nation.

D E C I S I O N

THE RECORDS OF THIS OFFICE SHOW: That at Muskogee, Indian Territory, January 18, 1901, application was received by the Commission to the Five Civilized Tribes for the enrollment of Mollie Delano as a citizen by intermarriage of the Cherokee Nation. Further proceedings in the matter of said application were had at Muskogee, Indian Territory, October 2, 1902, and January 5 and February 6, 1907.

THE EVIDENCE IN THIS CASE SHOWS: That the applicant herein, Mollie Delano, a white woman, married in November 1873, one Charles H. Delano, who was, at the time of said marriage, a recognized citizen by blood of the Cherokee Nation, who is identified on the Cherokee authenticated tribal roll of 1880, Canadian District, No. 372 as a native Cherokee, and whose name is included on the approved partial roll of citizens by blood of the Cherokee Nation opposite No. 16909. It is further shown that from the time of said marriage the said Charles H. Delano and Mollie Delano resided together as husband and wife, and continuously lived in the Cherokee Nation up to and including

Cherokee Intermarried White 1906
Volume VII

September 1, 1902. Said applicant is identified on the Cherokee authenticated tribal roll of 1880, and the Cherokee census roll of 1896 as an intermarried citizen of the Cherokee Nation.

IT IS, THEREFORE, ORDERED AND ADJUDGED: That in accordance with the decision of the Supreme Court of the United States, dated November 5, 1906, in the cases of Daniel Red Bird, et al., vs. the United States, Nos. 125, 126, 127, and 128, the said applicant, Mollie Delano, is entitled, under the provisions of Section twenty-one of the Act of Congress approved June 28, 1898 (30 Stats. 495) to enrollment as a citizen by intermarriage of the Cherokee Nation, and her application for enrollment as such is accordingly granted.

Tams Bixby
Commissioner.

Dated at Muskogee, Indian Territory,
this   FEB 19 1907

◇◇◇◇◇

Cherokee 7091

Muskogee, Indian Territory, February 19, 1907.

W. W. Hastings,
    Attorney for the Cherokee Nation,
        Muskogee, Indian Territory.

Dear Sir:

There is enclosed herewith copy of the decision of the Commissioner to the Five Civilized Tribes, dated February 19, 1907, granting the application for the enrollment of Mollie Delano as a citizen by intermarriage of the Cherokee Nation.

Respectfully,

Enc I-106   Commissioner.

RPI

◇◇◇◇◇

Cherokee Intermarried White 1906
Volume VII

Cherokee 7091.

Muskogee, Indian Territory, February 19, 1907.

The Commissioner to the Five Civilized Tribes,
Muskogee, Indian Territory.

Sir:

Receipt is acknowledged of the testimony and of your decision enrolling Mollie Delano as a citizen by intermarriage of the Cherokee Nation. Time for protesting said decision is waived and I consent that said person may be placed upon the schedule immediately.

Respectfully,
W. W. Hastings
Attorney for the Cherokee Nation.

◇◇◇◇◇

Cherokee 7091

Muskogee, Indian Territory, February 19, 1907.

Mollie Delano,
Texanna, Indian Territory.

Dear Madam:

There is enclosed herewith copy of the decision of the Commissioner to the Five Civilized Tribes, dated February 19, 1907, granting the application for your enrollment as a citizen by intermarriage of the Cherokee Nation.

You will be advised when your name has been placed upon a schedule of citizens of the Cherokee Nation and approved by the Secretary of the Interior.

Respectfully,

Commissioner.

Enc I-107

RPI

Cher IW 207

◇◇◇◇◇

Cherokee Intermarried White 1906
Volume VII

F.R.

DEPARTMENT OF THE INTERIOR

COMMISSIONER TO THE FIVE CIVILIZED TRIBES

In the matter of the application for the enrollment of

NANCY J. SANDERS

As a citizen by intermarriage of the Cherokee Nation.

Cherokee 7312

Department of the Interior,
Commission to the Five Civilized Tribes,
Muskogee, I. T. February 18th 1901.

In the matter of the application of Nancy J. Sanders for the enrollment of herself and one child as Cherokee citizens, she being sworn before Commissioner T. B. Needles, testified as follows:

Q What is your name? A. Nancy J. Sanders.
Q What is your age? A. 47.
Q What is your post office address? A. McLain.
Q What district do you reside in? A. Canadian.
Q Are you a recognized citizen of the Cherokee Nation? A. Yes sir.
Q By blood? A. No sir by inter-marriage.
Q Who do you desire to have enrolled? A. Myself and one child
Q What is the child's name? A. Sallie.
Q How old? A. Sixteen.
Q Are you married? A. No sir.
Q What was your husband's name? A. John
Q Is he living? A. No sir.
Q Was he a Cherokee by blood? A. Yes sir.
Q When did you marry him? A. About 30 years ago.
Q When did he die? A. 16 years ago.
Q Have you married since? A. Yes sir.
Q What is your present name? A. Sanders.
Q You and your last husband seperated[sic]? A. Yes sir.
Q Was your last husband a white man? A. No sir.
Q What was your last husbands[sic] name? A. Zeek[sic] Cline.
Q Is he living? A. Yes sir

Cherokee Intermarried White 1906
Volume VII

Q Did you live with John Sanders from the time you married him until his death?
A. Yes sir.
Q And afterwards married Cline? A. Yes sir.
Q Were you divorced from him? A. Yes sir.

> Upon an examination of the 1880 authenticated roll of the Cherokee Nation, there is found on page 49, #1356, the name of N. J. Sanders in Canadian district.

> Upon an examination of the 1896 census roll of the Cherokee Nation, page 93, #271 there appears the name of Nannie J. Sanders in Canadian district. Page 69, #1893 thereof appears the name of Sallie Sanders in Canadian district.

Q Did you sue Cline for divorce or did he sue you? A. I sued him; he tried to sue me first and failed to get it and afterwards I applied for a divorce from him and got it.
Q Do you claim citizenship by virtue of your marriage with Sanders or Cline? A. I go by the name of Sanders.
Q You stated that you lived with Mr. Sanders from the time of your marriage until his death? A. Yes sir.
Q And this child Sallie is a child by Sanders? A. Yes sir.
Q Is this child alive now? A. Yes sir.
Q How long have you lived in the Cherokee Nation? A. Ever since I was eight or ten years old.
Q Live here now? A. Yes sir.
Q Before what Court did Mr. Cline apply for a divorce? A. Cherokee Court at the Falls.
Q And then you sued? A. Yes sir.
Q On what grounds? A. I dont[sic] recollect now.
Q Had he left you? A. Yes sir.

Com'r Needeles[sic],-
    The name of Nancy J. Sanders if found on the authenticated 1880 roll as N. J. Sanders an intermarried white and on the census roll of 1896 as Nannie J. Sanders. The name of the child, Sallie, by her first husband John Sanders, a Cherokee citizen by blood, is found on the roll of 1896. The testimony shows that the applicant was married to one John Sanders, a Cherokee citizen, with whom she lived until his death. She afterwards married one Zeek Cline a Cherokee citizens[sic], from whom she was divorced on her own application. Consequently she and the child Sallie will be duly listed for enrollment, she as a Cherokee citizen by intermarriage and her child Sallie as a Cherokee citizen by blood.

==============================

Chas. von Weise, being sworn states that as stenographer to the Commission to the Five Civilized Tribes he reported in full all the proceedings in the above cause and that the foregoing is a full, true and correct transcript of his stenographic notes therein.

Cherokee Intermarried White 1906
Volume VII

Chas von Weise

Subscribed and sworn to before me this the 21st of February, 1901.

T B Needles
Commissioner.

◇◇◇◇◇

Cher
Supp'l to # 7312

Department of the Interior,
Commission to the Five Civilized Tribes,
Muskogee, I. T., October 15, 1902.

In the matter of the application of NANCY J. SANDERS, for the enrollment of herself as a citizen by intermarriage, and her daughter, SALLIE SANDERS, as a citizen by blood, of the Cherokee Nation.

NANCY J. SANDERS, being duly sworn and examined by the Commission, testified as follows:

Q What is your name ? A Nancy J. Sanders.
Q What is your age at this time, Mrs. Sanders ?
A I am going on forty nine,
Q What is your post office address ? A McLain.
Q Are you the same Nancy J. Sanders that applied to the Commission for enrollment as an intermarried citizen of the Cherokee Nation, in February, 1901 ?
A Yes sir.
Q What was your husband's name ? A John Sanders.
Q Is he living or dead ? A He is dead.
Q How long since he died ? A It will be seventeen years this next December.
Q When were you married to John Sanders ?
A I don't recollect.
Q Was it before 1880 ? A Yes sir.
Q Was he your first husband ? A Yes sir.
Q Were you his first wife ? A Yes sir.
Q Now, did you live with your husband John Sanders from the time of your marriage up till his death ? A Yes sir.
Q You never separated ? A No sir.
Q He died about seventeen years ago ? A Yes sir.
Q Have you ever married since his death ? A Yes sir.
Q What is your present husband's name ? A We have separated. He was divorced. His name was Zeke Cline.
Q When were you married to Mr. Cline ? A Six years last February.
Q Was he a citizen or a white man ? A He was a citizen.

155

Cherokee Intermarried White 1906
Volume VII

Q   Of the Cherokee Nation, and by Cherokee blood ?   A   Yes sir.
Q   Is he living at this time ?   A   Yes sir.
Q   How long did you and he live together ?   A   We were married in February, and parted in May.
Q   In May of the same year ?   A   Yes sir.
Q   You didn't live together very long ?   A   No sir.
Q   Since you separated, you have never lived together since May six years ago ?   A   No sir.
Q   Have you been divorced ?   A   Yes sir.
Q   Have you married since you and Mr. Cline were divorced ?   A   No sir.
Q   You were still a widow and a single woman on the first day of September, 1902 ?   A   Yes sir.
Q   Have you lived in the Cherokee Nation all the time since 1880 up to the present time?   A   Yes sir.

E. C. Bagwell, on oath states that, as stenographer to the Commission to the Five Civilized Tribes, he correctly recorded the testimony and proceedings had in the above entitled cause, and that the foregoing is an accurate transcript of his stenographic notes thereof.   E.C. Bagwell

Subscribed and sworn to before me this November 18, 1902.

                                                    BC Jones
                                                    Notary Public.

◇◇◇◇◇

                                                    Cherokee 7312

DEPARTMENT OF THE INTERIOR,
COMMISSION TO THE FIVE CIVILIZED TRIBES,
MUSKOGEE, IND. TER., OCT. 16, 1901.

In the matter of the application for the enrollment of Nancy J. Sanders et al. as citizens of the Cherokee Nation:

SUPPLEMENTAL STATEMENT.

An examination of the 1880 authenticated tribal roll of the Cherokee Nation shows that Ezekiel Clyne[sic] is identified on that roll at page 10, #259, Canadian District, as a native Cherokee.

It is ordered that copies of this statement be filed with and made a part of the record in this case.

                                                    TB Needles
                                                    Commissioner.

Cherokee Intermarried White 1906
Volume VII

◇◇◇◇◇

C. F. B.   Cherokee 7312.

DEPARTMENT OF THE INTERIOR,
COMMISSIONER TO THE FIVE CIVILIZED TRIBES.
Muskogee, Indian Territory, February 7, 1907.

In the matter of the application for the enrollment of Nancy J. Sanders as a citizen by intermarriage of the Cherokee Nation.

APPEARANCES:
        Applicant appears in person.

        Cherokee Nation represented by H. M. Vance in behalf of W. W. Hastings, Attorney.

Nancy J. Sanders being first duly sworn by Chas. E. Webster, Notary Public, testified as follows:

ON BEHALF OF COMMISSIONER.

Q What is your name?   A Nancy J. Sanders.
Q What is your age?   A 52.
Q What is your post office address?   A Wimer.
Q You are an applicant for enrollment as a citizen by intermarriage of the Cherokee Nation?   A Yes sir.
Q You have no Cherokee blood?   A No sir.
Q Your only claim to the right to enrollment as a citizen of the Cherokee Nation is by virtue of your marriage to a citizen by blood?   A Yes sir.
Q What is the name of the citizen through whom you claim the right to enrollment?
A John Sanders.
Q Is he living?   A No sir.
Q When did you marry him?
A It has been 38 years ago. I was married in Sequoyah District at Judge Faulkner's.
Q Was he a recognized citizen by blood of the Cherokee Nation at the time you married him?
A Yes sir.
Q Residing in the Cherokee country?
A Yes sir.
Q Was he your first husband?
A Yes sir.
Q Were you his first wife?
A Yes sir.
Q By whom were you married?
A Judge Frank Faulkner.

Cherokee Intermarried White 1906
Volume VII

Q Have you any evidence of a documentary character showing your marriage to your husband, John Sanders?
A No sir; you know they didn't get license then like they do now; we just went to the Judge.
Q Did this man Faulkner who married you, give you a certificate at that time?
A No sir.
Q When did you husband die?
A He died 20 years ago, the 10th of last December.
Q From the time of your marriage to him did you and he reside together continuously as husband and wife until the time of his death?
A Yes sir.
Q Since his death, have you married? A Yes sir.
Q What is the name of your second husband? A Klein.
Q When did you marry Mr. Klein?
[sic] About 7 years ago I reckon; married about 15 miles from here.
Q What was the full name of your second husband?
A Zeke Klein.
Q Was he a citizen by blood of the Cherokee Nation?
A Yes sir.
Q He was a Cherokee by blood? A Yes sir.
Q He was not a Shawnee or Delaware?
A No sir; he was a Cherokee by blood.
Q Are you living with him at the present time?
A No sir; we just lived together about 3 months.
Q He is living is he? A Yes sir.
Q And you and he lived together for a period of about three months?
A Yes sir.
Q And then you separated? A Yes sir; got a divorce.
Q Since that time you and he have lived separate and apart?
A Yes sir.
Q Did he leave you or did you leave him?
A He left me.
Q What was the cause of his leaving you, do you know?
A He wanted to sell my property, what my children had, and I wouldn't agree to it.
Q You owned the property, did you? A Yes sir.
Q Did you own the house in which you were living at the time he left you?
A No sir, it belonged to him; I had moved to one of his places.
Q At the time of your separation from him, did you continue to live in that house he owned?
A No sir; no longer than the renters got out of my place.
Q You left his house and went to your own place?
A Yes sir.
Q You say you secured a divorce from him? A Yes sir.
Q Have a copy of the decree of divorce? A No sir.
Q Where was it granted? A Webber's Falls.

Cherokee Intermarried White 1906
Volume VII

Q Did he appear against you at the time you sued him?
A He first sued me for a divorce and he had no graounds[sic] to get one on; then they all got at me to sue him for a divorce and they got up some papers for me to sign and I signed them; I didn't know what they was for; I can't read nor write myself. I got the divorce.
Q The divorce was granted you?   A Yes sir.
Q Was he present at the time you secured the divorce?
A Yes sir; he was there at the Falls. I think the papers they got up was a kind of a compromise some way.
Q There was a contract drawn up, was there, dividing your property, and mutually agreeing to separate?
A No sir; some of my friends got me to sue him for a divorce and for him to support me as long as I lived. I went to the Falls two or three times and they got up some king of papers, telling me what he would give me, and sent them out to me to sign, and after I signed it, that set him free and he never gave me nothing.
Q Has he contributed anything to your support since that divorce?
A No sir.
Q Has your residence been continuously in the Cherokee Nation since your marriage to your first husband?
A Yes sir; never lived no where else.

The applicant, Nancy J. Sanders, is identified on the Cherokee authenticated tribal roll of 1880, Canadian District, No. 1356, and on the Cherokee census roll of 1896, page 93, No. 271, as an intermarried citizen of the Cherokee Nation.

To the applicant: It will be necessary for you to introduce the testimony of some witness who was present at the time of your marriage to John Sanders, or who has actual personal knowledge that you were living together as husband and wife shortly after the time that you state you married John Sanders.

Q What is the name of your oldest child?
A Cherokee; she died when she was three months old.
Q What was the name of the oldest one living in 1880?
A Walter Cornelius.
Q What was the name of the next one?   A Dora Sanders.
Q Was your oldest child living in 1880 ever known as E. C. Sanders?
A Not that I know of.
Q What is the name of your next child after Dora?   A Lillie.
Q Is your child, Cherokee Sanders living at this time?
A She was just three weeks old when she died. That was my oldest child.
Q What was the name of the next one?
A Cornelius, -- Walter Cornelius.
Q Is Cornelius living at this time?   A Yes sir.
Q Is your son, Cornelius, married?   A Yes sir.
Q What is his wife's name?   A Maud.
Q Has he any children?   A Yes sir.

Cherokee Intermarried White 1906
Volume VII

Q Give their names please.
A Clyde, Corinne, Nannie, Edward and Jessie.

Immediately following the name of the applicant herein, Nancy J. Sanders, who is identified on the Cherokee authenticated tribal roll of 1880 as above mentioned, appears the name of E. C. Sanders, whose age is given at that time as 7 years. The said E. C. Sanders is listed for enrollment on Cherokee card 4383, under the name of Corinne Sanders, and his name is included in the approved partial roll of citizens by blood of the Cherokee Nation, opposite No. 10475. The name of the husband of the applicant, John Sanders, by virtue of her marriage to whom Nancy J. Sanders claims the right to enrollment as a citizen by intermarriage of the Cherokee Nation, is identified on said roll at No. 1355, Canadian District, marked "dead".

The undersigned being first duly sworn states that as stenographer to the Commissioner to the Five Civilized Tribes, she recorded the testimony taken in this case and that the foregoing is a true and correct transcript of her stenographic notes thereof.

Myrtle Hill

Subscribed and sworn to before me this the 7th day of February, 1907.

John E. Tidwell
Notary Public.

◇◇◇◇◇

E.C.M. Cherokee 7312.

DEPARTMENT OF THE INTERIOR,
COMMISSIONER TO THE FIVE CIVILIZED TRIBES.
Muskogee, Indian Territory, February 7, 1907.

In the matter of the application for the enrollment of NANCY J. SANDERS as a citizen bu[sic] intermarriage of the Cherokee Nation.

Supplemental testimony.

W. W. BREEDLOVE, being first duly sworn by Walter Chappell testifies as follows:

Q What is your name.[sic] A Walter W. Breedlove, is the way it is on the roll I guess.
Q What is your age? A I am 46.
Q What is your post office address? A I would say Fairland.
Q You come here for the purpose of giving testimony in the case of Nancy J. Sanders in the application before the Commissioner for her enrollment as an intermarried citizen of the Cherokee Nation? A Yes sir.

Cherokee Intermarried White 1906
Volume VII

Q You are acquainted with the applicant Nancy J. Sanders?
A Yes sir.
Q How long have you know[sic] her? A I have known her since '67 I believe or '68.
Q '67 or '68? A Yes sir.
Q Were you acquainted with her first husband, John Sanders?
A Her first husband, yes sir.
Q Do you know about what time they were married?
A Well I think I do.
Q What was the date of the marriage? A Well it must have been in '68 or 9.
Q Were you present at the marriage? A No I was not present at the marriage.
Q You lived in the community? A Yes sir, I did but I was not at the marriage.
Q Can you testify positively that Nancy J. Sanders was married to her husband, John Sanders in '68 or '69? A I know that they were married in '68 or '69.
Q What reason have you for fixing this marriage in '68 or '69?
A Well I had a cousin that married a sister of this woman about two years after.
Q Is John Sanders living? A No he has been dead a good while.
Q Did John Sanders and Nancy J. Sanders reside together as husband and wife and live continuously in the Cherokee Nation from the time of their marriage until the death of John Sanders?
A Yes sir.
Q Has she remarried since the death of John Sanders?
A I do not think she has.
Q If she has you do not know anything about it.[sic] A No sir.
Q Are you sure that Nancy J. Sanders and John Sanders resided together as husband and wife until his death?
A No I am not sure about his death, but I know both of them before they were married and while they lived in Sequoyah District they lived as man and wife. They moved up into Canadian District and I have never known the family since then.

BY THE ATTORNEY FOR THE CHEROKEE NATION:

Q How old are you? A I was born in '61, on the 12th day of January.
Q Were you present at the marriage of John Sanders to his wife Nancy J. Sanders.
A No sir.
Q Do you know whether or not Nancy J. Sanders had been married prior to her marriage to John Sanders? A I don't understand, what is the question.
Q Do you know whether or not Nancy J. Sanders was married prior to her marriage to John Sanders? A Yes sir, I do.
Q Had she been married? A No sir.
Q Do you know whether John Sanders had been married prior to his marriage to Nancy J. Sanders? A No, he had never been married.
Q How long had you been acquainted with them before they were married? A Well I had known John Sanders pretty near all my life, and I had known this girl from the time they came here from Arkansas.

Cherokee Intermarried White 1906
Volume VII

Q How many years prior to their marriage did you know them?
A I had known John Sanders I should think about--I had known him eight or ten years, ever since we came back from the South.
Q Well you think you had known them for as long as ten years before they were married? A No sir I can not say that.
Q How long did you know them? A I had known them from 4 to 5 years, just right after the War when they came back.
Q Then you were mistaken when you said you had known them for ten years before they were married? A I do not think I made that statement. Did I? I was mistaken if I made that statement, for we came back in '65, I knew them from then on. I had known John Sanders.
Q Have you been acquainted with Nancy J. Sanders ever since she was married to John Sanders in '68 ot[sic] '69? A I never saw her after she moved away. I never saw her any more until I met her here two years ago.
Q You do not know then whether she is remarried? A No sir I do not.
Q You are mot[sic] prepared to say whether she is remarried? A No sir, I am not.
Q When were you married? A I was married in '87.
Q When was your cousin married to a sister of Nancy J. Sanders?
A When was my cousin married?
A Yes I believe you said your cousin married a sister of the woman. A Yes, Jack Webb.
Q When was Jack Webb married to a sister of Nancy J. Sanders.[sic]
A In '68 or '67 I am not sure about that.
Q Can you state positively that Jack Webb and a sister of Nancy J. Sanders were married before the marriage of John Sanders and Nancy J. Sanders.[sic] A About the same time, I believe John married first.
Q Can you state which couple was married first?
A No I cannot, I was only ten years old then.
Q You are not positive about these dates at all are you?
A Yes sir, I am positive about the date, but I do not know which were married first.
Q You not related in any way to John or Nancy J. Sanders?
A No sir.
Q You are a cousin of Jack Webb? A Yes sir.
Q Do you know whether Nancy J. Sanders had any children by John Sanders?
A Yes sir.
Q What is the first child's name? A I believe he is a boy, I believe his name is Nelius[sic] Sanders.
Q You are not able to state when he was born? A No sir.

BY COMMISSIONER:

Q How long after they were married did they move away?
A I do not think it was more than two or three years.
Q Then this child was born after they had moved away?
A No sir, that child was born in Sequoyah District.
Q Can you tell if it is living now? A I do not know.

Cherokee Intermarried White 1906
Volume VII

BY ATTORNEY FOR CHEROKEE NATION:

Q How did you fix the date of the marriage of John Sanders and Nancy J. Sanders?
A I fixed it from a circumstance like this: I went with my father to Louisiana when I was six years old and just when we came back these people were in the Cherokee Nation, at Wilson's Rock, Wilson's Ferry some call it, it was in '68, the winter of '68 or '69.
Q How long were you gone to Louisiana? A I was gone just one winter.
Q You were there one winter? A I went down in December and came back in April, yes sir.
Q When you got back you learned that they were married?
A No sir they were not married.
Q You say they were not married when you got back?
A No they were not married when I came back. I came back in '68 I reckon. I was eight years old when I came back and they were married after that.
Q How long after that? A Only a short time one and a half or two years.
Q Was it as much as two years? A No I do not think it was two years.
Q Then they were married when you were about 10 or 11 years old? A Yes sir, they were married when I was nine or ten years old.
Q That makes them married in 1870 or 1871? A No sir they were married before '71 for I went away from there before '71. They must have been married in '68 or '69, that is just to the best of my belief.

The undersigned, being first duly sworn states that as stenographer to the Commission to the Five Civilized Tribes he reported the proceedings had in the above entitled cause and that the same is a full true and correct transcript of his stenographic notes thereof.

Homer J Councilor

Subscribed and sworn to before me this February 8, 1907.

Walter W. Chappell
Notary Public.

◇◇◇◇◇

Cherokee Intermarried White 1906
Volume VII

E.C.M.   Cherokee 7312.

DEPARTMENT OF THE INTERIOR,
COMMISSIONER TO THE FIVE CIVILIZED TRIBES.
Muskogee, Indian Territory, February 8, 1907.

In the matter of the application for the enrollment of Nancy J. Sanders as a citizen by intermarriage of the Cherokee Nation.

SUPPLEMENTAL TESTIMONY.

WILLIAM McLAIN being first duly sworn by Walter E[sic]. Chappell testified as follows:

BY THE COMMISSIONER:

Q What is your name?   A William McLain.
Q What is your age?   A 57.
Q What is your post-office?   A Muskogee.
Q You come here for the purpose of giving testimony in the matter of the application of Nancy J. Sanders for enrollment as a citizen by intermarriage of the Cherokee Nation?
A That is what I understand.
Q How long have you known Nancy J. Sanders?   A I have known her ever since about the year 1888 or 9.
Q Was she married at the time you knew her?   A Yes sir.
Q What was the name of her husband?   A John Sanders.
Q Is John Sanders living now?   A No sir.
Q When did he die?   A It must have been along in 1880.
Q Were they residing together as husband and wife at the time of his death?
A Yes sir.
Q Was she remarried after the death of John Sanders?
A I was told she was I was not at the marriage ceremony. I was not at the marriage ceremony but they lived together as man and woman.
Q Have you ever held an official position in the Cherokee Nation[sic]
A Yes sir, I have. I have had several but at this time I was Circuit judge of the Southern Judicial District.
Q What was the name of Nancy J. Sanders' second husband?
A Cline, Ezekiel Cline.
Q While you were acting as Circuit judge of the Southern Judicial District were any divorce proceedings instituted for divorce by the applicant Nancy J. Sanders, to get a divorce from her husband Ezekiel Cline.[sic]   A Yes sir.
Q The proceedings were instituted by the Nancy J. Sanders?
A Yes sir.
Q Did she secure the divorce?   A Yes sir, I granted the divorce.

Cherokee Intermarried White 1906
Volume VII

Q Do you remember what the grounds of the divorce were?
A The case did not come to trial. The parties got together and came to terms. She sued for divorce and alimony. I--I do not remember the exact contention but he admitted certain allegations of willful desertion and failure to support.
Q These were the grounds on which you granted the divorce of Nancy J. Sanders?
A Yes sir.
Q Since securing the divorce from Ezekiel Cline has Nancy J. Sanders remarried?
A Not that I know of, she moved to Canadian District, I don't known what has become of her since then.
Q I will ask if you know whether or not John Sanders was a recognized citizen by blood of the Cherokee Nation? A Yes sir.
Q Was he born and raised in the Cherokee Nation?   A Yes sir.
Q Never lived out of the Cherokee Nation. A Not that I know of, he moved from Sequoyah to Canadian District, that is all.
Q Was Ezekiel Cline a white man or an Indian?   A He was an Indian.
Q Cherokee?
A Yes sir, Like I am, he did not show his Indian blood much but he was Indian.
Q He was regarded as an Indian?   A Yes sir his rights were never disputed.

Homer J. Councilor being first duly sworn states that as stenographer to the Commission to the Five Civilized Tribes he reported the testimony in the above entitled cause and the above and foregoing are a full, true and correct transcript of his stenographic notes thereof.

Homer J Councilor

Subscribed and sworn to before me this February 9, 1907.

Walter W. Chappell
Notary Public.

Cherokee Intermarried White 1906
Volume VII

E. C. M.   Cherokee 7312.

DEPARTMENT OF THE INTERIOR,
COMMISSIONER TO THE FIVE CIVILIZED TRIBES.
Muskogee, Indian Territory, February 9, 1907.

In the matter of the application for the enrollment of Nancy J. Sanders as a citizen by intermarriage of the Cherokee Nation.

SUPPLEMENTAL.

Moses L. Morris being first duly sworn by Walter W. Chappell, Notary Public, testified as follows:

Q What is your name?   A Moses L. Morris.
Q What is your age?   A 51 years.
Q What is your post office address?   A   Muskogee.
Q Mr. Morris, I will ask you if you are acquainted with the applicant, Nancy J. Sanders?
A Yes sir.
Q How long have you known her?
A I first met her the 25th day of December, '73; this man was a small boy.
Q Where did you meet her?
A In Sequoyah District about 10 miles west of Fort Smith.
Q Was she married at that time?
A She was married to this young man's father.
Q What was the name of her husband at that time?
A John Sanders.
Q Was John Sanders her first husband?
A First I ever knew anything about.
Q John Sanders is dead now, is he not?   A   Yes sir.
Q Did Nancy and John Sanders reside together as husband and wife until his death?
A Yes sir.
Q And lived in the Cherokee Nation all that time?
A Yes sir.
Q John Sanders was recognized as a citizen of the Cherokee Nation?
A Yes sir.
Q Now, Mr. Morris, after the death of John Sanders, can you tell me whether or not Nancy Sanders re-married?
A Yes, she married the second time.
Q Who was she married to?   A Zeke Klein.
Q Was Zeke Klein a Cherokee Indian?   A   Yes sir.
Q Since that time, has she been residing with Zeke Clein?
A No sir; I disremember about how long they lived together; each of them had some grown children.
Q Were they divorced?   A Yes sir.

Cherokee Intermarried White 1906
Volume VII

Q   Which one secured the divorce?
A   I can't say; I am not sure.
Q   Did she leave Klein or did Klein leave her or was it just a mutual agreement?
A   I can't tell you that, my friend.
Q   She has never been married to any other man, has she?
A   Not to my knowledge; no sir.

The undersigned being first duly sworn states that as stenographer to the Commission to the Five Civilized Tribes, she recorded the testimony taken in this case and that the foregoing is a true and correct transcript of her stenographic notes thereof.

Myrtle Hill

Subscribed and sworn to before me this the 13th day of February, 1907.

Walter W. Chappell
Notary Public.

F. R.   Cherokee 7312.

DEPARTMENT OF THE INTERIOR,

COMMISSIONER TO THE FIVE CIVILIZED TRIBES.

In the matter of the application for the enrollment of Nancy J. Sanders as a citizen by intermarriage of the Cherokee Nation.

D E C I S I O N

THE RECORDS OF THIS OFFICE SHOW: That at Muskogee, Indian Territory, February 18, 1901, application was received by the Commission to the Five Civilized Tribes for the enrollment of Nancy J. Sanders as a citizen by intermarriage of the Cherokee Nation. Further proceedings in the matter of said application were had at Muskogee, Indian Territory, October 15, 1902, February 1, 1907, February 7, 1907, February 8, 1907, and February 9, 1907.

THE EVIDENCE IN THIS CASE SHOWS: That the applicant herein, Nancy J. Sanders, a white woman, was lawfully married in 1869 to one John Sanders, who was at the time of said marriage a recognized citizen, by blood of the Cherokee Nation, and who

Cherokee Intermarried White 1906
Volume VII

is identified upon the Cherokee authenticated tribal roll of 1880, Canadian District, Page 49, No. 1355, as a native Cherokee; that from the time of said marriage, the said John Sanders and Nancy J. Sanders resided together as husband and wife until the death of the said John Sanders on December 10, 1886.

It is further shown that in February, 1895, the said applicant was married to one Ezekiel Cline, who was at the time of said marriage a recognized citizen by blood of the Cherokee Nation, and who is identified on the Cherokee authenticated tribal roll of 1880, Canadian District, Page 10, No. 259, as a native Cherokee, and whose name is included on the approved partial roll of citizens by blood of the Cherokee Nation opposite No. 17437; that the said Ezekiel Cline and the applicant herein resided together as husband and wife until May, 1895; that they then separated and thereafter, the said Nancy J. Sanders obtained a divorce from the said Ezekiel Cline. The decree of divorce in this case appears to have been rendered in accordance with an agreement entered into between the applicant and the said Ezekiel Cline. It also appears that since the said applicant was divorced from the said Ezekiel Cline, she has not remarried.

Since the applicant's marriage to her husband, John Sanders, in the year 1869, she has continuously lived in the Cherokee Nation up to and including September 1, 1902. Said Nancy J. Sanders is identified upon the Cherokee authenticated tribal roll of 1880 and the Cherokee census roll of 1896, as an intermarried citizen of the Cherokee Nation.

IT IS, THEREFORE, ORDERED AND ADJUDGED: That in accordance with the decision of the Supreme Court of the United States, dated November 5, 1906, in the cases of Daniel Red Bird, et al., vs. the United States, Nos. 125, 126, 127, and 128, the said applicant, Nancy J. Sanders, is entitled under the provisions of Section 21 of the Act of Congress approved June 28, 1898 (30 Stats. 495), to enrollment as a citizen by intermarriage of the Cherokee Nation, and her application for enrollment as such is accordingly granted.

                Tams Bixby
                  Commissioner.

Dated at Muskogee, Indian Territory,
this   FEB 20 1907

Cherokee Intermarried White 1906
Volume VII

Cherokee 7312

Muskogee, Indian Territory, February 20, 1907.

W. W. Hastings,
    Attorney for the Cherokee Nation,
        Muskogee, Indian Territory.

Dear Sir:

    There is enclosed herewith a copy of the decision of the Commissioner to the Five Civilized Tribes, dated February 20, 1907, granting the application for the enrollment of Nancy J. Sanders as a citizen by intermarriage of the Cherokee Nation.

        Respectfully,

Enc I-225   Commissioner.

RPI

◇◇◇◇◇

Cherokee 7312

Muskogee, Indian Territory, February 20, 1907.

The Commissioner to the Five Civilized Tribes,
    Muskogee, Indian Territory.

Sir:

    Receipt is acknowledged of the testimony and of your decision enrolling Nancy J. Sanders as a citizen by intermarriage of the Cherokee Nation. Time for protesting said decision is waived and I consent that said person may be placed upon the schedule immediately.

        Respectfully,
        W. W. Hastings
        Attorney for the Cherokee Nation.

◇◇◇◇◇

Cherokee Intermarried White 1906
Volume VII

Cherokee 7312

Muskogee, Indian Territory, February 20, 1907.

Nancy J. Sanders,
    Wimer, Indian Territory.

Dear Madam:

    There is enclosed herewith a copy of the decision of the Commissioner to the Five Civilized Tribes, dated February 20, 1907, granting the application for your enrollment as a citizen by intermarriage of the Cherokee Nation.

    You will be advised when your name has been placed upon a schedule of citizens of the Cherokee Nation and approved by the Secretary of the Interior.

                  Respectfully,

Enc I-226   Commissioner.

RPI

Cher IW 208

◇◇◇◇◇

F.R.   Cherokee 8358.

DEPARTMENT OF THE INTERIOR,
COMMISSIONER TO THE FIVE CIVILIZED TRIBES.
Muskogee, I. T., February 2, 1907.

    In the matter of the application for the enrollment of George W. Currey as a citizen by intermarriage of the Cherokee Nation.
Cherokee Nation represented by H. M. Vance.

    George W. Currey being first duly sworn by Frances R. Lane, a Notary Public for the Western District of Indian Territory, testified as follows:

By the Commissioner:
Q What is your name.[sic] A George W. Currey.
Q Your age?   A I was born in 1842.
Q And your postoffice address?   A Southwest City, Missouri.
Q You are a white man, are you?   A Yes sir.

Cherokee Intermarried White 1906
Volume VII

Q You claim the right to enrollment as a citizen by intermarriage of the Cherokee Nation?   A Yes sir.
Q Your claim to such right is solely by virtue of your marriage to a citizen of that nation?   A Yes sir.
Q What is the name of the citizen through whom your[sic] claim?
A Frances S. Prock. Her maiden name was McGhee.
Q When were you married to Frances S. Prock?   A 2nd day of January, 1874.
Q Where were you married to her?   A In Delaware District.
Q Was the marriage under license of the Cherokee Nation?
A Yes sir.
Q Have you any documentary evidence showing that marriage?
A I have a license, yes.

> Applicant presents certificate signed by S. N. Melton, clerk of the District Court of Delaware District, Cheroke[sic] nation[sic], showing that a marriage license was issued to G. W. Currey and Alsy Prock on January 1, 1874, and that said marriage license was returned executed January 2, 1874.
> The certificate of said S. N Melton bears date January 9, 1874, and does not bear the seal of the nation.
> Applicant also presents a certificate of T. J McGhee, Clerk of Delaware District, dated April 7, 1870, showing that Andrew Prock and Francis McGhee were married on said date.

Q Had you been married before you married Frances S. Prock?
A No sir.
Q Had she been married before she married you?   A Yes sir.
Q How many times?   A Once.
Q What was the name of her first husband?   A Andrew Prock.
Q Was Andrew Prock ~~married~~ living at the time she married you?
A No sir.
Q At the time you married Frances S. Prock was she a citizen by blood of the Cherokee Nation?   A Yes sir.
Q Is she living at this time?   A Yes sir.
Q Have you and Frances Prock resided together as husband and wife and lived continuously in the Cherokee nation from 1874 until the present time?   Yes, I have never been away from the nation at any time.
Q You gave your postoffice address as Southwest City, Missouri; do you live in the Cherokee nation: A Yes sir, four miles and a half west of the town of Southwest city[sic].
Q And in the Cherokee Nation   A Yes two miles west of the line.
Q Have you been out of the nation on any trips?   A Nothing only on business. I went out once and was gone about four weeks with some cattle.
Q But your home has ben[sic] in the Cherokee nation all the time?
A Yes sir.
Q You have never been separated from Frances S. Currey?
A No, we have lived together all the time; she is there yet.

Cherokee Intermarried White 1906
Volume VII

Witness excused/[sic]

Thomas J. McGhee, being first duly sworn by Frances R. Lane, testified as follows:
By the Commissioner.
Q What is your name?   A Thomas J. McGhee.
Q What is your postoffice address?   A Afton, I. T.
Q And your age?   A Sixty-two.
Q Did you ever know Frances S. Prock?   A Yes sir.
Q Are you related to her?   A She is my sister.
Q When was she married to Mr. Prock?
A About 1870.
Q When did Mr. Prock die?   A He died in 1872 as I remember.
Q And then your sister was married to George W. Currey?
A Yes, later on, in 1874.
Q And they have resided together as husband and wife and lived continuously in the Cherokee nation from the time of their marriage up to the present time?   A Yes, been together from that date up to the present time.

The applicant, George W. Currey, is identified on the Cherokee authenticated tribal roll of 1880, Delaware district, No. 532, as G. W. Currie[sic], and on the Cherokee census roll of 1896, page 567, No. 73, as George W. Curry[sic].
The applicant's wife, Frances S. Currie, is identified on the 1880 roll, Delaware District, No. 533 as F. S. Currie, and on the 1896 census roll of 1896, page 450, opposite No. 595, as Francis S. Currey.
Q Mr. McGhee, what is Mrs. Currey's full name?   A Frances Saphronia McGhee, and her present name is Frances S. Currey.
Q Mr. Currey presents a marriage license here showing that he was licensed to marry Alsy Prock?   A Alsy is her Cherokee name.
Q Then Alsy Prock and Frances S. Prock are one and the same person?
A Yes, the same person; that is her Cherokee name, Alsy.
Q Do you know who performed the marriage ceremony of Frances S. Prock and George W. Currey?   A On New Years[sic] Day her sister told me she was going to get married--that she had gone to Robertsons[sic] now to get married. I have no reason to think that they were not married.
Q You were not present at that marriage, however?   A No sir.

Statement by Mr. McGhee: The Clerks were not commissioned by the Cherokee Nation. The law authorized the judges to appoint their own clerks and Melton was appointed by me. And I further state that that writing in this certificate is his. I am familiar with his writing.

In Book S., Marriage Record Delaware District now in the possession of this office, there appears record showing that license was issued to G. W. Currie, a citizen of the United States to marry Alsy Prock, a citizen of the Cherokee Nation,

Cherokee Intermarried White 1906
Volume VII

on January 1, 1874; that the license was returned executed on January 2, 1874, and properly recorded.

Frances R., Lane, upon oath, states that as stenographer to the Commission to the Five Civilized Tribes she reported the testimony in the above entitled cause and that the foregoing is an accurate transcript of her stenographic notes thereof.

Francis R. Lane

Subscribed and sworn to before me this February 4, 1907.

Walter W. Chappell
Notary Public.

◇◇◇◇◇◇

(The below typed as given.)

CERTIFIED COPY.

Cherokee Nation, Del. Dc.

This is to certify that G.W. Curry a citizen of the United States was licnd to marry Alcy Prock a female Cherokee of Del. Dc Cn Licens issued Jan 1st 1874 and returned Jan 2nd 1874, Executd as the laws directs Bein in accordance with an Act passed By the National Council Bearin date of Oct 15" 1855. in Regard to White Men "Intermarriage in the Cherokee Nation this Jan 9th 1874.

(Signed) S.N. Melton,

Clerk of Dic
Court in Del Dc Cn.

I, Harriett E. Arbuckle on oath state that the above and foregoing is a true and correct copy of the original instrument now on file with the records of this office.

Harriett E Arbuckle

Subscribed and sworn to before me this 8 day of February, 1907.

Frances R Lane
Notary Public.

◇◇◇◇◇◇

Cherokee Intermarried White 1906
Volume VII

E C M Cherokee 8358.

DEPARTMENT OF THE INTERIOR,

COMMISSIONER TO THE FIVE CIVILIZED TRIBES.

In the matter of the application for the enrollment of GEORGE W. CURREY as a citizen by intermarriage of the Cherokee Nation.

D E C I S I O N

THE RECORDS OF THIS OFFICE SHOW: That at Zena, Indian Territory May 14, 1902 application was received by the Commission to the Five Civilized Tribes for the enrollment of George W. Currey as a citizen by intermarriage of the Cherokee Nation. Further proceedings in the matter of said application were had at Tahlequah, Indian Territory, October 29, 1902 and at Muskogee, Indian Territory, February 2, 1907.

THE EVIDENCE IN THIS CASE SHOWS: That the applicant herein, George W. Currey, a white man was married in accordance with Cherokee law January 2, 1874 to his wife, Francis S. Currey, formerly Prock, who was at the time of said marriage a recognized citizen by blood of the Cherokee Nation, who is identified on the Cherokee authenticated tribal roll of 1880, Delaware District No. 533, as a native Cherokee, and whose name is included on the approved partial roll of citizens by blood of the Cherokee Nation opposite No. 19428. It is further shown that from the time of said marriage the said George W. Currey and Francis S. Currey resided together as husband and wife and continuously lived in the Cherokee Nation up to and including September 1, 1902. Said applicant is identified on the Cherokee authenticated tribal roll of 1880 and the Cherokee census roll of 1896 as an intermarried citizen of the Cherokee Nation. .[sic]

IT IS, THEREFORE, ORDERED AND ADJUDGED: That in accordance with the decision of the Supreme Court of the United States dated November 5, 1906 in the cases of Daniel Red Bird et al. vs. the United States, Nos. 125, 126, 127, and 128, the said applicant, George W. Currey is entitled, under the provisions of Section Twenty-one of the Act of Congress approved June 28, 1898 (30 Stats. 495), to enrollment as a citizen by intermarriage of the Cherokee Nation and his application for enrollment as such is accordingly granted.

Tams Bixby
Commissioner.

Dated at Muskogee, Indian Territory,
this FEB 18 1907

Cherokee Intermarried White 1906
Volume VII

Cherokee 8358

Muskogee, Indian Territory, February 18, 1907.

W. W. Hastings,
    Attorney for the Cherokee Nation,
        Muskogee, Indian Territory.

Dear Sir:

    There is enclosed herewith a copy of the decision of the Commissioner to the Five Civilized Tribes, dated February 18, 1907, granting the application for the enrollment of George W. Currey as a citizen by intermarriage of the Cherokee Nation.

        Respectfully,

Encl. H-33   Commissioner.
JMH

Cherokee 8358

Muskogee, Indian Territory, February 18, 1907.

The Commissioner to the Five Civilized Tribes,
        Muskogee, Indian Territory.

Sir:

    Receipt is acknowledged of the testimony and of your decision enrolling George W. Curry[sic] as a citizen by intermarriage of the Cherokee Nation. Time for protesting said decision is waived, and I consent that said person may be placed upon the schedule immediately.

        Respectfully,
           W. W. Hastings
           Attorney for Cherokee Nation.

Cherokee Intermarried White 1906
Volume VII

Cherokee 8358

Muskogee, Indian Territory, February 18, 1907.

George W. Currey,
    Southwest City, Missouri.

Dear Sit:

    There is enclosed herewith a copy of the decision of the Commissioner to the Five Civilized Tribes, dated February 18, 1907, granting the application for your enrollment as a citizen by intermarriage of the Cherokee Nation.

    You will be advised when your name has been placed upon a schedule of citizens of the Cherokee Nation and approved by the Secretary of the Interior.

                    Respectfully,

Encl. H-34   Commissioner.
JMH

◇◇◇◇◇

Cherokee
I.W. 208.

Muskogee, Indian Territory, April 16, 1907.

George W. Curry,
    Southwest City, Missouri.

Dear Sir:

    Your marriage license and certificate filed in connection with your application for enrollment as a citizen by intermarriage of the Cherokee Nation is returned to you herewith, copies of the same being retained in the files of this office.

                    Respectfully,

Encl. W-3   Commissioner.
S.W.

Cher IW 209

Cherokee Intermarried White 1906
Volume VII

G.

C.

Department of the Interior.
Commission to the Five Civilized Tribes.
Zena, I. T., May 21, 1902.

In the matter of the application of ANNIE WALKER for the enrollment of herself as a citizen by blood of the Cherokee Nation.

ANNIE WALKER, being first duly sworn, and being examined, testified as follows:

BY COMMISSION: What is your name?   A Annie Walker.
Q What is your full name?   A Annie Walker. They have it Hester Ann Walker. My son, I suppose, had it out[sic] down that way.
Q Your correct name is Annie Walker?   A Yes sir.
Q How old are you?   A I am about eighty or ninety. I don't know my age exactly, but the way I keep it I must be that old.
Q What is your post office address?   A Well, sometimes at the Grove and sometimes here at Zena.
Q Where do you get your mail and papers.[sic] [sic] Get it here at Zena, and sometimes at the Grove.
Q How do you want your post office put down, Zene[sic], or Grove, or both.
A Either one, sometimes I stay here with Mr. Wicker, and sometimes with Mr Wright, wherever they find my mail, at either place.
Q What district do you live in?   A I don't know as I can [sic] recollect it right now. My mind is not very good. Delaware District, I guess it is.
Q Are you a citizen by blood of the Cherokee Nation?   A That is the way I was raised by my parents.
Q Are you a citizen by blood, or are you a white woman?   A I am not a white woman, never was.
Q Are you a Cherokee Indian by blood?   A I say I was taught that by my parents, but I could not say.
Q What is the name of your father?   A Mt[sic] dather's[sic] name was Randolph Carter.
Q Is he living?   A No sir, he has been dead for years.
Q Was he a Cherokee by blood?   A That is what he claimed.
Q What is the name of your mother?   A Her name was Fannie Carter.
Q How long has she been dead?   A She died the year before the war ended, you know how long that is better than I do.
Q Was she a Cherokee by blood?   A That is what she claijed[sic].
Q Does you name appear upon all the rolls if[sic] the citizens of the Cherokee Nation?
A I could not tell you.
Q Does your name appear upon the 1880 roll, if you know?
A I don't know. I guess it appears upon the 1880 roll.

Cherokee Intermarried White 1906
Volume VII

Q Do you know whether lr[sic] not you were enrolled in 1896? [sic] I could not tell you just when it was. My recollection is not very good.
Q You were not, or you don't know? A I don't know whether i[sic] was or not.
Q Did you ever draw any money with the Cherokee Indians?
A Never drew any money but bread money.
Q Abut[sic] when did you draw bread money, if you remember? [sic] I could not tell you just when it was. My recollection is not very good.
Q We just want you to tell the best you can. How much did you draw when you drew the money? A I don't know, about fifteen dollars, wasn't it.
Q Did you draw the Strip money in 1894? A No sir.
Q Why didn't you get that money? A Becuase[sic] they did not want to give to me, I reckon.
Q Were you living here at that time? A Yes sir, and for many a year before.
Q When did you first come to the Cherokee Nation? A I could not tell you. I was very small, and I could not tell you just when I did come.
[sic] Did you know when old Grand daddy[sic] Ridge was killed? Q[sic] No, I wasn't here myself then? A About the time he was killed, I suppose it was, that I came here.
Q Since you first came to the Cherokee Nation, have you ever been out of it?
A No sir.
W[sic] Do you live in the Cherokee Nation now? A Yes sir.
Q What was the name of your first husband? A The first husband that I was married to was Steen Walker.
Q When did he die? A He died two years since the war, I think.
Q Who did you marry after he died? A Nobody.
Q You have never married since then? A No sir, I have not.
Q Do you sometimes go by the name of Hester Ann Walker?
A I suppose I have. Hester Ann Walker, I guess that is my name that my parents gave me, that I went by, and I suppose it is there on the record that way. I guess they gave it in that way, some of them I don't know.
Q Give me the names of your children, beginning with the oldest one.
A Asa K. Carter was the oldest, Julia Ann Walters was the next, and her is Hattie Hall, Hattie Wright is her name now.
Q Is that all? A That is all.
Q Have you no more children? A Sarah Wicked.
Q You have always borne the name of Walker, have you, since before 1880?
A Yes sir.
Q Those rolls upon which your name appears, you appear there as Walker, Annie Walker, or Hester Ann Walker? A Either one will do I guess. I never give my nzme Hester Ann Walker, I give it in[sic] Annie.

1880 authenticated roll of citizens of the Cherokee Nation examined, and applicant identified as follows:

Page 334, #2832, Hester Ann Walker, Delaware District, age 55, Intermarried white.

Cherokee Intermarried White 1906
Volume VII

1896 census rll[sic] of citizens of the Cherokee Nation examined, and applicant identified as follows:

Page 593, #567, Hester Ann Walker, Delaware District, age 71, intermarried white.

Q Do you know what degree of Cherokee blood you have?   A No sir, could not tell you?
Q Do you know whether or not you are a half breed, or a quarter blood?   A No sir. But I never was called a white woman.
Q Ca[sic] you explain why your name appears on the rolls as Hester Ann instead of Annie?   A My name being on the roll as Hester Ann, that was the name my parents gave me, but I never give my name in that way. When I sign it I just sign it Annie.
Q How do you want to be enrolled, by the name of Annie, or Hester Ann Walker.
A Just enroll me by Annie. Doubles names, I don't see any sense in them.

The applicant's daughter, Sarah Wicked, appears upon straight card 2840.

Annie Walker will be listed for enrollment upon straight card.

Wm. Hutchinson, being first duly sworn, states that as stenographer to the Commission to the Five Civilized Tribes, he correctly recorded the testimony and proceedings in this case, and the foregoing is a true and complete transcript of the stenographic notes thereof.

Wm Hutchinson

Subscribed and sworn to before me this 26th day of May, 1902.

MD Green
NP

◇◇◇◇◇

Cherokee Intermarried White 1906
Volume VII

Statement of Applicant Taken Under Oath. **Zena I.T. H-245**

CHEROKEE BY BLOOD AND ADOPTION.

Date **May 21** 190**2**

Name ....
District .... Year .... Page .... No. ....
Citizen by blood .... Mother's citizenship ....
Intermarried citizen ....
Married under what law .... Date of marriage ....
8½License .... Certificate ....
Wife's name........**Annie Walker, Zena, I.T.**
District **Delaware** Year **1880** Page **334** No. **2832**
Citizen by blood **Yes** Mother's citizenship **Randolph Carter C -d**
Intermarried citizen..**Fannie Carter C -d**
Married under what law........... Date of marriage ....
License .... Certificate ....

Names of Children:

.... Dist........... Year........... Page........... No........... Age...........
.... Dist........... Year........... Page........... No........... Age...........
.... Dist........... Year........... Page........... No........... Age...........
.... Dist........... Year........... Page........... No........... Age...........
.... Dist........... Year........... Page........... No........... Age...........

On 1880 Roll as Hester Ann Walker.
" 1896 " p 593 #567 as Hester A. Walker Delaware Dist.

◇◇◇◇◇

JOR.
Cher. 8510.

Department of the Interior.
Commission to the Five Civilized Tribes.
Tahlequah, I. T., October 27, 1902.

SUPPLEMENTAL TESTIMONY in the matter of the application for the enrollment of ANNIE WALKER as a citizen by intermarriage of the Cherokee Nation.

HARRIET WRIGHT, being first duly sworn, and being examined testified as follows:

BY COMMISSION: What is your name?   A Harriet Wright.
Q How old are you?   A As well as I remember, I think about forty-seven.
Q What is your post office address?   A Grove.
Q You are a white woman, are you?   A Yes sir.

Cherokee Intermarried White 1906
Volume VII

Q You have just given testimony in your own case, have you, as an intermarried citizen?
A Yes sir.
Q In whose case do you now desire to give testimony?   A My mother's.
Q What is her name?   A Annie Walker.
Q About how old is she?   A I don't know, I guess she is pretty near ninety.
Q Is she a white woman?   A Yes sir.
Q Is she a citizen by intermarriage of the Cherokee Nation?   A Yes sir.
Q What is the reason she is not here in person?   A Because she is so old she could not get here very handy, and she is blind besides.
Q Is she very feeble?   A Yes sir.
Q Is she able to walk around?   A Yes sir, she knocks around in the yard and about the house.
Q Does she travel anywhere?   A No sir, only as we take her. She can not stand it to travel very far.
Q What is the name of the name through whom she claims her citizenship[sic]
A Steen Walker.
Q Is he living?   A No sir.
Q He is your step-father?   A Yes sir.
Q How long has Steen Walker been dead?   A He has been dead, as well as I remember, about a year after the war. That is as good as I can recollect. It may have been a year or two, after the war, I can't recollect.
Q Was your mother ever married before she married Steen Walker?
A Yes sir, she had been married before that[sic]
Q What was the name of her first husband?   A I could not tell you.
Q Was he living when she and Steen Walker were married?   A No sir.
Q Has your mother only been married twice?   A Yes sir.
Q Was her first husband your father?   A No sir.
Q Then she has been married three times?   A Yes sir, it is three times. Hall was my father's name.
Q Was she married to Hall before or after she married Steen Walker?
A It was before. Steen Walker was her last man.
Q Was your father living when she married Steen Walker?   A No sir.
Q Did you mother and Steen Walker live together continuously until the time of his death?   A Yes sir.
Q Were they living together when he died?   A Yes sir.
Q Has your mother married since Steen Walker died?   A No sir.
Q She has never lived with any other man?   A No sir.
Q Continued to live single?   A Yes sir.
Q Her name appears upon the 1880 roll does it?   A Yes sir.
Q Has she resided in the Cherokee Nation continuously for the last twenty-five or thirty years?   A Yes sir, she has been here since I can recollect.
Q Has she ever been out?   A No sir, nt[sic] that I know of.
Q She has no minor children, has she?   A No sir, she has only three children, that's all. Sallie is the youngest one, that is Walker's girl.

Cherokee Intermarried White 1906
Volume VII

ALCY BLACK, being first duly sworn, and being examined, testified as follows:

BY COMMISSION: What is your name?   A   Alcy Black.
Q How old are you?   A Twenty-four.
Q What is your post office address?   A Grove.
Q You are a recognized citizen by blood of the Cherokee Nation?   A Yes sir.
Q Do you know Annie Walker?   A Yes sir.
Q Is she related to you?   A Yes sir, she is my grandmother.
Q Do you know her present physical condition?   A Yes sir.
Q What is it?   A She is old and blind and can't see to get around, and she is feeble. She has to have help to take her around and show her how to get around.
Q Do you think it would be impossible for her to come before the Commission in person?   A Yes sir.
Q She is a citizen by intermarriage of the Cherokee Nation?
A Yes sir, so I have been told.
Q Recognized as such?   A Yes sir.
Q You, of course, don't know anything about her marriages?
A No sir.
Q Has she resided in the Cherokee Nation continuously during the time you have known her?   A Yes sir.
Q She has been single all the time you have known her?   A Yes sir.

Mrs. Wright, This testimony will be filed in your mother's case, and if the Commission finds it necessary she will be required to appear before the Commission in person at some future time.

This testimony will be filed with and made a part of the record in the matter of the application for the enrollment of Annie Walker as a citizen by intermarriage of the Cherokee Nation, Cherokee straight card field No. 8510.

Wm. Hutchinson, being first duly sworn, states that as stenographer to the Commission to the Five Civilized Tribes he correctly recorded the testimony and proceedings in this case, and the foregoing is a true and complete transcript of the stenographic notes thereof.

Wm Hutchinson

Subscribed and sworn to before me this 13th day of November, 1902.

BC Jones
Notary Public.

Cherokee Intermarried White 1906
Volume VII

E.C.M. Cherokee 8510.

DEPARTMENT OF THE INTERIOR,
COMMISSIONER TO THE FIVE CIVILIZED TRIBES.
Muskogee, I. T., February 14, 1907.

In the matter of the application for the enrollment of Annie Walker as a citizen by intermarriage of the Cherokee Nation.

Annie Walker being first duly sworn by Frances R. Lane, a Notary Public for the Western District of Indian Territory, testified as follows:

Examination by the Commissioner.

Q What is your name? A Annie Walker.
Q Your age? A I can't tell you how old I am.
Q What is your postoffice address? A Zena, I. T.
Q You appear here today for the purpose of giving testimony relative to your right to enrollment as a citizen by intermarriage of the Cherokee Nation? A Yes sir.
Q Through whom do you claim your right? (No answer.)
Q What is your husband's name? A Steen Walker.
Q Was he a Cherokee by blood? A Yes, I suppose he was.
Q He was recognized as a citizen by blood of the Cherokee Nation, was he? A Yes sir.
Q Is he dead now? A Yes sir.
Q When did he die? A Well, I couldn't just tell you.
Q About how long ago? (No answer)
Q With reference to the war when did he die? A Two years after the war ended.
Q Do you know when you were married? A I was married to him for a year before the war.
Q Was you his first wife? A No, he had been married before.
Q Who was his first wife? A Well, I don't know.
Q Was she dead when he married you? A Yes, dead two or three years before I married him.
Q Was he your first husband? A Yes, the first man I was ever married to.
Q Then you were his second wife, and he was your first husband?
A Yes, by marriage he was my first husband and the last.
Q From the time of your marriage until his death did you continuously reside together as husband and wife and live in the Cherokee nation? A Yes, we both lived here in the Cherokee Nation.
Q Was he born in the Cherokee nation? A I guess he must have been.
Q Since his death have you continuously resided in the Cherokee Nation? A Yes, I have been nowhere[sic] else.
Q You have not been married since his death? A No, I have not.
Q Are you a white woman? A Well, I don't know that I am a white woman.
Q What other blood did you have in your[sic] besides white? A I can't tell you what other blood. My parents told me I was part Cherokee.

Cherokee Intermarried White 1906
Volume VII

Q You have never been recognized as a Cherokee by blood? A No, I aint[sic].

Witness excused.

Sarah Wickett, being first duly sworn by Frances R. Lane, testified as follows:

By the Commissioner:
Q What is your name? A Sarah Wickett.
Q Your age? A About 43.
Q Your postoffice address? A Zena, I. T.
Q What relation are you to the applicant in this case? A She is my mother.
Q What is the name of your father? A Steen Walker.
Q Has your mother always been regarded as a white woman or as a woman having some Cherokee blood? A She always taught me she was Cherokee, but she never did try to prove it.
Q She has never been enrolled as a Cherokee by blood? A No.
Q Do you remember when your father died? A No sir.
Q Since the death of your father has your mother ever re-married? A No sir.
Q Since you can remember has she continuously lived in the Cherokee nation?
A Yes sir.
Q Your father was a recognized citizen by blood of the Cherokee nation, was he?
A Yes sir.

Witness excused.

The applicant here presents in evidence an affidavit of one Joseph Fox, sworn to before T. S. Remson on the 22nd day of January 1907. This affidavit will be filed and made a part of the record in this case.

Frances R. Lane upon oath states that as stenographer to the Commissioner to the Five Civilized Tribes she reported the testimony in the above entitled cause and that the foregoing is an accurate transcript of her stenographic notes thereof.

Frances R Lane

Subscribed and sworn to before me this February 14, 1907.

Walter W. Chappell
Notary Public.

Cherokee Intermarried White 1906
Volume VII

(Below was originally a handwritten affidavit on the microfilm and is typed as given.)

Affidavit of
Joseph Fox
and
Jane Toyaman(?)

Northern Dist ⎫
Indian Territy ⎬   Grove   January 22nd 1907

       Personally appears before me a Notary Public in and for said Dist and Territory Joseph Fox age 64 years whose Post office is Grove, I. Ty. and Jane Toyaman age 63 years Post office Grove I.Ty. After being duly sworn declare as follows that they have been personally acquainted with Annie Walker during the Civil War and ever since. We knew her husband Steen Walker who died about 1867. And she has not remarried since his death. She is about blind. Hardly able to go any where

	his
	Joseph x Fox
Witness to Mark	mark
	her
Joseph England	Jane x Toyaman
Jacob DuBois	mark

                      The within affidavits subscribed and sworn to this 22d day of January A D 1907

                                   T S Remson
                                   Notary Public
                           My Comp Expires May 2d 1908

                                                        <u>8510</u>

◇◇◇◇◇

E. C. M.   Cherokee 8510

DEPARTMENT OF THE INTERIOR,

COMMISSIONER TO THE FIVE CIVILIZED TRIBES.

    In the matter of the application for the enrollment of ANNIE WALKER as a citizen by intermarriage of the Cherokee Nation.

<u>D E C I S I O N</u>

Cherokee Intermarried White 1906
Volume VII

THE RECORDS OF THIS OFFICE SHOW: That at Zena, Indian Territory, May 21, 1902, application was received by the Commission to the Five Civilized Tribes for the enrollment of Annie Walker as a citizen by intermarriage of the Cherokee Nation. Further proceedings in the matter of said application were had at Tahlequah, Indian Territory, October 27, 1902, and Muskogee, Indian Territory, February 14, 1907.

THE EVIDENCE IN THIS CASE SHOWS: That the applicant herein, Annie Walker, a white woman, married about 1860 one Steen Walker, since deceased, who was at the time of said marriage a recognized citizen by blood of the Cherokee Nation. It is further shown that from the time of said marriage until the death of Steen Walker, which occurred about 1867, the said Steen Walker and Annie Walker resided together as husband and wife and continuously lived in the Cherokee Nation; that since the death of said Steen Walker the said Annie Walker has remained unmarried and continuously lived in the Cherokee Nation up to and including September 1, 1902. Said applicant is identified on the Cherokee authenticated tribal roll of 1880 and the Cherokee census roll of 1896 as an intermarried citizen of the Cherokee Nation.

IT IS, THEREFORE, ORDERED AND ADJUDGED: That in accordance with the decision of the Supreme Court of the United States, dated November 5, 1906, in the cases of Daniel Red Bird, et al. vs. the United States, Nos. 125, 126, 127, and 128, the said applicant, Annie Walker, is entitled, under the provisions of Section twenty-one of the Act of Congress approved June 28, 1898 (30 Stats. 495), to enrollment as a citizen by intermarriage of the Cherokee Nation, and her application for enrollment as such is accordingly granted.

Tams Bixby
Commissioner.

Dated at Muskogee, Indian Territory,
this   FEB 20 1907

(Copy of original document from case.)

Cherokee Intermarried White 1906
Volume VII

Cherokee
8510

Muskogee, Indian Territory, December 27, 1906.

Annie Walker,
    Zena, Indian Territory.

Dear Madam:

November 6, 1906, the United States Supreme Court held that white persons who intermarried with Cherokee citizens according to Cherokee law prior to November 1, 1875, are entitled to enrollment and allotments of land as citizens of the Cherokee Nation.

You are advised that to properly determine your right to enrollment as a citizen by intermarriage of the Cherokee Nation, it will be necessary for you to appear before the Commissioner for the purpose of giving testimony as to the date of your marriage and whether or not your husband, by reason of your marriage to whom you claim the right to enrollment as a citizen by intermarriage of the Cherokee Nation, was a recognized Cherokee citizen at the time of your marriage to him.

You are therefore directed to appear before the Commissioner at Muskogee, Indian Territory, at 9 o'clock A. M., on Saturday, January 5, 1907, and give testimony as above indicated.

                Respectfully,

GHL   Acting Commissioner.

◇◇◇◇◇

Cherokee 8510.

Muskogee, Indian Territory, February 20, 1907.

W. W. Hastings,
    Attorney for the Cherokee Nation,
        Muskogee, Indian Territory.

Dear Sir:

There is enclosed herewith a copy of the decision of the Commissioner to the Five Civilized Tribes, dated February 20, 1907, granting the application for the enrollment of Annie Walker as a citizen by intermarriage of the Cherokee Nation.

Cherokee Intermarried White 1906
Volume VII

Respectfully,

Enc I-233   Commissioner.
RPI

◇◇◇◇◇

Cherokee 8510.

Muskogee, Indian Territory, February 20, 1907.

The Commissioner to the Five Civilized Tribes,
    Muskogee, Indian Territory.

Sir:

    Receipt is acknowledged of the testimony and of your decision, enrolling Annie Walker as a citizen by intermarriage of the Cherokee Nation. Time for protesting said decision is waived and I consent that said person may be placed upon the schedule immediately.

Respectfully,
W. W. Hastings
Attorney for the Cherokee Nation.

◇◇◇◇◇

Cherokee 8510.

Muskogee, Indian Territory, February 20, 1907.

Annie Walker,
    Zena, Indian Territory.

Dear Madam:

    There is enclosed herewith a copy of the decision of the Commissioner to the Five Civilized Tribes, dated February 20, 1907, granting the application for your enrollment as a citizen by intermarriage of the Cherokee Nation.

    You will be advised when your name has been placed upon a schedule of citizens of the Cherokee Nation and approved by the Secretary of the Interior.

Respectfully,

Enc I-234   Commissioner.
RPI

Cherokee Intermarried White 1906
Volume VII

Cher IW 210

◇◇◇◇◇

Department of the Interior,
Commission to the Five Civilized Tribes,
Westville, I. T., July 18, 1900.

In the matter of the application of Jennie Scott et al for enrollment as Cherokee citizens; being sworn and examined by Commissioner Breckinridge she testifies as follows:

George Crittenden, Interpreter:

Q What is your name? A Jennie Scott.
Q How old is she? A She don't know for certain, she is about forty-six, she thinks.
Q What is her post-office address? A Baptist.
Q Goingsnake District? A Yes sir.
Q Who does she apply for? A Herself and seven children, she has nine, but there are two of them married.
Q Is her husband dead? A He is living. He is out west working some place, she don't say where.

Examined by Hastings, attorney for Cherokee Nation:

Q Is he living with her? A Yes, they live together.

Examined by Com'r Breckinridge:

Q Ask her if she wants to apply for her husband? A She don't know how that would be, she says that their marriage license was worn out and destroyed, he is an adopted citizen.

(Applicant is advised that she can apply for him if she want to, and says she will do so then.)
Q Does she apply as a Cherokee by blood? A Yes sir.
Q How long has she been married? A Something about twenty-five years.
   Note: 1880 roll examined, page 470, #1480, as Jane Scott. 1896 roll examined, page 788, #1906, as Jane Scott, Goingsnake District.

Mr. Walkingstick, Official Interpreter, interprets:

Q Ask her how long she has been living in this District? A Born and raised here.
Q She is still living here? A Yes sir.
Q Ask her to give the names of her children unmarried and living with her? A She says this young lady here is her daughter, and has been married, but is not married now, and is living with her, and she wants to enroll her, she says she has some children of her own.

Note: Applicant is advised that this child had better apply for herself.
Q Give the names of her other children? A Henry Scott, aged twenty.
   Note:- 1880 roll examined, name not found.
      1896 roll examined, page 788, #1908, Henry Scott.

Cherokee Intermarried White 1906
Volume VII

Dennis Scott, seventeen. (On 1896 roll, page 788 #1908[sic], Denis Scott. Ella Scott, fourteen. On 1896 roll, page 788, #1910, as Ella Scott, Goingsnake District.) Susan Scott, twelve years old. (On 1896 roll, page 788, #1911, as Susan Scott, Goingsnake District) Thomas Scott, nine years old. (On 1896 roll, page 788, #1912, as Thomas Scott, Goingsnake District.) Rufus Scott, six years old. (On 1896 roll, page 788, #1913, Rufus Scott.) Margaret Scott, two year old.

Q Is that all?   A That's all.
Q Has she got certificate of birth of that child?   A Yes sir.
(Produces certificate of birth.)
Q She wants to apply for her husband?   A Yes sir.
Q Where is her husband?   A He is out west somewhere, out at work.
Q How long has he been gone?   A Three weeks to-day.
Q When is he expected back?   A In about three weeks more.
Q What's his name?   A John Scott.
   Note: 1880 roll examined, page 470, #1479, John Scott, Goingsnake District. 1896 roll, page 828, #178, John Scott.

Com'r Breckinridge: Say to her, Mr. Walkingstick, that she is duly enrolled in 1880 and 1896, and her children are duly enrolled in 1896, except the youngest child, for which she presents properly executed certificate of birth, and she and all of her children will be enrolled as Cherokees by blood.
Say that her husband is identified on the roll of 1880 and likewise on the roll of 1896, and he will be enrolled as a Cherokee by adoption.

M. D. Green, being first duly sworn, states that as stenographer to the Commission to the Five Civilized Tribes he reported the foregoing case and that the above and foregoing is a full true and complete transcript of his stenographic notes in said case.

MD Green

Subscribed and sworn to before me this 18th day of July 1900.

Clifton R. Breckinridge
Commissioner.

◇◇◇◇◇

Cherokee Intermarried White 1906
Volume VII

H.
Cher. 336.

Department of the Interior.
Commission to the Five Civilized Tribes.
Tahlequah, I. T., October 6, 1902.

SUPPLEMENTAL TESTIMONY AND PROCEEDINGS in the matter of the application for the enrollment of John Scott as a citizen by intermarriage of the Cherokee Nation.

JOHN SCOTT, being first duly sworn, and being examined, testified as follows:

BY COMMISSION: What is your name?   A John Wesley Scott is my name. I sign it John W.
Q You are enrolled as John Scott, and you say your full name is John W. Scott?
A Yes sir.
Q Do you desire to have it changed?   A Yes sir.
Q You are a white man, are you?   A Yes sir.
Q Have you heretofore made application to this Commission for enrollment as a citizen by intermarriage of the Cherokee Nation?
A Yes sir. My wife did for me.
Q What is the name of your wife?   A Jennie.
Q Is she living?   A Yes sir.
Q Is she a Cherokee by blood?   A Yes sir.
Q When were you and she married?   A Could not give the exact date. We have been living together twenty-seven or -eight years.
Q Have you and she lived together continuously since the date of your marriage?
A Yes sir.
Q Are you living together now?   A Yes sir.
Q Do you claim your right to enrollment by reason of your marriage to her?   A Yes sir.
Q Were you ever married before you married her?   A No sir.
Q Was she ever married before she married you?   A No sir.
Q Did she make satisfactory proof, at the time of her application for your enrollment, of your marriage to her according to Cherokee law?   A Yes sir.
Q Have you resided in the Cherokee Nation continuously since the date of your application for enrollment?   A Yes sir.

This testimony will be filed with and made a part of the record in the matter of the application for the enrollment of John Scott as a citizen by intermarriage of the Cherokee Nation, Cherokee straight card field No. 336.

Cherokee Intermarried White 1906
Volume VII

Wm. Hutchinson, being first duly sworn, states that as stenographer to the Commission to the Five Civilized Tribes he correctly recorded the testimony and proceedings in this case, and the foregoing is a true and complete transcript of the stenographic notes thereof.

Wm Hutchinson

Subscribed and sworn to before me this 9th day of October, 1902.

John O Rosson
Notary Public.

◇◇◇◇◇

C.F.B.   Cherokee 336.

DEPARTMENT OF THE INTERIOR,
COMMISSIONER TO THE FIVE CIVILIZED TRIBES.
MUSKOGEE, I. T., JANUARY 3, 1907.

In the matter of the application for the enrollment of John Scott as a citizen by intermarriage of the Cherokee Nation.

APPEARANCES: Applicant appears in person.

JOHN SCOTT, being first duly sworn by B. P. Rasmus, Notary Public, testified as follows:

ON BEHALF OF THE COMMISSIONER:

Q What is your name?   A John Wesley Scott.
Q When you appeared here before you gave your name imply as John Scott. Do you want to be considered as John Scott, or as John Wesley Scott?   A I think I gave it as John Wesley Scott.
Q You want it, then, to go down as John Wesley Scott?   A Yes sir.
Q What is your age?   [sic] I dont[sic] know just exactly my age, but I think I will be 54 the 29th of this month.
Q What is your post office address?   A Chance.
Q Do you claim the right to enrollment as a citizen by intermarriage of the Cherokee Nation?   A I do.
Q You have no Cherokee blood?   A No sir.
Q Through whom do you claim the right to enrollment as a citizen by intermarriage of the Cherokee Nation?   A My wife before she was married Jennie Corntassell.
Q She was a recognized citizen of the Cherokee Nation at the time you married her, was she?   A Yes sir.
Q Living in the Cherokee Nation?   A Yes sir.
Q When were you married to her?   A I was married March 14, 1875.

Cherokee Intermarried White 1906
Volume VII

Q Did you comply with Cherokee law regulating marriage? A Yes sir, I got out a license from Ben Goss, Clerk of Going Snake District. I taken[sic] out a license and got 10 signers, the law required 10 signers at that time. Judge Johnson Whitmire married me.

Q Have you any documentary evidence with you to show your marriage? A No sir.

Q But it is a matter of record, is it? A I never have come across the record of it; I sent my marriage certificate back to the Clerk to have it recorded, but I have not been able to find whether it was recorded or not.

Q Since your marriage, where have you lived? A I have lived in Going Snake District, all except 6 years, when I lived in Tahlequah District.

Q You have continuously lived in the Cherokee Nation since your marriage? A Yes sir.

Q Your wife is living? A Yes sir.

Q And she has continuously lived with you as your wife since your marriage, has she? A Yes sir.

The applicant, John W. Scott, is identified on the Cherokee authenticated tribal roll of 1880, Going Snake District, No. 1479. His wife, Jennie Scott, is included in the approved partial roll of citizens by blood of the Cherokee Nation, at No. 1031.

The undersigned, being first duly sworn, states that as stenographer to the Commission to the Five Civilized Tribes, she correctly reported the above and foregoing testimony, and that the same is a full, true and correct transcript of her stenographic notes thereof.

Sarah Waters

Subscribed and sworn to before me this 4th day of Jan. 1907.

John E. Tidwell
Notary Public.

Cherokee Intermarried White 1906
Volume VII

Cherokee 336.

DEPARTMENT OF THE INTERIOR.

COMMISSIONER TO THE FIVE CIVILIZED TRIBES.

Muskogee, I.T., January 26, 1907.

....

Supplemental proceedings in the matter of the application for the enrollment of John Scott as a citizen by intermarriage of the Cherokee Nation.

....

Witnesses sworn by John E. Tidwell, a Notary Public.

....

Watt Whitmire being first duly sworn, testifies as follows:

By the Commissioner:

Q What is your name? A Watt Whitmire.
Q What is your age? A 54.
Q What is your Post Office address? A Westville, I.T.
Q Are you a citizen by blood of the Cherokee Nation? A Yes sir.
Q Do you know a man in the Cherokee Nation by the name of John Scott? A Yes sir.
Q How long have you known him? A I have known him 25 years or longer--longer than that I guess, I don't remember the first time I did see him.
Q Was he living in the Cherokee Nation when you become[sic] acquainted with him? A Yes sir.
Q You have always known him as a white man, have you? A Yes sir.
Q Has he ever been married? A Yes sir.
Q What is the name of his wife? A Jennie Corntassel.
Q Did you know her prior to her marriage to John Scott? A Yes sir.
Q She has always been a recognized citizen by blood of the Cherokee Nation has she? A Yes sir.
Q She is living now is she? A Yes sir.
Q Do you know of your own personal knowledge when John Scott was married to his wife Jennie Corntassel? A What year it was--no sir.
Q Were you living in the immediate vicinity when they were married?
A Yes sir, they were married at my father's house--my father was judge, he married them.
Q Were you at home? A Yes sir.

Cherokee Intermarried White 1906
Volume VII

Q   Did you witness the ceremony?   A   Yes sir.
Q   Did you see the marriage license?   A   No sir.
Q   Was your father an official of the Cherokee Nation at that time?
    A   He was District Judge at that time.
Q   Judge of what district?   A   Going Snake District.
Q   you don't remember the year in which this marriage occurred?
    A   No sir, I do not.
Q   Since the marriage of John Scott to his wife Jennie Scott do you know of your own personal knowledge that he has been recognized as a citizen by intermarriage of the Cherokee Nation?   A   Yes sir he has been recognized as a citizen of the Cherokee Nation and voted in the elections.
Q   He has enjoyed all the rights and privileges of a citizen of the Cherokee Nation?
    A   Yes sir.
Q   Did he ever hold any office in the Cherokee Nation?   A   Not that I know of.
Q   But you say that you know of your own personal knowledge that he has voted at elections?   A   Yes sir.
Q   Did you ever hear of his right as a citizen by intermarriage of the Cherokee Nation questioned in any way?   A   No sir I never do.
Q   Was Jennie Scott ever married before she married John Scott?   A   No sir, not as I know of.
Q   And he, to your knowledge, was never married before he married her?   A   Not to my knowledge.
Q   Can you approximate the date of their marriage?   A   No sir, I cannot.
Q   You have no idea as to when the marriage occurred?   A   I can't recollect the year or the month at all,
Q   But he was married by your father who was judge at that time, the judge of Going Snake District?   A   Yes sir.
Q   Married at your father's home and you were present and witnessed the ceremony?
    A   Yes sir.
Q   You know nothing about his license?   A   No sir, I never saw his license at all. All I know was that they was required to get a license --white men was required to get a license to marry a Cherokee at that time but I never saw his license.
Q   And your father as judge of Going Snake District would have had no authority to have married these parties had not John Scott presented a license?   A   No sir that was the Cherokee law that when a white man married a Cherokee they was required to get license from the Clerk of the district.
Q   You don't remember who was clerk of the district at that time do you?   A   Well since I have been studying the matter over I have a recollection a man by the name of Joe Stout was clerk at that time. I may be mistaken.
Q   Do you know the years during which your father was judge of Going Snake District?
    A   I don't remember exactly, but he was judge one time in 1876 but whether it was in 1876 and 1877 or 1875 and 1876 I can't tell. He was elected for two years but whether it was '75 and '75 or '76 and 77 I can't remember.
Q   Was that the only period that your father ever served as judge of Going Snake District?   A   Yes sir.

Cherokee Intermarried White 1906
Volume VII

Q And will you give his name again please? A Johnson Whitmire, they call him-- his real name was Jonothan[sic] Whitmire.
Q Is your father, Johnson Whitmire living at this time? A No sir.
Q Do you know or have you known John Scott and Jennie Scott-continuously since their marriage? A Yes sir.
Q Do you know their children? A Yes sir.
Q What is the name of their oldest child? A Lizzie, as I remember.
Q Do you know of your own personal knowledge that they have lived together as husband and wife continuously and lived together all these years in the Cherokee Nation? A Yes sir.

Witness excused.

John Scott being duly sworn by B. P. Rasmus, a Notary Public, testifies as follows:

By the Commissioner:

Q What is your name? A John Scott.
Q What is your age? A 54.
Q What is your Post office address? A Chance, I.T.
Q You are an applicant for enrollment as a citizen by intermarriage of the Cherokee Nation? A Yes sir.
Q When were you married to your wife, Jennie Scott? A I was married March 14, 1875.
Q Who married you? A Johnson Whitmire.
Q Who issued your marriage license? A As well as I remember it was Ben Goss.
Q Are any of the people living who signed your petition? A I can't remember any of them. I remember one, a full blood by the name of Silas Holland, and what made me remember him he said he wouldn't sign it, he wouldn't sign a whiteman's petition.
Q Then you can't give the Commissioner the names or name of any one who signed your petition? A No sir.
Q But you secured the signatures did you and obtained the license before you married her? A Yes sir, they only required ten I went to work to get signers--we were having a stable-raising, and when I got ten there was another man said "I'll sign it" and I had thirteen signers.
Q What is the name of your oldest child? A Lizzie.
Q When was Lizzie born? A April 15, 1876 as well as I can recollect.

The name of Lizzie Scott given by the applicant as his oldest child appears upon the Cherokee authenticated tribal roll of 1880 immediately following the names of John Scott and Jane Scott her age appearing thereon as four years.

Cherokee Intermarried White 1906
Volume VII

Q   Are there any other witnesses to your marriage living at this time?   A   Why not that I know of, there was one woman there but I never could remember who she was. The parties that went with us are dead.
Q   Did John Blackfox see you married?   A   No sir.
Q   Was he living in the immediate vicinity at the time you were married?   A   I don't k now right where he was living--he had been living there in the neighborhood all the time and saw well as I recollect he was at old Uncle Billy Harnages[sic].

    The applicant presents an affidavit signed by John Blackfox in which John Blackfox states that John Scott married Jennie Corntassel on March 14, 1875; This affidavit will be filed and made a part of the record in this case.

Q   Why did you not bring this John Blackfox before the Commissioner in Charge. order that he might testify in your case?   A   Well, he couldn't well come and Mr. Dore said his affidavit would do just as well. Mr. Dore questioned him.
Q   Is it possible for you to bring this man before the Commissioner to testify in your case?   A   Why I could have him summonsed I guess and he would come but I don't know that he would come without. One reason I have been to right smart expense and had to borrow the money to make this trip.

Witness Excused.

Mr. Whitmire recalled,

Q   Mr. Whitmire, do you remember when John Scott's oldest child was born?
A   No sir.
Q   But you could swear positively that it was some time, perhaps a year after his marriage?   A   I do not know.
Q   You could swear positively that it was after he was married?   A   Yes sir.
Q   But as to how long after his marriage you wouldn't be positive?
A   No sir.

Witness Excused.

    I, Cora E. Glendenning, a stenographer to the Commissioner to the Five Civilized Tribes, on oath state that I reported the proceedings in the above entitled cause on January 26, 1907, and that the foregoing is a true and complete transcript of my stenographic notes therein.

Cora E. Glendenning

Subscribed and sworn to before me this 31 day of January, 1907.

Chas E Webster
Notary Public.

Cherokee Intermarried White 1906
Volume VII

DEPARTMENT OF THE INTERIOR,
COMMISSIONER TO THE FIVE CIVILIZED TRIBES.
WESTVILLE, I. T., FEBRUARY 8, 1907.

In the matter of the application for the enrollment of JOHN SCOTT as a citizen by intermarriage of the Cherokee Nation.

(Below was originally a handwritten affidavit on the microfilm and is typed as given.)

Benjamin F. Goss being first duly sworn by William R. Bass a Notary Public testifies as follows:

What is your name?   A - Benjamin F Goss.   What is your age?   A - Seventy nine years past.   An you are a Cherokee by blood.   A - Yes sir.   How long have you lived in the Indian Territory?   A - Have lived here since the year 1839.   Do you know a man by the name of John W Scott?   A - Yes sir   How long have you known him?   A - I have known him since about the year 1870.   Where has he lived since you first know?   A - He has lived in the Territory all that time   -   About how old was he when you first became acquainted with him?   A - Was quite a young man.   What do you know about his marriage?   A - I was clerk of the Goingsnake District in the years 1874 - 5 - 6 - 7 and during the year 1874 or 1875 issued him a license to marry Jennie Corntassell a Cherokee by blood.   His license never was returned to be recorded   About what time of the year did you issue this license to John W Scott?   A - In the spring of the year I think in March.   What is your best recollection as to whether it was in 1874 or 1875?   A - I can not say positively as to the year, but am certain that it was in the spring of the year. Have you known John W Scott since that time?   A - Yes sir.   Been intimately acquainted with with[sic] him?   A - Yes sir.   Did you also know his wife Jennie?   A - Have known her since she was a little girl   How soon after you issued the license to John W Scott did you see him again?   A - I saw him very shortly after   Where was he living right after his marriage?   A - Near Westville I.T.   Was that woman Jennie Corntassell or Jennie Scott living with him at that time as his wife?   A - Yes sir they were living together as man and wife   You did not see them married?   A - No sir but I always supposed they were and they could not well have lived here together if they had

198

Cherokee Intermarried White 1906
Volume VII

not been. It was understood by his neighbors and acquaintances that they were husband and wife and they certainly lived together as such.

Charles B. Wilson, being first duly sworn, doth depose and say that the above and foregoing are the original questions propounded by him to, and the answers returned thereto by <u>Benjamin F. Goss</u> the above name witness.

Charles B. Wilson

Subscribed and sworn to before me this 11th day of February, 1907.

Walter W. Chappell
Notary Public.

(Below was originally a handwritten affidavit on the microfilm and is typed as given.)

John W. Scott being first duly sworn by P. J. Dore a Notary Public testified as follows

What is your name?   A - John W. Scott.
What is your wife's name?   A - Jennie Scott her maiden name was Jennie Corntassell
What is the name of your oldest child?   A - Lizzie Scott -- About how old is she?
A - She will be thirty two years old next April.   Have you ever kept a record of the births of your children?   A - Yes.   In what did you keep it?   A - In our family bible. Have you that bible now?   A - Yes sir.   Will you attach the original record of the birth of your daughter Lizzie Scott to this your evidence?   A - I will, together with the record of the birth of my other children.

Cherokee Intermarried White 1906
Volume VII

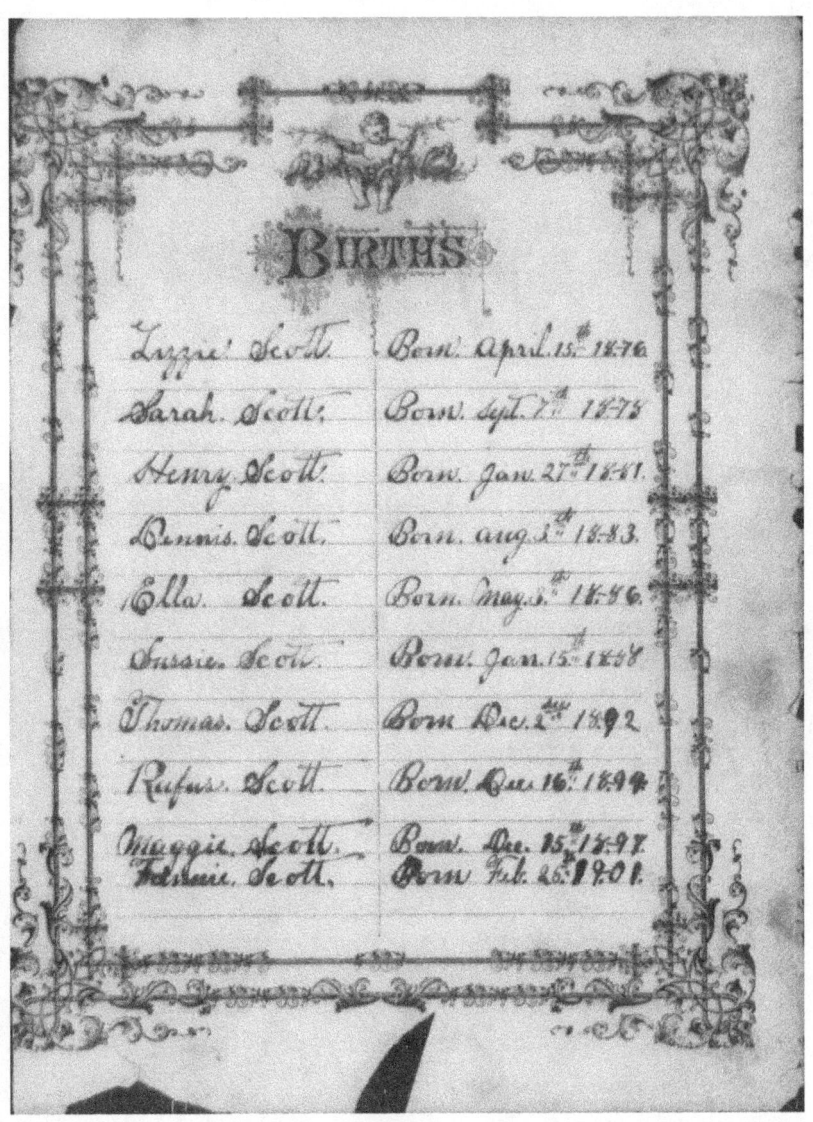

(Copy of original document from case.)

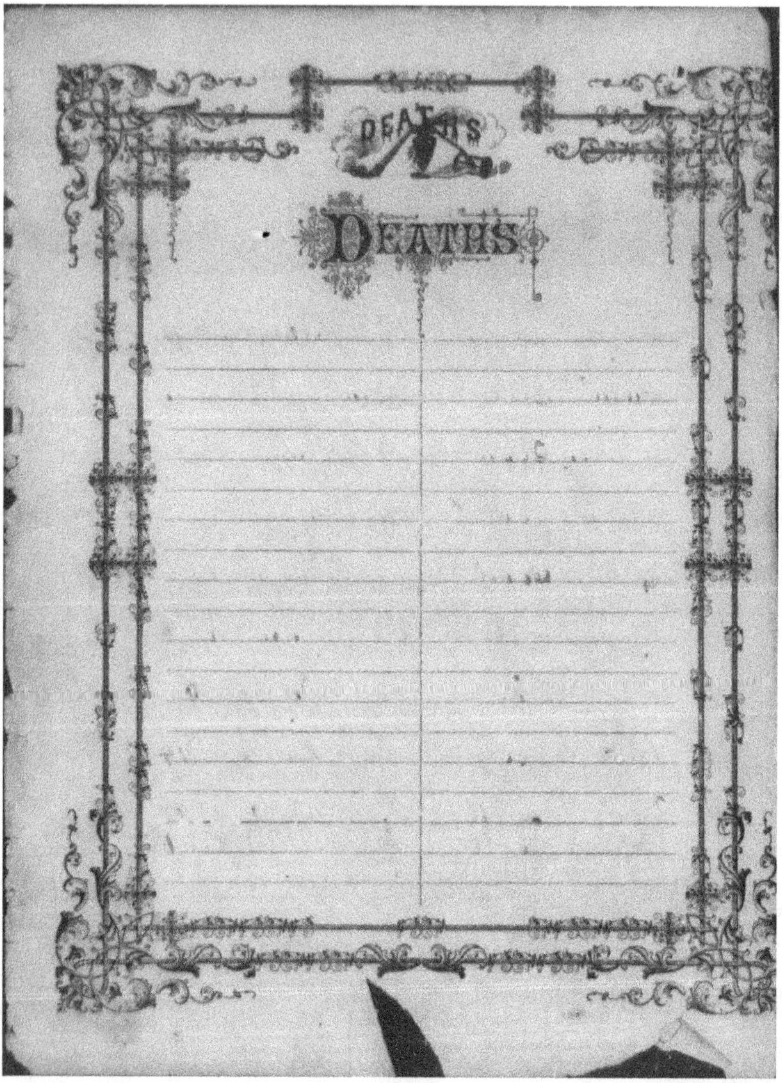

Cherokee Intermarried White 1906
Volume VII

(Copy of original document from case.)

Cherokee Intermarried White 1906
Volume VII

Charles B. Wilson, being first duly sworn, doth depose and say that the above and foregoing are the original questions propounded by him to, and the answers returned thereto by <u>John W. Scott</u> the above named witness.

Charles B Wilson

Subscribed and sworn to before me this to 11th day of February, 1907.

Walter W. Chappell
Notary Public.

◇◇◇◇◇

CERTIFIED COPY.

P. J. DORE,

GENERAL MERCHANDISE.

Westville, Ind. Ter. Jany. 25/1907.

United States of America)
) ss
Northern Dept. Ind. Ter.)

John Black fox being first duly sworn Depose and says:
He knows John Scott Married Jennie Corntossel[sic] on March 14th 1875.

Witness to mark,

(Signed) John X Black fox
                       his / mark

Sam Foreman,

J. A. Bryant

Subscribed and sworn to before me this 25th Day of Jany 1907.

(Signed) P. J. Dore,
Notary Public.

My Com exp. June 4, 1908.

Cherokee Intermarried White 1906
Volume VII

This certifies that the undersigned, being duly sworn, states that as stenographer to the Commission to the Five Civilized Tribes she made the aboce[sic] and foregoing copy and that the same is a full, true and correct copy of the original instrument now on file in this office.

Georgia Coberly
Stenographer.

Subscribed and sworn to before me this 14th day of February, 1907.

Walter W. Chappell
Notary Public.

◇◇◇◇◇

E C M   Cherokee 336.

DEPARTMENT OF THE INTERIOR,
COMMISSIONER TO THE FIVE CIVILIZED TRIBES.

In the matter of the application for the enrollment of JOHN SCOTT as a citizen by intermarriage of the Cherokee Nation.

D E C I S I O N

THE RECORDS OF THIS OFFICE SHOW: That at Westville, Indian Territory, July 18, 1900 application was received by the Commission to the Five Civilized Tribes for the enrollment of John Scott as a citizen by intermarriage of the Cherokee Nation. Further proceedings in the matter of said application were had at Tahlequah, Indian Territory, October 6, 1902, Muskogee, Indian Territory, January 3, 1907 and January 26, 1907 and at Westville, Indian Territory, February 8, 1907.

THE EVIDENCE IN THIS CASE SHOWS: That the applicant herein, John Scott, a white man, was married in accordance with Cherokee law March 14, 1875, to his wife, Jennie Scott, nee Corntassell, who was at the time of said marriage a recognized citizen by blood of the Cherokee nation, who is identified on the Cherokee authenticated tribal roll of 1880, Going Snake District opposite No. 1480, as a native Cherokee, and whose name is included on the approved partial roll of citizens by blood of the Cherokee Nation opposite No. 1031. It is further shown that from the time of said marriage the said John Scott and Jennie Scott resided together as husband and wife and continuously lived in the Cherokee Nation up to and including September 1, 1902. Said applicant is identified on the Cherokee authenticated tribal roll of 1880 and the Cherokee census roll of 1896 as an intermarried citizen of the Cherokee Nation.

IT IS, THEREFORE, ORDERED AND ADJUDGED: That in accordance with the decision of the Supreme Court of the United States dated November 5, 1906 in the cases of Daniel Red Bird, et al. vs. the United States, Nos. 125, 126, 127, and 128, the said

Cherokee Intermarried White 1906
Volume VII

applicant, John Scott, is entitled, under the provisions of Section Twenty-one of the Act of Congress approved June 28, 1898, (30 Stats. 495), to enrollment as a citizen by intermarriage of the Cherokee Nation, and his application for enrollment as such is accordingly granted.

Tams Bixby
Commissioner.

Dated at Muskogee, Indian Territory,
this   FEB 20 1907

◇◇◇◇◇

Cherokee
336.

Muskogee, Indian Territory, February 20, 1907.

John Scott,
Baptist, Indian Territory.

Dear Sir:

There is enclosed herewith a copy of the decision of the Commissioner to the Five Civilized Tribes, dated February 20, 1907, granting your application for enrollment of as a citizen by intermarriage of the Cherokee Nation.

You will be advised when your name has been placed upon a schedule of citizens of the Cherokee Nation and approved by the Secretary of the Interior.

Respectfully,

Encl. JH-39.
HJC

Commissioner.

◇◇◇◇◇

Cherokee Intermarried White 1906
Volume VII

Cherokee
336.

Muskogee, Indian Territory, February 20, 1907.

The Commissioner to the Five Civilized Tribes,
    Muskogee, Indian Territory.

Sir:

Receipt is acknowledged of the testimony and of your decision enrolling John Scott as a citizen by intermarriage of the Cherokee Nation. Time for protesting said decision is waived and I consent that said person may be placed upon the schedule immediately.

Respectfully,
W. W. Hastings
Attorney for Cherokee Nation.

◇◇◇◇◇

Cherokee
336.

Muskogee, Indian Territory, February 20, 1907.

W. W. Hastings,
    Attorney for the Cherokee Nation,
        Muskogee, Indian Territory.

Dear Sir:

There is enclosed herewith a copy of the decision of the Commissioner to the Five Civilized Tribes, dated February 20, 1907, granting the application for the enrollment of John Scott, as a citizen by intermarriage of the Cherokee Nation.

Respectfully,

Encl. HJ-40.

HJC   Commissioner.

Cherokee Intermarried White 1906
Volume VII

Cher IW 211

◇◇◇◇◇

F.R.

DEPARTMENT OF THE INTERIOR,

COMMISSIONER TO THE FIVE CIVILIZED TRIBES.

In the matter of the application for the enrollment of

AMANDA ALBERTY

as a citizen by intermarriage of the Cherokee Nation.

Cherokee 573.

◇◇◇◇◇

DEPARTMENT OF THE INTERIOR,
COMMISSION TO THE FIVE CIVILIZED TRIBES,
STILWELL, I.T. JULY 24, 1900.

In the matter of the application of Andrew J. Alberty et als., for enrollment as Cherokee citizens, said Alberty being sworn by Commissioner Needles, testified as follows:

Q What is your name? A Andrew J. Alberty.
Q Your age? A 55.
Q Your postoffice? A Stilwell.
Q What district do you reside? A Goingsnake.
Q How long have you lived there? A Born and rised[sic] there.
Q Lived there always ever since? A Yes.
Q Are you a Cherokee? A Yes.
Q Make application as a Cherokee by blood? A Yes.
Q What is the name of your father? A Johnson Alberty.
Q Is he living? A No sir.
Q Did he die before '80? A Yes, '64.
Q What is the name of your mother? A Katie.
Q Is she living? A No sir.
Q Did she die before '80? A ~~Yes~~. No sir, she died last July.

206

Cherokee Intermarried White 1906
Volume VII

     Applicant, Andrew J. Albert[sic], on '80 roll, page 403, number 4 as Andy Alberty.

Q What degree of blood do you claim?   A I expect I am about 1/4.
Q Are you married?   A Yes.
Q Was your wife a citizen by blood?   A No sir, white woman.
Q When were you married?   A '70.
Q What is your wife's name?   A Amanda Alberty.
     On '80 roll, page 403, number 5 as Mandy.
        On '96 roll, page 817, number 1, as Amanda B. Alberty.
Q Is your wife living?   A Yes.
Q What is the name of the oldest child at home under 21 years of age?   A Thedocia[sic], 18 years old.
     On '96 roll, page 719, number 9 as Theodocia.
Q What is the name of the next one?   A William L., 16 years old.
     On '96 roll, page 719, number 10 as William P.
Q Next one?   A Ada, 14 years old.
     On '96 roll, page 719, number 11 as Ada May.
Q Next one?   A Bishop M., 12 years old.
     On '96 roll, page 719, number 12.
Q Next one?   A Samuel J. 10 years old, page 719, number 13.
Q Are these children all alive and living with you?   A Yes.

     The name of Andrew J. Alberty being found upon the authenticated roll of '80 as well as upon the census roll of '96, and Amanda, his wife, being also found upon the authenticated roll of '80 and on the census roll of '96 as an intermarried citizen, she, Amanda, will be admitted as an intermarried citizen. Andrew J. Alberty and his children, as enumerated above, and said children's name being found upon the census rolls of '96, and sufficient proof being made as to their residence, they, as well as their father, are ordered enrolled as Cherokee citizens by blood, and their names will be entered upon the roll now being made by this Commission.

     Brown McDonald, being duly sworn, says as Stenographer to the Commission to the Five Civilized Tribes, he reported in full the testimony of the above named witness, and the foregoing is a full, true and correct transcript of his notes.

                                                  Brown McDonald

Sworn to and subscribed before me this 30th day of July, 1900, at Bunch, I.T.

                                                  TB Needles
                                                 Commissioner.

Cherokee Intermarried White 1906
Volume VII

JOR.
Cher. 573.

Department of the Interior.
Commission to the Five Civilized Tribes.
Tahlequah, I. T., October 21, 1902.

SUPPLEMENTAL TESTIMONY in the matter of the application for the enrollment of AMANDA ALBERTY as a citizen by intermarriage of the Cherokee Nation.

AMANDA ALBERTY, being first duly sworn, and being examined, testified as follows:

BY COMMISSION: What is your name?   A Amanda Alberty.
Q How old are you?   A Forty.
Q What is your post office address?   A Stilwell.
Q You are a white woman, are you?   A Yes sir.
Q Has application been made to this Commission for your enrollment as a citizen by intermarriage of the Cherokee Nation?   A Yes sir.
Q What is the name of your husband?   A Andrew Jackson Alberty.
Q Is he living?   A Yes sir.
Q Is he a Cherokee by blood?   A Yes sir.
Q When were you and he married?   A In 1870.
Q Do you claim your right to enrollment by reason of your marriage to him?   A Yes sir.
Q Does your name appear upon the roll of 1880?   A Yes sir.
Q Were you ever married before you married him?   A No sir.
Q Was he ever married before he married you?   A Yes sir.
Q What was the name of his first wife?   A Elizabeth Folsom.
Q Is she living?   A No sir.
Q Was she living at the time you and your present husband were married?   A No sir, she was dead.
Q Was that the only time your husband as ever married before he married you?
A Yes sir.
Q He is your first husband and your are his second wife?   A Yes sir.
Q Have you and he lived together continuously since your marriage?   A Yes sir.
Q Were you living together on the 1st day of September, 1902?   A Yes sir.
Q You have never been separated?   A No sir.
Q Have you resided in the Cherokee Nation continuously since you and he married?
A Yes sir.
Q Has he also?   A Yes sir.
Q You have how [sic] minor children that application was mad for?
A Six. Seven with the one that is dead.
Q How many minor children had you--under twenty-one years of age--and unmarried, at the time you made application for enrollment?   Application was made for the enrollment of five children, was it no[sic]   A Yes sir.
Q One of those died since?   A Yes sir.

Cherokee Intermarried White 1906
Volume VII

Q You have just executed an affidavit as to one of those children, Adam. A Yes sir.
Q Are those other fur[sic] children living?   A Yes sir.

    This testimony will be filed with and made a part of the record in the matter of the application for the enrollment of Amanda Alberty as a citizen by intermarriage of the Cherokee Nation, Cherokee straight card field No. 573.

Wm. Hutchinson, being first duly sworn, states that as stenographer to the Commission to the Five Civilized Tribes he correctly recorded the testimony and proceedings in this case, and the foregoing is a true and complete transcript of the stenographic notes thereof.

                                                         Wm Hutchinson

Subscribed and sworn to before me this 8th day of November, 1902.

                                                        BC Jones
                                                              Notary Public.

◇◇◇◇◇◇

THE STILWELL
DRUG COMPANY

                                      STILWELL, I. T. Dec. 28" 1906.

Will O Beall Esq.
       Sir:
This certified that Mrs. Amanda Alberty, whom you have summoned to appear before the Commissioner on Jan. 3" 07, will not be physically able to make the trip by that time.
    She has been very sick for the last 3 or 4 weeks but is better now. She will possible be able to make the trip in Spring. If she could make her proof at home it would be much better for her. Can she do so?   If so advise her.
                                         Your etc.
                                         T. S. Williams M. D.
                                         Her physician.

    The undersigned upon oath states that she made the above copy and that same is a true and correct copy of the original letter on file in this office.

                                                        Myrtle Hill

Cherokee Intermarried White 1906
Volume VII

Subscribed and sworn to before me this the 16th day of February, 1907.

John E. Tidwell
Notary Public.

◇◇◇◇◇

I Andrew J. Alberty says that I was married in Ind. Ter. Feb. 16th, 1870 and have lived as man and wife ever since and have lived in the Cherokee Nation since 1873.

Witness my hand this 11th day of Feb. 1907.

(Signed) Andrew J. Alberty.

Sworn to and subscribed before me this 11th day of Feb 1907.

(Signed) Hugh M. Adair
Notary Public.

(SEAL)

My Commission expires Nov. 21st, 1908.
THIRD TERM.

The undersigned upon oath states that she made the above copy and that same is a true and correct copy of the original affidavit on file in this office.

Myrtle Hill

Subscribed and sworn to before me this the 16th day of February, 1907.

John E. Tidwell
Notary Public.

◇◇◇◇◇

(The Affidavit below typed as given.)

Personally appeared this 11th day of Feb. 1907 Benj. F. Paden of near Stilwell I. T. Northern District. Who deposeth and says. That I am 70 years of age That I live 3 miles S. E. of Stilwell Ind Ter. I have been acquainted Andrew J. Alberty and wife Amanda Alberty for about 35 years and that they have lived together as man and wife ever since I knew them and has always been recognized by the Cherokee Laws as man and wife and that their marriage has been considered as legal.
In witness whereof I have set my hand this 11th day of Feb. 1907.

Signed   Benj. F. Paden.

Cherokee Intermarried White 1906
Volume VII

Sworn to and subscribed before me this 11th day of Feb. 1907.

(Signed)   Hugh M. Adair
(SEAL)   Notary Public

My Commission expires Nov. 21st, 1908.
   THIRD TERM.

The undersigned upon oath states that she made the above copy and that same is a true and correct copy of the original affidavit on file in this office.

Myrtle Hill

Subscribed and sworn to before me this the 16th day of February, 1907.

John E. Tidwell
Notary Public.

◇◇◇◇◇

Personally appeared this 11th day of Feb. 1907 John B. Paden of Stilwell Ind. Ter. Northern District, who says. That I am about 45 years of age. That I live in Stilwell, Ind. Ter. That I have been acquainted with Andrew J. Alberty and wife Amanda Alberty for about 32 years and that they were married in the Ind. Ter. That they lived here ever since and have lived together as man and wife ever since I knew them and has always been recognized by all as well as Cherokee laws. Tha[sic] their marriage has been considered legal.

(Signed)   John B. Paden.

Sworn to and subscribed before me this 11th day of Feb. 1907.

(Signed)   Hugh M. Adair
(SEAL)   And   Notary Public.

My Commission expires Nov. 21st, 1908.
   THIRD TERM.

The undersigned upon oath states that she made the above copy and that same is a true and correct copy of the original affidavit on file in this office.

Myrtle Hill

Subscribed and sworn to before me this the 16th day of February, 1907.

John E. Tidwell
Notary Public.

◇◇◇◇◇

Cherokee Intermarried White 1906
Volume VII

F. R.   Cherokee 573.

DEPARTMENT OF THE INTERIOR,

COMMISSIONER TO THE FIVE CIVILIZED TRIBES.

In the matter of the application for the enrollment of Amanda Alberty as a citizen by intermarriage of the Cherokee Nation.

D E C I S I O N

THE RECORDS OF THIS OFFICE SHOW: That at Stilwell, Indian Territory, July 24, 1900, application was received by the Commission to the Five Civilized Tribes for the enrollment of Amanda Alberty as a citizen by intermarriage of the Cherokee Nation. Further proceedings in the matter of said application were had at Tahlequah, Indian Territory, October 21, 1902.

THE EVIDENCE IN THIS CASE SHOWS: That the applicant herein, Amanda Alberty, is a white woman, who claims her right to enrollment as a citizen by intermarriage of the Cherokee Nation, by virtue of her marriage in the year 1870 to one Andrew J. Alberty, who is alleged to have been a recognized citizen by blood of the Cherokee Nation at the time of said marriage, and who is identified upon the Cherokee authenticated tribal roll of 1880, Going Snake District, Page 403, No. 4, as a native Cherokee, and whose name is included on the approved partial roll of citizens by blood of the Cherokee Nation opposite No. 1682.

It is further shown that since said marriage, the said Andrew J. Alberty and Amanda Alberty resided together as husband and wife and continuously lived in the Cherokee Nation up to and including September 1, 1902.

It further appears from the records in the possession of this office that John Alberty, who is identified on the Cherokee authenticated tribal roll of 1880, Going Snake District, Page 403, No. 6, as a native Cherokee, and whose name is included on the approved partial roll of citizens by blood of the Cherokee Nation, opposite No. 22570, is the son of said Andrew J. Alberty and Amanda Alberty, the applicant herein, and that the said John Alberty was born in the year 1873. An examination of the Cherokee authenticated tribal roll of 1880 shows the said John Alberty to have been seven years of age at the date of the making of said roll.

The applicant herein is identified upon the Cherokee authenticated tribal roll of 1880 and the Cherokee census roll of 1896 as an intermarried citizen of the Cherokee Nation.

In view of the foregoing, it is considered that the applicant, Amanda Alberty, was married in accordance with Cherokee law, to a citizen by blood of the Cherokee Nation, prior to November 1, 1875.

IT IS, THEREFORE, ORDERED AND ADJUDGED: That in accordance with the decision of the Supreme Court of the United States, dated November 5, 1906, in the cases

Cherokee Intermarried White 1906
Volume VII

of Daniel Red Bird, et al., vs. the United States, Nos. 125, 126, 127, and 128, the said applicant, Amanda Alberty, is entitled under the provisions of Section 21 of the Act of Congress approved June 28, 1898 (30 Stats., 495), to enrollment as a citizen by intermarriage of the Cherokee Nation and her application for enrollment as such is accordingly granted.

Tams Bixby
Commissioner.

Dated at Muskogee, Indian Territory,
this   FEB 21 1907

◇◇◇◇◇

Cherokee
573.

Muskogee, Indian Territory, February 21, 1907.

Amanda Alberty,
Stilwell, Indian Territory.

Dear Madam:

There is enclosed herewith a copy of the decision of the Commissioner to the Five Civilized Tribes, dated February 21, 1907, granting your application for enrollment as a citizen by intermarriage of the Cherokee Nation.

You will be advised when your name has been placed upon a schedule of citizens of the Cherokee Nation and approved by the Secretary of the Interior.

Respectfully,

Encl. HJ-41.
HJC   Commissioner.

◇◇◇◇◇

Cherokee Intermarried White 1906
Volume VII

Cherokee
573.

Muskogee, Indian Territory, February 21, 1907.

The Commissioner to the Five Civilized Tribes,
    Muskogee, Indian Territory.

Sir:

Receipt is acknowledged of the testimony and of your decision enrolling Amanda Alberty as a citizen by intermarriage of the Cherokee Nation. Time for protesting said decision is waived and I consent that said person may be placed upon the schedule immediately.

    Respectfully,
    W. W. Hastings
    Attorney for Cherokee Nation.

◇◇◇◇◇

Cherokee
573.

Muskogee, Indian Territory, February 21, 1907.

W. W. Hastings,
    Attorney for the Cherokee Nation,
        Muskogee, Indian Territory.

Dear Sir:

There is enclosed herewith a copy of the decision of the Commissioner to the Five Civilized Tribes, dated February 15, 1907, granting the application for the enrollment of Amanda Alberty as a citizen by intermarriage of the Cherokee Nation.

    Respectfully,

Encl. HJ-42.
  HJC   Commissioner.

Cher IW 212

Cherokee Intermarried White 1906
Volume VII

Department of the Interior,
Commission to the Five Civilized Tribes,
Stillwell[sic], I.T., July 26, 1900.

In the matter of the application of Esther Roberts for the enrollment of herself and child as Cherokees by blood, and her husband by intermarriage; being duly sworn and examined by Commissioner Breckenridge[sic], she testified as follows:

Q What is your name? A Esther S Roberts.
Q How old are you? A 56.
Q What is your post office? A Dutch Mills, Ark.
Q What district do you live in? A Going Snake.
Q How long have you lived in that district? A I have been living there all my life, 56 years.
Q For whom do you apply for enrollment? A For myself and one child and my husband, he is sick and can't be here.
Q Do you apply as a Cherokee by blood? A Yes, sir.
Q Is your husband a Cherokee by blood? A No, sir.
Q Is your husband much sick? A Yes, sir, he has been awful bad off, but he is getting a little better.
Q How long has he been sick? A It will soon be a month.
Q Are you on the roll of 1880? A Yes, sir.
Q Under what name were you enrolled in 1880, were you Roberts then?
A Yes, sir, I guess so, we have been married 34 years.
(On 1880 roll, page 466, No. 1403, Ester Roberts, Going Snake dist.
On 1880 roll, page 780, No. 1882, Esther S. Roberts, Going Snake dist.)
Q Give me your husband's full name? A Solon H. Roberts.
Q How old is he? A He is 57 to-day.
Q When were you married? A In 1866.
Q Is he on the roll of 1880? A Yes, sir.
(On 1880 roll, page 466, No. 1402, S. H. Roberts, Going Snake dist.
On 1896 roll, page 827, No. 159, Solon H. Roberts, Going Snake dist.)
Q Are you and he living together at this time? A Yes, sir.
Q He has been making his home right along in the Nation? A Yes, sir.
Q Is this child under age? A Yes, sir.
Q What is the name of the child? A Martha Ellen Roberts.
Q How old is the child? A 16.
(On 1896 roll, page 780, No. 1684, Martha E. Roberts, Going Snake district.)

Mrs. Roberts, you and your husband are both duly identified on the roll of 1880 and the roll of 1896, and your child is identified on the roll of 1896, and you and your child will be enrolled as a Cherokee by blood and your husband as a Cherokee by intermarriage.

-------0---------

Cherokee Intermarried White 1906
Volume VII

     Bruce C. Jones, being duly sworn, says that as stenographer to the Commission to the Five Civilized Tribes he reported the testimony of the above named witness, and that the foregoing is a full, true and correct translation of his stenographic notes.

Bruce C Jones

Sworn to and subscribed before me this the 1st day of August, 1900.

Clifton R. Breckinridge
Commissioner.

◇◇◇◇◇

JOR.
Cher. 686.

Department of the Interior.
Commission to the Five Civilized Tribes.
Tahlequah, I. T., October 8, 1902.

    SUPPLEMENTAL TESTIMONY AND PROCEEDINGS in the matter of the application for the enrollment of SOLON H. ROBERTS as a citizen by intermarriage of the Cherokee Nation.

    SOLON H. ROBERTS, being first duly sworn, and being examined, testified as follows:

BY COMMISSION: What is your name?   A Solon Harrison Roberts.
Q How old are you?   A I am in my fifty-ninth year.
Q What is your post office address?   A Dutch Mills, Arkansas.
Q You are a white man, are you?   A Yes sir.
Q Have you heretofore made application to this Commission for enrollment as a citizen by intermarriage of the Cherokee Nation?   A Yes sir.
Q What is the name of your wife?   A Hester[sic] S. Roberts.
Q She is your present wife?   A Yes sir.
Q Is she living?   A Yes sir.
Q Is she a Cherokee by blood?   A Yes sir.
Q When were you and she married?   A In 1866, February 4th.
Q Were you married at that time under Cherokee law?   A No sir, under the state laws of Arkansas.
Q When did you come to the Cherokee Nation?   A In 1868, February.
Q Were you remarried according to the laws of the Cherokee Nation?
A I applied for a license and got it and was married by Judge Adair of Goingsnake District.
Q Have you filed your Cherokee marriage license with the Commission[sic]
A No sir.

Cherokee Intermarried White 1906
Volume VII

Q Did you exhibit it to the Commission?   A No sir, they said it was not necessary. My wife applied for me. I was sick with rheumatism.
Q Does your name appear upon the roll of 1880?   A Yes sir.
Q Have you and your wife lived together continuously since the date of your marriage?
A Yes sir.
Q Were you living together on the 1st day of September, 1902?
A Yes sir.
Q Have you resided in the Cherokee Nation continuously since 1868?
A Yes sir.
Q Has your wife also?   A Yes sir.
Q Were you ever married before you married your present wife?   A No sir.
Q Was she ever married before she married you?   A No sir.
Q You are her first husband and she is your first wife?   A Yes sir.
Q You made application for the enrollment of how many children?   [sic] One.
Q Is that child living now?   A Yes sir.

      This testimony will be filed with and made a part of the record in the matter of the application for the enrollment of Solon H. Roberts as a citizen by intermarriage of the Cherokee Nation, Cherokee straight card field No. 686.

Wm. Hutchinson, being first duly sworn, states that as stenographer to the Commission to the Five Civilized Tribes he correctly recorded the testimony and proceedings in this case, and the foregoing is a true and complete transcript of the stenographic notes thereof.

Wm Hutchinson

Subscribed and sworn to before me this 14th day of October, 1902.

John O Rosson
Notary Public.

Cherokee Intermarried White 1906
Volume VII

DEPARTMENT OF THE INTERIOR
COMMISSIONER TO THE FIVE CIVILIZED TRIBES
MUSKOGEE, IND. TER.
JAN. 3, 1907

CHEROKEE 686.

IN THE MATTER OF THE APPLICATION FOR THE ENROLLMENT OF SOLON H. ROBERTS AS A CITIZEN BY INTERMARRIAGE OF THE CHEROKEE NATION.

SOLON H. ROBERTS BEING FIRST DULY SWORN BY B. P. RASMUS, A NOTARY PUBLIC TESTIFIED AS FOLLOWS:

EXAMINATION BY THE COMMISSIONER:

Q What is your name.[sic] A Solon H. Roberts.
Q What is your age. A Sixty three in my sixty fourth year
Q What is your post office address? A Dutch Mills, Washington County, Arkansas.
Q Are you an applicant for enrollment as a citizen by intermarriage of the Cherokee Nation. A Yes sir.
Q You have no Cherokee blood. A No sir.
Q Your only claim to a right to enrollment as a citizen of the Cherokee Nation is by virtue of your marriage to a citizen by blood of the nation is it. A Yes sir.
Q What is the name of the citizen thru whom you claim the right to enrollment. A Her maiden name was Esther S. Bigsby.
Q Was she a recognized citizen of the Cherokee Nation at the time you married her.
A She was a refugee from the war to Fayetteville Arkansas at the latter end of the war; I got acquainted with her and married her under the laws of Arkansas February 4th, '66, February, I don't remember the day of the month but it was February '68 we removed to the Cherokee Nation; in May of that year I applied to the clerk with a petition of the citizens of the neighborhood for a license which was issued, and I disremember the date of the marriage; J. T. Adair, and John Thornton; John Thomas Adair, Supreme Judge of the Nation at that time performed the ceremony; I got the certificate of marriage and turned it over to the clerk.
Q What district was that license issued from. A It was issued in Goingsnake District.
Q And you were married in Goingsnake District. A Yes sir
Q Were you ever married prior to your marriage to her? A No sir.
Q Was she ever married prior to her marriage to you? A No sir.
Q Is your wife living at this time. A Yes, when I left home
Q Have you and she continuously lived in the Cherokee Nation as man and wife since your marriage. A Yes sir.

Cherokee Intermarried White 1906
Volume VII

The applicant Solon H. Roberts is identified on the Cherokee authenticated tribal roll of 1880 Goingsnake District, No. 1402; his wife Esther S. Roberts is included in the approved partial roll of citizens by blood of the Cherokee Nation opposite No. 22646.

Q Have you your marriage license and certificate with you
A No sir I haven't them with me; they were lost.
Q You have no documentary evidence of your marriage.
A No sir I have not.
Q Are there any persons living who were witnesses to your marriage?
A Mrs. Penelope, Adair's wife is living; also Mrs. Nanie Bigbee is living and Miss Jennie Bigbee my sisterinlaw[sic]; those three parties were present when I was married if I'm not mistaken; I don't think I am.
Q They are all living. A Yes sir.

ooOoo

Clara Mitchell Wood being first duly sworn upon her oath states that as stenographer to the Commissioner to the Five Civilized Tribes she reported the above and foregoing proceedings and that this is a correct transcript of her stenographic notes.

Clara Mitchell Wood

Subscribed and sworn to before me this 3rd day of January 1907

B.P. Rasmus
Notary Public.

DEPARTMENT OF THE INTERIOR,
COMMISSIONER TO THE FIVE CIVILIZED TRIBES.
STILWELL, I. T., FEBRUARY 9, 1907.

In the matter of the application for the enrollment of SOLON ROBERTS as a citizen by intermarriage of the Cherokee Nation.

(Below was originally a handwritten Affidavit on the microfilm and is typed as given.)

Penelope Adair being first duly sworn by William R. Bass a Notary Public testified as follows:

What is your full name? A - Penelope Adair. About how old are you Mrs. Adair? A - I will be eighty three years old the 12th day of next May. I was born in the

Cherokee Intermarried White 1906
Volume VII

year 1824. How long have you lived in the Indian Territory? A - Came here in 1839 from Tennessee Are you a Cherokee by blood? A - Yes sir
Are you acquainted with Solon H. Roberts and his wife Ester S. Roberts? A - Yes sir.
How long have you known them? A - I have known both of them since 1868
Were they married at that time? A - Yes sir.
What was her maiden name? A - Ester S Bigby Do you know in what year they were married? A - I think they were married in 1868 in May How do you know that they were married in 1868? A - I was present and saw them married.
Who performed the marriage ceremony? A- My husband Judge Adair who was at that time Supreme judge of the Cherokee Nation
Was this marriage ceremony solemnized in accordance with Cherokee law and under a license issued by the Cherokee Nation? A - Yes sir
Have they resided in the Cherokee Nation continuously since their marriage?
A - Yes sir never lived any where else to my knowledge
Is Mrs Roberts a Cherokee by blood? A - Yes sir.

Charles B. Wilson, being first duly sworn, doth depose and say that the above and foregoing are the original questions propounded by him to, and the answers returned thereto by <u>Penelope Adair</u> the above name witness.

Charles B Wilson

Subscribed and sworn to before me this 11th day of February, 1907.

Walter W Chappell
Notary Public.

(Below was originally a handwritten Affidavit on the microfilm and is typed as given.)

Nancy Bigby being duly sworn by William R. Bass a Notary Public testified as follows

What is your name? A - Nancy Bigby but I am on the Cherokee Roll as Nannie J. Bigby. How old are you Mrs Bigby? A - I am fifty five years old Are you acquainted with Solon H Roberts and his wife Esther S Roberts? A - Yes sir.
How long have you known them? A - I have known them since they were married.
What year were they married? A - In 1868. What do you know about their marriage?

Cherokee Intermarried White 1906
Volume VII

A - I saw them married.   Who performed the marriage ceremony?   A - Judge Adair Was this marriage ceremony solemnized in accordance with Cherokee law and under a license issued by the Cherokee Nation?   A - I think it was.

Charles B. Wilson, being first duly sworn, doth depose and say that the above and foregoing are the original questions propounded by him to, and the answers returned thereto by <u>Nancy Bigby</u> the above named witness.

Charles B. Wilson

Subscribed and sworn to before me this 11th day of February, 1907.

Walter W. Chappell
Notary Public.

◇◇◇◇◇

CERTIFIED COPY.

Affidavit of Penelope Adair, endorsed by
Nannie J. Bigby, nee Williams.

Jan. 30, 1907

I Penelope Adair make the following Statement:

That I was preasant[sic] when Solon H. Roberts and his wife Ester S. Roberts, nee Bigby was married in the year of 1868 in my House in Going Snake Dist. Cherokee Nation by my Husband J. T. Adair who was at that time Supream[sic] Judge of the Cherokee Nation

(Signed)   Penelope Adair

Subscribed and sworn to before me this befor[sic] me this 31 day of Jan 1907.

(Signed)   Hugh M. Adair,
Notary Public.

(SEAL)

My term expires Nov. 21st, 1908
  THIRD TERM

Cherokee Intermarried White 1906
Volume VII

This certifies that the undersigned, being duly sworn, states that as stenographer to the Commission to the Five Civilized Tribes she made the above and foregoing copy and that the same is a full, true and correct copy of the original instrument now on file in this office.

Georgia Coberly
Stenographer.

Subscribed and sworn to before me this 14th day of February, 1907.

Walter W. Chappell
Notary Public

◇◇◇◇◇

E C M   Cherokee 686.

DEPARTMENT OF THE INTERIOR,

COMMISSIONER TO THE FIVE CIVILIZED TRIBES.

In the matter of the application for the enrollment of SOLON H. ROBERTS as a citizen by intermarriage of the Cherokee Nation.

D E C I S I O N

THE RECORDS OF THIS OFFICE SHOW: That at Stillwell[sic], Indian Territory, July 26, 1900 application was received by the Commission to the Five Civilized Tribes for the enrollment of Solon H. Roberts as a citizen by intermarriage of the Cherokee Nation. Further proceedings in the matter of said application were had at Tahlequah, Indian Territory, October 8, 1902, Muskogee, Indian Territory, January 3, 1907 and at Stillwell[sic], Indian Territory, February 9, 1907.

THE EVIDENCE IN THIS CASE SHOWS: That the applicant herein, Solon H. Roberts, a white man, was married in accordance with Cherokee law in 1868 to one Esther A[sic]. Roberts, nee Bigby, who was at the time of said marriage a recognized citizen by blood of the Cherokee Nation, who is identified on the Cherokee authenticated tribal roll of 1880, Going Snake District, No. 1403 as a native Cherokee, and whose name is included on the approved partial roll of citizens by blood of the Cherokee Nation opposite No. 22646. It is further shown that from the time of said marriage the said Solon H. Roberts and Esther A. Roberts resided together as husband and wife and continuously lived in the Cherokee Nation up to and including September 1, 1902. Said applicant is identified on the Cherokee authenticated tribal roll of 1880 and the Cherokee census roll of 1896 as an intermarried citizen of the Cherokee Nation.

IT IS, THEREFORE, ORDERED AND ADJUDGED: That in accordance with the decision of the Supreme Court of the United States, dated November 5, 1906 in the cases

Cherokee Intermarried White 1906
Volume VII

of Daniel Red Bird, et al. vs. the United States, Nos. 125, 126, 127, and 128, the said applicant, Solon H. Roberts, is entitled, under the provisions of Section Twenty-one of the Act of Congress approved June 28, 1898)30 Stats. 495)[sic], to enrollment as a citizen by intermarriage of the Cherokee Nation, and his application for enrollment as such is accordingly granted.

Tams Bixby
Commissioner.

Dated at Muskogee, Indian Territory,
this   FEB 23 1907

◇◇◇◇◇

Cherokee 686   **COPY**

Muskogee, Indian Territory, February 23, 1907.

W. W. Hastings,
    Attorney for the Cherokee Nation,
        Muskogee, Indian Territory.

Dear Sir:

There is enclosed herewith a copy of the decision of the Commissioner to the Five Civilized Tribes, dated February 23, 1907, granting the application for the enrollment of Solon H. Roberts as a citizen by intermarriage of the Cherokee Nation.

Respectfully,

SIGNED Tams Bixby
Commissioner.

Encl. A-16
    RA

◇◇◇◇◇

Cherokee Intermarried White 1906
Volume VII

Cherokee 686

Muskogee, Indian Territory, February 23, 1907.

The Commissioner to the Five Civilized Tribes,
  Muskogee, Indian Territory.

Sir:

Receipt is acknowledged of the testimony and of your decision, enrolling Solon H. Roberts as a citizen by intermarriage of the Cherokee Nation. Time for protesting said decision is waived, and I consent that said person may be placed upon the schedule immediately.

Respectfully,
W. W. Hastings
Attorney for the Cherokee Nation.

◇◇◇◇◇

Cherokee 686   **COPY**

Muskogee, Indian Territory, February 23, 1907.

Solon H. Roberts,
  Dutch Mills, Arkansas.

Dear Sir:

There is enclosed herewith a copy of the decision of the Commissioner to the Five Civilized Tribes, dated February 23, 1907, granting the application for your enrollment as a citizen by intermarriage of the Cherokee Nation.

You will be advised when your name has been placed upon a schedule of citizens of the Cherokee Nation and approved by the Secretary of the Interior.

Respectfully,

SIGNED *Jams Bixby*
Commissioner.

Encl. A-17
  RA

Cher IW 213

Cherokee Intermarried White 1906
Volume VII

◇◇◇◇◇

DEPARTMENT OF THE INTERIOR

COMMISSIONER TO THE FIVE CIVILIZED TRIBES

In the matter of the application for the enrollment of

JERRY H. VESTAL

As a citizen by intermarriage of the Cherokee Nation.

Cherokee 1652

◇◇◇◇◇

Statement of Applicant Taken Under Oath.

CHEROKEE BY BLOOD AND ADOPTION.

(62)   Date **AUG 20 1900**   1900.
Name **Jerry H. Vestal**   **Webbers Falls I.T.**
District **Canadian**   Year **1880**   Page **52**   No. **1426**
Citizen by blood   Mother's citizenship
Intermarried citizen **Yes**
Married under what law   Date of marriage
License   Certificate
Wife's name
District   Year   Page   No.
Citizen by blood   Mother's citizenship
Intermarried citizen
Married under what law   Date of marriage
License   Certificate

    Names of Children:

	Dist.	Year	Page	No.	Age
	Dist.	Year	Page	No.	Age
	Dist.	Year	Page	No.	Age
	Dist.	Year	Page	No.	Age
	Dist.	Year	Page	No.	Age

on 1880 roll as J.H. Vestal

                                                       #1652

Cherokee Intermarried White 1906
Volume VII

Cher-1652.

DEPARTMENT OF THE INTERIOR.
Commission to the Five Civilized Tribes.
Muskogee, I.T., October 29, 1902.

In the matter of the application of Jerry H. Vestal for enrollment as a citizen by intermarriage of the Cherokee Nation.

James J. Severs, called as a witness, and being first duly sworn and examined by the Commission, testified as follows:

Q What is your name?   A James J. Severs.
Q What is your postoffice address?   A Webbers Falls, I.T.
Q How old are you?   A Fifty years.
Q Are you acquainted with Jerry H. Vestal?   A Yes sir.
Q You appear for the purpose of giving testimony in the matter of the application of Jerry H. Vestal for enrollment as an intermarried citizen?
A Yes, I have a certificate here.
Q Why does he not appear in person?   A He is not able to get here.
Q He is physically unable to come?   A Yes, here is a certificate from the doctor.

> Applicant presents to the Commission a certificate from H. B. Burns, M.D., certifying that the applicant John[sic] H. Vestal is physically unable to come to Muskogee at this time, which certificate is dated October 27, 1902, and is sworn to before Justice of the Peace Buchannan the same day. The same is filed herewith and the testimony of this witness will be taken and submitted before the Commission.

Q Are you a citizen of the Cherokee nation?   A Yes sir.
Q How long have you known Mr. Vestal?   A Ever since January, 1873.
Q All the time since 1873?   [sic] Yes sir.
Q Where has Mr. Vestal lived during that time, since you have known him?
A In Canadian District, near Webbers Falls.
Q He is a white man, is he?   A Yes sir.
Q And an applicant for enrollment as a citizen of the Cherokee nation, by intermarriage?   A Yes sir.
Q What is his wife's name?   A Eliza Jane I believe.
Q Was she a Cherokee citizen by blood?   A Yes sir.
Q Is she living or dead?   A She is dead.
Q Do you know about how long she has been dead?   A She died along about the first day of July, 1881, I think. I don't know just the day of the month.
Q Mr. Vestal and she were married prior to the making of the 1880 roll?
A Yes, sometime. I don't know just when.

Cherokee Intermarried White 1906
Volume VII

Q And he appears on the 1880 roll with her as her husband? A Yes, they was both enrolled.
Q Did Mr. Vestal and his wife live together from the time you knew them in 1873 up to the date of her death, as husband and wife? A Yes sir.
Q Never were separated? A No sir.
Q Since her death has Mr. Vestal married again? A No, he has never been married.
Q You have lived right in the neighborhood with him all the time and know that to be a fact? A Yes, I can give you my reasons more fully which would explain to you if you like.
Q Well, now, you say Mr. Vestal has never married since the death of his Cherokee wife in 1881? A Yes.
Q He was still a widower and a single man on the first day of September, 1902, was he? A Yes, and is yet. I was at his home yesterday.
Q Has he lived in the Cherokee nation all the time since 1880 up to the present time?
A Yes sir.
Q Never has lived out of the Cherokee nation since the? A No, if you like I can give you my means of being acquainted with him and knowing this much about him.
Q No, I don't care for that. You know of your own knowledge that he has lived in the Cherokee nation since 1880 up to the present time? A Yes
Q Never lived anywhere else? A No, we both lived in the same neighborhood.
Q This testimony will be submitted to the full Commission and in case it is not deemed sufficient by them Mr. Vestal will be further notified.

----o----

Frances R. Lane upon oath states that as stenographer to the Commissioner to the Five Civilized Tribes she correctly recorded the testimony in the above entitled cause, and that the foregoing is an accurate transcript of her stenographic notes thereof.

Frances R. Lane

Subscribed and sworn to before me this November 7th, 1902.

BC Jones
Notary Public.

Cherokee Intermarried White 1906
Volume VII

H. B. BURNS, M. D.
J. I. BAILEY, M. D.

BURNS & BAILEY,
SPECIALISTS ON DRUG AND LIQUOR HABITS.

WEBBERS FALLS, I.T. Oct 27   190 2

To Whom it May Concern -

This is to certify that I have examined Jerry H. Vestal and know that he is unable to go to Muscogee[sic] or even leave his home.

H. B. Burns M.D.

Subscribed and sworn to before me this 27" day of October 1902

J.C. Buchanan
Notary Public.

◇◇◇◇◇

F. R.   Cherokee 1652.

DEPARTMENT OF THE INTERIOR,
COMMISSIONER TO THE FIVE CIVILIZED TRIBES.
Muskogee, Indian Territory, January 15, 1907.

In the matter of the application for the enrollment of Jerry H. Vestol[sic] as a citizen by intermarriage of the Cherokee Nation.

APPEARANCES:
Tom Owen, Attorney for applicant.
Cherokee Nation represented by
W. W. Hastings, Attorney.

James Neale being first duly sworn by Chas. E. Webster, Notary Public, testified as follows:

ON BEHALF OF COMMISSIONER.

Q What is your name?   A James Neale.
Q What is your age?   A 75 in February.
Q What is your post office address?
A McLain, Indian Territory.
Q In whose behalf do you appear here?
A In behalf of Jerry Vestol.

Cherokee Intermarried White 1906
Volume VII

Q Jerry Vestol claims the right to enrollment as a citizen by intermarriage of the Cherokee Nation?
A That's the way I understand it.
Q James H. Vestol is not living at this time?
A No sir.
Q When did he die?
A I don't remember the date.
Q Do you know about when it was?
A About a year ago.
Q His claim to the right to enrollment was by virtue of his marriage to a citizen of the Cherokee Nation?
A Yes sir.
Q Do you know the name of the citizen through whom he claimed such right?
A I do.
Q Through whom?
A Eliza J. Vestol after she was married; Neale was her maiden name.
Q When was Jerry H. Vestol married to Eliza J. Neale?
A To the best of my knowledge, about 1856 or 1857.
Q Where were they married?   A In Alabama.
Q When did they remove to the Cherokee Nation?
A I am not certain about that. I was not here then.
Q Was it before the war or after the war?
A Before the war.
Q Do you know whether or not Jerry H. Vestol and Eliza J. Neale upon their removal to the Cherokee Nation, were married in accordance to the laws of the Cherokee Nation?
A I don't know anything about that.
Q Do you know when Eliza J. Neale was admitted to citizenship in the Cherokee Nation?
A I can't swear to that either.
Q Is Eliza J. Neale who became Mrs. J. H. Vestol, living?
A She is not.
Q When did she die?
A About 1881; to the best of my recollection in July.
Q Did Jerry H. Vestol marry after that time?
A Not that I have any knowledge of.
Q Was Jerry H. Vestol married previous to his marriage to Eliza J. Neale?
A Not that I have any knowledge of.
Q Was Eliza J. Neale married previous to her marriage to Jerry H. Vestol?
A No sir.
Q They removed to the Cherokee Nation just before the war?
A Before the war; it might have been 3 or 4 years; I have no definite idea about that.
Q Did Jerry H. Vestol and Eliza J. Vestol reside together as husband and wife from the time of their removal to the Cherokee Nation until the time of her death in 1881?
A Yes sir.

Cherokee Intermarried White 1906
Volume VII

Q   They lived continuously in the Cherokee Nation all that time?
A   To the best of my knowledge they moved out once.
Q   When was that?
A   I can't be positive about that because I was not here.
Q   When did you come to this country?
A   In '53 the first time and in 1874 the second time.
Q   Do you know whether or not from 1874 until her death, they lived continuously in the Cherokee Nation?
A   Yes sir.
Q   And Jerry H. Vestol continued to reside in the Cherokee Nation until his death?
A   He did.
Q   Of your own knowledge, you have no information whatever as to whether or not they were married in accordance with Cherokee law when they came to the Cherokee country?
A   I have not.
Q   Was it understood that they had been married in accordance with such law? :
A   I didn't understand it that way.
Q   It was your understanding then that they had not been married according to the Cherokee law?
A   I just heard Vestol say that there was something he hadn't complied with and other parties said so too, but what that was, I don't know.
Q   Was Jerry H. Vestol recognized as an intermarried citizen of the Cherokee Nation the Nation; that is, was he permitted to vote?
A   Yes sir.
Q   When was the first time you remember he was permitted to vote?
A   I have no definite recollection about that. I don't recollect about the first election that was held after I got back.

BY MR. HASTINGS.

Q   Did you say that you heard Mr. Vestol say there was some part of the Cherokee law he didn't comply with?
A   I heard him talking about a certain certificate and I understood from his conversation that he didn't have it.
Q   Did you understand from him through that he had procured a license and married in accordance with Cherokee law after he came to this country.
A   No, I never heard him say as to that.
Q   What you want to testify to, then, is that since you came to the Cherokee Nation in '74, you know that he and his wife were living together, recognized as husband and wife, and continued to live together until her death,- until about July, '81?
A   Yes, I can testify positively as to that.
Q   Did you live back in Alabama?
A   Born and raised in Alabama. I left there in 1853.
Q   Where did you go?
A   I came out to the Cherokee Nation and stayed about 10 months and then went to California.

Cherokee Intermarried White 1906
Volume VII

Q   Then you were in California when he married?
A   Yes.

BY MR. OWEN.

Q   What relation are you to Mrs. Vestol?
A   Full brother.
Q   Was she older or younger than you?
A   Six years younger than me.
Q   Where did you live when you came to the Cherokee Nation in 1874?
A   I lived about one or two months at Webber's Falls with Vestol; then I moved out on the prairie.
Q   Where did Vestol and your sister live?
A   Webber's Falls bottoms; about 8 or 10 miles.
Q   Did you ever her Vestol say whether or not he was married after he came here to the Cherokee Nation?
A   I never heard him say he was.
Q   Did you ever hear him say he was not?
A   To the best of my knowledge, I never heard him say he was or was not.
Q   What certificate was it he was talking about?
A   The marriage certificate as I understand it.
Q   He had failed to get a marriage certificate?
A   Yes sir.
Q   A certificate of what marriage?
A   To Cherokees as I understand it; I heard that white persons marrying Cherokees outside of the Cherokee Nation,- the law required them to marry again after they got in the Cherokee Nation; and I never heard him say that he did.
Q   What certificate was it he did not have?
A   Pertaining, I suppose, to a marriage certificate; that is the way I understood it.
Q   Were you readmitted after you came back in '74?
A   Yes sir.
Q   When?
A   Between '75 and '80.
Q   Do you know whether your sister, Mrs. Vestol, was re-admitted?
A   To the best of my knowledge she was.
Q   Do you know whether she was admitted before or after the war?
A   After the war.

John Lane being first duly sworn by Chas. E. Webster, Notary Public, testified as follows:

ON BEHALF OF COMMISSIONER.

Q   What is your name?   A   John Lane.
Q   What is your age?   A   54.

Cherokee Intermarried White 1906
Volume VII

Q   What is your post office address?
A   Webber's Falls.
Q   You appear here for the purpose of giving testimony relative to the right to enrollment of Jerry H. Vestol as a citizen by intermarriage of the Cherokee Nation?
A   Yes sir.
Q   When did you first know Jerry H. Vestol?
A   About '73.
Q   Was he married at that time?
A   Yes sir; supposed to be.
Q   Do you know to whom he was married?
A   To one of Mr. Neale's sisters.
Q   Do you know whether or not his wife was recognized as a citizen by blood of the Cherokee Nation at the time you first knew her?
A   Yes sir; claimed to be.
Q   Do you know whether or not Jerry H. Vestol and his wife were ever married in accordance with the Cherokee law; that is, under a license of the Cherokee Nation?
A   No sir; I don't.
Q   When you first knew them in 1873, was it the understanding that they had been married in accordance with such license?
A   Well, I heard Mr. Vestol say they had been married in the Cherokee Nation.
Q   Did you hear him say when?   A   No sir; I didn't.
Q   Or where?
A   He said it was at Chief John Ross' house up above Tahlequah.
Q   Was that when you first knew him in 1873 that you heard him make those statements?
A   No sir; it was along after that; about '74 or '75. I wasn't well acquainted with him when he first came in there.
Q   Is Jerry H. Vestol living at this time?
A   No sir.
Q   When did he die?
A   A little over a year ago.
Q   When did his wife die?
A   She has been dead about 24 or 25 years.
Q   From the time you first knew Jerry H. Vestol and his wife in the Cherokee Nation in 1873, did they reside together as husband and wife and live continuously in the Cherokee Nation up until her death?
A   Yes sir.
Q   Since her death, has Jerry H. Vestol re-married?
A   Not that I know of.
Q   Has he continued to reside in the Cherokee Nation since her death?
A   Yes sir; up until his death.

BY MR. OWEN.

Q   Do you know whether Vestol was recognized as a citizen from the time you knew him in '73?

Cherokee Intermarried White 1906
Volume VII

A   His wife was and also he was; he first moved on the Drew farm down there and Drew wanted to sell him the farm and he wouldn't by a place until his wife was re-admitted.
Q   Do you know if she was re-admitted?
A   I suppose she was. He bought the place I was living on.
Q   Do you know whether he ever sat as a juror in any cases down there in the Cherokee courts?
A   Yes sir.
Q   Did he hold any office in the Cherokee Government?
A   No sir; not any more than serving as juryman and grand juryman. He was allowed to vote and in '75, the paid him what they called bread money.
Q   How do you know that?
A   He told me they did and I know what he bought; he said he bought a cow with the money.
Q   Did you ever see him acting as a juror in the Cherokee Nation?
A   Yes sir.
Q   You know then that he was recognized as a citizen of the Cherokee Nation?
A   Yes sir; always had been.
Q   What relation was Mrs. Vestol to you?
A   None at all that I know of.
Q   Was he any relation to you?
A   No sir; if he was I didn't know it.
Q   When did they move into the Cherokee Nation?
A   In '73.
Q   Did they ever move out of the Cherokee Nation after that?
A   No sir.
Q   They have lived right there in the vicinity of Webber's Falls?
A   Yes sir.
Q   After Mrs. Vestol died, did the old man re-marry before he died?
A   No sir; if he did, I don't know it.
Q   Did you continue to live there as a neighbor to him?
A   Yes sir.
Q   You would have known it if he had married?
A   Yes sir.

ON BEHALF OF COMMISSIONER.

Q   You states just now that Jerry H. Vestol purchased a farm from you and it was your understanding that he wouldn't purchase it until his wife was re-admitted to citizenship?
A   Drew tried to sell him a farm. I had rented a place and lived on it two years, '74 and '75; it belonged to Dr. Lindsey, and he bought it in '75.

BY MR. OWEN.
Q   Did you ever hear Mr. or Mrs. Vestol say anything about getting married in the Cherokee Nation?

Cherokee Intermarried White 1906
Volume VII

A   No sir.

ON BEHALF OF COMMISSIONER.

Q   You having been a neighbor of them, it was always understood that they had been married in the Cherokee Nation?
A   Yes sir; he always told me he had been married at Chief Ross'.

     J. J. Sevier being first duly sworn by Chas. E. Webster, Notary Public, testified as follows:

ON BEHALF OF COMMISSIONER:

Q   What is your name?   A   J. J. Sevier.
Q   What is your age?   A   54.
Q   What is your post office address?
A   Webber's Falls.
Q   You appear here to give testimony relative to the right to enrollment of Jerry H. Vestol, a citizen by intermarriage of the Cherokee Nation?
A   Yes sir.
Q   When did you first know Jerry H. Vestol?
A   I first got acquainted with him in January, 1873, but had known of him a long time before that.
Q   He was a married man in 1873?   A   Yes sir.
Q   You knew his wife?   A   Yes sir.
Q   Do you know whether or not they had been married under the laws of the Cherokee Nation?
A   Nothing only what he told himself.
Q   What statements did he make to you regarding any Cherokee Marriage?
A   He told me the first marriage was in 1857 under the laws of Alabama and they afterwards came to the Nation and they went up near Tahlequah and while there, Chief Ross advised him he had better marry again under Cherokee law, and he did so.
Q   Do you know about the date of that marriage under the Cherokee law?
A   Nothing only he said 1857.
Q   Was it prior to the war?   A   Yes sir.
Q   From the time when you first knew them personally in 1873, was it the understanding that they had been married in accordance with the Cherokee law?
A   Well, from what he said about it; yes sir.
Q   They resided together as husband and wife until her death?
A   Yes sir.
Q   And Mr. Vestol did not re-marry after that time?
A   No sir; I think not.
Q   He lived continuously all that time in the Cherokee Nation?
A   Yes sir.

Cherokee Intermarried White 1906
Volume VII

BY MR. OWEN.

Q Do you know whether he ever acted as a juror in Cherokee courts?
A Yes sir; he did.
Q He was generally recognized as a citizen?
A Yes sir; he served both as grand juror and petit juror. I had him in my courts there.
Q What office did you hold?
A District Attorney; Cherokee Court.
Q Do you know when Mrs. Vestol was re-admitted to citizenship?
A It seems to me it was '75; either '74 or '75.
Q How do you fix that date?
A I went off to school in September, '75, to Fayetteville, Arkansas, and after father went to Tahlequah, Indian Territory he was admitted to council and had Mrs. Vestol's case; and he sent the paper to me and the proceedings of the Council were published every week and I noticed Mrs. Vestol's name among those admitted.
Q Was she any relation of yours?
A First cousin.
Q Your recollection is that it was in the fall of '75?
A Yes sir; that's my recollection.
Q Might you be mistaken about that and it was '74?
A Well, I think not; I don't know though; of course, I could be mistaken.

  Applicant presents in evidence certificate of A. B. Cunningham, Executive Secretary Cherokee Nation, dated January 11, 1907, showing in the criminal records of the Canadian District, 1868 to 1875, that Jerry Vestol was one of the jurors in the case of Cherokee Nation vs. George Simmons, at a special term held January 4, 1875.

  The applicant is identified on the Cherokee authenticated tribal roll of 1880, Canadian District, opposite No. 1426, and on the 1896 roll opposite No. 293.

  The undersigned being first duly sworn states that as stenographer to the Commission to the Five Civilized Tribes. she recorded the testimony taken in this case and that the foregoing is a full, true and correct transcript of her stenographic notes thereof.

                  Myrtle Hill

Subscribed and sworn to before me this the 21st day of January, 1907.

                  John E. Tidwell
                  Notary Public.

Cherokee Intermarried White 1906
Volume VII

AN Act Granting Certain Persons therein Named Cherokee Citizenship.

Be It Enacted by the National Council:-

That the following named persons be and they are admitted to Cherokee Citizenship: John Jordan and wife and Children, J.P. Thompson, L. Thompson, Jessie Thompson, W. W. Thompson, W.J. McMaking, wife and child, James Glazier, Sarah McUhel, Joseph Gaylor, and family and J. H. Vestal and wife; Provided, That this act shall not take effect until the before named persons, shall remove into the Cherokee Nation as citizens thereof.

L.B.Bell,　　　　　　　　　　　　William Wilson,
Clerk of Senate.　　　　　　　　　President of Senate.

Concurred in

Geo. O. Sanders,　　　　　　　　Jno. R. Duval,
Clerk of Council.　　　　　　　　Speaker of Council,

Approved:
Dec. 5th, 1874.

Will P. Ross.

Executive Department,

Cherokee Nation,

Tahlequah, Indian Territory.

I, A. B. Cunningham, Executive Secretary of the Cherokee Nation, do hereby certify that the above and foregoing is a true and correct copy of an act of the National Council, entitled,

"An act granting certain persons therein named Cherokee Citizenship."

As of record in this office.

Said Act being approved by the Principal Chief and recorded on page 215 of "Record of Laws of Cherokee Nation, 1872, 1873, and 1874,".

Cherokee Intermarried White 1906
Volume VII

In testimony whereof, I haveunto set my hand and affix the seal of the Cherokee Nation, this the 16th day of January, 1907.

        A.B. Cunningham
        Executive Secretary,
        Cherokee Nation.

◇◇◇◇◇

(The below typed as given.)

W. C. ROGERS, PRINCIPAL CHIEF
D. M. FAULKNER, ASSISTANT CHIEF
W. W. HASTINGS, NATIONAL ATTORNEY
J. H. COVEL, INTERPRETER

A. B. CUNNINGHAM, EXECUTIVE SECRETARY
C. J. HARRIS, ASSISTANT SECRETARY
W. H. WALKER, ASSISTANT SECRETARY

CHEROKEE NATION
TAHLEQUAH, INDIAN TERRITORY

I, hereby certify that the "Record of Permits issued, for Canadian District: show that Jery Vestal procured a permit for L.H.Olliver for the term of four months, beginning March,I,and ending July,Ist,I895.

 I further certify that the record that the "Criminal record of Canadian District, I868to I875, shows Jerry Vestal was one of the jurors in the case of the Cherokee Nation, vs. George Simmons, charged with murder, before the Circuit Court in and for Canadian District,at a special term held January--4-the, I875, and case continued until January,25th,I875.

 I further certify that both of the above mentioned records of Canadian District, Cherokee Nation, were by an Act of the Cherokee National Council,transferred to and made a part of the records of this department, and that the same is in my custody.

 In testimony whereof, I hereunto set may hand and affix the seal of the Cherokee Nation, this the IIth,day of January,I907.

        A.B. Cunningham
        Executive Secretary.

◇◇◇◇◇

Cherokee Intermarried White 1906
Volume VII

DEPARTMENT OF THE INTERIOR,
COMMISSIONER TO THE FIVE CIVILIZED TRIBES.

F.R.   Cherokee 1652.

Muskogee, I.T., January 31, 1907.

In the matter of the application for the enrollment of Jerry H. Vestol as a citizen by intermarriage of the Cherokee Nation.

Applicant represented by Tom. Owen.

W. H. Barker, being first duly sworn by Frances R. Lane, a Notary Public for the Western District of Indian Territory, testified as follows:

By Mr. Owen:
Q   Your name is W. H. Barker?   A   Yes sir.
Q   Your residence is Muskogee?   A   Yes sir.
Q   What is your age?   A   Fifty-six.
Q   Are you a citizen of the Cherokee Nation?   A   Yes sir.
Q   Have you held any official position under Cherokee government?
A   Yes sir.
Q   What?   A   Well, I was a member of the Cherokee Council and Judge of the Southern Judicial Circuit.
Q   What part of the Cherokee Nation was included in your circuit while you were judge?   A   Canadian District.
Q   Did you know a many by the name of Jerry H. Vestol?   A   Yes sir.
Q   Where did he reside?   A   Webbers Falls.
Q   Was he a recognized citizen of the Cherokee nation?   A   Yes sir.
Q   To what extent did you have an acquaintance over the Cherokee nation with the citizens?   What I mean, were you pretty generally acquainted all over the nation?   A   I was pretty generally acquainted all over the Cherokee Nation, that is, among the people.
Q   Did you know any other Vestol in the Cherokee nation except the one who resided near Webbers Falls?   A   No, I never did.
Q   How many terms were you in the council?   A   I was speaker of the house two years; I was in, was re-elected to the Cherokee council, Cherokee National Council.
Q   What district were you elected from?   A   Canadian District.
Q   This man Vestol lived in your district did he?   A   Yes sir.
Q   Did you know any more than this one man by that name that lived in that district?
A   No, I didn't know any other one.
Q   Were you acquainted with his wife?   A   No, I was not.

Frances R. Lane upon oath states that as stenographer to the Commissioner to the Five Civilized Tribes she reported the testimony in the above entitled case and that the foregoing is an accurate transcript of her stenographic notes thereof.

Frances R Lane

Cherokee Intermarried White 1906
Volume VII

Subscribed and sworn to before me this January 31, 1907.

Edward Merrick
Notary Public.

◇◇◇◇◇

UNITED STATES OF AMERICA.)
    WESTERN DISTRICT   )
    INDIAN TERRITORY.   )

IN RE APPLICATION OF JERRY H VESTAL FOR ENROLLMENT AS AN ADOPTED CITIZEN OF THE CHEROKEE NATION.
AFFIDAVIT OF FRANKLIN GRITTS.

Franklin Gritts having been first duly sworn upon oath states that he is 73 or 74 years of age, he is not certain which; that his residence and Post Office is Gritts Indian Territory; that he is almost a full blood Chereokee[sic] citizen and is enrolled as such or full blood by the Commissioner to the Five Civilized Tribes; that during the year 1874 he was a member of the Cherokee Council as one of the Councilmen from the Canadian District of the Cherokee Nation; that while serving in such capacity as Councilman that Jerry H. Vestal and wife were re-admitted by the Council as shown by the records thereof, and that he has lived in the same neighborhood as the said Jerry H Vestal since 1873 or from the time the said Vestal moved into this district up to the time of his death, and knows that the act of the Council re-admitting Vestal and wife was re-admitting the said Jerry H Vestal and wife of Webbers Falls or the Canadian District; that to the best of his knowledge there has never been but the one Vestal made application for admission or been recognized as a citizen of the Cherokee Nation; that he served upon a jury with the said Jerry H Vestal in the George Simmons murder trial which was held in Webbers Falls during the latter part of 1875 or the first part of 1876. Further affiant saith not.

Witness to mark.

J. J. Sevier
  B F Burr

his
Franklin x Gritts
mark

Cherokee Intermarried White 1906
Volume VII

Subscribed and sworn to before me this 31st day of January 1907.

J C Buchanan
Notary Public

My Com Ex
6/29/10

◇◇◇◇◇

UNITED STATES OF AMERICA.)
    WESTERN DISTRICT   )
    INDIAN TERRITORY.   )

IN RE APPLICATION OF JERRY H VESTAL FOR ENROLLMENT AS AN ADOPTED CITIZEN OF THE CHEROKEE NATION.

STATEMENT OF J. J. SEVIER and B. F. BURR AS TO RELIABILITY OF FRANKLIN GRITTS.

J. J. Sevier and B. F. Burr each of lawful age having been first duly sworn upon oath state that they were present and saw Franklin Gritts make his mark to signature to statement made in reference to the application of Jerry H Vestal and that they believe from the best of their knowledge that the said statements are true and that the said Franklin Gritts is a resident of Gritts Indian Territory, a citizen of the Cherokee Nation and worthy of belief.

J J Sevier
B.F. Burr

Subscribed and sworn to before me this 31st day of January 1907.

J.C. Buchanan
Notary Public.

My Com. Ex
6/29/10

◇◇◇◇◇

Cherokee Intermarried White 1906
Volume VII

T.W.L.   Cherokee 1652

DEPARTMENT OF THE INTERIOR

COMMISSIONER TO THE FIVE CIVILIZED TRIBES

In the matter of the application for the enrollment of Jerry H. Vestal as a citizen by intermarriage of the Cherokee Nation.

DECISION

THE RECORDS OF THIS OFFICE SHOW: That at Fort Gibson, Indian Territory, August 20, 1900, application was received by the Commission to the Five Civilized Tribes for the enrollment of Jerry H. Vestal as a citizen by intermarriage of the Cherokee Nation. Further proceedings in the matter of said application were had at Muskogee, Indian Territory, October 29, 1902, January 15, 1907, and January 31, 1907.

THE EVIDENCE IN THIS CASE SHOWS: That the applicant herein, Jerry H. Vestal, a white man, was married in the State of Alabama, prior to November 1, 1875, to his wife, Eliza J. Vestal, since deceased, who is identified on the Cherokee authenticated tribal roll of 1880, Canadian District, No. 1427, as a native Cherokee, marked "Dead"; that the applicant herein, Jerry H. Vestal and his wife, Eliza J. Vestal, were admitted to citizenship in the Cherokee Nation on December 5, 1874, as "J. N. Vestal and wife", upon the condition that they remove to the Cherokee Nation; that said applicant and his said wife removed to the Cherokee Nation in 1874; that from the time of said marriage the said Jerry H Vestal and Eliza J. Vestal resided together as husband and wife, and continuously lived in the Cherokee Nation since the year 1874, until the death of said Eliza J. vestal which occurred in 1881; that after the death of said Eliza J. Vestal said Jerry H. Vestal remained unmarried and continuously lived in the Cherokee Nation up to and including September 1, 1902. Said applicant is identified on the Cherokee authenticated tribal roll of 1880 and the Cherokee census roll of 1896 as an intermarried citizen of the Cherokee Nation.

IT IS THEREFORE ORDERED AND ADJUDGED: That in accordance with the decision of the Supreme Court of the United States dated November 5, 1906, in the cases of Daniel Red Bird. et al., vs. the United States, Nos. 125, 126, 127, and 128, the said applicant, Jerry H. Vestal, is entitled, under the provisions of section 21, of the Act of Congress approved June 28, 1898 (30 Stats. 495), to enrollment as a citizen by intermarriage of the Cherokee Nation, and his application for enrollment as such is accordingly granted.

                                        Tams Bixby
                                                Commissioner.
Dated at Muskogee, Indian Territory,
this   FEB 21 1907

Cherokee Intermarried White 1906
Volume VII

Department of the Interior.
COMMISSIONER TO THE FIVE CIVILIZED TRIBES.

In the matter of the death of _____ a citizen of the _____ Nation, who formerly resided at or near _____, Ind. Ter., and died on the _____ day of _____, 1____

AFFIDAVIT OF RELATIVE.

I, _____, on oath state that I am _____ years of age and a citizen by _____, of the _____ Nation; that my postoffice address is _____, Ind. Ter.; that I am _____ of _____ who was a citizen, by _____, of the _____ Nation and that said _____ died on the _____ day of _____, 1____

WITNESSES TO MARK:

Subscribed and sworn to before me this _____ day of _____, 190___

_____ Notary Public.

AFFIDAVIT OF ACQUAINTANCE.

Western Dist.
Ind Ter

I, **H. L. Sanders**, on oath state that I am **37** years of age, and a citizen ~~by~~ _____ of the **U.S.** Nation; that my postoffice address is **Webbers Falls**, Ind. Ter.; that I was personally acquainted with **Jerry H. Vestal** who was a citizen, by **Intermarriage**, of the **Cherokee** Nation; and that said **Jerry H Vestal** died on the **18** day of **November**, **1905**

Cherokee Intermarried White 1906
Volume VII

H L Sanders

WITNESSES TO MARK:

{ _____

Subscribed and sworn to before me this **21st** day of **June**, 1907

Walter W Chappell
Notary Public.

◇◇◇◇◇

Department of the Interior.
COMMISSIONER TO THE FIVE CIVILIZED TRIBES.

In the matter of the death of **Jerry H Vestal**
a citizen of the **Cherokee** Nation, who formerly resided at or near
Webbers Falls, Ind. Ter., and died on the **18th** day of
November, **1905**

AFFIDAVIT OF RELATIVE.

{ _____

I, _____, on oath state that I am _____ years of age and a citizen by _____, of the _____ Nation; that my postoffice address is _____, Ind. Ter.; that I am _____ of _____ who was a citizen, by _____, of the _____ Nation and that said _____ died on the _____ day of _____, 1_____

WITNESSES TO MARK:

{ _____

Subscribed and sworn to before me this _____ day of _____, 190___

_____
Notary Public.

Cherokee Intermarried White 1906
Volume VII

AFFIDAVIT OF ACQUAINTANCE.

Indian Territory }
Western District

I, **Mary Rogers**, on oath state that I am **56** years of age, and a citizen by **Blood** of the **Cherokee** Nation; that my postoffice address is **Webbers Falls**, Ind. Ter.; that I was personally acquainted with **Jerry H. Vestal** who was a citizen, by **adoption**, of the **Cherokee** Nation; and that said **Jerry H Vestal** died on the **18th** day of **November**, 1905

                                        her
                                   Mary x Rogers

WITNESSES TO MARK: mark

   HL Sanders
   Joe Shiffield

Subscribed and sworn to before me this **24** day of **June**, 1907

                                  JC Buchanan
                                        Notary Public.

◇◇◇◇◇

Cherokee 1652

                       Muskogee, Indian Territory, February 21, 1907.

W. W. Hastings,
    Attorney for the Cherokee Nation,
        Muskogee, Indian Territory.

Dear Sir:

    There is enclosed herewith a copy of the decision of the Commissioner to the Five Civilized Tribes, dated February 21, 1907, granting the application for the enrollment of Jerry H. Vestal as a citizen by intermarriage of the Cherokee Nation.

                           Respectfully,

Encl. H-57   Commissioner.
JMH

◇◇◇◇◇

Cherokee Intermarried White 1906
Volume VII

Cherokee 1652

Muskogee, Indian Territory, February 21, 1907.

The Commissioner to the Five Civilized Tribes,
    Muskogee, Indian Territory.

Sir:

    Receipt is acknowledged of the testimony and of your decision enrolling Jerry H. Vestal as a citizen by intermarriage of the Cherokee Nation. Time for protesting said decision is waived and I consent that said person may be placed upon the schedule immediately.

                  Respectfully,
                  W. W. Hastings
                  Attorney for the Cherokee Nation.

◇◇◇◇◇

Cherokee 1652

Muskogee, Indian Territory, February 21, 1907.

The Commissioner to the Five Civilized Tribes,
    Muskogee, Indian Territory.

Sir:

    Receipt is acknowledged of the testimony and of your decision enrolling Jerry H. Vestal as a citizen by intermarriage of the Cherokee Nation. Time for protesting said decision is waived, and I consent that said person may be placed upon the schedule immediately.

                  Respectfully,
                  W. W. Hastings
                  Attorney for Cherokee Nation.

◇◇◇◇◇

Cherokee Intermarried White 1906
Volume VII

Cherokee 1652

Muskogee, Indian Territory, February 21, 1907.

Administrator of Estate of Jerry H. Vestal,
  Webbers Falls, Indian Territory.

Dear Sir:

There is enclosed herewith a copy of the decision of the Commissioner to the Five Civilized Tribes, dated February 21, 1907, granting the application for the enrollment of Jerry H. Vestal as a citizen by intermarriage of the Cherokee Nation.

You will be advised when the name of said Jerry H. Vestal has been placed upon a schedule of citizens of the Cherokee Nation and approved by the Secretary of the Interior.

Respectfully,

Encl. H-58
JMH

Commissioner.

◇◇◇◇◇

Cherokee 1652

Muskogee, Indian Territory, February 21, 1907.

Thomas Owen,
  Attorney for Jerry H. Vestal,
    Muskogee, Indian Territory.

Dear Sir:

There is enclosed herewith a copy of the decision of the Commissioner to the Five Civilized Tribes, dated February 21, 1907, granting the application for the enrollment of Jerry H. Vestal as a citizen by intermarriage of the Cherokee Nation.

You have heretofore been furnished a copy of the record of proceedings had in this case.

Respectfully,

Encl. H-58 1/2
JMH

Commissioner.

Cherokee Intermarried White 1906
Volume VII

Cher IW 214

◇◇◇◇◇

DEPARTMENT OF THE INTERIOR.
COMMISSION TO THE FIVE CIVILIZED TRIBES.
FT/[sic] GIBSON, I. T., AUGUST 21st, 1900.

IN THE MATTER OF THE APPLICATION OF Wilson Cordrey, wife and son, for enrollment as citizens of the Cherokee Nation, and he being sworn by Commissioner, C. R. Breckinridge, testified as follows:

Q What is your name? A Wilson Cordrey.
Q What is your age? A Going on eighty-eight.
Q What is your Postoffice? A Braggs.
Q What is your District? A Illinois.
Q For whom do you make application for enrollment; yourself?
A Yes sir; myself, my wife, and one boy if you will allow me to enroll him.
Q Is he your son? A Yes sir.
Q Is he twenty one? A I expect he is.
Q Do you apply for yourself as a Cherokee by blood? A Yes sir.
Q Is your wife a Cherokee by blood? A My first wife was.
Q This wife? A she is a white woman.
Q How long have you lived in the Cherokee Nation? A All my life.
Q Have you lived in Illinois District all the time? A No sir.
Q How long have you lived in Illinois? A About twenty five years.
Q You are on the 1880 roll, are you? A Yes sir.
Q What is your wifes[sic] name? A Nancy Hall, before I married her.
Q When did you marry her? A 1863.
Q She is on the roll of 1880 with you then? A Yes sir.
Q What is your father's name? A Dave Cordrey.
Q Indian or white man? A Indian.
Q Dead, is he? A Yes sir.
Q How long ago? A During the year the Treaty of 1835 was made.
Q Your mother? A My mother, she has been dead
Q What is her name? A Charlotte Cordrey.
Q Was she a white woman or an Indian? A White woman.
Q Dead? A Yes sir.
Q What is the name of her mother? A She was a white woman.
Q What was her given name? A Susie, I think they called her.
Q White woman? A Yes sir.
Q Dead? A Yes sir.
(Applicant identified on the roll of 1880, Page 514, #353, Wilson Cordray[sic], Illinois District)
(Applicant's wife identified on the roll of 1880, Page 514, #354, Nancy Cordray, Illinois District)

Cherokee Intermarried White 1906
Volume VII

(Applicant identified on the roll of 1896, Page 851, #472, Wilson Cordrray[sic], Illinois District)
(Applicant's wife identified on the roll of 1896, Page 926, #35, Nancy Cordry[sic], Illinois District)

This applicant is duly identified on the rolls of 1880, and 1896; hiw[sic] wife is identified on both of the rolls; and he will be enrolled now as a Cherokee by blood; and she as a Cherokee by adoption.

R. R. Cravens, being sworn, states that as stenographer to the Commission to the Five Civilized Tribes, he reported the foregoing testimony and proceedings in full, and that same is a true, full and correct transcript of his stenographic notes in said case.

R R Cravens

Sworn to and subscribed before me this 28th day of August, 1900.

T B Needles
COMMISSIONER.

◇◇◇◇◇

Cherokee 1716.

DEPARTMENT OF THE INTERIOR,
COMMISSION TO THE FIVE CIVILIZED TRIBES.
Muskogee, I. T., October 17, 1902.

In the matter of the application of Wilson Cordray for the enrollment of himself as a citizen by blood of the Cherokee Nation, and for the enrollment of his wife, Nancy Cordray, as a citizen by intermarriage, of the Cherokee Nation.

SUPPLEMENTAL PROCEEDINGS.

NANCY CORDRAY, being sworn, testified as follows:

By the Commission,

Q Your name is Nancy Cordray, is it?   A Yes, sir. There's two Nancy Cordrays.
Q What's your husband's name?   A Wilson M. Cordray.
Q What's your age?   A I don't know my age exactly.
Q About seventy-seven?   A My brother said seventy-eight; he lived in the State.
Q What is your postoffice?   A Braggs.
Q Are you a white woman?   A Yes, sir, the Indians raised me.
Q Your name is on the roll of 1880?   A Yes, sir, it's on every roll since peace was made.
Q What's your husband's name?   A Wilson Cordray

Cherokee Intermarried White 1906
Volume VII

Q Was he your husband in 1880? A Yes, sir, when peace was made.
Q He the husband through whom you claim your citizenship? A Yes, he's at home.
Q You and your husband been living together since '80? A Yes, sir.
Q Never been separated? A Only when he goes off and stays among the children.
Q Does he just go off and visit the children? A He's just old and childish. He gets vexed and goes off and gets vexed and comes back.
Q Have you lived in the Cherokee Nation all your life? A Yes, sir, was never no where else in my life.
Q Is your husband living? A Yes, sir.

By Mr. Starr,

Q Living with you now? A Yes, he was when I left home.

      Retta Chick, being first duly sworn, states that, as stenographer to the Commission to the Five Civilized Tribes, she recorded the testimony and proceedings in the matter of the foregoing application, and that the above is a true and complete transcript of her stenographic notes thereof.

                                                                   Retta Chick

Subscribed and sworn to before me this 14th day of November, 1902.

                                                                   PG Reuter
                                                                    Notary Public.

◇◇◇◇◇

                                                                   Cherokee 1715.

DEPARTMENT OF THE INTERIOR,
COMMISSIONER TO THE FIVE CIVILIZED TRIBES.
MUSKOGEE, I. T., JANUARY 22, 1907.

      In the matter of the application for the enrollment of NANCY CORDRAY as a citizen by intermarriage of the Cherokee Nation.

      LOUISA ANDERSON, being first duly sworn by B. P. Rasmus, Notary Public, testified as follows on behalf of applicant:

ON BEHALF OF THE COMMISSIONER:

Q What is your name? A Louisa Anderson.
Q What is your age? A My mother said I was 46, I don't know whether I am that old or not, but she said I was.
Q What is your postoffice address? A Fort Gibson, Indian Territory

Cherokee Intermarried White 1906
Volume VII

Q You are a citizen by blood of the Cherokee Nation, are you?   A Yes sir.
Q You appear here today for the purpose of giving testimony relative to the right of Nancy Cordray to enrollment as a citizen by intermarriage of the Cherokee Nation, do you?   A Yes sir, I am a witness here to get it fixed up today if I can.
Q Is Nancy Cordray your mother?   A Yes sir.
Q She is a white woman is she?   A Yes sir, she has been in the Nation ever since she was 8 years old.
Q She had no Cherokee blood?   A No sir, not as I know of.
Q She only claimed the right to enrollment as a citizen of the Cherokee Nation by virtue of her marriage to a Cherokee by blood?   A That is all.
Q Is she living?   A No sir.
Q When did she die?   A The day before last Christmas.
Q What is the name of the citizen through whom she claims the right to enrollment?
A Wilson Cordray.
Q Is he your father?   A Yes sir.
Q When was Wilson Cordray married to Nancy Cordray?   A They were married before the war.
Q Do you know where they were married?   A No sir, I don't; Uncle Vanhoy is my witness, he said he would come in and tell where he was married at; I don't know, they were married before the war though.
Q Where were you living when you can first remember?   A I was living right where I am living now, in the bottom ever since I can remember.
Q Were you living when[sic] your father and mother when you can first remember?
A Yes sir.
Q From the time you can first remember did your father and mother reside together continuously as husband and wife until the death of your father in 1905?   A Yes sir.
Q And lived all the time in the Cherokee Nation?   A Yes sir, ever since I have been big enough to recollect.
Q Have you any evidence in a documentary character showing the marriage of Wilson Cordray to Nancy Cordray?   A No sir, I haven't got any papers or anything because his house got burned down twice and if they had any papers or anything they were burned up in the house. Just witnesses is all I can bring up.

The applicant, Nancy Cordray, is identified on the Cherokee Authenticated tribal roll of 1880; her husband, Wilson Cordray is identified on said roll at No. 353, and his name appears upon an approved partial roll of citizens by blood of the Cherokee Nation opposite No. 4552.

(Witness excused)

------------------------oOo------------------------

Cherokee Intermarried White 1906
Volume VII

    Geo. H. Lessley, being first duly sworn, states that as stenographer to the Commission to the Five Civilized Tribes, he reported the proceedings had in the above entitled cause, and that the above and foregoing is a true and correct transcript of his stenographic notes thereof.

                                            Geo. H. Lessley

Subscribed and sworn to before me this 22nd day of January, 1907.

                                              John E. Tidwell
                                              Notary Public.

E.C.M.   Cherokee 1715.

DEPARTMENT OF THE INTERIOR,
COMMISSIONER TO THE FIVE CIVILIZED TRIBES.
MUSKOGEE, I. T., FEBRUARY 9, 1907.

    SUPPLEMENTAL proceedings in the matter of the application for the enrollment of NANCY CORDRAY as a citizen by intermarriage of the Cherokee Nation.

CHARLES HARRIS, being first duly sworn by Walter W. Chappell, Notary Public, testified as follows:

ON BEHALF OF THE COMMISSIONER:

Q   What is your name?   A Charles Harris.
Q   What is your age?   A 65.
Q   What is your post office address?   A Muskogee, I.T.
Q   Mr. Harris, do you appear here today for the purpose of giving testimony relative to the right of Nancy Cordray to enrollment as a citizen by intermarriage of the Cherokee Nation? A Yes sir.
Q   Were you acquainted with Nancy Cordray?   A Yes sir.
Q   Were you acquainted with her husband, Wilson Cordray?   A Yes sir.
Q   Are they alive now?   A The wife is.
Q   How long have you known Nancy and Wilson Cordray?   A Since about '72 or '73.
Q   Were they married when you first knew them?   A Yes sir.
Q   Where were they living?   A In the Bottoms, over near Gibson.
Q   What District is that? A Illinois.
Q   Was Wilson Cordray a citizen by blood of the Cherokee Nation, at that time? A Yes sir.
Q   Do you know whether or not Wilson Cordray had ever been married prior to his marriage to Nancy Cordray? A Not that I know of.

Cherokee Intermarried White 1906
Volume VII

Q   Had Nancy Cordray been married prior to her marriage to Wilson Cordray?
    A Not that I ever heard of.
Q   You say they were living together as husband and wife when you first became acquainted with them?   A Yes sir.
Q   After that did they continuously reside in the Cherokee Nation, and live together as husband and wife until the time of his death?   A Yes sir, that is my understanding.

(Witness excused).

THOMAS CORDRAY, being first duly sworn by Walter W. Chappell, Notary Public, testified as follows:

Q   What is your name?   A Thomas Cordray.
Q   What is your age?   A About 58.
Q   What is your post office address?   A Muskogee, I. T.
Q   Do you appear here today for the purpose of giving testimony relative to the right of Nancy Cordray to enrollment as a citizen by intermarriage of the Cherokee Nation?   A Yes sir:
Q   Are you any relation to Nancy Cordray?   A No sir, nothing more than step-mother.
Q   She is your step-mother?   A Yes sir.
Q   Who was your father?   A Wilson Cordray.
Q   He had been married before he married Nancy Cordray?   A Yes sir, he married this lady after my mother died.
Q   When were Wilson Cordray and Nancy Cordray married?   A They commenced living together like people did in them times in '62.
Q   That was after the death of your mother?   A Yes sir.
Q   They were regarded as husband and wife, were they?   A Yes sir.
Q   Has Wilson Cordray always been recognized as a citizen of the Cherokee Nation?   A Yes sir.
Q   From the time of their marriage until his death, did Wilson and Nancy Cordray reside together as husband and wife, and live in the Cherokee Nation?
    A Yes sir, I suppose they did; sometimes he was away from home.
Q   Were those absences temporary?   A I guess they was; he would go back.
Q   To where some of his children lived.
Q   Just on visits?   A I guess so.

BY MR. HASTINGS, ATTORNEY FOR CHEROKEE NATION:

Q   He never lived out of the Cherokee Nation?   A No sir.
Q   After the death of Wilson Cordray, did Nancy Cordray remarry?   A No sir.
Q   She never remarried up to the time of her death?   A No sir.
Q   Do you know whether or not they were ever married at all?
    A Can't swear to it; I was there 2 or 3 weeks.
Q   Were they said to have been legally married?   A I didn't ask any questions.

Cherokee Intermarried White 1906
Volume VII

Q Did you ever hear that they were married, or that they just took up with each other?
A I never asked no questions.
Q Did you ever hear anything about it?   A People taken up together in them times.
Q Did you ever know anything about it one way or the other?
A No sir.
Q Were they said to have been married by a preacher, or an officer, or that they were married at all?   A No sir.
Q Was either of them ever married before?   A Nancy Cordray had been married to a Cherokee Indian named Dick Jumper, and my father had been married to my mother.
Q Was her first husband dead at the time?   A Yes sir, he had been dead several years.
Q This is your step-mother you are testifying about?   A Yes sir.
Q She is living with your father?   A Yes sir.
Q When did you say they commenced living together?   A In '62.
Q How old were you then?   A About 13 or 14.
Q Do you mean to say that you never heard, one way or the other, as to whether they were lawfully married?   A I asked no questions; it was a general rule that people lived together.
Q I want to know if you had any information about it?   A No sir.
Q You dont[sic] know whether your father married her or not?   A No sir.
Q Where were you living at the time?   A In the Choctaw Nation.
Q Where were they living then?   A Right there in the Choctaw Nation; during the war; I lived with the old man off and on.
Q Were you there when they commenced living together?   A No sir.
Q Where were you?   A I dont[sic] know just exactly.
Q Were you there in the neighborhood?   A Not then I was not.
Q You do not remember how far away your were at the time?   A No sir, because I didn't have nothing to do with it.
Q You were in the Choctaw Nation?   A Yes sir.
Q Was your father's home your home?   A When I was at home.
Q Your headquarters?   A Yes sir, general headquarters.

(Witness excused).

The undersigned, being first duly sworn, states that, as stenographer to the Commissioner to the Five Civilized Tribes, she correctly reported the above and foregoing testimony, and that the same is a full, true and complete transcript of her stenographic notes thereof.

Sarah Waters

Subscribed and sworn to before me this 11th day of February, 1907.

Frances R Lane
Notary Public.

Cherokee Intermarried White 1906
Volume VII

◇◇◇◇◇

E C M   Cherokee 1715.

DEPARTMENT OF THE INTERIOR,

COMMISSIONER TO THE FIVE CIVILIZED TRIBES.

In the matter of the application for the enrollment of NANCY CORDRAY as a citizen by intermarriage of the Cherokee Nation.

D E C I S I O N

THE RECORDS OF THIS OFFICE SHOW: That at Fort Gibson, Indian Territory, August 21, 1900 application was received by the Commission to the Five Civilized Tribes for the enrollment of Nancy Cordray as a citizen by intermarriage of the Cherokee Nation. Further proceedings in the matter of said application were had at Muskogee, Indian Territory, October 17, 1902, January 22, 1907 and February 9, 1907.

THE EVIDENCE IN THIS CASE SHOWS: That the applicant herein, Nancy Cordray, nee Hall, a white woman, was married in the year 1863 to one Wilson Cordray, who was at the time of said marriage a recognized citizen by blood of the Cherokee Nation, who is identified on the Cherokee authenticated tribal roll of 1880, Illinois District, No. 353, as a native Cherokee, and whose name is included on the approved partial roll of citizens by blood of the Cherokee Nation opposite No. 4552. It is further shown that from the time is said marriage the said Wilson Cordray and Nancy Cordray resided together as husband and wife and continuously lived in the Cherokee Nation up to and including September 1, 1902. Said applicant is identified on the Cherokee authenticated tribal roll of 1880 and tha[sic] Cherokee census roll of 1896 as an intermarried citizen of the Cherokee Nation.

IT IS, THEREFORE, ORDERED AND ADJUDGED: That in accordance with the decision of the Supreme Court of the United States dated November 5, 1906 in the cases of Daniel Red Bird, et al. vs. the United States, Nos. 125, 126, 127, and 128, the said applicant, Nancy Cordray, is entitled, under the provisions of Section Twenty-one of the Act of Congress approved June 28, 1898 (30 Stats. 495), to enrollment as a citizen by intermarriage of the Cherokee Nation, and her application for enrollment as such is accordingly granted.

                                                                Tams Bixby
                                                                Commissioner.

Dated at Muskogee, Indian Territory,
this   FEB 21 1907

◇◇◇◇◇

Cherokee Intermarried White 1906
Volume VII

Cherokee
1715.

Muskogee, Indian Territory, February 21, 1907.

W. W. Hastings,
    Attorney for the Cherokee Nation,
        Muskogee, Indian Territory.

Dear Sir:

    There is enclosed herewith a copy of the decision of the Commissioner to the Five Civilized Tribes, dated February 21, 1907, granting the application for the enrollment of Nancy Cordray as a citizen by intermarriage of the Cherokee Nation.

Respectfully,

Encl. HJ-45.
  HJC

Commissioner.

◇◇◇◇◇

Cherokee
1715

Muskogee, Indian Territory, February 21, 1907.

The Commissioner to the Five Civilized Tribes,
    Muskogee, Indian Territory.

Sir:

    Receipt is acknowledged of the testimony and of your decision enrolling Nancy Cordray as a citizen by intermarriage of the Cherokee Nation. Time for protesting said decision is waived and I consent that said person may be placed upon the schedule immediately.

Respectfully,
W. W. Hastings
Attorney for Cherokee Nation.

◇◇◇◇◇

Cherokee Intermarried White 1906
Volume VII

Cherokee
1715

Muskogee, Indian Territory, February 21, 1907.

Louisa Anderson,
Fort Gibson, Indian Territory.

Dear Madam:

There is enclosed herewith a copy of the decision of the Commissioner to the Five Civilized Tribes, dated February 21, 1907, granting the application for the enrollment of your mother Nancy Cordray as a citizen by intermarriage of the Cherokee Nation.

You will be advised when her name has been placed upon a schedule of citizens of the Cherokee Nation and approved by the Secretary of the Interior.

Respectfully,

Encl. HJ-50.
HJC
Commissioner.

◇◇◇◇◇

GAW.

DEPARTMENT OF THE INTERIOR,

OFFICE OF INDIAN AFFAIRS,

I. T. 34106-1907   WASHINGTON.   May 25, 1907.

Richard F. Boudinot, Esq.
Braggs, Indian Territory.

Sir:

The Office in in receipt of your letter of April 5, 1907, asking that the name of Nancy Cordry[sic], wife of Wilson Cordry, be stricken from the roll of intermarried citizens of the Cherokee Nation, and saying that the Department has certainly been misinformed as to the identity of this person or she would not have been enrolled.

In reply you are advised that the records of this office show that the name of Nancy Cordray has been stricken from the roll of intermarried Cherokee citizens.

Cherokee Intermarried White 1906
Volume VII

Very Respectfully,

(Signed) Frank M. Conser.

EWE-EH   Chief Cler.

Cher IW 215

Department of the Interior,
Commission to the Five Civilized Tribes,
Pryor Creek, I. T., Sept. 13, 1900.

In the matter of the application of Albert G. Gass for the enrollment of himself and wife as Cherokee citizens; being sworn and examined by Commissioner Needles he testified as follows:

Q What is your name?   A Albert G. Gass.
Q What is your age?   A Fifty-nine.
Q What is your post-office address?   A Inola, Indian Territory.
Q What district do you live in?   A Cooweescoowee.
Q Are you a recognized citizen of the Cherokee Nation?   A Yes sir.
Q By blood or intermarriage?   A Intermarriage.
Q How long have you resided in the Cherokee Nation?   A Ever since 1867.
Q What is your wife's name?   A Her maiden name was Lucy Ann Ward.
Q You were married before 1880?   A Yes sir.
Q Have you any children that you desire to enroll?   A No sir.
1880 roll page 435 #767 Albert Gass Goingsnake District;
1880 roll page 435 #768 Lucy Gass   "
1896 roll page 1280 #92 Albert Gass Tahlequah District;
1896 roll page 1178 #1323 Lucy Gass Tahlequah District.

Com'r Needles: The name of Albert G. Gass is found upon the authenticated roll of 1880 as Albert Gass and the name of his wife Lucy is also found upon the authenticated roll of 1880, his name is also found upon the census roll of 1896 as Albert Gass, and the name of his wife is also found upon the census roll of 1896; he having been duly identified according to page and number of the rolls as indicated in the testimony and having made satisfactory proof as to residence, said Albert G. Gass will be duly listed for enrollment as a Cherokee citizen by intermarriage, and his wife Lucy as a Cherokee citizen by blood.

Cherokee Intermarried White 1906
Volume VII

M. D. Green, being first duly sworn, states that as stenographer to the Commission to the Five Civilized Tribes he correctly recorded the testimony and proceedings in this case and the foregoing is a true and complete transcript of his stenographic notes thereof.

MD Green

Subscribed and sworn to before me this 17 day of September 1900.

TB Needles
Commissioner.

◇◇◇◇◇

Cher
Supp'l to # 2725

Department of the Interior,
Commission to the Five Civilized Tribes,
Muskogee, I. T., October 13, 1902.

In the matter of the application of ALBERT G. GASS, for the enrollment of himself as a citizen by intermarriage, and his wife, LUCY A. GASS, as a citizen by blood, of the Cherokee Nation.

ALBERT G. GASS, being duly sworn and examined by the Commission, testified as follows:

Q What is your name ? A Albert G. Gass.
Q How old are you ? A Sixty one years old.
Q What is your post office address ? A Inola.
Q You are a white man ? A Yes sir.
Q Does your name appear upon the 1880 roll as an intermarried white ? A Yes sir.
Q What is your wife's name ? A Lucy A.
Q Was she your wife in 1880 ? A Yes sir.
Q Have you and your wife been living together in the Cherokee Nation ever since 1880? A Yes sir.
Q Never been separated ? A No sir.
Q You never made your home outside the Cherokee Nation ? A No sir.
Q Have you any children living with you ? A NO sir.

E. C. Bagwell, on oath states that, as stenographer to the Commission to the Five Civilized Tribes, he correctly recorded the testimony and proceedings had in the above entitled cause, and that the foregoing is an accurate transcript of his stenographic notes thereof.

E.C. Bagwell

Cherokee Intermarried White 1906
Volume VII

Subscribed and sworn to before me this October 30, 1902.

BC Jones
Notary Public.

◇◇◇◇◇

Cherokee No. 2725.

DEPARTMENT OF THE INTERIOR, COMMISSIONER TO THE FIVE CIVILIZED TRIBES.

Muskogee, Indian Territory. January 7, 1907.

In the matter of the application of Albert G. Gass for enrollment as a citizen by intermarriage of the Cherokee Nation.

Albert G. Gass, being first duly sworn by Frances R. Lane, Notary Public, testified as follows:

BY THE COMMISSIONER:

Q What is your name?   A Albert G. Gass.
Q What is your age? A 65 years old.
Q What is your postoffice address? A Peggs, Indian Territory.
Q You claim citizenship in the Cherokee Nation by intermarriage do you? A Yes, sir.
Q Through whom do you claim such citizenship? A By Lucy A Ward.
Q She was a citizen by blood of the Cherokee Nation? A Yes, sir.
Q When were you married to Lucy A. Gass? A Married to her in 1864,
Q Where? A In the state of Texas.
Q At what place? A In Hopkins County.
Q That marriage was under a license of the state of Texas? A Yes, sir.
Q The ceremony performed by a preacher? A Yes, sir, hard-shell Baptist preacher.
Q The license recorded? A Yes, sir, sent back to the office.
Q You haven't a copy of that license with you? A No, sir.
Q When did you move to the Cherokee Nation with Lucy A. Gass? A '67.
Q Upon your removal to the Cherokee Nation were you again married to her in accordance with the Cherokee laws? A In august 1868 I married her again according to the laws of the Cherokee Nation.
Q Where did this second marriage take place? A In Going Snake District near the state line of Kansas.

Cherokee Intermarried White 1906
Volume VII

Q That was under a license of the Cherokee Nation? A Yes, sir, that is what they called a license.
Q What was the name of the judge who married you? A Johnson Robins, fullblood Cherokee.
Q What became of that certificate? A Can't tell you; he took it. Don't know what he done with it.
Q Is Lucy A. Gass living at this time? A Yes, sir, or she was yesterday evening at 2 o'clock.
Q Have you and Lucy A. Gass lived together continuously as man and wife within the Cherokee Nation from the date of your removal to said Nation in 1868 until the present time? A Yes, sir.
Q Was Lucy A. Gass married prior to the time she married you? A No, sir.
Q Were you married prior to the time you married her? A No, sir.
Q Is there anyone here today who was present at your marriage in the Cherokee Nation? A Yes, sir, he is here.
Q What is his name? A Joe Thornton.
Q You have nothing at this time in the way of documentary evidence covering either the marriage in Texas or the marriage in the Cherokee Nation? A Not unless I go back to the records.

The applicant's name appears on field card 2725, and is listed on the authenticated roll of Cherokee citizens of 1880, Going Snake District, opposite No. 767. Lucy A. Gass, the applicant's wife, is also listed on the 1880 roll opposite No. 768, and is included in an approved partial roll of citizens of the Cherokee Nation by blood, opposite No. 6945. The name of the applicant and his wife also appear on the 1896 roll opposite Nos. 92 and 1323.

Q Is there anyone else living at this time who was present at this marriage in the Cherokee Nation? A The only witness I had is dead. I asked her brother about her and he said she was dead.

WITNESS EXCUSED.

F. Elma Lane, upon oath, states that as stenographer to the Commission to the Five Civilized Tribes, she reported the proceedings in the above entitled and numbered cause, and that the foregoing is a true and correct transcript of her stenographic notes therein.

F. Elma Lane

Subscribed and sworn to before me this 8th day of January, 1907.

Edward Merrick
Notary Public.

Cherokee Intermarried White 1906
Volume VII

⋄⋄⋄⋄⋄

C. F. B.   Cherokee 2725.

DEPARTMENT OF THE INTERIOR,
COMMISSION TO THE FIVE CIVILIZED TRIBES.
Muskogee, Indian Territory, January 11, 1907.

Supplemental proceedings in the Matter of the Application for the Enrollment of Albert G. Gass as a citizen by intermarriage of the Cherokee Nation.

APPEARANCES: E. L. C. Ward for Applicant.
Cherokee Nation represented by
W. W. Hastings, Attorney.

E. L. C. Ward being first duly sworn by B. P. Rasmus, Notary Public, testified as follows:

ON BEHALF OF COMMISSIONER.

Q What is your name? A E. L. C. Ward.
Q What is your age? A 50 years.
Q What is your post office address?
A Siloam Springs.
Q Do you know a person in the Cherokee Nation by the name of Albert G. Gass?
A Yes sir.
Q How long have you known him?
A I recollect him since 1864.
Q He is a white man? A Yes sir.
Q He claims the right to enrollment as a citizen of the Cherokee Nation by virtue of his marriage to a Cherokee by blood?
A Yes sir.
Q What was his wife's name? A Lucy Ann Ward.
Q Did you know her before her marriage to Gass?
A Yes sir; she was my half sister.
Q When were they married? A In 1864.
Q Where were they married at that time?
A State of Texas.
Q Was Lucy A. Gass living in the State of Texas at that time?
A Yes sir.
Q Was she making that her home or was her home in the Cherokee Nation?
A Her home was in the Cherokee Nation.
Q Was she a recognized citizen of the Nation?
A She was quick as she came back.

Cherokee Intermarried White 1906
Volume VII

Q   When did they come to the Cherokee Nation after their marriage?
A   In '67.
Q   On coming to the Cherokee Nation, was Lucy A. Gass recognized as a citizen of the Nation or was she admitted by the Cherokee authorities?
A   She was recognized as a citizen.
Q   Were they married in accordance with the laws of the Cherokee Nation, subsequent to the coming to the Nation?
A   They went up to get married in '68. They lived there 6 or 8 months to get acquainted, so as to get signers to their petition.
Q   After they had resided in the Cherokee Nation for 6 or 8 months, they were married in accordance with the laws of the Cherokee Nation?
A   They went off to get married and came back and said they were married.
Q   You didn't see them married?
A   No sir.
Q   Did you see the petition he got for the purpose of securing his license?
A   I was a small boy then; couldn't read; I just heard he got it.
Q   It was your understanding and belief that he did secure a license?
A   Yes sir.
Q   They came back and you have known them since that time as husband and wife?
A   Yes sir.
Q   And you understood that that was their purpose,- being married again,- was to comply with the laws of the Cherokee Nation?
A   Yes sir.
Q   Since their marriage in 1868, has Albert G. Gass enjoyed all the privileges and exercised all the rights of a citizen by intermarriage of the Cherokee Nation?
A   I don't think he got all the monies but he enjoyed all the rights of a citizen by intermarriage.
Q   Do you know of his voting at elections?
A   Yes sir.
Q   Did he ever hold any office?
A   Not that I know of.
Q   But he has been recognized as a citizen by intermarriage by the Cherokee authorities?
A   Yes sir.

The undersigned being first duly sworn states that as stenographer to the Commission to the Five Civilized Tribes, she recorded the testimony taken in this case and that the foregoing is a full, true and correct transcript of her stenographic notes thereof.

                                            Myrtle Hill

Subscribed and sworn to before me this the 14th day of January, 1907

                                            John E. Tidwell
                                            Notary Public.

Cherokee Intermarried White 1906
Volume VII

◇◇◇◇◇

Cherokee 2725.

DEPARTMENT OF THE INTERIOR.

COMMISSIONER TO THE FIVE CIVILIZED TRIBES.

Muskogee, I.T. February 19, 1907.

SUPPLEMENTAL:

In the matter of the application for the enrollment of Albert G. Gass as a citizen by intermarriage of the Cherokee Nation.

S. E. Parris being first duly sworn by W. W. Chappell, a Notary Public, testifies as follows:

By the Commissioner:

Q   What is your name? A S. E. Parris.
Q   What is your age? A 57.
Q   What is your Post office address? A Tahlequah.
Q   Do you appear here today for the purpose of giving testimony relative to the right of Albert G. Gass to enrollment as a citizen by intermarriage of the Cherokee Nation? A Yes sir.
Q   How long have you been acquainted with Albert G. Gass? A About 30 years.
Q   Is he a white man? A I suppose so, he's said to be.
Q   Are you acquainted with his wife? A Yes sir.
Q   What is her name? A Lucy Ann Ward before she married Gass.
Q   Is she a citizen by blood of the Cherokee Nation? A I think so, I guess she is, we have been in the Nation all our lives; played together.
Q   Were you acquainted with these parties before they married? A I was with the woman, but not with the man.
Q   Were you present at their marriage? A No sir, he married this girl in Texas first, and my brother got the signers for him and they was married again.
Q   Did you see the petition? A No sir.
Q   Do you know positively that they got a license from the authorities of the Cherokee Nation? A No sir, I know they had the petition.
Q   When were they married? A I don't know; it was a long time ago.
Q   About how long ago? A It was in '66 or '68 or somewhere along there.
Q   Since the date of their marriage have they continuously resided together as husband and wife and remained in the Cherokee Nation? A Yes sir.

Witness Excused.

Cherokee Intermarried White 1906
Volume VII

Alec Ward being first duly sworn by W. W. Chappell, a Notary Public, testifies as follows:

By the Commissioner:

Q What is your name? A Alec Ward.
Q Your age? A 68.
Q Your Post Office address? A Claremore.
Q Do you appear here today for the purpose of giving testimony relative to the right of Albert G. Gass to enrollment as a citizen by intermarriage of the Cherokee Nation? A Yes sir.
Q How long have you been acquainted with the applicant in this case, Albert G. Gass? A About the middle of the war and ever since.
Q Is he a white man? A I suppose he is.
Q You say he married your sister? A Yes sir.
Q She was a citizen by blood of the Cherokee Nation? A Yes sir.
Q When did he marry your sister? A Two years after the war and at the time of the war, the middle of the war, in Texas.
Q After moving to the Nation was your sister admitted to citizenship in the nation? A Yes sir.
Q When? A She didn't have to be, she was already a citizen. They were married in Texas and they come back here and were married over.
Q Were they married under a license issued by the authorities of the Cherokee Nation? A Yes sir.
Q Did you see the license? A I didn't know what a license was but they called them a license.
Q Did you see a paper purporting to be a license? A No sir, I don't think I did.
Q Was you at the marriage? A Yes sir, I was right there.
Q Did they secure a license? A That's what they said it was.
Q Did they get up a petition? A Yes sir.
Q You are positive of that? A Yes sir.
Q From the time of the marriage have they continuously resided together as husband and wife and remained in the Cherokee Nation? [sic] Yes sir.

By Mr. Hastings:

Q What was the purpose of this second marriage? A To get them a right to territory, I guess.
Q In order to be married in accordance with Cherokee law? A Yes sir.
Q Now you people went out of the Nation at the beginning of the war, were out during the war and came back at the end of the war and never lost your citizenship at all? A No sir.

Witness Excused.

Cherokee Intermarried White 1906
Volume VII

I, Cora E. Glendenning, a stenographer to the Commissioner to the Five Civilized Tribes on oath state that I reported the proceedings in the above entitled cause, and that the foregoing is a true and correct transcript of my stenographic notes therein.

Cora E Glendenning

Subscribed and sworn to before me this 20 day of February 1907.

Walter W. Chappell
Notary Public.

◇◇◇◇◇

E.C.M.   Cherokee 2725

DEPARTMENT OF THE INTERIOR,

COMMISSIONER TO THE FIVE CIVILIZED TRIBES.

In the matter of the application for the enrollment of Albert G. Gass as a citizen by intermarriage of the Cherokee Nation.

D E C I S I O N

THE RECORDS OF THIS OFFICE SHOW: That at Pryor Creek, Indian Territory, September 13, 1900, application was received by the Commission to the Five Civilized Tribes for the enrollment of Albert G. Gass as a citizen by intermarriage of the Cherokee Nation. Further proceedings in the matter of said application were had at Muskogee, Indian Territory, October 13, 1902, January 7 and 11, and February 19, 1907.

THE EVIDENCE IN THIS CASE SHOWS: That the applicant herein, Albert G. Gass, a white man, was married in accordance with Cherokee law, in August, 1868, to one Lucy A. Gass, nee Ward, who was at the time of said marriage, a recognized citizen by blood of the Cherokee Nation, who is identified upon the Cherokee authenticated tribal roll of 1880, Going Snake District, No. 768, as a native Cherokee, and whose name is included on the approved partial roll of citizens by blood of the Cherokee Nation opposite No. 6945. It is further shown that from the time of said marriage the said Albert G. Gass and Lucy A. Gass resided together as husband and wife and continuously lived in the Cherokee Nation up to and including September 1, 1902. Said applicant is identified on the Cherokee authenticated tribal roll of 1880, and the Cherokee census roll of 1896 as an intermarried citizen of the Cherokee Nation.

IT IS, THEREFORE, ORDERED AND ADJUDGED: That in accordance with the decision of the Supreme Court of the United States, dated November 5, 1906, in the cases of Daniel Red Bird, et al., vs. the United States, Nos. 125, 126, 127, and 128, the said applicant, Albert G. Gass, is entitled, under the provisions of Section twenty-one of the

Cherokee Intermarried White 1906
Volume VII

Act of Congress approved June 28, 1898 (30 Stats. 495), to enrollment as a citizen by intermarriage of the Cherokee Nation, and his application for enrollment as such is accordingly granted.

          Tams Bixby
            Commissioner.

Dated at Muskogee, Indian Territory,
this   FEB 23 1907

◇◇◇◇◇

Cherokee 2725   COPY

         Muskogee, Indian Territory, February 23, 1907.

W. W. Hastings,
   Attorney for the Cherokee Nation,
      Muskogee, Indian Territory.

Dear Sir:

   There is enclosed herewith a copy of the decision of the Commissioner to the Five Civilized Tribes, dated February 23, 1907, granting the application for the enrollment of Albert G. Gass as a citizen by intermarriage of the Cherokee Nation.

         Respectfully,
          SIGNED *Tams Bixby*
           Commissioner.

Encl.A-14
 RA

◇◇◇◇◇

Cherokee 2725

         Muskogee, Indian Territory, February 23, 1907.

The Commissioner to the Five Civilized Tribes,
   Muskogee, Indian Territory.

Sir:

   Receipt is acknowledged of the testimony and of your decision, enrolling Albert G. Gass as a citizen by intermarriage of the Cherokee Nation. Time for protesting said

Cherokee Intermarried White 1906
Volume VII

decision is waived and I consent that said person may be placed upon the schedule immediately.

Respectfully,
W. W. Hastings
Attorney for the Cherokee Nation.

◇◇◇◇◇

Cherokee 2725

COPY

Muskogee, Indian Territory, February 23, 1907.

Albert G. Gass,
Peggs, Indian Territory.

Dear Sir:

There is enclosed herewith a copy of the decision of the Commissioner to the Five Civilized Tribes, dated February 23, 1907, granting the application for your enrollment as a citizen by intermarriage of the Cherokee Nation.

You will be advised when your name has been placed upon a schedule of citizens of the Cherokee Nation and approved by the Secretary of the Interior.

Respectfully,
SIGNED *Tams Bixby*
Commissioner.

Encl. A-15
RA

Cher IW 216

◇◇◇◇◇

DEPARTMENT OF THE INTERIOR.
COMMISSION TO THE FIVE CIVILIZED TRIBES.
VINITA, I. T., SEPTEMBER 17th, 1900.

IN THE MATTER OF THE APPLICATION OF Tredwell S. Remsen, wife and child, for enrollment as citizens of the Cherokee Nation, and he being sworn by Commissioner, T. B. Needles, testified as follows:

Q What is your name? A Tredwell S. Remsen.
Q What is your age? A Fifty six/[sic]
Q What is your Postoffice? A Groves.

Cherokee Intermarried White 1906
Volume VII

Q What District do you live in? A Delaware.
Q Are you a recognized citizen of the Cherokee Nation? A Yes sir.
Q By blood or intermarriage? A Intermarriage.
Q How long have you been a resident of the Cherokee Nation?
A Twenty eight years.
Q What is the name of your wife? A Julia E. Remsen.
Q When did you marry her? A Febuary[sic] 6th, 1875.
Q For whom do you apply? A Myself, wife and one child.
Q What is the name of your child? A Alvie M. Remsen.
Q How old is he? A She is sixteen.
Q Is she living and living with you? A Yes sir.
Q What is the age of your wife? A She is forty three.

  (1880 Roll, Page 304, #2147, Treadwell[sic] Rinson[sic], Delaware Dis't)
  (1880 Roll, Page 304, #2148, Esther Rinson, Delaware   ")
  (1896 Roll, Page 587, #457, Tredwell S. Remsen, Delaware Dis't)
  (1896 Roll, Page 523, #2588, Julia E. Remsen, Delaware   ")
  (1896 Roll, Page 523, #2589, Alvie M. Remsen, Delaware Dis't)

  The name of Tredwell S. Remsen appears upon the authenticated roll of 1880, as Treadwell Rinson, and the name of his wife, Julia E. Remsen appears on the authenticated roll of 1880, as Ester Rinson: Their names appear upon the census rolls of 1896, they being fully identified according to the page and number of the rolls, and having made satisfactory proof of their residence; the said Tredwell S. Remsen will be duly listed for enrollment by this Commission as a Cherokee citizen by intermarriage, and his wife, Julia E. Remsen, and daughter, Alvie M. Rensen as Cherokee citizens by blood.

  The undersigned, being sworn, states that as stenographer to the Commission to the Five Civilized Tribes, he correctly recordd[sic] the testimony and proceedings in this case, and that the foregoing is a true and complete transcript of his stenographic notes thereof.

                       R R Cravens

Subscribed and sworn to before me
this 17th day of September, 1900.

                     T B Needles
                     C O M M I S S I O N E R .

Cherokee Intermarried White 1906
Volume VII

Cherokee 2841.

Department of the Interior,
Commission to the Five Civilized Tribes,
Muskogee, I. T., October 21, 1902.

In the matter of the application of Tredwell S. Remsen for the enrollment of himself as a citizen by intermarriage, and for the enrollment of his wife, Julia E. Remsen, an child, Alvie M. Remsen, as citizens by blood of the Cherokee Nation; he being sworn and examined by the Commission, testified as follows:

Q   What is your name? A Tredwell S. Remsen.
Q   How old are you? A Fifty-nine years old.
Q   What is your postoffice? A Grove, Indian Territory.
Q   Are you a white man? A Yes sir.
Q   Is your name on the roll of 1880 as an intermarried white man? A Yes sir.
Q   What is your wife's name? A Julia E.
Q   Is she a Cherokee by blood? A Yes sir.
Q   How long has she been living in the Cherokee Nation? A She was born here.
Q   Was she your wife in 1880? A Yes sir.
Q   Is she the wife through whom you claim your citizenship? A Yes sir.
Q   Have you and your wife been living together since 1880? A Yes sir.
Q   Never been separated? A No sir.
Q   Are you living together now? A Yes sir.
Q   Has the Cherokee Nation been your home since 1880? A Yes sir.
Q   Never been anywhere else? A No sir.

The undersigned, being duly sworn, states that as stenographer to the Commission to the Five Civilized Tribes he correctly recorded the testimony and proceedings in this case, and that the foregoing is a true and correct transcript of his stenographic notes thereof.

E.G. Rothenberger

Subscribed and sworn to before me this 19th day of November, 1902.

BC Jones
Notary Public.

Cherokee Intermarried White 1906
Volume VII

Cher 2841

Department of the Interior,
Commission to the Five Civilized Tribes,
Cherokee Land Office.
Tahlequah, I. T., September 24, 1903.

In the matter of the application of Tredwell S. Remsen for the enrollment of himself and his wife, Julia E., and his minor child, Alvie M. Remsen, as citizens by blood of the Cherokee Nation.

LEE VANDAGRIFF, personally appearing, and being first duly sworn and examined, testified as follows:

Q What is your name? A Lee Vandagriff.
Q How old are you? A 28.
Q What is your post office address? A Grove, I. T.
Q Are you a citizen by blood of the Cherokee Nation? A Yes, sir.
Q Is your wife a citizen? A Yes, sir.
Q What is her name? A Alvie M. Vandagriff.
Q How old is she? A Nineteen.
Q Under what name was she enrolled by the Commission? A Alvie M. Remsen.
Q Have you married her since she was enrolled? A Yes, sir.
Q When were you married? A January 7, 1903.
Q Do you and she live together now? A Yes, sir.
Q You present here a power of attorney, signed by Alva M. Vandagriff, authorizing you to slect[sic] her allotment in the Cherokee Nation, is that the same person as Alvie M. Vandagriff? A Yes, sir.

o---------------------------o

I, George R. Smith, being first duly sworn, state that, as stenographer to the Commission to the Five Civilized Tribes, I recorded the testimony as given above, and that the same is a true and accurate transcript of my stenographic notes thereof.
A part of my notes containing testimony in the matter of this application were lost, and no record can, therefore, be made of that portion of it.

George R. Smith

Subscribed and sworn to before me this 1 day of November, 1903.

Samuel Foreman

Cherokee Intermarried White 1906
Volume VII

Cherokee No. 2841.

DEPARTMENT OF THE INTERIOR,
COMMISSIONER TO THE FIVE CIVILIZED TRIBES.
Muskogee, I. T., January 2, 1907.

In the matter of the application of Tredwell S. Remsen for enrollment as a citizen by intermarriage of the Cherokee Nation.

Tredwell S. Remsen, being first duly sworn by Frances R. Lane, a Notary Public for the Western District, Indian Territory, testified as follows:

By the Commissioner:
Q What is your name? A Tredwell S. Remsen.
Q How old are you? A Sixty-three.
Q What is your postoffice address? A Grove, I. T.
Q You claim to be a citizen by intermarriage of the Cherokee Nation? A Yes sir.
Q Through whom do you claim that right? A Julia E. Monroe.
Q When were you married to her? A 6th of February, 1875.
Q Did you marry her under Cherokee law? A Yes sir.
Q Have you got a license? A No, I havn't[sic] got no license. I havn't[sic] got no marriage certificate. The marriage license was lost or burned 7 or 8 years ago. The marriage license is lost.

> The applicant presents for consideration a family bible containing the following certificate:
> "This certifies that the rite of holy matrimony was celebrated between Tredwell S. Remsen of Valley Spring, N.Y., and Julia E. Monroe of Careys Ferry, Cherokee Nation, on February 6, 1875 at T. J. McGhee's by T. J. McGhee, Judge of Delaware District. Witness T. J. McGhee and Rebecca Monroe."

Q Who filled out this certificate? A I filled it out myself.
Q When did you fill this out? A I filled it out sometime I think probably in 1883 or 1884. I don't know exactly when.
Q Did you obtain a license to marry your wife before you marriage? A Yes sir.
Q Who did you get it from? A James E. Holland.
Q What did you pay for that license? A $10
Q Did you present a petition to secure that license?
A Yes, I had a petition with ten signers, Cherokees by blood.
Q What became of it? A It was lost in the fire at below Chetopa, Kansas or else we lost it when we moved, and my wife got that other affidavit from McGhee.
Q Have you and your wife lived together continuously as husband and wife, in the Cherokee Nation, from the time of your marriage in 1875 up to and including the present time? A Yes sir.
Q And are still living together? A No sir.
Q When did you separate? A October 5, 1905.

Cherokee Intermarried White 1906
Volume VII

Q Did you obtain a divorce from her or did she from you? A She got one from me I guess; I never got any notice of it though.
Q Did you live together up until that time, or had you ever been separated before>
A No, never been separated before.
Q Did she leave you or did you leave her? A She left me--well, she has not left me; she is there yet; we don't live together as man and wife and havn't[sic] since Oct. 5th. 1905.
Q You live in the same neighborhood? A Yes, in the same house. Our daughter is there with us, and her family.
Q Were you ever married before you married Julia E. Monroe? A No sir.
Q Was she ever married before she married you? A No, she was about 17 years old, and I took her on east and showed her all my folks out in New York, after we were married, a few years afterwards.
Q You have not married again since you separated from her? A No sir.

Applicant is identified on the 1880 Cherokee roll opposite No. 2147. His wife, through whom he claims his right to be enrolled as a citizen of the Cherokee Nation by intermarriage, is identified on said roll opposite No. 2148. She is also identified on the final roll of citizens by blood of the Cherokee Nation opposite No. 3172.

It will be necessary for you to furnish additional proof of the fact that you obtained a license to marry your wife in accordance with the Cherokee law, and that said license and certificate have been lost or destroyed, and also, to present secondary evidence to establish the fact that you were married according to Cherokee law.

Frances R. Lane upon oath states that as stenographer to the Commissioner to the Five Civilized Tribes she reported the testimony in the above entitled cause and that the foregoing is an accurate transcript of her stenographic notes thereof.

Frances R Lane

Subscribed and sworn to before me this January 4, 1907.

Edward Merrick
Notary Public.

Cherokee Intermarried White 1906
Volume VII

Cherokee 2841.

DEPARTMENT OF THE INTERIOR,
COMMISSION TO THE FIVE CIVILIZED TRIBES.
Muskogee, Indian Territory, January 4, 1907.

Additional Evidence taken in the Matter of the Application for the Enrollment of Tredwell S. Remson[sic], as a citizen by intermarriage of the Cherokee Nation. Census Card Number 2841.

David A. McGee being first duly sworn testified as follows:

ON BEHALF OF COMMISSIONER.

Q What is your name?
A David A. McGee.
Q How old are you?
A About 58 years old.
Q What is your post office address?
A Dodge, Indian Territory.
Q Are you a citizen of the Cherokee Nation?
A Yes sir.
Q By blood?
A Yes sir.
Q Do you know Tredwell S. Remson?
A I know T. S. Remson.
Q Did you know Julia E. Monroe?
A Yes sir.
Q Do you know when she and T. S. Remson were married?
A I know about.
Q About when were they married?
A As well as I can remember, sometime in February, 1875.
Q Do you know whether they were married under a Cherokee license or not?
A I don't know; I heard they were.
Q Did you ever see the license?
A No sir.
Q Who married them?
A I don't know; I did know but I don't remember.

BY APPLICANT.

Q Do you remember signing the petition for the license?
A I signed so many petitions, I don't remember' I might; if you had asked me I would have signed.
Q What was the first time you ever saw me in the Cherokee Nation, there about Grove?
A About '74.

Cherokee Intermarried White 1906
Volume VII

Q   I have always boarded there, haven't I, and been recognized as a citizen of the Cherokee Nation?
A   Yes sir; I served on the Jury several times with you in our Courts.

Applicant states that he drew bread money in 1875 and 1880 as a citizen of the Cherokee Nation.

The undersigned being first duly sworn states that as stenographer to the Commission to the Five Civilized Tribes, she correctly recorded the testimony taken in this case and that the foregoing is a full, true and correct transcript of her stenographic notes thereof.

Myrtle Hill

Subscribed and sworn to before me this the 5th day of January, 1907.

John E. Tidwell
Notary Public.

◇◇◇◇◇

C. F. B.   Cherokee 2841.

DEPARTMENT OF THE INTERIOR,
COMMISSION TO THE FIVE CIVILIZED TRIBES.
Muskogee, Indian Territory, January 7, 1907.

In the Matter of the Application for the Enrollment of Tredwell S. Remson as a citizen by intermarriage of the Cherokee Nation.

APPEARANCES:
Thomas J. McGee for Applicant.

Cherokee Nation represented by H. M. Vance, in behalf of W. W. Hastings, Attorney.

Thomas J. McGee being first duly sworn by John E. Tidwell, Notary Public, testified as follows:

ON BEHALF OF COMMISSIONER.

Q   What is your name?   A   Thomas J. McGee.
Q   What is your age?   A   62.
Q   What is your post office address?
A   Afton, Indian Territory.

Cherokee Intermarried White 1906
Volume VII

Q   Are you a citizen by blood of the Cherokee Nation?
A   Yes sir.
Q   You desire to give testimony relative to the right to enrollment of Tredwell S. Remson as a citizen by intermarriage of the Cherokee Nation?
A   Yes sir.
Q   Tredwell S. Remson has no Cherokee blood?
A   No sir.
Q   His only claim to the right to enrollment as a citizen of the Cherokee Nation is by virtue of his marriage to a citizen by blood?
A   Yes sir.
Q   What is the name of the citizen through whom he claims that right?
A   Julia E. Remson.
Q   When were they married?
A   In 1875.
Q   What time of the year in 1875?
A   As well as I remember, it was in the fore part of the year. I can't give the exact date. I married them myself. I was Judge of the District.
Q   Was she a recognized citizen of the Cherokee Nation at the time he married her?
A   Yes sir.
Q   Did he procure a license?
A   Yes sir; from one of my clerks, James E. Holland.
Q   He was married then in accordance with the law of the Cherokee Nation, by you?
A   Yes sir.
Q   You were then Judge of what District?
A   Delaware District, Cherokee Nation.
Q   Do you know of your own personal knowledge that after their marriage they lived together as husband and wife continuously up to the present time?
A   Well, they lived together until right here of late; I think they were divorced.
Q   How long ago?
A   I think it has been in the last six months; I just heard that; I am not positive.
Q   Do you know where you obtained that information?
A   I heard it there in Grove through their neighbors.
Q   They were living together on September 1, 1902?
A   Yes sir.
Q   Have they continuously lived in the Cherokee Nation since their marriage?
A   Yes sir.
Q   Do you know of your own personal knowledge that they were married in accordance with the laws of the Cherokee Nation?
A   Yes sir; I do.
Q   Was there any record made of this marriage?
A   Yes sir; I think there was.
Q   Where is it to be found?
A   It should be found in the Executor's office, of the Cherokee Nation.

Cherokee Intermarried White 1906
Volume VII

The undersigned being first duly sworn states that as stenographer to the Commission to the Five Civilized Tribes, she correctly recorded the testimony taken in this case and that the foregoing is a full, true and correct transcript of her stenographic notes thereof.

Myrtle Hill

Subscribed and sworn to before me this the 8th day of January, 1907.

John E. Tidwell
Notary Public.

◇◇◇◇◇

CERTIFIED COPY.

Grove, I. T.
Dec. 31st, 1906.

This is to certify that Nancy A. Harlin who is about 66 Years of age, a resident of Grove, I. T. is very feeble and Infirm not able to do any thing.

(Signed) J. C. Holland -
M. D.

I have been a Practicing Physician for about 13 years.

The within affidavit Subscribed and
sworn to this 8th day of January A.D. 1907.

(SEAL)
(Signed) T. S. Remsen
Notary Public.

My Comss. expires May 2d, 1908.

This certifies that the undersigned, being duly sworn, states that as stenographer to the Commission to the Five Civilized Tribes she made the above and foregoing copy and that the same is a full, true and correct copy of the original instrument now on file in this office.

Georgia Coberly
Stenographer.

Cherokee Intermarried White 1906
Volume VII

Subscribed and sworn to before me this 20th day of February, 1907.

> Oliver C Hinkle
> Notary Public.

◇◇◇◇◇

CERTIFIED COPY.

2d Recording District)   Cherokee - 2841.
)
Indian Territory   )   Grove, January 9th, 1907.

       Personally appeared before me a Notary Public in and for said District and Territory Nancy A. Harlin, to me known and entitled to credit, who after being duly sworn declares as follows:

I am 64 years of age in 1872, I married James E. Harlin, a Cherokee by blood in February 1873. My husband issued a Marriage License to Tredwell S. Remsen, a white man, to marry Julia E. Monroe, a Cherokee woman by blood, and a recognized Citizen of the Cherokee Nation. I know this was in 1875 as during that spring we drew bread money at Vinita. Rebecca Monroe, Mother of Julia E. lived neighbor to me and when they came back from T. J. McGhee after being married I gave them their wedding dinner. And they were married sometime before we drew Our read money. I am in feeble health and not able to go any where.

> (Signed) Nancy A. Harlin

Subscribed and sworn to this 9th day of January 1907.

> (Signed) W. E. Ross,
> Notary Public.

My Commission expires Oct. 17th, 1909.

(SEAL)

       This certifies that the undersigned, being duly sworn, states that as stenographer to the Commission to the Five Civilized Tribes she made the above and foregoing copy and that the same is a full, true and correct copy of the original instrument now on file in this office.

> Georgia Coberly
> Stenographer.

Cherokee Intermarried White 1906
Volume VII

Subscribed and sworn to before me this 20th day of February, 1907.

Oliver C Hinkle
Notary Public.

◇◇◇◇◇

CERTIFIED COPY.

Cherokee 2841.
Grove, Ind. Tery. Jan. 11th 1907.

Comss. to the 5 Civilised[sic] Tribes. I enclose a letter to you from A. B. Cunningham, Ex. Secty. Cherokee Nation. From what he says my record of marriage may be found in some Other Book or the Book Kept by the Clerk of Tahlequah Dist.

Resp.

(Signed) T. S. Remsen.

Grove - Ind Tery. - January 9, 1907.

Comss. to the 5 Civilized Tribes:

I would be pleased to have a copy of T. J. McGhee's testimony in my case - Cherokee No. 2841.

Resp.

(Signed) T. S. Remsen.

Grove, Ind Tery.
January 6th, 1906.

Comss. to the 5 Civilised[sic] Tribes:

T. J. McGhee, who married me will be at your office tomorrow 7 or 8 to testify for Lewis Moore and Samuel C. Glenn. Please have him to testify in my case.

Cherokee No. 2841.

Resp. (Signed) Tredwell S. Remsen.

N. B. let me know if his testimony is sufficient.

Cherokee Intermarried White 1906
Volume VII

This certifies that the undersigned, being duly sworn, states that as stenographer to the Commission to the Five Civilized Tribes she made the above and foregoing copy and that the same is a full, true and correct copy of the original instrument now on file in this office.

             Georgia Coberly
              Stenographer.

Subscribed and sworn to before me this 20th day of February, 1907.

             Oliver C Hinkle
              Notary Public.

◇◇◇◇◇

CERTIFIED COPY.

EXECUTIVE DEPARTMENT
Cherokee Nation.

W.C. Rogers, Principal Chief	A.B. Cunningham, Ex. Secretary.
D.M. Faulkner, Assistant Chief	C.J. Harris, Assistant Secretary
W.W. Hastings, National Attorney	W.M. Walker, Assistant Secretary.
J H. Covel, Interpreter	

            TAHLEQUAH, INDIAN TERRITORY
               January 9th, 1907.

T. S. Remson

  Grove, Indian Territory,

Sir:-

Replying to your letter of the 7,inst, you are advised that all the marriage records were sent to the Commission late last month. I think possibly they were looking in the Delaware records for you, I think if they will examine a small record of Tahlequah District, this is a small book about 4 by 6 inches, they will find your record, as this little book contains a record of many of those old marriages from various districts in the Nation. I suppose it was the custom to send the license to the Clerk of Tahlequah district for record.

          Very respectfully,
           (Signed) A. B. Cunningham
                Secretary.

Cherokee Intermarried White 1906
Volume VII

This certifies that the undersigned, being duly sworn, states that as stenographer to the Commission to the Five Civilized Tribes she made the above and foregoing copy and that the same is a full, true and correct copy of the original instrument now on file in this office.

            Georgia Coberly
            Stenographer.

Subscribed and sworn to before me this 20th day of February, 1907.

            Oliver C Hinkle
            Notary Public.

◇◇◇◇◇

CERTIFIED COPY.

            Grove, I. T.
            Dec. 31st, 1906.

This is to certify that James E. Harlin who is about 75 years of age, a resident of Grove, I. T., who is afected[sic] very much with Rheumatism & Diabetis[sic]-: not able to go any where, almost Impossible to get out of the house without &[sic] assistant[sic].

       (Signed) J. C. Holland,
           M. D.

I have been a Practicing Medicine for about 13 years:-
The within affidavit subscribed and sworn to this 8th day of January, 1907.

       (Signed) G. S. Remsen,
           Notary Public.

My Comss. expires May 2nd, 1908.

(SEAL)

This certifies that the undersigned, being duly sworn, states that as stenographer to the Commission to the Five Civilized Tribes she made the above and foregoing copy and that the same is a full, true and correct copy of the original instrument now on file in this office.

            Georgia Coberly
            Stenographer.

Cherokee Intermarried White 1906
Volume VII

Subscribed and sworn to before me this 20th day of February, 1907.

Oliver C Hinkle
Notary Public.

◇◇◇◇◇

C E R T I F I E D C O P Y .

Cherokee - 2841.

2d Recording Dist)
)
Indian Territory)   Grove, January 9th, 1907.

    Personally appeared before me a Notary Public in and for said Dist, and Territory, James E. Harlin, a resident of Grove, to me known, and entitled to credit, who after being duly sworn declares as follows:- I am Over 75 years of age I married Nancy A. Harlin, nee Bell in 1872 I was Clerk of Delaware District, Cherokee Nation in 1874 and 5. In February 1875 I issued a Marriage License to Tredwell S. Remsen, a white man to Marry Julia E. Monroe, a Cherokee woman by blood and a recognized citizen as such. This license was issued in accordance with the Laws of the Cherokee Nation Existing at that time, they were duly executed by T. J. McGhee, Judge of Delaware District, returned to my office and recorded in a Book Kept by Clerks for that purpose. Some three days after the License were issued this Book was turned Over to my Successor in office, November, 1875, Mr. Cunningham.

I am afflicted with rheumatism, can hardly walk around the house.

                      (Signed)   James E. Harlin.

Subscribed and sworn to before me this 9th day of January, 1907.

                      (Signed)   W. E. Ross,

Notary Public.

My Commission expires Oct. 17th, 1909.
(SEAL)

    This certifies that the undersigned, being duly sworn, states that as stenographer to the Commission to the Five Civilized Tribes she made the above and foregoing copy and that the same is a full, true and correct copy of the original instrument now on file in this office.

Georgia Coberly
Stenographer.

Cherokee Intermarried White 1906
Volume VII

Subscribed and sworn to before me this 20th day of February, 1907.

Oliver C Hinkle
Notary Public.

◇◇◇◇◇

E C M   Cherokee 2841.

DEPARTMENT OF THE INTERIOR,
COMMISSIONER TO THE FIVE CIVILIZED TRIBES.

In the matter of the application for the enrollment of TREDWELL S. REMSEN as a citizen by intermarriage of the Cherokee Nation.

D E C I S I O N

THE RECORDS OF THIS OFFICE SHOW: That at Vinita, Indian Territory September 17, 1900 application was received by the Commission to the Five Civilized Tribes for the enrollment of Tredwell S. Remsen as a citizen by intermarriage of the Cherokee Nation. Further proceedings in the matter of said application were had at Muskogee, Indian Territo[sic] October 21, 1902, Tahlequah, Indian Territory, September 24, 1903 and Muskogee, Indian Territory, January 2, January 4 and January 7, 1907.

THE EVIDENCE IN THIS CASE SHOWS: That the applicant herein, Tredwell S. Remsen, a white man, was married in accordance with Cherokee law February 6, 1875 to his wife, Julia A. Remsen nee Monroe, who was at the time of said marriage a recognized citizen by blood of the Cherokee Nation, who is identified on the Cherokee authenticated tribal roll of 1880, Delaware District No. 2148 as a native Cherokee and whose name is included on the approved partial roll of citizens by blood of the Cherokee Nation opposite No. 7132. It is further shown that from the time of said marriage the said Tredwell S. Remsen and Julia A. Remsen resided together as husband and wife and continuously lived in the Cherokee Nation up to and including September 1, 1902. Said applicant is identified on the Cherokee authenticated tribal roll of 1880 and the Cherokee census roll of 1896 as an intermarried citizen of the Cherokee Nation citizen.

IT IS, THEREFORE, ORDERED AND ADJUDGED: That in accordance with the decision of the Supreme Court of the United States, dated November 5, 1906, in the cases of Daniel Red Bird, et al. vs. the United States, Nos. 125, 126, 127, and 128, the said applicant, Tredwell S. Remsen is entitled, under the provisions of Section Twenty-one of the Act of Congress approved June 28, 1898 (30 Stats. 495), to enrollment as a citizen by intermarriage of the Cherokee Nation, and his application for enrollment as such is accordingly granted.

Cherokee Intermarried White 1906
Volume VII

Tams Bixby
Commissioner.

Dated at Muskogee, Indian Territory,
this   FEB 23 1907

◇◇◇◇◇

Cherokee 2841

COPY

Muskogee, Indian Territory, February 23, 1907.

W. W. Hastings,
     Attorney for the Cherokee Nation,
          Muskogee, Indian Territory.

Dear Sir:

     There is enclosed herewith a copy of the decision of the Commissioner to the Five Civilized Tribes, dated February 23, 1907, granting the application for the enrollment of Tredwell S. Remsen as a citizen by intermarriage of the Cherokee Nation.

Respectfully,
SIGNED Tams Bixby
Commissioner.

Encl. A-9
    RA

◇◇◇◇◇

Cherokee 2841

Muskogee, Indian Territory, February 23, 1907.

The Commissioner to the Five Civilized Tribes,
     Muskogee, Indian Territory.

Sir:

     Receipt is acknowledged of the testimony and of your decision enrolling Tredwell S. Remsen as a citizen by intermarriage of the Cherokee Nation. Time for protesting said decision is waived and I consent that said person may be placed upon the schedule immediately.

Respectfully,
W. W. Hastings
Attorney for the Cherokee Nation.

◇◇◇◇◇

Cherokee Intermarried White 1906
Volume VII

Cherokee 2841

COPY

Muskogee, Indian Territory, February 23, 1907.

Tredwell S. Remsen,
    Grove, Indian Territory.

Dear Sir:

    There is enclosed herewith a copy of the decision of the Commissioner to the Five Civilized Tribes, dated February 23, 1907, granting the application for your enrollment as a citizen by intermarriage of the Cherokee Nation.

    You will be advised when your name has been placed upon a schedule of citizens of the Cherokee Nation and approved by the Secretary of the Interior.

                     Respectfully,
                       SIGNED *Tams Bixby*
                       Commissioner.

Encl. A-8
RA

Cher IW 217

◇◇◇◇◇

DEPARTMENT OF THE INTERIOR,
COMMISSION TO THE FIVE CIVILIZED TRIBES,
VINITA, I.T., SEPTEMBER 19, 1900.

    In the matter of the application of Robert C Miller for the enrollment of himself, wife and children as citizens of the Cherokee Nation, said Miller being sworn by Commissioner T. B. Needles, testified as follows:

Q What is your name? A Robert C. Miller.
Q What is your age? A 66.
Q What is your post office address? A Grove.
Q What district do you live in? A Delaware.
Q Are you a recognized citizen of the Cherokee Nation? A Yes, sir
Q By blood? A No, sir.
Q By inter-marriage? A Yes, sir.
Q Your father and mother are non-citizens? A Yes, sir.
Q For whom do you apply for enrollment? A Myself, wife and family
Q What is the name of your wife? A Mary E. Lamar.

Cherokee Intermarried White 1906
Volume VII

Q That was her name when you married her? A Yes, sir.
Q When did you marry her? A April 1st, 1869.
Q Have you been living with her continuously since that time? A Yes, sir.
Q Is she living now? A Yes, sir.
Q She was born in '50? A Yes, sir.
Q Do you know the name of her father? A Yes, sir, J. R. Lamar.
Q Is he living? A No, sir.
Q What is the name of her father[sic]? A Elizabeth.
Q Is she living? A No, sir.
Q Felix F. was born in 1883? A Yes, sir.
Q He would be 17 years old would not he? A Yes, sir.
Q Emma M., she is 13 years old? A Yes, sir.
Q James C., he would be 11 years old? A Yes, sir.
Q William E., he is nine years old? A Yes, sir.
Q These children alive and living with you? A Yes, sir.
Q How long have you been a resident of the Cherokee Nation? A About 34 years.
Q You been living with your wife continuously since that time? A Yes, sir.

1880 enrollment; page 288, #1739, Robert Mellir[sic], Delaware.
1880 enrollment; page 288, #1740, Mary Mellit[sic],   "
1896 enrollment; page 562, #376, Robert Miller,   "
1896 enrollment; page 502, #2013, Mary E. "   "
1896 enrollment; page 502, #2016, Felix Miller,   "
1896 enrollment; page 502, #2017, Emma   "   "
1896 enrollment; page 502, #2018, James   "   "
1896 enrollment; page 502, #2019, William "   "

Com'r Needles:

The name of Robert C. Miller appears upon the authenticated roll of 1880 as Robert Mellir, and upon the census roll of 1896 as Robert Miller. The name of his wife appears upon the authenticated roll of 1880 as Mary Mellir, and upon the census roll of 1896 as Mary Miller. The name of his children, Felix F., Mary, James F. appear upon the census roll of 1896. They all being duly identified according to the page and number as indicated in the testimony and having made satisfactory proof of their residence, said Robert C. Miller will be duly listed for enrollment by this Commission as a Cherokee citizen by inter-marriage. The name of his wife Mary, and his children, Felis[sic], Emma M., James C[sic]. and William C., will be duly listed for enrollment by this Commission as Cherokee citizens by blood.

J. O. Rosson, being first duly sworn, states that as stenographer to the Commission to the Five Civilized Tribes, he correctly recorded the testimony and proceedings in this case, and that the foregoing is a true and complete transcript of his stenographic notes thereof.

JO Rosson

Cherokee Intermarried White 1906
Volume VII

Subscribed and sworn to before me this 21st day of September, 1900.

TB Needles
Commissioner.

◇◇◇◇◇

File with Cherokee straight No. 3008.

Department of the Interior,
Commission to the Five Civilized Tribes,
Vinita, I.T., October 26, 1901.

In the matter of the application of Robert C. Miller et al for enrollment as Cherokee citizens.

STATEMENT AND ORDER.

Commissioner Breckinridge: In Cherokee straight case No. 3008, the application of Robert C. Miller, et al., the age of the child, Felix F. Miller, is given in the testimony as 17 years at the time of application, September 19, 1900, and on the enrollment card and in the enrollment memorandum the age of this child is given as 13 years. Upon consulting the roll of 1896 this child is found there recorded as 13 years of age, which would make his age at the present time 17. It is ordered that the enrollment card be corrected to correspond with the testimony and the roll of 1896, and that this child's name be entered as 17 years old.

There are marked variations in the names of some of these applicants.

In the case of the applicant's wife she is given upon the card, upon the enrollment memorandum and in the testimony as Mary E; in the field judgment her name is mentioned simply as Mary. It is obvious that the former is correct and the card as it now stands is considered to be correct.

As regards the child, Felix F., his name is mentioned in the judgment as Felia, which is obviously a stenographic error, and the card is considered correct, he having been recorded as Felix F.; this corresponds with the rendering of his name in the judgment and one form given in the testimony and on the enrollment memorandum.

The child, William E. as given in the testimony and on the enrollment card, is mentioned in the field judgment as William C. It is evident that the initial C. in the latter case is a typographical[sic] error and the present form of the enrollment card is correct.

It is ordered that a copy of the foregoing be attached to each copy of the testimony in this case.

--**--

Cherokee Intermarried White 1906
Volume VII

M. D. Green, being firs duly sworn, states that as stenographer to the Commission to the Five Civilized Tribes he correctly recorded the testimony and proceedings in this case and that the foregoing is a true and complete transcript of his stenographic notes thereof.

MD Green

Subscribed and sworn to before me this October 28, 1901.

C.R. Breckinridge

Commissioner.

◇◇◇◇◇

Cherokee 3008.

DEPARTMENT OF THE INTERIOR,
COMMISSION TO THE FIVE CIVILIZED TRIBES.
Muskogee, I. T., October 20, 1902.

In the matter of the application of Robert C. Miller for the enrollment of himself as a citizen by intermarriage, and for the enrollment of his wife, Mary E. Miller, and his four children, Felix F. Miller, Emma M. Hopkins, James C. Miller and William E. Miller, as citizens by blood, of the Cherokee Nation.

SUPPLEMENTAL PROCEEDINGS.

ROBERT C. MILLER, being sworn, testified as follows:

By the Commission,

Q What is your name, please? A Robert C. Miller.
Q What's your age, Mr. Miller, at this time? A Well, about sixty-eight, as well as I recollect.
Q What's your postoffice? A Grove.
Q Are you the same Robert C. Miller for whom application was made in September, 1900 for enrollment as an intermarried citizen? A At Vinita?
Q Yes. A Yes, sir.
Q Who made the application for you? A Who made it?
Q Yes, who appeared before the Commission? A I did.
Q You did, yourself? A Yes, sir.
Q Well, at that time you gave your age as sixty, is that right or was that a mistake?
A Well, now, I made a mistake just now, I guess. You see, I taken[sic] it off the family record and the children's ages and all.
Q Well, now, what would you say your age is at this time? A Well I give it in correct. I took it off the family record.
Q At that time? A Yes, I handed it to the Commission.

Cherokee Intermarried White 1906
Volume VII

Q So your age now would be about sixty-two? A Yes, about sixty-two. My head's in a bad shape.
Q What is your wife's name? A Mary E.
Q Is she a citizen by blood? A Yes, sir, I guess she is.
Q When were you married to your wife, Mary E.? A April 1, '69.
Q To this wife? A Yes, sir.
Q Never been married to any other woman? A No.
Q You are on the '80 roll with her as her husband? A Yes, sir, I am on the '70[sic] roll.
Q Have you and your wife, Mary E., lived together since 1880 up to the present time? A Yes, sir.
Q Never been separated? A No, sir, stayed right there and aim to take care of her as long as she lives.
Q Were you and she living together as husband and wife on the first day of September, 1902? A Yes, sir.
Q Have you and she lived together in the Cherokee Nation all the time since 1880 up to the present time? A Yes, sir.
Q Are these children, Felix F., Emma M., James C. and William E., all your children by your wife, Mary E.? A Yes, sir.
Q All these four children living at this time? A All living.
Q Have they lived in the Cherokee Nation all their lives? A All but Emma, she lives in Washington.
Q She's married? A Emma is married and Felix is married and both have a boy apiece.
Q You say Felix has a child, and Emma? A Yes, sir.
Q It is about time they were on the roll then. A They are on the roll, they sent them down here. Felix and his woman have been with me and my woman fourteen months. He made a crop there.

Retta Chick, being first duly sworn, states that, as stenographer to the Commission to the Five Civilized Tribes, she recorded the testimony and proceedings in the matter of the foregoing application, and that the above is a true and complete transcript of her stenographic notes thereof.

Retta Chick

Subscribed and sworn to before me this 18th day of November, 1902.

BC Jones
Notary Public.

Cherokee Intermarried White 1906
Volume VII

F.R.   Cherokee 3008.

DEPARTMENT OF THE INTERIOR,
COMMISSIONER TO THE FIVE CIVILIZED TRIBES.
Muskogee, I. T., January 28, 1907.

In the matter of the application for the enrollment of Robert C. Miller as a citizen by intermarriage of the Cherokee Nation.

Robert C. Miller being first duly sworn by Frances R. Lane a Notary Public for the Western District of Indian Territory, testified as follows:

By the Commissioner:
Q What is your name? A Robert C. Miller.
Q What is your age? A I was born in 1834 I think.
Q That makes you about 73 years old? A Yes sir.
Q What is your postoffice address? A Grove, I. T.
Q You are a white man are you? A Yes sir.
Q Not possessed of any Indian blood? A Not a bit.
Q You claim your right to enrollment by virtue of your marriage to a citizen by blood of the Cherokee Nation? A Yes sir.
Q What is the name of the citizen through whom you claim? A My wife, Mary E. Miller, now. Mary E. Lamar was her name.
Q When were you married to Mary E. Lamar? A April 1, 1869.
Q That marriage was under a license of the Cherokee Nation, was it? A Yes sir.
Q What district was that? A Flint District.
> In Book B., Marriage Records of Flint District, page 120, now in possession of this office, appears a record showing that a marriage license was issued by James W. Adair Clerk of the District Court, Flint District, to Robert Miller and Mary Lamar on March 30, 1869, and that said parties were married on April 1, 1869, by M. Ghormley, minister of the Gospel. Said marriage license and certificate of marriage were filed for record on April 3, 1869.

Q At the time you married Mary Lamar, she was a citizen by blood of the Cherokee nation? A Yes sir.
Q Had you ever been married before you married Mary Lamar? A No sir.
Q Had she ever been married before she married you? A I don't know whether she had or not. She lived with a man down in the Choctaw Nation awhile. One of her cousins, and he wouldn't work and she made him hike.
Q When was that? A During the war.
Q It is your understanding though, that she was never lawfully married to this man in the Choctaw Nation. A No--you see they all took up when they first come to this country; they just took up and lived together.
Q Is your wife living at this time? A Yes, she is at home.
Q From the time of your marriage to Mary Lemar[sic] in 1869, have you resided as husband and wife and continuously lived in the Cherokee Nation up until the present time? A Yes sir.

Cherokee Intermarried White 1906
Volume VII

Q You have never been separated and have never moved out of the Cherokee Nation.[sic]
A No, I have got as good woman as anyone' if she hadn't have been a good woman I wouldn't have been here today. I fell 12 feet and when I got that fall---
Q At the time you married Mary Lamar she was regarded as a single woman? They didn't regard her as being married to this man in the Cherokee[sic] Nation? A No, everybody called her Mary Lamar and recommended her to me as a good woman

>The applicant, Robert C. Miller, is identified on the Cherokee authenticated tribal roll of 1880, Delaware District, opposite No. 1739, and on the Cherokee census roll 1896, Delaware District, No. 376.
>
>The applicant's wife, Mary E. Miller, is identified on the Cherokee authenticated tribal roll of 1880, Delaware District, opposite No. 1740, and on the Cherokee census roll of 1896, Delaware District, opposite 2013.
>
>She is also included in the approved partial roll of citizens by blood of the Cherokee nation opposite No. 7474.

Frances R. Lane upon oath states that as stenographer to the Commissioner to the Five Civilized Tribes she reported the testimony in the above entitled cause and that the foregoing is an accurate transcript of her stenographic notes thereof.

Frances R Lane

Subscribed and sworn to before me this January 29, 1907.

Edward Merrick
Notary Public.

◇◇◇◇◇

E. C. M.   Cherokee 3008.

DEPARTMENT OF THE INTERIOR,
COMMISSIONER TO THE FIVE CIVILIZED TRIBES.
Muskogee, Indian Territory, February 6, 1907.

In the matter of the application for the enrollment of Robert C. Miller as a citizen by intermarriage of the Cherokee Nation.

SUPPLEMENTAL.

Martha Evans being first duly sworn by Mrs. Lyman K. Lane, Notary Public, testified as follows:

Q What is your name?   A   Martha Evans.
Q You came here for the purpose of giving testimony in the case of Robert C. Miller, now pending before this Commission?
A Yes sir.

Cherokee Intermarried White 1906
Volume VII

Q Are you acquainted with the applicant in this case, Robert C. Miller, and his wife, Mary E. Miller?
A Yes sir.
Q How long have you known them?
A I have known her all her life.
Q Was she ever married prior to her marriage to Robert C. Miller?
A Yes sir.
Q Who was her first husband? A John Inlow.
Q Was she married more than once before she married Robert C. Miller?
A No sir.
Q She was married in accordance with the law to this John Inlow?
A Yes sir.
Q They lived together as husband and wife?
A Yes sir.
Q Was he dead when she married Robert C. Miller?
A Yes sir; he was dead.
Q Was John Inlow any relation to Mary E. Miller?
Q They were second cousins.
Q They were living together at the time he died?
A No.
Q They had separated had they? A Yes sir.
Q Was Mary E. Miller a recognized citizen by blood of the Cherokee Nation?
A Yes sir.
Q Was she born in the Cherokee Nation?
A No, she was born in Alabama.
Q When did she come to this Nation?
A Why, it was '56 I reckon.
Q After coming to the Cherokee Nation she was admitted to citizenship?
A O yes.
Q Did Mary E. Lamar come to this Nation on the general invitation issued by the Cherokee Nation to the Cherokees in Alabama?
A No.
Q Was she recognized as a citizen of the Cherokee Nation prior to her marriage to Robert C. Miller?
A Why, yes.
Q What was her father's name? A James Lamar.
Q Her mother's name? A Elizabeth Lamar.

Richard L. Taylor being first duly sworn by Mrs. Lyman K. Lane, testified as follows:

Q What is your name? A Richard L. Taylor.
Q What is your age? A 52.
Q What is your post office address?
A Stilwell, Indian Territory.

Cherokee Intermarried White 1906
Volume VII

Q What district? A Flint District.
Q Are you acquainted with the applicant herein, Robert C. Miller, and his wife, Mary E. Miller?
A Yes sir.
Q How long have you known them?
A Ever since along about '68 or '69; somewheres[sic] along there.
Q Were you acquainted with the wife of Robert C. Miller before she was married?
A Yes sir.
Q Were you acquainted with her at the time she was married to John Inlow?
A No sir; I wasn't acquainted with her. I think they married somewhere on Red River at the time of the war.
Q Have you any knowledge as to whether he was dead or not before she married Robert C Miller?
A That was my understanding. They had separated and then he died up there in the Choctaw Nation.
Q He was dead at the time she married Robert C. Miller?
A Yes sir.
Q Mary E. Miller has always been recognized as a citizen of the Cherokee Nation?
A Yes sir.
Q Was she recognized as such before she married Robert C. Miller?
A Yes sir.
Q Have they continuously lived in the Cherokee Nation since you have known them?
A As far as I know. You see they lived up in the country where I live a good long while and then they moved North and this is the first time I have seen the old man for about 15 years.
Q So far as you know they have always lived in the Cherokee Nation?
A Yes sir.

Robert C. Miller being first duly sworn, testified as follows:

Q What is your name? A Robert C. Miller.
Q What is your age? A 73 or 74.
Q What is your post office address? A Grove.
Q You are the applicant in this case? A Yes sir.
Q You were the husband of Mary E. Miller?
A Yes sir.
Q Have you any positive knowledge, Mr. Miller, as to whether the former husband of Mary E. Miller was dead at the time she was married to your or not?
A Yes sir; Devine brought the news west of Grand River; he lived in Arkansas and he got him to carry the news to John Inlow's brother.
Q Mr. Miller, when your wife, Mary E. Lamar, came to this country, was she admitted to citizenship in the Cherokee Nation or was she always recognized as a citizen without being admitted?
A She was always recognized as being a citizen.
Q You don't know whether they ever made application?
A No, I can't tell you.

Cherokee Intermarried White 1906
Volume VII

Q How long were you acquainted with her before you were married?
A I guess a couple of years.
Q Had she been recognized as a citizen of the Cherokee Nation before you married her?
A Yes sir.
Q Mr. Miller, since your marriage to Mary E. Miller, have you and she resided together as husband and wife and continuously lived in the Cherokee Nation?
A Yes sir.

The undersigned being first duly sworn states that as stenographer to the Commission to the Five Civilized Tribes, she recorded the testimony taken in this case and that the foregoing is a true and correct transcript of her stenographic notes thereof.

Myrtle Hill

Subscribed and sworn to before me this the 11th day of February, 1907.

J. L. Gary
Notary Public.

◇◇◇◇◇

E.C.M.   Cherokee 3008.

DEPARTMENT OF THE INTERIOR,

COMMISSIONER TO THE FIVE CIVILIZED TRIBES.

In the matter of the application for the enrollment of Robert C. Miller as a citizen by intermarriage of the Cherokee Nation.

D E C I S I O N

THE RECORDS OF THIS OFFICE SHOW: That at Vinita, Indian Territory, September 19, 1900, application was received by the Commission to the Five Civilized Tribes for the enrollment of Robert C. Miller as a citizen by intermarriage of the Cherokee Nation. Further proceedings in the matter of said application were had at Muskogee, Indian Territory, matter of said application were had at Vinita, Indian Territory, October 26, 1901, and at Muskogee, Indian Territory, October 20, 1902, January 28 and February 6, 1907.

Cherokee Intermarried White 1906
Volume VII

THE EVIDENCE IN THIS CASE SHOWS: That the applicant herein, Robert C. Miller, a white man, was married in accordance with Cherokee law, April 1, 1869 to one, Mary E. Miller, nee Lamar, who was at the time of said marriage a recognized citizen by blood of the Cherokee Nation who is identified upon the Cherokee authenticated tribal roll of 1880, Delaware District, No. 1740, as a native Cherokee, and whose name is included on the approved partial roll of citizens by blood of the Cherokee Nation opposite No. 7474. It is further shown that from the time of said marriage the said Robert C. Miller and Mary E. Miller resided together as husband and wife and continuously lived in the Cherokee Nation up to and including September 1, 1902. It is also shown that at the time of her marriage to Robert C Miller, the said Mary E. Miller was the widow of one John Inlow. Said applicant is identified upon the Cherokee authenticated tribal roll of 1880 and the Cherokee census roll of 1896 as an intermarried citizen of the Cherokee Nation.

IT IS, THEREFORE, ORDERED AND ADJUDGED: That in accordance with the decision of the Supreme Court of the United States, dated November 5, 1906, in the cases of Daniel Red Bird, et al., vs. the United States, Nos. 125, 126, 127, and 128 the said applicant, Robert C. Miller, is entitled, under the provisions of Section 21 of the Act of Congress approved June 28, 1898 (30 Stats. 495), to enrollment as a citizen by intermarriage of the Cherokee Nation and his application for enrollment as such is accordingly granted.

Tams Bixby
Commissioner.

Dated at Muskogee, Indian Territory,
this   FEB 23 1907

Cherokee 3008

COPY

Muskogee, Indian Territory, February 23, 1907.

W. W. Hastings,
    Attorney for the Cherokee Nation,
        Muskogee, Indian Territory.

Dear Sir:

There is enclosed herewith a copy of the decision of the Commissioner to the Five Civilized Tribes, dated February 23, 1907, granting the application for the enrollment of Robert C. Miller as a citizen by intermarriage of the Cherokee Nation.

Respectfully,

SIGNED *Tams Bixby*
Commissioner.

Encl. A-11
RA

Cherokee Intermarried White 1906
Volume VII

◇◇◇◇◇

Cherokee 3008

Muskogee, Indian Territory, February 23, 1907.

The Commissioner to the Five Civilized Tribes,
   Muskogee, Indian Territory.

Sir:

   Receipt is acknowledged of the testimony and of your decision enrolling Robert C. Miller as a citizen by intermarriage of the Cherokee Nation. Time for protesting said decision is waived, and I consent that said person may be placed upon the schedule immediately.

                    Respectfully,
                    W. W. Hastings
                    Attorney for the Cherokee Nation.

◇◇◇◇◇

Cherokee 3008

COPY

Muskogee, Indian Territory, February 23, 1907.

Robert C. Miller,
   Grove, Indian Territory.

Dear Sir:

   There is enclosed herewith a copy of the decision of the Commissioner to the Five Civilized Tribes, dated February 23, 1907, granting the application for your enrollment as a citizen by intermarriage of the Cherokee Nation.

   You will be advised when your name has been placed upon a schedule of citizens of the Cherokee Nation and approved by the Secretary of the Interior.

                    Respectfully,
                    SIGNED *Tams Bixby*
Encl. A-10   Commissioner.
   RA

Cher IW 218

◇◇◇◇◇

Cherokee Intermarried White 1906
Volume VII

F.R. Cherokee 6461.

DEPARTMENT OF THE INTERIOR
COMMISSIONER TO THE FIVE CIVILIZED TRIBES.

In the matter of the application for the enrollment of Elzina Ross as a citizen by intermarriage of the Cherokee Nation.

◇◇◇◇◇

FOUR copies with mother's case, ELZINA ROSS:

Department of the Interior,
Commission to the Five Civilized Tribes,
Tahlequah, I.T., December 11, 1900.

In the matter of the application of Andrew E. Ross for the enrollment of himself and his mother, Elzina Ross, as Cherokee citizens; being sworn and examined by Commissioner Needles he testified as follows:

Q What is your name? A Andrew E. Ross.
Q What is your age? A 28.
Q What is your post-office? A Locust Grove.
Q In what district do you live? A Saline District.
Q Are you a recognized citizen of the Cherokee Nation by blood?
A Yes sir.
Q What is your father's name? A Oliver Ross.
Q Is he living? A Yes sir.
Q What is your mother's name? A Anna Ross.
Q Is she living? A Yes sir.
1880 roll page 660 #966 Andrew Ross Saline Dist native Cher
1896 roll page 1013 #960 Andrew Ross Saline.
Q Do you want to enroll anybody but yourself? A My mother, she isn't able to get here; she is old and feeble; got a terrible cold and not able to come.
Q What is her name? A Elzina Ross.
Q How old is she? A 58.
Q You swear she is unable to come on account of bodily infirmaties[sic]
A Yes sir; she isn't able to come over the rough road.
1880 roll page 660 #962 as Elizina[sic] Ross Saline native Cher
Applicant: My mother is a white woman.
1896 roll page 1035 #32 Elizina Ross Saline Dist.

296

Cherokee Intermarried White 1906
Volume VII

Q You know whether your mother lived with your father until the time of his death?
A Yes sir, she did.
Q She ever married since? A No sir.

Com'r Needles: The name of Elzina Ross, the mother of the applicant, appears upon the authenticated roll of 1880 as Elizina Ross and upon the census rll[sic] of 1896 she is also identified; having made satisfactory proof as to her residence, also given satisfactory reasons why she is not able to be here in person, she will be duly listed for enrollment as a Cherokee citizen by intermarriage;
xxxxxx[sic] to Andrew E. Ross, his name appears upon the authenticated roll of 1880 as well as the census roll of 1896; he is duly identified and having made satisfactory proof as to residence, he will be duly listed for enrollment as a Cherokee citizen by blood.

M.D. Green, being first duly sworn, states that as stenographer to the Commission to the Five Civilized Tribes he correctly recorded the testimony and proceedings in this case and the foregoing is a true and complete transcript of his stenographic notes thereof.

MD Green

Subscribed and sworn to before me this December 12, 1900.

T B Needles
Commissioner.

⬦⬦⬦⬦⬦

Statement of Applicant Taken Under Oath.

CHEREKEE BY BLOOD AND ADOPTION.

Date DEC 11 1900   1900.

Name
District   Year   Page   No.
Citizen by blood   Mother's citizenship
Intermarried citizen
Married under what law   Date of marriage
License   Certificate

Wife's name **Elzina Ross**   **Locust Grove IT.**
District **Saline**   Year **1880** Page **660** No. **962**
Citizen by blood ~~Yes~~   Mother's citizenship
Intermarried citizen **Yes**
Married under what law   Date of marriage
License   Certificate

Names of Children:

	Dist.	Year	Page	No.	Age
	Dist.	Year	Page	No.	Age

Cherokee Intermarried White 1906
Volume VII

	Dist.	Year	Page	No.	Age
	Dist.	Year	Page	No.	Age
	Dist.	Year	Page	No.	Age

On 1880 roll as Elzina Ross

◇◇◇◇◇

Cherokee 6461.

Department of the Interior,
Commission to the Five Civilized Tribes,
Muskogee, I. T., October 15, 1902.

In the matter of the application of Elzina Ross for the enrollment of herself as a citizen by intermarriage of the Cherokee Nation; she being sworn and examined by the Commission, testified as follows:

Q What is your name? A Elzina Ross.
Q How old are you? A Going on sixty.
Q What is your postoffice? A Locust Grove.
Q Are you a white woman? A Yes sir.
Q Are you on the roll of 1880 as an adopted citizen? A Yes sir.
Q What was the name of your husband in 1880? A Oliver Ross.
Q Is he dead? A Yes sir.
Q When did he die? A He has been dead two years last April 6th.
Q Did you and your husband Oliver live together in the Cherokee Nation from 1880 up until the time he died? A Yes sir.
Q Never were separated were you? A No sir.
Q Of course, you haven't married since he died? A No sir.
Q Have you been living in the Cherokee Nation all the time since 1880? A Yes sir.
Q Oliver Ross was your first husband was he? A Yes sir.

The undersigned, being duly sworn, states that as stenographer to the Commission to the Five Civilized Tribes he correctly recorded the testimony and proceedings in this case, and that the foregoing is a true and correct transcript of his stenographic notes thereof.

E.G. Rothenberger

Subscribed and sworn to before me this 10th day of November, 1902.

BC Jones
Notary Public.

Cherokee Intermarried White 1906
Volume VII

◇◇◇◇◇

F.R. Cherokee 6461.

DEPARTMENT OF THE INTERIOR,
COMMISSIONER TO THE FIVE CIVILIZED TRIBES.
MUSKOGEE, I. T., FEBRUARY 15, 1907.

In the matter of the application for the enrollment of ELZINA ROSS as a citizen by intermarriage of the Cherokee Nation.

ANDREW ROSS, being first duly sworn by Walter W. Chappell, Notary Public, testified as follows:

ON BEHALF OF THE COMMISSIONER:

Q What is your name? A Andrew Ross.
Q What is your age? A 35.
Q What is your post office address? A Locust Grove.
Q Do you know Elzina Ross? A Yes sir.
Q Are you related to her? A Yes sir.
Q What relation? A Son.
Q Is Elzina Ross living at this time? A Yes sir.
Q What is the condition of her health? A It is not very good.
Q She is not able to appear here? A No sir; the trip is too hard for her.
Q Elzina Ross claims the right to enrollment as a citizen by intermarriage of the Cherokee Nation, does she? A Yes sir.
Q Is she a white woman? A Yes sir.
Q Does she claim the right to enrollment by virtue of her marriage to a citizen of the Cherokee Nation? A Yes sir.
Q What is the name of the citizen through whom she claims the right to enrollment? A Oliver Ross.
Q Is Oliver Ross living at this time? A No sir.
Q When did he die? A In 1900.
Q When were Elzina and Oliver Ross married? A February 1, 1865.
Q Have you any documentary evidence showing their marriage? A Yes sir.

Witness presents certificate of Jno. N. Cox, Clerk, County Court of Hopkins County, Texas, showing that a marriage license was issued to Oliver Ross and Elzina Goonin January 31, 1865, and that said certificate was returned executed February 1, 1865.

Q Elzina Ross' name before marriage was Goonin, was it? A Yes sir.
Q Do you know when they removed to the Cherokee Nation? A In '66.

Cherokee Intermarried White 1906
Volume VII

Q   Upon their return to the Nation to[sic] you know whether or not Oliver Ross was readmitted to citizenship?   A   He was always recognized as a citizen of the Cherokee Nation.
Q   Where did he live prior to his marriage?   A   In the Indian Territory; he was in Texas at the end of the war, but he came back here after the war.
Q   Did he serve in the war?   A   Yes sir.
Q   Did Oliver Ross and Elzina Ross reside together as husband and wife, and live in the Cherokee Nation from the time of their removal to the Nation in 1866?
    A   Yes sir.
Q   Has Elzina Ross continued to live in the Cherokee Nation since his death?
    A   Yes sir.
Q   She has not remarried?   A   No sir.
Q   It is your understanding that Oliver Ross was not married previous to his marriage to Elzina Ross?   A   Yes sir, he was married, but his wife was dead.
Q   He had been married once before?   A   Yes sir.
Q   Who was his first wife?   A   Susie Vann.
Q   Was his first wife a citizen of the Cherokee Nation?   A   Yes sir.
Q   What is your understanding as to the date of her death?
    A   I dont[sic] know the date.
Q   But it is your understanding that she died prior to the marriage of Oliver Ross to Elzina Goonin?   A   Yes sir.
Q   Was Elzina Ross married prior to her marriage to Oliver Ross?   A   No sir.
Q   It is your understanding, is it, that from the time of their removal to Indian Territory from Texas in 1866 that they were regarded as husband and wife?   A   Yes sir.
Q   Did Oliver Ross exercise all the rights accorded to citizens by blood of the Cherokee Nation?   A   Yes sir.
Q   Did he ever hold office?   A   Yes sir.
Q   What office?   A   District Clerk, I think.
Q   What year?   A   I dont[sic] know.
Q   What District?   A   Saline District.

JOSHUA ROSS, being first duly sworn by Walter W. Chappell, Notary Public, testified as follows:

Q   What is your name?   A   Joshua Ross.
Q   What is your age?   A   74.
Q   What is your post office address?   A   Muskogee.
Q   Do you appear here today for the purpose of giving testimony relative to the right to enrollment as a citizen by intermarriage of the Cherokee Nation of Elzina Ross?
    A   I do.
Q   Are you related to Elzina Ross by marriage?   A   I am.
Q   What is the relationship?   A   She is the widow of my brother, Oliver Ross.
Q   Do you know when Oliver Ross and Elzina Ross were married?
    A   In 1865.
Q   Where were they married?   A   In Texas.
Q   When did they remove to the Cherokee Nation?   A   In 1866.

Cherokee Intermarried White 1906
Volume VII

Q How near were you living to Oliver Ross immediately subsequent to his removal to the Cherokee Nation? A First at Ft. Gibson, and on his way he came to my house and stayed all night.

Q Well, during the next few years? A In the same District awhile.

Q From the time of his removal to the Cherokee Nation in 1866 was Oliver Ross recognized as a citizen by blood of the Cherokee Nation? A Yes sir.

Q Do you know if any steps were taken by him to be readmitted?
A No sir, it was not necessary because he had always lived in and been a citizen of the Cherokee Nation, and immediately after the war he came back.

Q The only time, then, he was out of the Cherokee Nation was when he served in the war? A Yes sir.

Q Did Oliver Ross and Elzina Ross reside together as husband and wife, and live continuously in the Cherokee Nation from 1866 until the death of Oliver Ross? A Yes sir.

Q And since that time Elzina Ross has continuously lived in the Cherokee Nation? A Yes sir.

Q Oliver Ross was married prior to his marriage to Elzina Ross, was he?
A Yes sir, his wife died; he was married to Susan Vann and she died in 1860 and was buried at Butler's Creek, 10 miles from here.

Q What office in the Cherokee Nation did Oliver Ross hold?
A He was Clerk of the District after the war.

Q Saline District? A Yes sir.

Q What year? A '67, I think it was.

Q No one but recognized citizens by blood of the Cherokee Nation can hold office in the Nation, can they? A Recognized citizens can hold office.

Q Did Oliver and Elzina Ross have any children? A Yes sir.

Q What is the name of the oldest child? A Mary.

Q Do you know in what year she was born? A I dont[sic] remember.

Q Is she living at this time? A Yes sir, up near Chelsea.

Q What is her name? A Mary Jones.

JAMES M. BELL, being first duly sworn by Joshua W. Ross, Notary Public, testified as follows:

Q What is your name? A James M Bell.

Q What is your age? A 74.

Q What is your post office address? A Needmore.

Q Do you appear here today to give testimony relative to the right to enrollment of Elzina Ross as a citizen by intermarriage of the Cherokee Nation? A Yes sir.

Q How long have you known Elzina Ross? A I dont[sic] know her at all.

Q Did you ever know one Oliver Ross in the Cherokee Nation? A Yes.

Q When did you first become acquainted with Oliver Ross?
A I have known him since childhood.

Q When did you first know him? A In the old Nation, in the old country; it was at my father's house, and he was home from school.

Q In about what year was that? A About '37 or '38; along there.

Cherokee Intermarried White 1906
Volume VII

Q When did Oliver Ross come to the Cherokee Nation? A Under the Treaty of 1835.
Q With his parents? A Yes sir.
Q What are the name[sic] of his parents? A Andrew Ross, and his mother was a Miss Lowry.
Q When did you come to the Cherokee Nation?
A My father brought me here in 1839.
Q Did you live in the same District with Oliver Ross after coming here?
A For awhile, in Saline District.
Q When you first knew him in Saline District did Oliver Ross exercise all the rights and privileges of a citizen of the Cherokee Nation? A Yes sir, he was Clerk of the District at one time, if I am not mistaken.
Q You say you know there was never any question about his citizenship?
A No sir.

The applicant is identified on the Cherokee authenticated tribal roll of 1880, Saline District, No. 962, and on the Cherokee census roll of 1896, Saline District, Page 1035, No. 32.

The undersigned, being first duly sworn, states that as stenographer to the Commission to the Five Civilized Tribes, she correctly reported the above and foregoing testimony, and that the same is a full, true and complete transcript of her stenographic notes thereof.

Sarah Waters

Subscribed and sworn to before me this 16th day of February, 1907.

Oliver C. Hinkle
Notary Public.

◇◇◇◇◇

Oliver Ross, |
453 TO | ss
Elzina Goonin. | BE IT REMEMBERED, That on this 31 day of Janny[sic] 1865 the following marriage license was issued, to-wit:

TEXAS, TO-WIT: Hopkins County, ss:

To all who shall see these presents, Greeting:

Know ye, that any person legally authorized to celebrate the rites of matrimony, is hereby licensed to join in marriage as husband and wife, Oliver Ross and Elzina Goonin and for so doing this shall be his sufficient authority.

Cherokee Intermarried White 1906
Volume VII

In testimony whereof, I, Z. G. Matthews, Clerk of the Hopkins County Court, hereunto subscribe my name, and affix the seal of said Court, this 31st day of January, 1865.

Z. G. Matthews.

BE IT REMEMBERED, That on this 10 day of Feby, 1865, the following certificate was filed in my office, to-wit:

TEXAS, TO-WIT: Hopkins County:

This certified, That I joined in marriage as husband and wife Oliver Ross and Elzina Goonin on the 1st day of Feby, 1865.

Wm Chapman, M. G.

xxxxxxxxxxxxxxxxxxxxx

THE STATE OF TEXAS, |
|
CIUNTY[sic] OF HOPKINS. | I, Jno. N. Cox, Clerk of the County Court in and for Hopkins County, Texas, do hereby certify that the above and foregoing is a true and correct copy of a marriage license issued to Oliver Ross and Eliza[sic] Goonin and the certificate of return thereon, as appears of record in Vol. 2 page 222 Marriage License of Hopkins County, Texas. I further certify that I have carefully compared this copy with the original record thereof.

Witness my hand and seal of office at office in Sulphur Springs, Texas, this 28th day of January, A. D. 1907.

Jno N Cox   Clerk County Court,
Hopkins County, Texas.

By   J L Mothershed   Deputy.

◇◇◇◇◇

Cherokee Intermarried White 1906
Volume VII

F.R.   Cherokee 6461.

DEPARTMENT OF THE INTERIOR,

COMMISSIONER TO THE FIVE CIVILIZED TRIBES.

In the matter of the application for the enrollment of Elzina Ross as a citizen by intermarriage of the Cherokee Nation.

D E C I S I O N

THE RECORDS OF THIS OFFICE SHOW: That at Tahlequah, Indian Territory, December 11, 1900, application was received by the Commission to the Five Civilized Tribes for the enrollment of Elzina Ross as a citizen by intermarriage of the Cherokee Nation. Further proceedings in the matter of said application were had at Muskogee, Indian Territory, October 15, 1902, and February 17, 1907.

THE EVIDENCE IN THIS CASE SHOWS: That the applicant herein, Elzina Ross was lawfully married in 1865, in the State of Texas to one Oliver Ross who was, at the time fo[sic] said marriage, a recognized citizen by blood of the Cherokee Nation and who is identified on the Cherokee authenticated tribal roll of 1880, Saline District, Page 660, No. 961, as a native Cherokee.

It is further shown that the said Oliver Ross and Elzina Ross resided together as husband and wife and continuously lived in the Cherokee Nation from 1866, until the death of said Oliver Ross in 1900; that since the death of her said husband the said Elzina Ross has not remarried and has continued to reside in the Cherokee Nation up to and including September 1, 1902.

The applicant is identified on the Cherokee authenticated tribal roll of 1880, Saline District, Page 660, No. 962, as a native Cherokee. She is also identified on the Cherokee census roll of 1896, as an adopted white citizen of the Cherokee Nation.

The evidence shows that the applicant is a white woman and claims her right to enrollment as a citizen of the Cherokee Nation by virtue of her marriage to said Oliver Ross.

It is considered, therefore, that the enrollment of Elzina Ross as a native Cherokee on the Cherokee authenticated tribal roll of 1880 is an erroneous classification.

IT IS, THEREFORE, ORDERED AND ADJUDGED: That in accordance with the decision of the Supreme Court of the United States, dated November 5, 1906, in the cases of Daniel Red Bird, et al., vs. the United States, Nos. 125, 126, 127, and 128, that the applicant herein, Elzina Ross, is entitled under the provisions of Section 21 of the Act of Congress approved June 28, 1898 (30 Stats., 495), to enrollment as a citizen by intermarriage of the Cherokee Nation and her application for enrollment as such is accordingly granted.

Cherokee Intermarried White 1906
Volume VII

Tams Bixby
Commissioner.

Dated at Muskogee, Indian Territory,
this FEB 21 1907

◇◇◇◇◇

Cherokee 6461

Muskogee, Indian Territory, February 21, 1907.

W. W. Hastings,
    Attorney for the Cherokee Nation,
        Muskogee, Indian Territory.

Dear Sir:

    There is enclosed herewith a copy of the decision of the Commissioner to the Five Civilized Tribes, dated February 21, 1907, granting the application for the enrollment of Elzina Ross as a citizen by intermarriage of the Cherokee Nation.

Respectfully,

Encl. H-59
JMH
Commissioner.

◇◇◇◇◇

Cherokee 6461

Muskogee, Indian Territory, February 21, 1907.

The Commissioner to the Five Civilized Tribes,
    Muskogee, Indian Territory.

Sir:

    Receipt is acknowledged of the testimony and of your decision enrolling Elzina Ross as a citizen by intermarriage of the Cherokee Nation. Time for protesting said decision is waived, and I consent that said person may be placed upon the schedule immediately.

Respectfully,
W. W. Hastings
Attorney for Cherokee Nation.

◇◇◇◇◇

Cherokee Intermarried White 1906
Volume VII

Cherokee 6461

Muskogee, Indian Territory, February 21, 1907.

Elzina Ross,
    Locust Grove, Indian Territory.

Dear Madam:

    There is enclosed herewith a copy of the decision of the Commissioner to the Five Civilized Tribes, dated February 21, 1907, granting the application for your enrollment as a citizen by intermarriage of the Cherokee Nation.

    You will be advised when your name has been placed upon a schedule of citizens of the Cherokee Nation and approved by the Secretary of the Interior.

                Respectfully,

Encl. H-60   Commissioner.
JMH

Cher IW 219

◇◇◇◇◇◇

(No information given.)

Cher IW 220

◇◇◇◇◇◇

                                                        F.R.

DEPARTMENT OF THE INTERIOR

COMMISSIONER TO THE FIVE CIVILIZED TRIBES

In the matter of the application for the enrollment of

LUCINDA WELCH

As a citizen by intermarriage of the Cherokee Nation.

Cherokee 10030.

Cherokee Intermarried White 1906
Volume VII

◇◇◇◇◇

DEPARTMENT OF THE INTERIOR,
COMMISSION TO THE FIVE CIVILIZED TRIBES,
VINITA, I T., SEPTEMBER 27, 1900.

In the matter of the application of John Cobb Welch for the enrollment of his mother, Lucinda Welch, as a citizen of the Cherokee Nation; said Welch being sworn by Commissioner T. B. Needles, testified as follows:

Q   What is the name of your mother?   A   Lucinda Welch.
Q   How old is your mother?   A   75, too old and infirm to come here.
Q   What is her post office address?   A   Grove.
Q   Is she full blood Cherokee?   A   No, sir.
Q   What degree of blood has she?   A   She is a white woman.
Q   What is the reason she is not here?   A   She is too old and feeble to come.
Q   What is her name?   A   Lucinda Welch.

1880 enrollment; page 338, #2949, Lucinda Welch, Delaware.
1896 enrollment; page 593, #558, Lucinda Welch, Delaware.

Q   Is your father living?   A   No, sir, he has been dead 14 years.

Com'r Needles:--Upon examination of the records of the Dawes Commission it is found that the said Lucinda Welch made application to said Commission in the year 1896, in case No. 4436, for enrollment as a citizen of the Cherokee Nation, and the record shows that said application was denied. No appeal was taken. The facts in the case are that the said Lucinda Welch's name appears upon the authenticated roll of 1880 as an intermarried citizen of the Cherokee Nation white, and she has lived in the Cherokee Nation ever since the year 1867, and is now 75 years is age. Her name also appears, as stated, upon the records of the Dawes Commission as having applied, as stated above, and having been denied; consequently final judgment as to the application of the said Lucinda Welch will be suspended and her name will be placed upon a doubtful cars

))) oooOOOooo---[sic]

J. O. Rosson, being first duly sworn, states that as stenographer to the Commission to the Five Civilized Tribes, he correctly recorded the testimony and proceedings in this case, and the foregoing is a true and complete transcript of his stenographic notes thereof.

J O Rosson

Subscribed and sworn to before me this 1st day of October, 1900.

TB Needles
Commissioner.

Cherokee Intermarried White 1906
Volume VII

◇◇◇◇◇

Statement of Applicant Taken Under Oath.

CHEROKEE BY BLOOD AND ADOPTION.

Date **SEP 27 1900** 1900.

Name .... **Grove I T**
District .... Year .... Page .... No. ....
Citizen by blood .... Mother's citizenship ....
Intermarried citizen ....
Married under what law .... Date of marriage ....
License **(75)** .... Certificate ....
Wife's name .... **Lucinda Welch**
District .... **DELAWARE** .... Year **1880** Page **338** No. **2949**
Citizen by blood .... Mother's citizenship ....
Intermarried citizen **Yes**
Married under what law .... Date of marriage ....
License .... Certificate ....

Names of Children:

	Dist.	Year	Page	No.	Age
	Dist.	Year	Page	No.	Age
	Dist.	Year	Page	No.	Age
	Dist.	Year	Page	No.	Age
	Dist.	Year	Page	No.	Age

D455

◇◇◇◇◇

D-455.

Department of the Interior.
Commission to the Five Civilized Tribes.
Tahlequah, I. T., December 17, 1900.

In the matter of the enrollment of Lucinda Welch.

SUPPLEMENTARY TESTIMONY

Witness, J. C. Welch, being sworn and examined by Commissioner T. B. Needles, testified as follows:

Q   What is your name?   A J. C. Welch.
Q   What is your age?   A I will be 51 years old.

Cherokee Intermarried White 1906
Volume VII

Q   You know Lucinda Welch?   A   Yes sir, she is my mother.
Q   What is your postoffice?   A   Grove.
Q   What statement do you desire to make now in regard to her enrollment?   A   All the statement I have to make is that she wasn't able to appear in person. She is too old and crippled up and cannot come.

By W. W. Hastings, representative of the Cherokee Nation-
Q   Did she apply to the Dawes Commission in 1896?   A   She says she didn't, and didn't know anything about it.
Q   She is too old to come and make that statement to the Commission?
A   Yes sir; she is crippled up and couldn't come here herself.
Q   With whom was she living in 1896; four years ago?   A   She was living by herself. Her brothers were staying there with her.
Q   You know whether she authorized anyone to make an application for her?   A   I don't think so; I don't know anything about it myself.
Q   What did she say about it?   A   She said she didn't authorize anybody to.
Q   Did she know anything about it?   A   She said she didn't.
Q   Was her first knowledge of it after you had told her after you went back to Vinita?   A   That was the first she knew.
Q   You went back and advised her of it?   A   She didn't know anything about it, and I told her her name appears on that roll, and she said she didn't know anything about it.
Q   Did some of yours, or her relatives, living up near there, make an application?
A   Yes sir, her brothers. She had three brothers living there.
Q   What do they say about this - what explanation do they make?   A   They all deny it, never could find out. They all deny it is all I know. I don't know anything about it. I have an idea that old Uncle Johnny Parker and Harvey Hampton sent them in, but I don't know.

Commissioner Needles-
Q   Your mother claims citizenship as an intermarried citizen?   A   Yes sir.
Q   Her husband's dead?   A   Yes sir.
Q   Has she ever married since?   A   No sir.
Q   Your father was an Indian by blood?   A   Yes sir.

E. G. Rothenberger, being duly sworn, states that as stenographer to the Commission to the Five Civilized Tribes, he reported in full the supplementary testimony in the above case, and that the foregoing is a full, true and correct transcript of his stenographic notes in said case.

                                             E.G. Rothenberger

Subscribed and sworn to before me this 10th day of January, 1901.

                                             TB Needles
                                                  Commissioner.

Cherokee Intermarried White 1906
Volume VII

D 455

Department of the Interior,
Commission to the Five Civilized Tribes.
Muskogee, I. T., February 27, 1902.

In the matter of the application of Lucinda Welch, for the enrollment of herself as a citizen of the Cherokee Nation:

The applicant was notified by registered letter February 11, 1902, that her application for the enrollment of herself as a citizen of the Cherokee Nation, would be taken up for final consideration by the Commission on the 27th day of February, 1902, and that she could on said date appear before the Commission either in person or by attorney, and an opportunity would be given her to introduce any further testimony affecting her application.
Receipt has been acknowledged of the Commission's letter.

Mr. Hastings, of counsel for the Cherokee Nation; The representatives of the Cherokee Nation desire to call attention to the affidavit made by her before J. C. Starr, Notary Public, filed in the original application before the Dawes Commission in 1896, she having introduced some testimony tending to show that she did not apply, or know of any application being made for her, and this reference is made for the purpose of calling attention of the Commission to the Five Civilized Tribes fact that she must have known of this application being made in her behalf, or else she would not have made the affidavit referred to.

The Commission: The applicant having this day, to-wit: the 27th day of February, 1902, been called three times, and failing to respond either in person or by attorney, it is ordered that this case be closed, and that the same be reported to the Commission for final decision based upon the evidence now of record.

TB Needles
Commissioner.

E. C. Bagwell, on oath states that, as stenographer to the Commission to the Five Civilized Tribes, he correctly recorded the testimony and proceedings had in the above entitled cause, and that the above and foregoing is an accurate transcript of his stenographic notes thereof.

E.C.Bagwell

Subscribed and sworn to before me this February 28, 1902.

(No Signature given.)
Commissioner.

Cherokee Intermarried White 1906
Volume VII

◇◇◇◇◇

Cherokee D-455.

Department of the Interior,
Commission to the Five Civilized Tribes,
Muskogee, I. T., September 25, 1902.

In the matter of the application of Lucinda Welch for the enrollment of herself as a citizen by intermarriage of the Cherokee Nation; -

J. C. Starr, being sworn and examined by the Commission, testified as follows:
Q What is your name?   A J. C. Starr.
Q How old are you?   A 32.
Q What is your postoffice?   A Vinita.
Q Are you one of eh representatives of the Cherokee Nation?   A Yes sir.
Q Are you acquainted with Lucinda Welch, the applicant in this case?   A I am.
Q Where does she live?   A She lives near Grove, I. T.
Q How long have you known her?   A Since 1880.
Q Where has she lived since you have known her?   A Near Grove, I. T., the same place where she is living now.
Q Has she lived there continuously from 1880 up until the present time?   A Yes sir.
Q She has never lived out of the territory or Cherokee Nation since you have known her in 1880?   A No sir, right where she is living now ever since I have known her. She is very feeble and unable to come before the Commission.

The undersigned, being duly sworn, states that as stenographer to the Commission to the Five Civilized Tribes he correctly recorded the testimony and proceedings in this case, and the foregoing is a true and correct transcript of his stenographic notes thereof.
E.G. Rothenberger

Subscribed and sworn to before me this 3rd day of October, 1902.

BC Jones
Notary Public.

◇◇◇◇◇

Cherokee Intermarried White 1906
Volume VII

Cherokee D 455.

DEPARTMENT OF THE INTERIOR,
COMMISSION TO THE FIVE CIVILIZED TRIBES.
Muskogee, I. T., October 10, 1902.

In the matter of the application of Lucinda Welch for the enrollment of herself as a citizen by intermarriage of the Cherokee Nation.

Supplemental Proceedings.

J. C. STARR, being sworn, testified as follows:

By the Commission,

Q   Your name, age and postoffice?   A   J. C. Starr, thirty-two, Vinita.
Q   You are one of the representatives of the Cherokee Nation?
A   Yes, sir.
Q   And a Cherokee by blood?   A   Yes, sir.
Q   How much blood have you got in you?   A   I don't know about that.
Q   Are you acquainted with Lucinda Welch, who was an applicant before the Commission for enrollment as an intermarried citizen of the Cherokee Nation citizen?
A   Yes, sir.
Q   How long had you known her?   A   I have known her since along about 1880, and it may be a year before that. I moved to the vicinity where she lived in '79, and I lived neighbors to her since until two years ago.
Q   What is her physical condition at this time?   A   She is very old and unable to go anywhere.
Q   What was her husband's name?   A   James Welch.
Q   Were they married prior to 1880?   A   Why, I suppose they were. They were living together as husband and wife when I knew them.
Q   They are both on the '80 roll as husband and wife?   A   Yes, sir.
Q   Did she live with her husband, James Welch, up to 1880?   A   Yes, sir.
Q   How long has James Welch been dead?   A   James Welch has been dead for several years -- ten years or more -- I don't remember just exactly when he died.
Q   Has Lucinda Welch married since her husband's death?   A   She has not.
Q   She was still a widow and single on the first day of September, 1902?   A   Yes, sir.

Retta Chick, being first duly sworn, states that, as stenographer to the Commission to the Five Civilized Tribes, she recorded the testimony and proceedings in the matter of the foregoing application, and that the above is a true and complete transcript of her stenographic notes thereof.

Retta Chick

Cherokee Intermarried White 1906
Volume VII

Subscribed and sworn to before me this 18 day of October, 1902.

                                        PG Reuter
                                        Notary Public.

◇◇◇◇◇

                                        Cherokee D-455.

DEPARTMENT OF THE INTERIOR,
COMMISSION TO THE FIVE CIVILIZED TRIBES.
---o---

In the matter of the application for the enrollment of Lucinda Welch as a citizen by intermarriage of the Cherokee Nation.

--o:o--

DECISION.

--:o:--

The record in this case shows that on September 27, 1900, John Cobb Welch appeared before the Commission at Vinita, Indian Territory, and made application for the enrollment of his mother, Lucinda Welch, as a citizen by intermarriage of the Cherokee Nation. Further proceedings were had in the matter of said application at Tahlequah, Indian Territory, on December 17, 1900, and again at Muskogee, Indian Territory, on September 12, 1902, and October 10, 1902.

The evidence shows that the said Lucinda Welch, a white woman, was married prior to 1880 to one James Welch, a native Cherokee, who is identified on the 1880 Authenticated Roll of the Cherokee Nation. Lucinda Welch is also identified on said roll. Her said husband had been dead about ten years when this application was made, and she had not remarried since his death up to and including September 1, 1902. The evidence further shows that this applicant has resided continuously in the Cherokee Nation since her marriage prior to 1880 up to and including September 1, 1902.

From the records of the Commission, it appears that the applicant filed her original petition, under the Act of Congress of June 10, 1896, (29 Stats., 321) with the Commission to the Five Civilized Tribes for admission as a citizen by blood of the Cherokee Nation, which was denied by the Commission, and no appeal was taken therefrom.

It is the opinion of this Commission that the applicant's right to enrollment as an intermarried citizen of the Cherokee Nation Cherokee is not prejudiced by the denial of her application for admission as a citizen by blood under the provisions of the said Act of June 10, 1896, (29 Stats., 321); and that the said Lucinda Welch should, therefore, be enrolled as a citizen by intermarriage of the Cherokee Nation, in accordance with the

Cherokee Intermarried White 1906
Volume VII

provisions of the Act of Congress approved June 28, 1898, (30 Stats., 495), and it is so ordered.

<u>COMMISSION TO THE FIVE CIVILIZED TRIBES.</u>

Tams Bixby
Acting Chairman.

TB Needles
Commissioner.

C. R. Breckinridge
Commissioner.

Dated at Muskogee, Indian Territory, this DEC 10 1902

◇◇◇◇◇

E C M /8 Cherokee 10030.

DEPARTMENT OF THE INTERIOR,
COMMISSIONER TO THE FIVE CIVILIZED TRIBES.
Muskogee, Indian Territory,
February 9, 1907.

In the matter of the application for the enrollment of LUCINDA WELCH as a citizen by intermarriage of the Cherokee Nation.

APPEARANCES:
Applicant represented by Mollie Henson, Grand-daughter.

Cherokee Nation represented by W.W. Hastings, Attorney.

MOLLIE HENSON, being first duly sworn by Walter W. Chappell, a Notary Public, testifies as follows:

ON BEHALF OF THE COMMISSIONER:

Q What is your name?
A Mollie E. Henson.
Q What is your age?
A 32 years old.
Q What is your post-office address?
A Grove, Indian Territory.

Cherokee Intermarried White 1906
Volume VII

Q   Where do you live?
A   At Grove.
Q   How long have you lived there?
A   I have lived in Grove and near Grove all my life.
Q   You come here for the purpose of giving testimony in the matter of the application for the enrollment of Lucinda Welch as a citizen by intermarriage of?
A   Yes sir.
Q   What relation are you to Lucinda Welch?
A   I'm her grand-daughter.
Q   Is Lucinda Welch living at this time?
A   No sir.
Q   When did she die?
A   She died the 18th day of March in 1905.
Q   Through whom does she claim her right to enrollment as a citizen by intermarriage of the Cherokee Nation?
A   James Welch, her husband.
Q   Is James Welch a Cherokee by blood?
A   Yes sir.
Q   Has he always lived in the Cherokee Nation?
A   No sir, he came to the Cherokee Nation in 1867, according to what I have heard them say.
Q   How do you account for his coming here in 1867?
A   The only way I have to account for it is what I heard my grand-mother say: She said that her nephew died at their house the year they came here, and I have the date of his death.
Q   What was the name of this nephew?
A   Markes[sic] Powell.

The witness presents in evidence a testament containing the statement that Markes Powell died August 12, 1867.

Q   Was your grand-father admitted to citizenship before their removal to the Cherokee Nation?
Q   I do not know.
Q   Do you know whether he has always been recognized as a citizen of the Cherokee Nation?
A   Yes sir, I think he has.
Q   Can you remember your grand-father prior to November 1, 1875?
A   No sir.
Q   How many wives has your grand-father had?
A   One.
Q   Had your grand-mother been married more than once?
A   No sir.
Q   She was his first wife and he was her first husband?
A   Yes sir.

Cherokee Intermarried White 1906
Volume VII

Q Do you know what District your grand-father lived in when he first came to this country?
A Flint District.
Q After that what District did he live in?
A He did'nt[sic] live in any except the Delaware that I ever knew.
Q Is your grand-father on the 1880 roll?
A Yes sir.

The applicant, Lucinda Welch is identified on the 1880 roll, Delaware District No. 2949, as an adopted white. The husband of the applicant, James Welch, is also identified on the 1880 roll, Delaware District No. 2948, as a native Cherokee.

Q How many children did your grand-father and grand-mother have?
A Three.
Q What were their names?
A Jonathan Housten Welch, John Cobb Welch, (that's my father), and Cornelia Welch.
Q Which one of these was your father?
A John Cobb Welch.
Q Is he living at this time?
A Yes sir.
Q Is he able to appear before the Commission and give testimony in this case?
A Yes sir.
Q Where were James Welch and Lucinda Welch married?
A They were married in the Old Country, I don't know now if it was North Carolina or Georgia.
Q They were married before they came here?
A Yes sir.
Q Do you know whether James Welch exercised all the rights of citizenship in the Cherokee Nation prior to his death?
A Yes sir, he did.
Q What did he do? Did he vote?
A He voted and run for office and drew money, and he owned land, or held land the same as all other Cherokees did
Q Was your father enrolled as a Cherokee by blood?
A Yes sir.
Q Have you been enrolled as a Cherokee by blood?
A Yes sir.
Q Do you know of any one who could come here and testify as to the marriage of your grand-father, how long he lived in the Cherokee Nation, whether he was regarded as a citizen of the Cherokee Nation and whether he was ever admitted to citizenship in the Cherokee Nation?
A I don't know, I suppose my father could testify to part of that?
Q Was your father born in this Nation?
A No sir.
Q How old was your father when he came to this country?
A I think he was 19 years old.

Cherokee Intermarried White 1906
Volume VII

Q   Do you think he could remember whether your grand-father had ever been admitted to citizenship or not?
A   He might remember, I can't say.
Q   Why does'nt[sic] he appear here today?
A   Well, I was appointed executor of her will and I suppose he thought I had the right to do it.

TO THE WITNESS:
It will be necessary that you have your father appear here and give testimony relative to the facts in this case, and also the testimony of other witnesses who have known your grand-father since his arrival in the Cherokee Nation. This is very inportant[sic] and you are requested to have them appear here at the earliest possible time.

Q   Do you care to make any further statement in this case?
A   I wanted to say that I 'phone one of the great-uncles and one of my grand-mother's first cousins, but they won't be here till tomorrow.

(Witness excused)

Case held open for further testimony.

February 8, 1907, 2 - P.M.

SUPPLEMENTAL TESTIMONY in the matter of the application for the enrollment of LUCINDA WELCH as a citizen by intermarriage of the Cherokee Nation.

AUGUSTUS C. SAGER, being first duly sworn by Walter W. Chappell, a Notary Public, testifies as follows:

ON BEHALF OF THE COMMISSIONER:

Q   What is your name?
A   Augustus C. Sager.
Q   What is your age?
A   71 years.
Q   What is your post-office address?
A   Grove, Indian Territory.
Q   You appear here for the purpose of giving testimony relative to the right of Lucinda Welch as a citizen by intermarriage of the Cherokee Nation?
A   Yes sir.

Cherokee Intermarried White 1906
Volume VII

Q   Were you acquainted with Lucinda Welch?
A   Yes sir.
Q   With her husband, James Welch?
A   Yes sir.
Q   Are they living now?
A   No sir.
Q   Both dead?
A   Yes sir.
Q   How long have you known James Welch and Lucinda Welch?
A   I got acquainted with them in '71.
Q   Where were they living at that time?
A   Near Grove in the Delaware District.
Q   Was James Welch a citizen of the Cherokee Nation?
A   I suppose he was, every body said he was.
Q   Did he exercise the rights of a citizen?
A   Yes sir.
Q   Was he regarded as a citizen at the time you knew him in 1871?
A   Yes sir.
Q   Did he hold any office?
A   No sir.
Q   Did he vote?
A   Yes sir.
Q   Did he own land in the Cherokee Nation?
A   Yes sir.
Q   He owned it as a citizen of the Cherokee Nation?
A   Yes sir.
Q   Was he born in the Cherokee Nation?
A   No sir, I think not.
Q   Where was he born?
A   I could'nt[sic] tell you.
Q   Do you know when he came to the Cherokee Nation?
A   Not exactly.
Q   Was he admitted to citizenship in the Cherokee Nation before his coming here?
A   Yes sir.
Q   Do you know what Court admitted him to citizenship?
A   The Court at Tahlequah. He got in before the Council I reckon.
Q   You are sure he has been a citizen and was admitted before 1875?
A   Yes sir.
Q   Had James Welch and Lucinda Welch resided together as husband and wife and continuously lived in the Cherokee Nation until the death of James Welch?
A   Yes sir.
Q   Since the death of James Welch has Lucinda Welch re-married?
A   No sir.
Q   She remained as a widow until her death?
A   Yes sir.

Cherokee Intermarried White 1906
Volume VII

Q Did you know Lucinda Welch before she was married to James Welch?
A No sir.
Q She was a white woman, was she?
A I suppose so, that's what they claim.
Q Did you know the Indian name of James Welch?
A No sir.
Q He went by an Indian name sometimes did'nt[sic] he?
A Yes sir, but I forget what it was.
Q Was it Oo - Ka - Mah, the name he went by?
A Yes sir, with the Indians.
Q Did they have any children?
A Yes sir.
Q How many?
A I reckon there was three.
Q Mr. Sager, are you a Cherokee by blood?
A No sir.
Q You claim as a citizen by intermarriage?
A Yes sir.
Q You never heard any one question the right of James Welch as a citizen of the Cherokee Nation, did you?
A No sir.
Q Had his right as a citizen been questioned you would have heard of it, would'nt[sic] you?
A Yes sir.

(Witness excused)

This certifies that the undersigned, being duly sworn, states that as stenographer to the Commission to the Five Civilized Tribes, she reported the proceedings had in the above entitled cause and that the above and foregoing is a full and correct transcript of her stenographic notes thereof.

Georgia Coberly
Stenographer.

Subscribed and sworn to before me this 9th day of February, 1907.

Frances R Lane
Notary Public.

Cherokee Intermarried White 1906
Volume VII

E.C.M.   Cherokee 10030.

DEPARTMENT OF THE INTERIOR, COMMISSIONER TO THE FIVE CIVILIZED TRIBES. MUSKOGEE, I. T., FEBRUARY 9, 1907.

SUPPLEMENTAL PROCEEDINGS in the matter of the application for the enrollment of LUCINDA WELCH as a citizen by intermarriage of the Cherokee Nation.

JOHN COBB WELCH, being first duly sworn by Walter W. Chappell, Notary Public, testified as follows:

ON BEHALF OF THE COMMISSIONER:

Q   What is your name?   A John Cobb Welch.
Q   What is your age?   A 56.
Q   What is your post office address?   A Grove.
Q   Are you the son of Lucinda Welch?   A Yes sir, I was born in '49.
Q   Do you appear here today for the purpose of giving testimony relative to the right to enrollment as a citizen by intermarriage of the Cherokee Nation of Lucinda Welch?   A Yes sir.
Q   Where were you born?   A In North Carolina.
Q   When did you come to this country?   A In '67.
Q   Did you come with your father and mother?   A Yes sir.
Q   Did you come when they did?   A Yes sir.
Q   Do you remember whether or not your father was admitted to citizenship upon his coming to this country?   A That was my understanding., You see, we came here on an invitation, and my father and Mack Morris went to Tahlequah, Indian Territory and it is my understanding that they were readmitted, because they come here in the invitation of the Chief.
Q   Then they were admitted shortly after coming to this country were they?   A In the fall of '67, to the best of my recollection
Q   Was your father always recognized as a citizen of the Cherokee Nation?
       A Always as an Indian, but not of this Nation, because he was not here until 1867.
Q   Was he regarded as a citizen of this Nation after coming here?
       A Yes sir.
Q   Did he exercise all the rights and privileges of a citizen?
       A Yes sir.
Q   Did he ever hold any office in the Cherokee Nation?   A No sir; they run him several time, but he got bear.
Q   Your father and mother of course were married in North Carolina. Did they reside together as husband and wife until the time of his death?   A Yes sir
Q   After his death did your mother ever remarry?   A No sir.
Q   When did your father die?   A I have forgotten.

Cherokee Intermarried White 1906
Volume VII

Q   About how many years has he been dead?   A His death is down in the Bible, but I have forgotten.
Q   Did you ever know anyone by the name of Arkansas Welch?   A I knew a Welch woman that came to our house where we lived in Flint, and claimed to be kin of ours.
Q   Did you know G. W. Welch?   A No sir.
Q   James M. Welch?   A No sir.
Q   Was you father's name James M. or just James?   A James Welch.
Q   Were you ever acquainted with any one by the name of L.E. Welch?
   A Now, there was some Welch's on the river, but I dont[sic] know their names.
Q   Do you know of any Welchs[sic] who came from North Carolina and were admitted to citizenship in the year 1876?
   A John Welch, but I dont[sic] know whether he was admitted or not, but he was a citizen here, and drawed aldn[sic] here.
Q   But you can testify positively that your father, from the time of his coming here until his death exercised all the rights and privileges of a citizen of the Cherokee Nation?   A Yes sir; drawed money after he come to this country of all money that was ever paid.
Q   He was enrolled on the 1867 roll, was he?   A I dont[sic] remember whether they were taking the census or not then, but in 1868 or 1869, maybe in 1870, they taken[sic] the census in Flint, and Eph Adair and Huckleberry Downing taken[sic] the census.
Q   He went under an Indian name, did he not?   A Yes sir.
Q   Can you spell it?   A It was Chi-my-no-ga-ma.

(Witness excused).

The undersigned, being first duly sworn, states that, as stenographer to the Commissioner to the Five Civilized Tribes, she correctly reported the above and foregoing testimony, and that the same is a full, true and complete transcript of her stenographic notes thereof.

Sarah Waters

Subscribed and sworn to before me this 13th day of February, 1907.

Frances R Lane
Notary Public.

Cherokee Intermarried White 1906
Volume VII

E. C. M.

Cherokee 10030.

DEPARTMENT OF THE INTERIOR,
COMMISSIONER TO THE FIVE CIVILIZED TRIBES.
Muskogee, Indian Territory, February 9, 1907.

In the matter of the application for the enrollment of Lucinda Welch as a citizen by intermarriage of the Cherokee Nation.

Cherokee Nation represented by W. W. Hastings, Attorney.

SUPPLEMENTAL.

H. H. Hampton being first duly sworn by Mrs. Lyman K. Lane, Notary Public, testified as follows:

ON BEHALF OF COMMISSIONER.

Q What is your name?
A H. H. Hampton.
Q What is your age?
A 80 years the 12th of April.
Q What is your post office address?
A Grove.
Q Are you a citizen of the Cherokee Nation?
A No sir.
Q Are you acquainted with the applicant in this case, Lucinda Welch?
A Yes sir.
Q Were you acquainted with her husband, James Welch?
A Him and me was boys together and went to school together.
Q Where did he live at that time?
A Cherokee County, North Carolina.
Q He removed to the Cherokee Nation, did he?
A Yes sir.
Q When did he come?
A About '67 I think.
Q Did you come here at the same time?
A No sir; he came before I did.
Q Was he admitted to citizenship in the Cherokee Nation on his coming to the Cherokee Nation?
A I suppose he was. He drew money here and was enrolled her and run for office.
Q When was that he ran for office?
A I don't know what year it was.
Q About how long ago?
A '75 or '76; somewhere along there.
Q You don't remember whether he was admitted to citizenship or not, do you?
A I suppose he was; he drew money.
Q But you have no positive knowledge of his being admitted?
A Nothing only what I got from his own mouth.

Cherokee Intermarried White 1906
Volume VII

Q   Did you live in the same community that he did?
A   Yes sir.
Q   Do you remember when he was married to Lucinda Welch?
A   Yes sir; I don't know whether I can give the date, right, about '46 or '47.
Q   They were married in Cherokee County, North Carolina, were they?
A   There was no marriage among the Indians at that time; if a white man married an Indian woman or an Indian man married a white lady, they had to take them to Georgia to get married. Welch took Lucinda Welch, his wife, and went over into Georgia and was married and came back.
Q   Was Lucinda Welch a white woman?   A   Yes sir.
Q   And James Welch a Cherokee Indian?   A   Yes sir.
Q   Did he bring her to the Cherokee Nation with him?
A   Yes sir.
Q   They resided together as husband and wife in the Cherokee Nation from their removal here until the time of his death?
A   Yes sir.
Q   Were any children born of that marriage?   A   Yes sir.
Q   Can you give me the names of the children?
A   Yes sir; Bud, Cobb and Cornelia.
Q   Are they living now?   A   There is one of them living.
Q   Which one?   A   Cobb, the father of this lady here.

J. P. Parker being first duly sworn by Mrs. Lyman K. Lane, Notary Public, testified as follows:

ON BEHALF OF COMMISSIONER.

Q   What is your name?   A   J. P. Parker.
Q   What is your age?   A   70 years old the 18th of next April.
Q   What is your post office address?
A   Grove, Indian Territory.
Q   Mr. Parker, were you acquainted with James Welch and his wife, Lucinda Welch?
A   Yes sir.
Q   When did you first become acquainted with them?
A   Lucinda Welch is my sister.
Q   When did you first become acquainted with James Welch?
A   I can remember him ever since I was old enough to remember. We were raised with a mile of each other.
Q   Where were you living at that time?
A   Cherokee County, North Carolina.
Q   How long did you live there?   A   Until I was grown.
Q   Then where did you go?   A   I went to Georgia.
Q   From there where did you go?   A   I came here.

Cherokee Intermarried White 1906
Volume VII

Q   When did you come here?
A   My first trip was in 1886; and I went back to Georgia and came back in 1893 and have been here ever since.
Q   Mr. Parker, when was your sister, Lucinda, and James Welch married?
A   I don't know that I can give the precise date; it was in the 1840's.
Q   Do you remember about what time they came to the Cherokee Nation?
A   Yes sir; 1867,
Q   Have they resided in the Cherokee Nation since their removal here?
A   Yes sir.
Q   Mr. Parker, I will ask you if you are acquainted with a man by the name of George Welch?
A   No, I can't say that I am.
Q   Do you know a man or woman by the name of Arkansas Welch?
A   No sir.
Q   Do you know what James Welch's middle name was?
A   I don't think he had any,
Q   Did you know a man by the name of Thomas Welch?
A   No sir.
Q   What is Lucinda Welch's middle name?
A   She had none, if she had I don't remember it.

H. H. Hampton, re-called, testified as follows:

ON BEHALF OF COMMISSIONER.

Q   Do you know what Lucinda Welch's middle name was?
A   I don't think she had any.
Q   Did you ever know anyone by the name of L. E. Welch?
A   No sir.
Q   Did you know a man by the name of George Welch?
A   There was a man back in the old Nation they called George Welch.
Q   Did you ever know anybody by the name of Thomas I. Welch?
A   No sir.
Q   Did you ever know a man or woman by the name of Arkansas Welch?
A   No sir.

The undersigned being first duly sworn states that as stenographer to the Commission to the Five Civilized Tribes, she recorded the testimony taken in this case and that the foregoing is a true and correct transcript of her stenographic notes thereof.

Myrtle Hill

Cherokee Intermarried White 1906
Volume VII

Subscribed and sworn to before me this the 13th day of February, 1907.

                 Walter W. Chappell
                 Notary Public.

◇◇◇◇◇

F. R.   Cherokee 10030.

DEPARTMENT OF THE INTERIOR,

COMMISSIONER TO THE FIVE CIVILIZED TRIBES.

In the matter of the application for the enrollment of Lucinda Welch as a citizen by intermarriage of the Cherokee Nation.

D E C I S I O N

THE RECORDS OF THIS OFFICE SHOW: That at Vinita, Indian Territory, September 27, 1900, application was received by the Commission to the Five Civilized Tribes for the enrollment of Lucinda Welch as a citizen by intermarriage of the Cherokee Nation. Further proceedings in the matter of said application were had at Tahlequah, Indian Territory, December 17, 1900, and at Muskogee, Indian Territory, February 27, 1902, September 25, 1902, October 10, 1902, February 8, 1907, and February 9, 1907. It further appears that on December 10, 1902, the Commission to the Five Civilized Tribes rendered its decision herein, granting the application of Lucinda Welch for enrollment as a citizen by intermarriage of the Cherokee Nation.

THE RECORDS[sic] OF THIS OFFICE SHOW: That the applicant herein, Lucinda Welch, a white woman, who is identified on the Cherokee authenticated tribal roll of 1880, Delaware District, Page 338, No. 2949, and on the Cherokee census roll of 1896, Delaware District, Page 593, No. 558, was married in about the year 1846 in the State of Georgia to one James Welch who is identified on the Cherokee authenticated tribal roll of 1880, Delaware District, Page 338, No. 2948, as a native Cherokee. It further appears that in the year 1867, the said James Welch and Lucinda Welch removed to the Cherokee Nation and resided together as husband and wife, and continuously lived in said Nation until the death of James Welch in 1886; that since the death of James Welch, the applicant herein, Lucinda Welch, has not remarried and has continuously lived in the Cherokee Nation up to and including September 1, 1902.

The evidence does not show the date of admission of James Welch to citizenship in the Cherokee Nation.

Mollie Henson testified on February 8, 1907, that it was her understanding that James Welch exercised all the rights of a citizen of the Cherokee Nation, that he drew money, voted in the elections and held land the same as other citizens.

Cherokee Intermarried White 1906
Volume VII

The same date, Augustus C. Sager testified that James Welch, when he first became acquainted with him in 1871, was regarded as a citizen of the Cherokee Nation.

John Cobb Welch on the same date testified that it was his understanding that James Welch was admitted to citizenship in the Cherokee Nation in the year 1867 and had thereafter been recognized as a citizen of such Nation and enjoyed the same rights and privileges accorded other citizens.

I am therefore of the opinion that it is shown by a preponderance of the evidence that the said James Welch was admitted to citizenship in the Cherokee Nation prior to November 1, 1875.

In view of the foregoing, it is considered that the applicant, Lucinda Welch, was lawfully married to a citizen by blood of the Cherokee Nation, prior to November 1, 1875.

IT IS, THEREFORE, ORDERED AND ADJUDGED: That the decision of the Commission to the Five Civilized Tribes dated December 10, 1902, granting the application of Lucinda Welch for enrollment as a citizen by intermarriage of the Cherokee Nation, should be affirmed; and that in accordance with the decision of the Supreme Court of the United States, dated November 5, 1906, in the cases of Daniel Red Bird, et al., vs. the United States, Nos. 125, 126, 127 and 128, the said applicant, Lucinda Welch, is entitled under the provisions of Section 21 of the Act of Congress approved June 28, 1898 (30 Stat. 495), to enrollment as a citizen by intermarriage of the Cherokee Nation, and her application for enrollment as such is accordingly granted.

Tams Bixby
Commissioner.

Dated at Muskogee, Indian Territory,
this   FEB 23 1907

◇◇◇◇◇

(The letter below typed as given. Extremely difficult to read)

Grove, I.T.
Oct. 3rd, 1900
Mr. J. C. Starr.
Vinita, I. T.

Dear Sir:- I went down to see mother the next day after I got home and I ask her about applying to the Dawes Com for citizenship she told me she knew nothing about it that she never did apply and never otherised any one else to send her name in she also told me that she never furnished a dollar to have her name put so you can see that Uncle Harvey Hampton and Dock Parker used *(illegible ...)* womans name in order to get in themselves. As we were Indians and ever one knows I supose they thought it would be a help to use her name, so you see it was a scheme of their own Well Cale you know as much about them as I could tell you in a week's time talking to you

So I will come to a close

As ever   J. C. Welch.

◇◇◇◇◇

(The letter below typed as given.)

Vinita I. T. October 6th 1900.

Mr. W. W. Hastings,

    Bartlesville, I. T.

        Dear Sir:

Plese read the inclosed letter and it might be that this old lady needs some help if facts are as stated. I was present when her application was made and I knew that an application had been made for her to the Dawes Commission in 1896. Her name is Lucinda Welch and she is the mother of Cobb Welch at Grove and is 75 years old and to reject her would rob her of house and home.

If you will get her card and testimony you will understand the case I am satisfied that Old Hary Hampton and Dock Parker at Grove put in her application in 1896 to the Dawes Commission to help themselves out and it may be true that she did not know anything about it (The chances are that she did know about it however.) You might look the matter up at any rate and see what you want to do with her case. She is an intermarried white her name is on 1880 roll and she has lived here ever since this country was a Nation practically and it looks rather hard to up set her in her old days.

I will be out there Thursday morning and is you need me before that time wire me and I will be there on first train.

                Yours truly,

                          JC Starr

Cherokee Intermarried White 1906
Volume VII

◇◇◇◇◇

COMMISSIONERS:
HENRY L. DAWES,
TAMS BIXBY,
THOMAS B. NEEDLES,
C. R. BRECKINRIDGE.

ALLISON L. AYLESWORTH,
SECRETARY.

ADDRESS ONLY THE
COMMISSION TO THE FIVE CIVILIZED TRIBES.

DEPARTMENT OF THE INTERIOR,
COMMISSION TO THE FIVE CIVILIZED TRIBES.

Muskogee, Indian Territory, **February 11,** 1902

Mrs. Lucinda Welch,
  Grove, Indian Territory,

Madam:-

You are hereby notified that the application of **yourself** for enrollment as citizen of the Cherokee Nation will be taken up for final consideration by the Commission to the Five Civilized Tribes, at its office in Muskogee, Indian Territory, on the **27th** day of **February**, 1902.

On said date, you may, if you desire, appear before the Commission, in person or by attorney, when an opportunity will be given you to introduce any additional testimony affecting your application.

You are further notified that the Representatives of the Cherokee Nation will also, at the same time, be afforded an opportunity to introduce testimony tending to disprove your right to enrollment, but said Representatives will be required to notify you of their intention to introduce such testimony before they will be permitted to do so.

Cherokee D-455

Register.

Yours truly,

Acting Chairman.

◇◇◇◇◇

Cherokee Intermarried White 1906
Volume VII

COPY   Cherokee D-455.

Muskogee, Indian Territory, December 15, 1902.

W. W. Hastings,
    Attorney for the Cherokee Nation,
        Muskogee, Indian Territory.

Dear Sir:

    There is herewith inclosed a copy of the decision of the Commissioner to the Five Civilized Tribes, dated December 10, 1902, granting the application of John Cobb Welch for the enrollment of his mother, Lucinda Welch, as a citizen by intermarriage of the Cherokee Nation.

    You are advised that you will be allowed fifteen days from date hereof in which to file such protest as you desire to make against the action of the Commission in this case, a copy of which protest you will be required to serve upon the applicant. If you fail to file protest within the time allowed this decision will be considered final.

Respectfully,

Tams Bixby
Acting Chairman.

Enc. H-235.

◇◇◇◇◇

Cherokee D-455

Muskogee, Indian Territory, January 15, 1903.

John Cobb Welch,
    Grove, Indian Territory.

Dear Sir:-

    There is herewith enclosed a copy of the decision of the Commission to the Five Civilized Tribes, dated December 10, 1902, granting your application for the enrollment of your mother, Lucinda Welch, as a citizen by intermarriage of the Cherokee Nation.

Respectfully,

Acting Chairman.

Enc. M-55

Register.

Cherokee Intermarried White 1906
Volume VII

◇◇◇◇◇

Cherokee
   10030

Muskogee, Indian Territory, January 22, 1907

Mollie E. Henson,
   Executrix of Estate of Lucinda Welch.
      Grove, Indian Territory.

Dear Madam :

      This office is in receipt of your letter of January 10, 1907, referring to the right to enrollment as a citizen by intermarriage of the Cherokee Nation of Lucinda Welch, deceased.

      In reply you are advised that the Supreme Court of the United States, by its decision of November 5, 1906, held that white persons who intermarried according to Cherokee law with Cherokee citizens, prior to November 1, 1875, are entitled to enrollment as citizens by intermarriage of the Cherokee Nation.

      If you claim that Lucinda Welch, deceased, is entitled to enrollment under the Court's decision, you will be permitted to appear before the Commissioner at Muskogee, Indian Territory, at once, and submit such testimony as you desire relative to her marriage to her Cherokee husband by reason of her marriage to whom she claimed the right to enrollment as a citizen by intermarriage of the Cherokee Nation, and as to the date of her marriage.

      The Act of Congress approved April 26, 1906, provides that the Secretary of the Interior shall have no jurisdiction to approve the enrollment of any person as a citizen of the Cherokee Nation, after March 4, 1907, and the matter of her enrollment should, therefore, receive immediate attention.

      Respectfully,

L M B   Commissioner

◇◇◇◇◇

Cherokee Intermarried White 1906
Volume VII

Cherokee
10030

Muskogee, Indian Territory, February 11, 1907

Mollie Henson,
    Grove, Indian Territory.

Dear Madam:

    Receipt is acknowledged of your letter of January 28, 1907, in which you state that your will appear before the Commissioner and submit evidence in the matter of the application of Lucinda Welch for enrollment as a citizen by intermarriage of the Cherokee Nation.

    You are advised that the Act of Congress approved April 26, 1906, (34 Stat. 137), provides that the Secretary of the Interior shall have no jurisdiction to approve the enrollment of any person as a citizen of the Cherokee Nation after March 4, 1907. This matter therefore demands your immediate attention.

                        Respectfully,

L M B   Commissioner.

◇◇◇◇◇

COPY

Cherokee 10030

Muskogee, Indian Territory, February 23, 1907.

W. W. Hastings,
    Attorney for the Cherokee Nation,
        Muskogee, Indian Territory.

Dear Sir:-

    There is enclosed herewith a copy of the decision of the Commissioner to the Five Civilized Tribes, dated February 23, 1907, granting the application for the enrollment of Lucinda Welch as a citizen by intermarriage of the Cherokee Nation.

                        Respectfully,

                                                  SIGNED *Tams Bixby*
Encl. E-87   Commissioner.
BLE

Cherokee Intermarried White 1906
Volume VII

◇◇◇◇◇

Cherokee 10030

Muskogee, Indian Territory, February 23, 1907.

The Commissioner to the Five Civilized Tribes,
    Muskogee, Indian Territory.

Sir:

    Receipt is acknowledged of the testimony and of your decision, enrolling Lucinda Welch as a citizen by intermarriage of the Cherokee Nation. Time for protesting said decision is waived and I consent that said person may be placed upon the schedule immediately.

                Respectfully,
                W. W. Hastings
                Attorney for the Cherokee Nation.

◇◇◇◇◇

Cherokee 10030   COPY

Muskogee, Indian Territory, February 23, 1907.

Lucinda Welch,
    Grove, Indian Territory.

Madam:-

    There is enclosed herewith a copy of the decision of the Commissioner to the Five Civilized Tribes, dated February 23, 1907, granting the application for your enrollment as a citizen by intermarriage of the Cherokee Nation.

    You will be advised when your name has been placed upon a schedule of citizens of the Cherokee Nation and approved by the Secretary of the Interior.

                Respectfully,

                SIGNED *Tams Bixby*

Encl. E-86   Commissioner.
BLE

Index

ADAIR
- Eph 321
- Hugh M 210,211,221
- J T 218,221
- James W 289
- John Thomas 218
- Judge 216,220,221
- Penelope 219,221
- Phoebe A 21

ALBERT
- Andrew J 207

ALBERTY
- Ada 207
- Ada May 207
- Adam 209
- Amanda 206,207,208,209,210,211, 212,213,214
- Amanda B 207
- Andrew J 206,207,210,211,212
- Andrew Jackson 208
- Bishop M 207
- John 212
- Johnson 206
- Katie 206
- Mandy 207
- Samuel J 207
- Thedocia 207
- Theodocia 207
- William L 207
- William P 207

ALEXANDER
- Cherokee 45,46,47,51,52
- Cherokee C 23
- Fay 23,24,25,26,29,34,39
- J H 48
- Jim 150
- Joe 29,45
- Joseph 23
- Joseph H 22,23,24,26,29,30,32,34, 45,46,47,48,49,50,51,52,53
- Kate 23,24,25,26,29,34,39
- Lillian 23,24,25,26,29,34,39
- Maud 23,24,25,26,29,34,39
- Maude 24
- Mr 27,28,33,38,39,40,41,42,43,44, 48,50
- Mrs 32
- Mrs C C 48
- Safrony 23
- Saphronia 29,30,34,46,47,51,52
- Silas 22
- Sophenia 23
- Sophronia 24,25,26,27,53
- Sophronia E 23

ANDERSON
- Louisa 249,256

ARBUCKLE
- Harriett E 173

BAGWELL
- E C 33,44,146,156,258,310

BAILEY
- Doctor 35,38
- Doctor W W 35
- Dr 34
- W W, MD 38

BARKER
- W H 105,238
- William 110

BASS
- William R 198,219,220

BAUGH
- Charlotte E 61
- Cynthia 55,56
- J H 55,56,59
- John H 55,56,57,58,59,60,61, 62,63,64
- Mitchell 55,56

BEALL
- Wm O 140,209

BECK
- Aaron H 5,6

BELL
- Hooley 72
- James M 81,84,301
- L B 236
- Mattie 80,82,84

BENGE
- George 48

BIGBEE
- Jennie 219
- Nanie 219

BIGBY
- Ester S 220,221
- Esther A 222

Index

Nancy 220,221
Nannie J 220,221
BIGSBY
Esther S 218
BIXBY
(Tams) 86
Nancy 254
Tams 10,53,62,75,87,96,99,100,
113,125,139,151,168,174,186,204,213
,223,224,241,266,267,283,284,294,
295,305,314,326,329,331,332
BLACK
Alcy 182
BLACK FOX
John 202
BLACKFOX
John 197
BOUDINOT
Richard F 256
William P 121,122
BOWERS
J H 46
Mr 48
BOWMAN
Lucy M 81
BRACKETT
Bessie 102
J T 102
John T 101,103,104,105,106,107,
108,111,112,113,114
John Thomas 102
Margaret 102,103,104,105,106,107,
109,110,111,112,113
Mr 108
BRAKETT
John T 103
BRECKINRIDGE
C R 56,77,101,102,116,129,247,
287,314
Clifton R 190,216
Commissioner 55,144,189,286
Com'r 56,189,190
BREEDLOVE
W W 160
Walter W 160
BRYAN
Charlotte 59,60

Charlotte E 58,61
J M 58
BRYANT
Charlotte 57
Edgar E 36,44
J A 202
BUCHANAN
J C 228,240,244
BUCHANNAN
(J C) 226
BUFFINGTON
T M 44
BURNS
H B, MD 226,228
BURR
B F 239,240
CAREY
Lucy Ann 71
Mary Ann 69,72,73
Nancy 72
CARR
Jesse O 26,67,68,79,91,92,117
CARTER
Asa K 178
Fannie 177,180
Margaret 105,111,112
Randolph 177,180
CARY
Mary Ann 65,74
CHANEY
J M 134
CHAPELL
Walter W 135
CHAPMAN
Wm 303
CHAPPELL
Chas W 83
W W 263
Walter 160
Walter E 164
Walter W 58,59,60,73,82,84,85,108,
123,134,135,136,138,150,163,165,166
,167,173,184,199,202,203,220,221,
222,243,251,252,265,299,300,314,317
,320,325
CHICK
Retta 29,103,249,288,312

CHI-MY-NO-GA-MA 321
CLINE
   Ezekiel 164,165,168
   Mr 156
   Zeek 153,154
   Zeke 155
CLINKSCALES
   A M 109,111
   A M, MD 111
CLOWRY
   Robert C 86,141
CLYNE
   Ezekiel 156
COBERLY
   Georgia 124,135,136,138,203,
   222,276,277,279,280,281,319
CONNER
   Caleb 64,65,66,67,68,69,70,71,
   75,76
   Jane 65,68
   Lucy 65
   Lucy J 66,67,68
   Lucy Jane 64,65,66
   Mary A 68
   Mrs 71
CONNOR
   Caleb 72,73,74
   Lucy 74
   Mary Ann 74
   Mrs 73
CONSER
   Frank M 257
CORDRAY
   Nancy 247,248,249,250,251,252,
   253,254,255,256
   Thomas 252
   Wilson 247,248,250,251,252,254
   Wilson M 248
CORDREY
   Charlotte 247
   Dave 247
   Fannie 89,93,95,99
   Wilson 247
CORDRRAY
   Wilson 248
CORDRY
   Nancy 248,256

   Wilson 256
CORNTASSEL
   Jennie 194,197
CORNTASSELL
   Jennie 192,198,199,203
CORNTOSSEL
   Jennie 202
COTTERMAN
   Lucy 73
COUNCILOR
   Homer J 163,165
COUNTRYMAN
   John 65
   Lucy 70,71,74
   Lucy Jane 65
COVE
   A J 94
COVEL
   J H 279
COWELLS
   Caleb W 66,67,68
   Caleb Willis 65
   Frank 65
   Jane 65
COWELS
   Caleb Willis 65
COWELSS
   Frank 65
COX
   Jno N 299,303
CRAVENS
   R R 24,66,90,102,248,268
CRITTENDEN
   George 189
CROWDER
   Mary 2
   Mr W P 6
   Nelson 1
   Polly 2,7,10
   W P 6
   William 1,2,3,4,7,10,11,12
   William P 2
   William Penn 2
CUNNINGHAM
   A B 235,236,237,278,279
   Mr 281
CURREY

Index

Frances S 171,172
Francis S 172,174
G W 171
George W 170,172,174,175,176
CURRIE
  F S 172
  Frances S 172
  G W 172
CURRY
  G W 173
  George W 172,175,176
DANIEL
  Dolphus 72
DAVENPORT
  James S 66,92
DE LANO
  Charles 145
  Charles Henry 145
  Mary 145
  Mary E 145
  Mollie 145
  Mollie Elizabeth 145
DELANO
  C E 149
  C H 144,147
  Charles E 149
  Charles H 144,147,148,150
  Charles Henry 144,148
  Mariah 144
  Mary 144
  Mary E 144
  Mollie 149,150,151,152
  Mollie E 146,147
  Mollie Elizabeth 146,148,149
DERRICK
  Charley B 20
  Edward 20
DORE
  Mr 197
  P J 199,202
DOWNING
  Huckleberry 321
DRAKE
  Dora 78
DREW
  (Unknown) 233
DUBOIS
  Jacob 185
DUNCAN
  Betsey 23
  John 23,73
  Safrony 24
  Saphronia 45,46,47,50,51,52
  Sophronia E 23
DUVAL
  Jno R 236
EIFFERT
  Henry 121
ELLIOTT
  G W 120,124
ENGLAND
  Joseph 185
EVANS
  Martha 290
FALKNER
  Franklin 48
FARGO
  C A 48
  Calvin 49
  Me 49
FAULKNER
  D M 279
  Frank 50,51,157
  John 50
  Judge 157,158
FOLSOM
  Elizabeth 208
FOREMAN
  David 58,59
  Polly 2,3,4,5,6
  Sam 202
  Samuel 91,270
FOX
  Joseph 184,185
GARY
  J L 293
GASS
  Albert 257
  Albert G 257,258,259,261,262,
  263,264,265,266,267
  Lucy 257
  Lucy A 258,259,260,265
  Lucy Ann 262,263
GAYLOR

Index

Joseph 236
GHOMLY
  W C 6
GHORMLEY
  M 289
GIBSON
  Joe 16
GLAZIER
  James 236
GLENDENNING
  Cora E 98,197,265
GLENN
  Samuel C 278
GOODMAN
  J B 43
GOONIN
  Eliza 303
  Elzina 299,300,302,303
GOSS
  Ben 193,196
  Benjamin F 198,199
GOTT
  Alfred M 115,116,117,118,119, 121,122,125,126,127,128
  A M 115,120
  Mr A M 120,124
  Sue T 115
  Susan 122,123
  Susan T 115,116,118,119,125
GRAY
  Matthew 44
GREEN
  M D 56,179,190,258,287,297
GRITTS
  Franklin 239,240
HALL
  (Unknown) 181
  Hattie 178
  Nancy 247,254
HAMPTON
  H H 322,324
  Harvey 309,327
  Hary 327
HARDIN
  Henry 40
HARLIN
  James E 277,280,281

Nancy A 276,277,281
HARNAGE
  Billy 197
HARRIS 121
  Byrd 118
  C J 279
  Charles 122,251
  Chas, MD 120,124
  Emma 115
  Lou 115
  Mr 123
  Susan 116,118,120,124
  Susan T 116,117,119,125
HASTINGS
  (W W) 189
  Mr 8,118,132,230,252,264,310
  Mr W W 327
  Pete 73
  W W .... 7,11,53,63,69,75,80,87,88, 100,109,113,114,117,121,126,127,131 ,142,143,151,152,157,169,175,187, 188,205,214,223,224,228,244,245,255 ,261,266,267,274,279,283,294,295, 305,309,314,322,329,331,332
HENSON
  Mollie 314,325,331
  Mollie E 314,330
HILL
  Myrtle .... 9,51,71,83,95,108,120,123, 133,150,160,167,209,210,211,235,262 ,274,276,293,324
HINKLE
  Oliver C 277,278,279,280,281, 282,302
HODSKINS
  Rev 133,137,138
HOLLAND
  J C, MD 276,280
  James E 271,275
  Silas 196
HOLT
  Henderson 110
HOPKINS
  Emma M 287
HUTCHINGS
  Mr 38,39,40,42,44
  W T 34

Index

HUTCHINSON
   Wm 4,179,182,192,209,217
INLOW
   John 291,292,294
JACKSON
   Capt 121,122
JACOBS
   W H 44
JONES
   B C 29,57,67,69,79,93,117,130, 146,156,182,209,227,259,269,288,298,311
   Bruce E 216
   Evan 118,120,124
   Mary 301
JORDAN
   Delia P 82,83
   J C 106
   John 110,236
   Mr 83
JORDON
   Dee 81
JUMPER
   Dick 253
KERR
   Minerva 120,124
KEYS
   James M 119
KLEIN
   (Zeke) 167
   Zeke 158,166
LAMAR
   Elizabeth 285,291
   Emma M 285
   Felix F 285
   J R 285
   James 291
   James C 285
   Mary 289,290
   Mary E 284,289,291,292,294
   William E 285
LANE
   F Elma 260
   Frances R 4,5,72,73,97,98,110, 124,170,172,173,183,184,227,238,253,259,271,272,289,290,319,321
   John 231

   Mrs Lyman K 149,290,291,322
LEMAR
   Mary 289
LESSLEY
   Geo H 251
LINDSEY
   Dr 233
   Mariah 59
   Mrs 58
   R W 60
LITTLEJOHN
   William N 13,15,16,21
LONDON
   Sarah 14
LOWRY
   Miss 302
MALLORY
   Mary Tabor 6
MARTIN
   Doc 14
MATTHEWS
   Z G 303
MCAFFREY
   Albert 90,96
   Albert M 90
   Andrew 96
   Fannie 89,90,91,92,94,95,96,98,99
   Hugh 89,90,91,92,93,94,95,96,97,98,99,100,101
   Hugh, Jr 89,90,92
   James A 89,90,92
   James Albert 89
   John 96
   Loran R 90,92
   Mary 96
   Napoleon 89,90,92
   Rhoda S 90,92
   Rhoda Savannah 89
   Walter T 89,90,92
MCCLURE
   Fannie E 149
MCDONALD
   Brown 2,207
MCDOWELL
   Lucy 70
MCGEE
   David A 273

Index

Thomas J 70,274
MCGHEE
   Frances S 171
   Frances Saphronia 172
   T J.....................171,271,277,278,281
   Thomas J 72,172
MCKNIGHT
   Jesse... 20
MCLAIN
   William... 164
MCMAKING
   W J.. 236
MCUHEL
   Sarah... 236
MEESHEAN
   Wm S.. 77
MELLIR
   Mary.. 285
   Robert... 285
MELLIT
   Mary.. 285
MELTON
   (Unknown)..................................... 172
   S N..171,173
MERRICK
   Edward 5,148,239,260,272,290
MERRILL
   Margaret 104
MILLER
   Emma 285,288
   Emma M 285,288
   Felia... 286
   Felis... 285
   Felix..285,288
   Felix F 285,286,287,288
   James 285
   James C 285,287,288
   James F 285
   Mary..285,286
   Mary E 285,286,287,288,289, 290,291,292,293,294
   Robert..285,289
   Robert C 284,285,286,287,289,290, 291,292,293,294,295
   William... 285
   William C 285,286
   William E 286,287,288

William H.. 94
MONROE
   Julia A 282
   Julia E.................271,272,273,277,281
   Rebecca 271,277
MOORE
   Lewis.. 278
MORRIS
   Mack.. 320
   Moses L 166
MOTHERSHED
   J L... 303
NEALE
   Eliza J 229
   James 228
   Mr... 232
NEEDELES
   Com'r 154
NEEDLES
   Commissioner..........................257,309
   Com'r 257,285,297,307
   T B.........2,24,64,66,76,89,90,115,128, 145,153,155,156,207,248,258,267,268 ,284,286,297,307,308,309,310,314
NORRID
   William H... 39
NORWOOD
   A H... 135
O'CONNELL
   Michael.. 44
OLLIVER
   L H 237
OO-KA-MAH 319
OWEN
   Judge.. 72
   Mr................................231,232,233,235
   Thomas 246
   Tom 228,238
PADEN
   Benj F 210
   John B... 211
PARKER
   Dock 327
   J P... 323
   Johnny 309
   Mr... 324
PARRIS

Henry 110
S E 263
PAYNE
Gabriel L 32
PHILLIPS
(Unknown) 70
PITTS
S C 121,122
POWELL
Markes 315
PROBASCO
E M 109,111,112
PROCK
Alcy 173
Alsy 171,172
Andrew 171
Frances S 171,172
Francis 171
Francis S 174
PROCTOR
(Zeke) 9
Zeke 3,4,5,7,8,10
RASMUS
B P 7,16,45,46,48,50,60,80,93,107, 120,192,196,218,219,249,261
RED BIRD
Daniel ..... 10,52,61,74,99,113,125,139, 151,168,174,186,203,213,223,241,254 ,265,282,294,304,326
REMSEN
Alvie M 268,269,270
G S 280
Julia A 282
Julia E 268,269,270
T S 276,278
Tredwell S 267,268,269,270,271, 277,278,281,282,283,284
REMSON
Julia E 275
T S 184,185,273,279
Tredwell S 273,274,275
REUTER
P G 26,33,103,249,313
RIDGE
(Unknown) 178
RILEY
Atwood 132,133

Bettie 129,132
Betty 129,131,139
Elizabeth 128,129,130,131,132, 134,135,136,139,140,141,142,143
George 132,133
Mr 150
Rufus ... 128,129,130,131,132,133,134, 135,136,139
Rufus R 133,137,138
Samuel 132,133
Samuel R 129
RINSON
Ester 268
Esther 268
Treadwell 268
RISNER
Elizabeth 133,137,138
ROBERTS
Ester 215
Ester S 220,221
Esther 215
Esther A 222
Esther S 215,219,220
Hester S 216
Martha E 215
Martha Ellen 215
S H 215
Solon 219
Solon H 215,216,217,218,219,220, 221,222,223,224
Solon Harrison 216
ROBINS
Johnson 260
ROGERS
Mary 244
W C 279
ROSS
Andrew 296,299
Andrew E 296,297
Anna 296
Chief 234
Elizina 296,297
Elzina 296,297,298,299,300,301, 304,305,306
John 232
Joshua 300
Joshua W 301

Index

Mary 301
Oliver 296,298,299,300,301, 302,303,304
W E 277,281
Will P 236
William P 109
ROSSON
  J O 285,307
  John O 4,192,217
ROTHENBERGER
  D G 57
  E G 116,129,130,269,298,309,311
RUSH
  Belle 107
  Mrs 110
RUSSELL
  Andrew 42
  Mr 43
SAGER
  Augustus C 317,326
  Mr 319
SANDERS
  Cherokee... 159
  Clyde 160
  Corinne 160
  Cornelius 159
  Dora 159
  E C 159,160
  Edward 160
  Geo O 236
  George 118,119
  H L 242,243,244
  Jessie 160
  John 153,154,155,157,158,159, 160,161,162,163,164,165,166,167,168
  Maud 159
  N J 154
  Nancy 166
  Nancy J .... 153,155,156,157,159,160, 161,162,163,164,165,166,167,168,169 ,170
  Nannie 160
  Nannie J 154
  Nelius 162
  Sallie 153,154,155
  Walter Cornelius 159
SCOTT
  Denis 190
  Dennis 190,200
  Ella 190,200
  Fannie 200
  Henry 189,200
  Jane 189,196
  Jennie 189,191,193,195,196, 198,199,203
  John 190,191,192,194,195,196,197, 198,202,203,204,205
  John W 191,193,198,199,202
  John Wesley 191,192
  Lizzie 196,199,200
  Maggie 200
  Margaret 190
  Rufus 190,200
  Sarah 200
  Susan 190
  Sussie 200
  Thomas 190,200
SEVERS
  James J 226
SEVIER
  J J 234,239,240
SHELTON
  Mr 73
SHIFFIELD
  Joe 244
SIMMONS
  George 235,237,239
SKINNER
  Frank 76,77,78,79,80,81,82,83, 84,85,86,87
  Katie 78
  Mattie 78,85
SMITH
  George R 270
  Rocky 109
SPRINGSTON
  (Unknown) 72
STARR
  J C 66,67,77,92,310,311,312,327
  Jeff 110
  Mr 78,249
  Mr J C 326
STOUT
  Joe 195

Index

TAYLOR 150
   Judge 148
   Richard L 291
THOMPSON
   Cherry C 25
   J P 236
   Jessie 236
   Judge 72
   L236
   W P 34,53
   W W 236
THORNTON
   Joe 260
   John 218
TIDWELL
   John E 9,51,70,81,94,95,105,
   106,108,119,120,133,146,148,160,193
   ,194,210,211,235,251,262,274,276
TOYAMAN
   Jane 185
TURNER
   Bill 93
VANCE
   H M 72,80,157,170,274
VANDAGRIFF
   Alva M 270
   Alvie M 270
   Lee 270
VANHOY
   Uncle 250
VANN
   Susan 301
   Susie 300
VESTAL
   Eliza J 241
   Eliza Jane 226
   J H 225,236
   J N 241
   Jerry 237
   Jerry H 225,226,228,239,240,241,
   242,243,244,245,246
   John H 226
   Mr 227
VESTOL
   Eliza J 229
   James H 229
   Jerry 228,229,235

Jerry H .. 228,229,230,232,233,234,238
Mr 233
Mrs 231,233,235
Mrs J H 229
VON WEISE
   Chas 145,154,155
WALKER
   Annie 177,179,180,181,182,183,
   185,186,187,188
   Emma 115
   Hester A 180
   Hester Ann 177,178,179,180
   Sallie 181
   Steen 178,181,183,184,185,186
   W M 279
WALKINGSTICK
   Mr 189,190
   S R 44
WALTERS
   Julia Ann 178
WARD
   Alec 264
   E L C 261
   Lucy A 259,265
   Lucy Ann 257,261,263
WATERS
   Sarah 85,110,193,253,302,321
WATTS
   Mr 46,48,49
   Thomas J 45
WEBB
   Jack 162
WEBSTER
   Chas E 6,71,104,131,157,197,
   228,231,234
WELCH
   Arkansas 321,324
   Bud 323
   Cobb 323,327
   Cornelia 316,323
   G W 321
   George 324
   J C 308,327
   James 312,313,315,316,318,319,
   321,322,323,324,325,326
   James M 321
   John 321

    John Cobb.... 307,313,316,320,326,329
    Jonathan Housten............................ 316
    L E..321,324
    Lucinda............... 306,307,308,309,310,
    311,312,313,314,315,316,317,318,319
      ,320,322,323,324,325,326,327,328,
    329,330,331,332
    Thomas 324
    Thomas I 324
WHITMIRE
    George 5,6
    Johnson....................................193,196
    Jonothan 196
    Mr.. 197
    Watt... 194
WICKED
    Sarah..178,179
WICKER
    Mr... 177
WICKETT
    Sarah.. 184
WILDER
    William L 22
WILLIAMS
    Nannie J.. 221
    T S, MD.. 209
WILLIAMSON
    (Unknown) 109
WILSON
    Charles B 199,202,220,221
    William.. 236
WOLFE
    Tom 93
WOOD
    Clara Mitchell................................. 219
WOODALL
    Judge................................104,110,111
WRIGHT
    Harriet.. 180
    Hattie 178
    Mr.. 177
    Mrs 182
    S T 60,148
YOUNGDUCK 144

www.ingramcontent.com/pod-product-compliance
Lightning Source LLC
Chambersburg PA
CBHW020240030426
42336CB00010B/563